20/11

ABSOLUTE RECOIL

ABSOLUTE RECOIL

TOWARDS A NEW FOUNDATION OF DIALECTICAL MATERIALISM

SLAVOJ ŽIŽEK

VERSO
London • New York

First published by Verso 2014
© Slavoj Žižek 2014

1 3 5 7 9 10 8 6 4 2

Verso
UK: 6 Meard Street, London W1F 0EG
US: 20 Jay Street, Suite 1010, Brooklyn, NY 11201
www.versobooks.com

Verso is the imprint of New Left Books

ISBN-13: 978-1-78168-682-9 (HB)
eISBN-13: 978-1-78168-683-6 (US)
eISBN-13: 978-1-78168-684-3 (UK)

British Library Cataloguing in Publication Data
A catalogue record for this book is available from the British Library

Library of Congress Cataloging-in-Publication Data

Žižek, Slavoj.
 Absolute recoil : towards a new foundation of
dialectical materialism / Slavoj Žižek.
   pages cm
 ISBN 978-1-78168-682-9 (hardback)
1. Dialectical materialism. 2. Hegel, Georg Wilhelm
Friedrich, 1770–1831. I. Title.
 B809.8.Z585 2014
 146'.32—dc23

2014015284

Typeset in Minion Pro by MJ & N Gavan, Truro, Cornwall
Printed in the US by Maple Press

For Jela, with a compulsion to repeat

Contents

Introduction:
"Certainly There Is a Bone Here"

In Chapter 5 of his *Materialism and Empirio-Criticism*, invoking Engels' claim that materialism has to change its form with each new scientific discovery, Lenin applies the point to Engels himself:

> Engels says explicitly that "with each epoch making discovery even in the sphere of natural science [not to speak of the history of mankind], materialism has to change its form." Hence, a revision of the "form" of Engels' materialism, a revision of his natural-philosophical propositions, is not only not "revisionism," in the accepted meaning of the term, but, on the contrary, is demanded by Marxism.[1]

Today, in turn, we should apply this motto to Lenin himself: if his *Materialism and Empirio-Criticism* clearly failed the task of raising philosophical materialism to the level of relativity theory and quantum physics, neither can it help us grasp other breakthroughs such as Freudian psychoanalysis, not to mention the failures of twentieth-century communism. The present book is an attempt to contribute to this task by way of proposing a new foundation for dialectical materialism. We should read the term "dialectics" in the Greek sense of *dialektika* (like *semeiotika* or *politika*): not as a universal notion, but as "dialectical [semiotic, political] matters," as an inconsistent (non-All) mixture. Which is why this book contains chapters *in*—not *on*—dialectical materialism: dialectical materialism is not the book's topic; it is, rather, practiced within these pages.

The book's title refers to the expression *absoluter Gegenstoss*, which Hegel uses only once, but at a crucial point in his logic of reflection, to designate the speculative coincidence of opposites in the movement by which a thing emerges out of its own loss. The most concise poetic formula of absolute recoil was provided by Shakespeare (no surprise here), in his uncanny *Troilus and Cressida* (Act 5, Scene 2):

---

1   V. I. Lenin, *Materialism and Empirio-Criticism*, available at marxists.org.

> O madness of discourse,
> That cause sets up with and against itself!
> Bi-fold authority! where reason can revolt
> Without perdition, and loss assume all reason
> Without revolt.

In the context of the play, these lines refer to Troilus' self-contradicting argumentation when he learns of Cressida's infidelity: he enumerates arguments for and against what he wants to demonstrate; his reasoning rebels against its own line of argument without seeming to undo itself; and his unreasonableness assumes the appearance of rationality without seeming to contradict itself. A cause that acts against itself, a reason that coincides with the revolt (against itself) ... Although these lines refer to feminine inconsistency, they can also be taken as a comment on the secret alliance between the dignity of the Law and its obscene transgression. Recall Shakespeare's standard procedure, in his royal chronicles, of supplementing the "big" royal scenes staged in a dignified way with scenes figuring common people who introduce a comic perspective. In the royal chronicles, these comic interludes strengthen the noble scenes by way of contrast; in *Troilus*, however, everyone, even the noblest of warriors, is "contaminated" by the ridiculing perspective, which invites us to see every character as either blind and pathetic or as involved in ruthless intrigues.

The "operator" of this de-tragicization, the single agent whose interventions systematically undermine tragic pathos, is Ulysses. This may sound surprising in view of Ulysses' first intervention, at the war council in Act 1, when the Greek (or "Grecian," as Shakespeare put it in what now may be called Bush mode) generals try to account for their failure to occupy and destroy Troy after eight years of fighting. Ulysses takes a traditional "old values" position, locating the cause of the Greeks' failure in their neglect of the centralized hierarchical order in which every individual has their proper place. What, then, causes this disintegration which leads to the democratic horror of everyone participating in power? Later in the play (Act 3, Scene 3), when Ulysses tries to convince Achilles to rejoin the battle, he mobilizes the metaphor of time as a destructive force that gradually undermines the natural hierarchical order: with the passing years, your heroic deeds will soon be forgotten, your reputation will be eclipsed by the new heroes—so if you want your warrior glory to continue to shine, you must rejoin the battle:

Time hath, my lord, a wallet at his back,
Wherein he puts alms for oblivion,
A great-sized monster of ingratitudes:
Those scraps are good deeds past; which are devour'd
As fast as they are made, forgot as soon
As done. Perseverance, dear my lord,
Keeps honour bright: to have done is to hang
Quite out of fashion, like a rusty mail
In monumental mockery …
        O, let not virtue seek
Remuneration for the thing it was;
For beauty, wit,
High birth, vigour of bone, desert in service,
Love, friendship, charity, are subjects all
To envious and calumniating time.

Ulysses' strategy here is profoundly ambiguous. In a first approach, he merely restates his argument about the necessity of "degrees" (ordered social hierarchy), and portrays time as a corrosive force which undermines the old true values—an arch-conservative motif. However, on a closer reading, it becomes clear that Ulysses gives his argument a singular cynical twist: how are we to fight against time, to keep the old values alive? Not by directly sticking to them, but by supplementing them with the obscene *Realpolitik* of cruel manipulation, of cheating, of playing one hero off against the other. Only this dirty underside, this hidden disharmony, can sustain harmony. Ulysses plays with Achilles' envy—with the very attitudes that work to destabilize the hierarchical order, since they signal that one is not satisfied with one's subordinate place within the social body. This secret manipulation of envy—in violation of the very rules and values Ulysses celebrates in his first speech—is needed to counteract the effects of time and sustain the hierarchical order of "degrees." This would be Ulysses' version of Hamlet's famous "The time is out of joint; O cursed spite, / That ever I was born to set it right!"—the only way to "set it right" is to counteract the transgression of Old Order with its *inherent transgression*, with a crime secretly made to serve the Order. The price to be paid is that the Order which survives is a mockery of itself, a blasphemous imitation of Order.

Hegel uses the term "absolute recoil" in his explanation of the category of "ground/reason (*Grund*)," where he resorts to one of his famous wordplays, connecting *Grund* (ground/reason) and *zu Grunde gehen* (to fall apart, literally "to go to one's ground"):

> The reflected determination, in falling to the ground, acquires its true meaning, namely, to be within itself the absolute recoil upon itself, that is to say, the positedness that belongs to essence is only a sublated positedness, and conversely, only self-sublating positedness is the positedness of essence. Essence, in determining itself as ground, is determined as the non-determined; its determining is only the sublating of its being determined. Essence, in being determined thus as self-sublating, has not proceeded from another, but is, in its negativity, self-identical essence.[2]

While these lines may sound obscure, their underlying logic is clear: in a relationship of reflection, every term (every determination) is posited (mediated) by another (its opposite), identity by difference, appearance by essence, and so on—in this sense, it "proceeds from another." When positedness is self-sublated, an essence is no longer directly determined by an external Other, by its complex set of relations to its otherness, to the environment into which it emerged. Rather, it determines itself, it is "within itself the absolute recoil upon itself"—the gap, or discord, that introduces dynamism into it is absolutely immanent.

To put it in traditional terms, the present work endeavors to elevate the speculative notion of absolute recoil into a universal ontological principle. Its axiom is that dialectical materialism is the only true philosophical inheritor of what Hegel designates as the speculative attitude of the thought towards objectivity. All other forms of materialism, including the late Althusser's "materialism of the encounter," scientific naturalism, and neo-Deleuzian "New Materialism," fail in this goal. The consequences of this axiom are systematically deployed in three steps: 1) the move from Kant's transcendentalism to Hegel's dialectics, that is, from transcendental "correlationism" (Quentin Meillassoux) to the thought of the Absolute; 2) dialectics proper: absolute reflection, coincidence of the opposites; 3) the Hegelian move beyond Hegel to the materialism of "less than nothing."

Part I begins with a critical analysis of two representative non-transcendental materialist theories of subjectivity (Althusser, Badiou). The second chapter deals with the transcendental dimension and describes the

---

2   G. W. F. Hegel, *Science of Logic*, Atlantic Heights: Humanities Press International 1989, p. 444.

move from the Kantian transcendental subject to the Hegelian subject as the "disparity" in the heart of Substance. The third chapter provides an extended commentary on Hegel's basic axiom according to which the Spirit itself heals the wounds it inflicts on nature.

Part II deals with the Hegelian Absolute. First, it describes the thoroughly evental nature of the Absolute which is nothing but the process of its own becoming. It then confronts the enigma of Hegelian Absolute Knowing: how should we interpret this notion with regard to the basic dialectical paradox of the negative relationship between being and knowing, of a being which depends on not-knowing? Finally, it considers the intricacies of the Hegelian notion of God.

Part III ventures an Hegelian expedition into the obscure terrain beyond Hegel. It begins by deploying the different, contradictory even, versions of the Hegelian negation of negation. It then passes to the crucial dialectical reversal of "there is no relationship" into "there is a non-relationship"— the passage which corresponds to the Hegelian move from dialectical to properly speculative Reason. The book concludes with some hypotheses about the different levels of antagonism that are constitutive of any order of being, delineating the basic contours of a renewed Hegelian "dentology" (the ontology of *den*, of "less than nothing").

In between these steps, two interludes—on Schoenberg's *Erwartung*, and on Ernst Lubitsch's masterpieces—offer artistic exemplifications of the book's conceptual content.

MATERIALISM, OLD AND NEW

Materialism appears today in four main versions: 1) reductionist "vulgar" materialism (cognitivism, neo-Darwinism); 2) the new wave of atheism which aggressively denounces religion (Hitchens, Dawkins, et al.); 3) whatever remains of "discursive materialism" (Foucauldian analyses of discursive material practices); 4) Deleuzian "new materialism." Consequently, we should not be afraid to look for true materialism in what cannot but appear as (a return to German) idealism—or, as Frank Ruda put it apropos Alain Badiou, true materialism is a "materialism without materialism" in which substantial "matter" disappears in a network of purely formal/ideal relations. This paradox is grounded in the fact that, today, it is idealism which emphasizes our bodily finitude and endeavors to demonstrate how this very finitude opens up the abyss of a transcendent divine Otherness beyond our reach (no wonder that the most spiritual of twentieth-century filmmakers, Tarkovsky, is simultaneously the one who was most obsessed with the impenetrable humid inertia of earth), while scientific materialists keep alive the techno-utopian dream of immortality, of getting rid of our bodily constraints.[3] Along these lines, Jean-Michel Besnier has drawn attention to the fact that contemporary scientific naturalism seems to revive the most radical idealist program of Fichte and Hegel: the idea that reason can make nature totally transparent.[4] Does not the biogenetic goal of reproducing humans scientifically through biogenetic procedures turn humanity into a self-made entity, thereby realizing Fichte's speculative notion of a self-positing I? Today's ultimate "infinite judgment" (coincidence of opposites) thus seems to be: absolute idealism is radical naturalist reductionism.[5]

This orientation marks a fourth stage in the development of anti-humanism: neither theocentric anti-humanism (on account of which US religious fundamentalists treat the term "humanism" as synonymous with secular culture), nor the French "theoretical anti-humanism" that accompanied the structuralist revolution in the 1960s (Althusser, Foucault, Lacan), nor the "deep-ecological" reduction of humanity to just one of the many animal species on Earth, but the one which has upset the balance of life on the planet through its *hubris*, and is now justifiably facing the revenge of Mother Earth. However, even this fourth stage is not without a history. In the first decade of the Soviet Union, so-called "bio-cosmism" enjoyed an extraordinary popularity—as a strange combination of vulgar materialism and Gnostic spirituality that formed the occult shadow-ideology, or obscene secret teaching, of Soviet Marxism. It is as if, today, "bio-cosmism" is reemerging in a new wave of "post-human" thought. The spectacular development of biogenetics (cloning, direct DNA interventions, etc.) is gradually dissolving the frontiers between humans and animals on the one side and between humans and machines on the other, giving rise to the idea that we are on the threshold of a new form of Intelligence, a "more-than-human" Singularity in which mind will no longer be subject to bodily constraints, including those of sexual reproduction. Out of this prospect

---

3   A decade or so ago, the Catholic Church condemned a woman who had a child in her early sixties for giving birth in an unnatural way, thereby elevating into an inviolable norm a fact of our biological nature.

4   Jean-Michel Besnier, *Demain les posthumains*, Paris: Fayard 2012.

5   We of course ignore here the fact that, on a closer look, an irreducible gap separates the dialectical "positing of presuppositions" from the scientific program of self-production.

a weird shame has emerged: a shame about our biological limitations, our mortality, the ridiculous way in which we reproduce ourselves—what Günther Anders has called "Promethean shame,"[6] ultimately simply the shame that "we were born and not manufactured." Nietzsche's idea that we are the "last men" laying the ground for our own extinction and the arrival of a new Over-Man is thereby given a scientific-technological twist. However, we should not reduce this "post-human" stance to the paradigmatically modern belief in the possibility of total technological domination over nature—what we are witnessing today is an exemplary dialectical reversal: the slogan of today's "post-human" sciences is no longer domination but surprise (contingent, non-planned emergence). Jean-Pierre Dupuy detects a weird reversal of the traditional Cartesian anthropocentric arrogance which grounded human technology, a reversal clearly discernible in today's robotics, genetics, nanotechnology, artificial life and Artificial Intelligence research:

> how are we to explain the fact that science became such a "risky" activity that, according to some top scientists, it poses today the principal threat to the survival of humanity? Some philosophers reply to this question by saying that Descartes' dream—"to become master and possessor of nature"—has turned out bad, and that we should urgently return to the "mastery of mastery." They understand nothing. They don't see that the technology profiling itself at our horizon through the "convergence" of all disciplines aims precisely at non-mastery. The engineer of tomorrow will not be a sorcerer's apprentice because of his negligence or ignorance, but by choice. He will "give" himself complex structures or organizations and will try to learn what they are capable of by exploring their functional properties—an ascending, bottom-up, approach. He will be an explorer and experimenter at least as much as an executor. The measure of his success will be more the extent to which his own creations will surprise him than the conformity of his realization to a list of pre-established tasks.[7]

Should we see an unexpected sign of hope in this reemergence of surprise at the very heart of the most radical naturalism? Or should we look for a way to overcome the impasses of cognitivist radical naturalism in Deleuzian "New Materialism," whose main representative is Jane Bennett

---

6   Gunther Anders, *Die Antiquiertheit des Menschen* (The Outdatedness of Human Beings), 2 vols., Munich: C. H. Beck 1956.

7   See Jean-Pierre Dupuy's contribution to *Le Débat*, No. 129 (March–April 2004), quoted in Besnier, *Demain les posthumains*, p. 195.

with her notion of "vibrant matter"? Fredric Jameson was correct to claim that Deleuzianism is today the predominant form of idealism: as did Deleuze, New Materialism relies on the implicit equation: matter = life = stream of agential self-awareness—no wonder New Materialism is often characterized as "weak panpsychism" or "terrestrial animism." When New Materialists oppose the reduction of matter to a passive mixture of mechanical parts, they are, of course, asserting not an old-fashioned teleology but an aleatory dynamic immanent to matter: "emerging properties" arise out of unpredictable encounters between multiple kinds of actants (to use Bruno Latour's term), and the agency for any particular act is distributed across a variety of kinds of bodies. Agency thereby becomes a social phenomenon, where the limits of sociality are expanded to include all material bodies participating in the relevant assemblage. For example, an ecological public is a group of bodies, some human, most not, that are subjected to harm, defined as a diminished capacity for action.[8] The ethical implication of such a stance is that we should recognize our entanglement within larger assemblages: we should become more sensitive to the demands of these publics and the reformulated sense of self-interest that calls upon us to respond to their plight. Materiality, usually conceived as inert substance, should be rethought as a plethora of things that form assemblages of human and non-human actors—humans are but one force in a potentially unbounded network of forces. We thereby move back to the enchanted world—no wonder Bennett's earlier work was on enchantment in everyday life. She concludes *Vibrant Matter* with what she calls (in no way wholly ironically) her "Nicene Creed for would-be materialists":

> I believe in one matter-energy, the maker of things seen and unseen. I believe that this pluriverse is traversed by heterogeneities that are continually doing things. I believe it is wrong to deny vitality to nonhuman bodies, forces, and forms, and that a careful course of anthropomorphization can help reveal that vitality, even though it resists full translation and exceeds my comprehensive grasp. I believe that encounters with lively matter can chasten my fantasies of human mastery, highlight the common materiality of all that is, expose a wider distribution of agency, and reshape the self and its interests.[9]

---

8   We can think of Auschwitz as an assemblage—in which the agents were not just the Nazi executioners but also the Jews, the complex network of trains, the gas ovens, the logistics of feeding the prisoners, separating and distributing clothes, extracting the gold teeth, collecting the hair and ashes and so on.

9   Jane Bennett, *Vibrant Matter*, Durham, NC: Duke University Press 2010, p. 122.

What vibrates in vibrant matter is its immanent life force or its soul (in the precise Aristotelian sense of the active principle immanent to matter), not subjectivity. New Materialism thus refuses the radical divide matter/ life and life/thought—selves or multiple agents are everywhere in different guises. A basic ambiguity nonetheless persists here: are these vital qualities of material bodies the result of our (the human observer's) "benign anthropomorphism," so that the vitality of matter means that "everything is, in a sense, alive,"[10] or are we effectively dealing with a strong ontological claim asserting a kind of spiritualism without gods, with a way of restoring sacredness to worldliness? If "a careful course of anthropomorphism" can help reveal the vitality of material bodies, it is not clear whether that vitality is a result of our perception being animistic or of an actual asubjective vital power—an ambiguity which is deeply Kantian.

Prior to Kant, and if we do not take into account the aleatory materialism of Democritus and Lucretius, the main opposition was that of external and internal teleology exemplified by the names of Plato and Aristotle. For Plato, the natural world is the product of a divine craftsman who looked to the world of eternal being for his model of the good and then created a natural order. The "externality" here is twofold: the agent whose goal is being achieved is external to the object, and the value is the agent's value, not the object's. Aristotle's notion differs from Plato's on both counts: the goal belongs to the organism rather than to an "external" designer, and the end to which a natural process is directed is simply the being, the life, of the natural object in question—it is not a "purpose," neither man's nor God's, but the actualization of the immanent potentials of an entity.

Kant breaks with this entire tradition and introduces an irreducible gap into our perception of reality. For him, the idea of purpose is immanent to our perception of living organisms: we ineluctably perceive them "as if a concept had guided its production" (an animal has eyes, ears and a nose in order to orient itself in its environment, it has legs in order to move itself, teeth in order to make eating easier, etc.). However, such teleological thinking does not relate to the objective reality of the observed phenomena: categories of teleology are not constitutive of reality (as are categories of linear material causality), they are merely a regulative idea—a pure *as if*, that is, we perceive living organisms "as if" they were structured in a teleological way. While efficiently causal explanations are always best (x causes y, y is the effect of x), there "will never be a Newton for a blade of grass," and

---

10   Ibid., p. 117.

so the organic must be explained "as if" it were constituted teleologically. Although the natural world gives an almost irresistible semblance of teleology, or adaptedness to goals, this is an anthropomorphic mode of thought, a subjective point of view under which we (have to) comprehend certain phenomena.[11]

The gap that separates modern science from Aristotelian descriptions of nature (experienced "natural" reality) concerns the status of the Real *qua* impossible. The commonsensical realist ontology opposes appearance and reality: the way things merely appear to us and the way they are in themselves, independently and outside of our relating to them. However, are not things already "in themselves" embedded in an environment, related to us? Is not their "in itself" the ultimate abstraction of our mind, the result of tearing things out of their network of relations? What science distils as "objective reality" is becoming more and more an abstract formal structure relying on complex scientific and experimental work. Does this mean, however, that scientific "objective reality" is just a subjective abstraction? Not at all, since it is here that one should mobilize the distinction between (experienced) reality and the Real. Alexandre Koyré pointed out how the wager of modern physics is to approach the real by means of the impossible: the scientific Real, articulated in letters and mathematical formulae, is "impossible" (also) in the sense that it refers to something we can never encounter in the reality within which we dwell. An elementary example: based on experiments, Newton calculated how fast, with how much acceleration, an object will move in free fall in an absolute vacuum, where there are no obstacles to slow down its movement; we, of course, never encounter such a pure situation in our reality, where tiny particles in the air always slow down the free fall, which is why a nail falls much faster than a feather, while in a vacuum the velocity of their fall would be identical. This is why, for modern science, we have to begin with an impossible-Real to account for the possible: we first have to imagine a pure situation in which stones and feathers fall with the same velocity, and only thereafter can we explain the velocity of actual objects falling as divergences or deviations due to empirical conditions. Another example: to explain the attenuation of the

---

11 Darwin could be described precisely as "a Newton for a blade of grass": the goal of his theory of evolution is to account for the phenomena of life in a non-teleological way. Although the notions he uses ("fitness," "selection," "struggle for existence," "survival of the fittest") have a plainly purposive character, natural selection provides design without the need for an intelligent designer: there is no inherent direction or teleology to evolution, all teleology in nature is an illusion.

movement of objects in our ordinary material reality, physics takes as its starting point the "principle of inertia" (again first formulated by Newton) which postulates that an object not subject to any net external force will move at a constant velocity—an object will continue moving at its current velocity until some force causes its speed or direction to change. On the surface of the Earth, inertia is as a rule masked by the effects of friction and air resistance which attenuate the speed of moving objects (usually to the point of rest), and this observable fact misled classical theorists such as Aristotle into assuming that objects move only as long as force is applied to them.[12] Lacan's notion of the Real as impossible should be applied here, including his opposition between reality and the Real: the "principle of inertia" refers to an impossible Real, something that never happens in reality but which has nonetheless to be postulated in order to account for what goes on in reality. It is in this sense that modern science is more Platonic than Aristotelian: Aristotelian approaches begin with empirical reality, with what is possible, while modern science explains this reality with reference to an ideal order which is found nowhere in reality.

Kant thus intervenes into the field of teleology as an agent of scientific modernity: purposes are imposed onto natural objects as organizational principles by us, the observing subjects; the role of teleological concepts is not constitutive but merely regulative, we apply them to make our experience meaningful. Kant thereby opens up an irreducible gap between chaotic nature "in itself" in its meaningless reality, and the meaning, the meaningful order, the purposefulness, we impose onto it. He

does not try to coerce nature into purposefulness, he doesn't try to obliterate its part of heterogeneity or contingency. On the contrary, he introduces the notion of purposefulness as a notion which retroactively makes nature purposeful. His point is thus not to transform chaotic nature into well-ordered one: he conceives of the notion of purposefulness in such a way that it reflects the notion of nature as chaotic. Perhaps, we should recognize here a discovery which corresponds to the discovery of the notion of fantasy in Freud and even more in Lacan. We are dealing with the invention of a notion which provides a name for the retroactive arrangement of successfulness or healing in a field in which a crack is gaping.[13]

---

12   See Alexandre Koyré, *Études de l'histoire de la pensée scientifique*, Paris: PUF 1966, p. 166.

13   Jela Krečič, *Philosophy, Fantasy, Film*, doctoral thesis, University of Ljubljana 2008.

New Materialism takes the step back into (what can only appear to us moderns as) premodern naivety, covering up the gap that defines modernity and reasserting the purposeful vitality of nature: "a careful course of anthropomorphization can help reveal that vitality, even though it resists full translation and exceeds my comprehensive grasp." Note the uncertainty of this statement: Bennett is not simply filling in the gap, she remains modern enough to register the naivety of her gesture, admitting that the notion of the vitality of nature is beyond our comprehension, that we are moving into an obscure area.

The move that defines New Materialism should be opposed to the properly Hegelian dialectical-materialist overcoming of the transcendental dimension or the gap that separates subject from object: New Materialism covers up this gap, reinscribing subjective agency into natural reality as its immanent agential principle, while dialectical materialism transposes back into nature not subjectivity as such but the very gap that separates subjectivity from objective reality.

If, then, New Materialism can still be considered a variant of materialism, it is materialist in the sense in which Tolkien's Middle-earth is materialist: as an enchanted world full of magical forces, good and evil spirits, etc., but strangely *without gods*—there are no transcendent divine entities in Tolkien's universe, all magic is immanent to matter, as a spiritual power that dwells in our terrestrial world. However, we should strictly distinguish the New Age topic of a deeper spiritual interconnection and unity of the universe from the materialist topic of a possible encounter with an inhuman Other with whom some kind of communication could be possible. Such an encounter would be extremely traumatic, since we would have to confront a subjectivized Other with whom no subjective identification is possible, it having no common measure with "being human." Such an encounter is not an encounter with a deficient mode of an Other Subject, but an encounter with an Other at its purest, with the abyss of Otherness not covered up or facilitated by imaginary identifications which make the Other someone "like us," someone we can emphatically "understand." There are many literary and cinema works which deal with this—suffice it here to mention three.

In Frank Schatzing's science fiction novel *The Swarm* (2004), scientists and journalists from across the world investigate what at first appear to be freak events related to the oceans: swimmers are driven from the coast by sharks and venomous jellyfish; commercial ships are attacked and sometimes destroyed in a variety of ways; France suffers an outbreak of an epidemic caused by contaminated lobsters, etc. When it becomes clear that all these events are related, an international task force is set up to deal with the problem. But the attacks continue: the east coast of North America is overrun by Pfiesteria-infested crabs, and the resulting epidemic causes millions of deaths and renders the affected cities uninhabitable; the Gulf Stream fails, threatening a global climate change that would destroy human civilization, and so on. During a task force meeting, a scientist offers his hypothesis: the phenomena are deliberate attacks by a hitherto unknown intelligent species from the depths of the sea; their goal is to eliminate the human race, which is devastating the Earth's oceans. The attackers—baptized the "yrr"—are single-cell organisms that operate in swarms, controlled by a single hive-mind that may have existed for hundreds of millions of years. Although the scientists succeed in making limited contact, the attacks do not cease, until a science journalist dives deep into the ocean and releases a corpse pumped full of the yrr's natural pheromone, hoping to trigger an "emotional" response. It works and the yrr end their attacks on humanity. The novel's epilogue reveals that a year later mankind is still recovering from its conflict with the swarm. The knowledge that humans are not the only intelligent life form on Earth has plunged most religious groups into chaos, while parts of the world still suffer from the epidemic sent by the yrr to destroy the threat to their marine homeland. Humanity now faces the difficult task of rebuilding its society and industry without coming into conflict with the ever-watchful superpower under the sea. While the novel deals with an ecological topic (the destruction and poisoning of maritime ecosystems), its actual focus is on our inability to understand aliens, on the impact the discovery of another intelligent species on Earth might have on us.

In the film *Ender's Game* (2013) an alien species called the Formics attacks Earth in the year 2086. The invasion is defeated, but the Formics continue to build up forces on their home planet. The story is about Andrew "Ender" Wiggin, a child genius trained in Battle School for the forthcoming war with the Formics. In the course of his military education, Ender trains with a computerized "mind game" in which characters that look like Formics materialize and dissolve before him. As the best student, Ender is nominated commander of the fleet and on Graduation Day leads the fleet in a battle simulation near the Formics' home planet. After eradicating the enemy forces he learns that the simulation was in fact a real battle and that he has destroyed the Formics in reality. Remembering his experience in the mind game, Ender realizes that the Formics had tried to communicate with him. He rushes to a mountain similar to the one he saw in the game and finds a Queen with a single Queen egg remaining. After promising the Queen that he will find a planet for the egg, he takes off in a spaceship, determined to colonize a new Formic World—a minimal ethical pact or bond is thus established between Ender and the Formic Queen.

A key feature shared by both these works is their imagining the Other as a maternal Other, as a swarm of pre-individual units subordinated to a single maternal collective Mind. In short, in both cases, the encounter is sexualized; it is the encounter of a male subject stumbling upon a feminine Other which is, as a rule, the pre-symbolic maternal Other of the psychotic closure, the absolute Other from whom no distance is tolerated, allowing no space for the subject's desire—an Other who just uses us as an instrument of its *jouissance*. A materialist approach should avoid not only this "maternal" temptation of imagining the Other as a pre-Oedipal Absolute without lack, but also the opposite temptation of reducing the Other to a mirror of our own disavowed interior ("all we find in the Other is our own repressed content that we have projected into it")—the temptation to which Tarkovsky succumbed in his cinema version of *Solaris*. The difference between Stanislaw Lem's classic science fiction novel and Tarkovsky's cinema version is crucial here. *Solaris* is the story of a space agency psychologist, Kelvin, sent to a half-abandoned spaceship orbiting a newly discovered planet, Solaris, where strange things have been taking place (scientists going mad, hallucinating and killing themselves). Solaris is a planet with an oceanic fluid surface that moves incessantly and, from time to time, imitates recognizable forms—not only elaborate geometric structures, but also gigantic child bodies or human buildings. All attempts to communicate with the planet have failed, but scientists entertain the hypothesis that Solaris is a gigantic brain which can somehow read human minds. Soon after his arrival, Kelvin finds his dead wife Hari at his side in bed. Years ago on Earth, Hari had killed herself after Kelvin had abandoned her. Now he is unable to shake her off, all attempts to get rid of her miserably fail as she rematerializes the next day. Analysis of her tissue reveals that she is not composed of atoms like normal human beings—past a certain micro-level, there is nothing, just a void. Finally, Kelvin grasps that Hari is a materialization of his own innermost traumatic fantasies.

Solaris, then, is a gigantic Brain that materializes in reality the innermost fantasies that support our desire, a machine that generates the ultimate fantasmatic objectal supplement or partner that we would never be ready to accept in reality, even though our entire psychic life turns around it. Read in this way, the story is really about the hero's inner journey, about his attempt to come to terms with his own repressed truth. Or, as Tarkovsky himself put it in an interview: "Maybe, effectively, the mission of Kelvin on Solaris has only one goal: to show that love of the other is indispensable to all life. A man without love is no longer a man. The aim of the entire 'solaristic' is to show humanity must be love."[14] In clear contrast to this, Lem's novel focuses on the inert external presence of the planet Solaris, of this "Thing which thinks" (to use Kant's expression, which fits perfectly here): the point of the novel is precisely that Solaris remains an impenetrable Other with which no communication is possible—true, it returns us to our innermost disavowed fantasies, but the "Che vuoi?" behind this remains thoroughly impenetrable (Why does It do it? As a purely mechanical response? To play demonic games with us? To help us—or compel us—to confront our disavowed truth?).[15]

AGAINST THE DEFLATED HEGEL

At the beginning of his *Encyclopaedia Logic* (the "Small Logic"), Hegel deploys the three elementary "attitudes [positions, *Stellungen*] of thought towards objectivity."[16] The first attitude is that of metaphysics, i.e., of naive realism, which directly presupposes the overlapping of the determinations of thought and determinations of being: metaphysics "has no doubts and no sense of the contradiction in thought, or of the hostility of thought against itself. It entertains an unquestioning belief that reflection is the means of ascertaining the truth, and of bringing the objects before the mind as they really are."[17] This first attitude of simply describing the universe in its rational structure is then undermined by the second attitude whose first form is empiricist skepticism, which doubts that we can ever form a consistent structure of what reality is out of the only thing we have access to, our dispersed and inconsistent experience, with its multiplicity of data.

---

14 Quoted from Antoine de Vaecque, *Andrei Tarkovski*, Paris: Cahiers du Cinéma 1989, p. 108.

15 For a more detailed reading of Tarkovsky's films, see Slavoj Žižek, "The Thing from Inner Space," in Renata Salecl, ed., *Sexuation (Sic 3)*, Durham, NC: Duke University Press 2000.

16 See "Introduction" in G. W. F. Hegel, *The Encyclopaedia Logic*, Indianapolis: Hackett 1991.

17 Ibid., p. 31.

Empiricist skepticism is then countered by the second form of this atti-tude: Kant's transcendental position. What transcendentalism shares with empiricist skepticism is that both accept the inaccessibility/unknowability of the Thing-in-itself. However, in contrast to empiricism, transcendental-ism as it were turns the obstacle itself into its own solution: it elevates the very forms of our mind, of subjectivity, which (de)form our access to the in-itself and thus deny us direct access to it, into an a priori, a positive fact constitutive of our phenomenal reality.

The question here is whether the transcendental horizon is the ultimate horizon of our thinking. If we reject (as we should) any naturalist or other return to naive realism, then there are only two ways to get over (or behind/ beneath) the transcendental dimension. The first form of this third atti-tude of thought towards objectivity is an immediate or intuitive knowing which posits a direct access to the Absolute beyond (or beneath) all discur-sive knowledge—Fichte's I = I, Schelling's Identity of Subject and Object, but also direct mystical intuition of God. The second form, of course, is Hegel's dialectics, which does exactly the opposite with regard to intuitive knowing: instead of asserting a direct intuitive access to the Absolute, it transposes into the Thing (the Absolute) itself the gap that separates our subjectivity from it.

As Hegel points out, this last position itself has two forms, dialecti-cal and speculative, and everything hinges here on the opposition between dialectical and speculative thinking—one might say that dialectics remains negative, while only speculation reaches the highest positive dimension. Dialectics which is not yet speculative is the vibrant domain of the tremor of reflection and reflexive reversals, the mad dance of negativity in which "all that is solid melts into air"—this is dialectics as eternal warfare, as a movement which ultimately destroys everything it gives birth to. In Marxist terms, we are dealing here with materialist dialectics and not dialectical materialism; in Hegelian terms, with determinate reflection and not reflex-ive determination; in Lacanian terms, with "there is no relationship" and not "there *is* a non-relationship."

So, in terms of the attitudes of thought towards objectivity, taken together we have not three but six such attitudes: 1) naive realist metaphys-ics, 2) empiricist skepticism, 3) transcendental criticism, 4) direct intuitive knowing of the Absolute, 5) dialectical thinking, and 6) speculative think-ing proper. These six positions, three of which are positive (1, 4, 6) and three negative (2, 3, 5), can be reduced in turn to three basic positions: objective-metaphysical, subjective-transcendental, dialectical-speculative.

Does not this matrix continue to determine our choices even today? Scientific naturalism (from quantum cosmology to evolutionary theory and the brain sciences), relativist historicism, versions of transcendentalism from Heidegger to Foucault, New Age intuitive knowing, "negative dialectics" from Trotskyist permanent revolution through Western Marxism (Adorno) up to today's forms of "resistance" … What would be the properly speculative position? Not Stalinism, since it clearly stands for the return to a naive realist metaphysics.

Can the main figure of Hegel that has emerged in recent decades—the "deflated" liberal Hegel of mutual recognition—do the job? It is crucial to see the political as well as the ontological limits of this deflated liberal Hegel—a figure who ultimately amounts to a weird Darwinian Hegel. The underlying ontological premise of Robert Pippin's reading of Hegel (rarely explicitly stated but nonetheless clearly indicated here and there) is that, in the evolution of animal life and of human animals on Earth, the human species somehow (this indeterminacy is crucial!) began to function in the modes of normativity and mutual recognition. On Pippin's interpretation, "spirit" thus refers neither to an extra-natural immaterial substance (along the lines of the Cartesian *res cogitans* opposed to the *res extensa*) nor to a Divine Mind or Cosmic Spirit which commandeers human agents as vehicles for the accomplishment of its own purposes. Here are some key passages from Pippin's *Hegel's Practical Philosophy* about "the capacity of some natural beings to be aware of themselves in a non-observational, but more self-determining way":[18]

> The suggestion Hegel seems to be making is simply that at a certain level of complexity and organization, natural organisms come to be occupied with themselves and eventually to understand themselves in ways no longer appropriately explicable within the boundaries of nature or in any way the result of empirical observation.

> Even though this finally achieved independence from nature is achieved only in objective spirit … it is never to be understood as something non-natural and it is still the case that a link with and partial determination by nature is always stressed by Hegel.

---

18   Robert B. Pippin, *Hegel's Practical Philosophy: Rational Agency as Ethical Life*, Cambridge: Cambridge University Press 2008, p. 56.

> It is the achievement of the sublating relation to nature that constitutes spirit; natural beings which by virtue of their natural capacities can achieve it are spiritual; having achieved it and maintaining it *is* being spiritual; those which cannot are not.[19]

The last quote indicates the thin line along which Pippin is treading here: although he writes that humans are "natural beings which by virtue of their natural capacities can achieve" spiritual self-relating, he by no means endorses the Aristotelian view according to which the human being is a substantial entity among whose positive features are potentials or powers of spiritual self-relating. For Pippin (following Hegel), spirit is not a substantial entity but a purely processual one, it is the result of its own becoming, it makes itself what it is—the only substantial reality there is is nature. The distinction between nature and spirit therefore stems not from the fact that spirit is a thing of a different kind from natural things, but rather has more to do with the different sets of criteria that are required for *explaining* them: spirit is "a kind of norm," "an achieved form of individual and collective mindedness, and institutionally embodied recognitive relations."[20] That is to say, free acts are distinguished by the *reason* to which a subject might appeal in *justifying* them, and justification is a fundamentally social practice, the practice of "giving of and asking for reasons" by participants in a set of shared institutions. Even at the individual level, expressing an intention amounts to "avowing a pledge to act, the content and credibility of which remains (*even for me*), in a way, suspended until I begin to fulfill the pledge."[21] It is not until my intention is recognized by others and myself as being fulfilled or realized in my deed that I can identify my act as my own.[22] Justification thus turns out to be more *retrospective* than prospective, a process in which the agent's own stance on her action is by no means authoritative. Being an agent, being able to provide reasons to others to justify one's deeds, is thus itself an "achieved social status such as, let us say, being a citizen or being a professor, a product or result of mutually recognitive attitudes."[23]

---

19   Ibid., pp. 46, 48, 53.

20   Ibid., p. 51.

21   Ibid., p. 52.

22   Note the radical implication of Pippin's position: the subject is constitutively decentered in Lacan's sense, its innermost status as a free agent is decided outside itself, in social recognition, and retroactively, with a delay, or after the (f)act.

23   Ibid., p. 52.

Is such a reading of Hegel appropriate to our historical moment? In his "Back to Hegel?," a critical review of my *Less Than Nothing*,[24] Pippin proceeds in four systematic steps, although his criticisms are interlinked across the different levels, from basic ontological questions about the fabric of being to the viability of the Welfare State today. His argument can be condensed as a paraphrase of de Quincey's famous passage on the "simple art of murder": "If once a man indulges himself in looking for gaps in the fabric of being, very soon he comes to think little of the notion of an abyssal act; and from this he comes next to abandon reliance on reason in our deliberations, and from that to reject that great dream of social democrats everywhere, Sweden in the Sixties." Pippin begins at the most basic level of ontology, problematizing my thesis on the ontological incompleteness of reality:

> I do not fully understand the claims about holes in the fabric of being, and at any rate, we do not need the claim if we go in the direction I am suggesting. For if that formulation of apperception is correct, it means we are able to account for the inappropriateness of psychological or naturalist accounts of such states, all without a gappy ontology (in the sense, if not in the same way, that Frege and the early Husserl criticized psychologism without an "alternate" ontology).

Pippin correctly reads my incompleteness thesis against the background of the status of subjectivity; he is well aware that I develop the topic of ontological incompleteness in order to answer the question "How should reality be structured so that (something like) subjectivity can emerge in it?" Pippin's solution is different: for him, Kantian transcendental apperception—the unity of awareness with self-awareness—suffices. Self-awareness means a minimal self-relating on account of which we, as humans, have to justify our acts with reasons. Pippin, of course, supplements Kant with the Hegelian account of the (transcendental, not empirical) genesis of self-awareness out of complex social relations focused on mutual recognition, or, to quote his acerbic critical remark: "'Spirit' emerges in this imagined social contestation, in what we come to demand of each other, not in the interstices of being." There is no need for holes in the fabric of the universe for this. From my standpoint, the problematic nature of this account is signaled by the fact that Pippin ends up with a standard transcendental dualism:

---

24   All further quotes from Pippin are taken from his review "Back to Hegel?," *Mediations: Journal of the Marxist Literary Group* 26:1–2 (2012–13), available at mediationsjournal.org (no pagination).

Of course, it is possible and important that some day researchers will discover why animals with human brains can do these things and animals without human brains cannot, and some combination of astrophysics and evolutionary theory will be able to explain why humans have ended up with the brains they have. But these are not philosophical problems and they do not generate any philosophical problems.

True, but such full scientific (self-)naturalization would have consequences for philosophy: if we could fully account for our moral acts in terms of natural causes, in what sense would we still experience ourselves as free? Kant's notion of freedom implies a discontinuity in the texture of natural causes, that is, a free act is an act which is ultimately grounded in itself and, as such, cannot be accounted for as an effect of the preceding causal network—in this sense, a free act *does* imply a kind of hole in the texture of phenomenal reality, the intervention of another dimension in the order of phenomenal reality. Of course, Kant does not claim that free acts are miracles which momentarily suspend natural causality—they just happen without violating any natural laws. However, the fact of freedom indicates that natural causality does not cover all there is but only the phenomenal reality, and that the transcendental subject, the agent of freedom, cannot be reduced to a phenomenal entity. Phenomenal reality is thus incomplete, non-All, a fact confirmed by the antinomies of pure reason which arise the moment our reason tries to comprehend phenomenal reality in its totality. One should always bear in mind that this "ontological scandal" is for Kant the necessary result of his transcendental turn.

This brings us to Pippin's second reproach: in his view, the thesis on the ontological incompleteness of reality opens up the space for abyssal acts of freedom, acts not grounded in any rational deliberation, since they are located in the interstices of being. That is to say, insofar as Spirit as a historical form of collective Reason, as a space within which rational deliberations take place, can be considered broadly synonymous with the Lacanian "big Other," and insofar as, following (the late) Lacan, I insist that there is no big Other, our acts lose their rational and normative foundation:

> The condition of modern atheism means for Žižek, in Lacanian terms, that there is and can be no longer any "big Other," any guarantor of at least the possibility of any resolution of normative skepticism and conflicts. But no transcendent guarantor is not the same thing as no possible reliance on reason in our own deliberations and in our claims on others.

Considered outside the big Other as shared symbolic substance, acts can only be irrational interventions with no collectively binding normative foundation; that is, they can be grounded only in direct brutal power, in the agent's resolve and will: "And if the act is 'abyssal,' then 'politics' simply means 'power,' power backed by nothing but resolve and will, likely met with nothing but resolve and will." I consider this a total misreading of my position: the fact that there is no big Other in no way implies that humans can operate outside the thick texture of symbolic coordinates. Lacan is more than aware of the weight of this texture—just recall his endless variations on decentered subjectivity, on the retroactive effect of meaning, on how a human being does not speak but is spoken, and so on. Lacan's point is just that the big Other is inconsistent, self-contradictory, thwarted, traversed by antagonisms, without any guarantee ("there is no Other of Other"), with no ultimate norm or rule totalizing it—in short, the big Other is not some kind of substantial Master who secretly pulls the strings but a stumbling malfunctioning machinery. In his reading of Hegel's ethical thought Pippin himself insists on the retroactivity of meaning: the meaning of our acts is not an expression of our inner intention, it emerges later, from their social impact, which means that there is a moment of contingency in every emergence of meaning. But there is another more subtle retroactivity involved here: an act is abyssal not in the sense that it is not grounded in reasons, but in the circular sense that it *retroactively posits its reasons*. A truly autonomous symbolic act or intervention never occurs as the result of strategic calculation, as I go through all possible reasons and then choose the most appropriate course of action. An act is autonomous not when it applies a preexisting norm but when it creates a norm in the very act of applying it. Take the act of falling in love: I don't fall in love when I meet a woman who meets my preestablished criteria; if it's true love, then I don't love the woman for her smile, eyes, legs, etc.—I love her smile, eyes, etc. because they are hers. So it is not that I act and make choices without reasons, rather that I freely choose which set of reasons will determine me.

And this brings us to the true focal point of the debate. Pippin's line of reasoning is that since, for me, bourgeois society is unreformable, a radical change is needed; however, since there is no big Other, this change cannot be a direct enactment of some historical necessity or teleology in the classical Marxist sense, but must be an abyssal voluntaristic act. Pippin here addresses what he sees as "the largest question of all," the one he "found the most dissatisfyingly addressed" in my book:

[Žižek] wants to say that bourgeois society is fundamentally self-contradictory, and I take that to mean "unreformable." We need a wholly new ethical order and that means "the Act." That society's pretense to being a rational form is undermined by the existence of a merely contingent particular, a figurehead at the top, the monarch. (A better question, it seems to me, is why Hegel bothers, given how purely symbolic and even pointless such a dotter of i's and crosser of t's turns out to be.)

Pippin immediately makes it clear in what sense bourgeois society is reformable—his reference is, as expected, "that great dream of social democrats everywhere—'Sweden in the Sixties!'" This, he continues,

> does not seem to me something that inevitably produces its own irrational and irreconcilable Unreason, or Other. More lawyers for the poor in Texas, affordable daycare, universal health care, several fewer aircraft carriers, more worker control over their own working conditions, regulated perhaps nationalized banks, all are reasonable extensions of that bourgeois ideal itself, however sick and often even deranged modern bourgeois society has become.

As to "unreformability," I am simply claiming that the demands in Pippin's list may appear as a series of "reasonable extensions" of the bourgeois ideal, but this appearance is *abstract* in a strictly Hegelian way, and ignores the general tendency of today's global capitalism.[25] At a more basic level, the claim that bourgeois society is "fundamentally self-contradictory" is a consequence of Hegel's universal thesis—it is a claim which holds for every society:

> The history of a single world-historical nation contains (a) the development of its principle from its latent embryonic stage until it blossoms into the self-conscious freedom of ethical life and presses in upon world history; and (b) the period of its decline and fall, since it is its decline and fall that signalizes the emergence in it of a higher principle as the pure negative of its own.[26]

---

25   Apropos Sweden in the 1960s, perhaps Pippin should read a Mankell or Larson detective novel to get an idea of what Sweden is like today, and how far it has been counter-reformed since the mythical '60s.

26   Hegel, *Philosophy of Right*, Third Part: Ethical Life, iii: The State, Remark to § 343, available at marxists.org.

In this simple and elementary sense, *every* particular form of state and society is by definition "self-contradictory" and, as such, condemned to disappear—as Pippin himself points out, the rational state articulated in Hegel's *Philosophy of Right* had itself already entered into a state of decay, the proof being that Hegel was able to articulate its notional structure.[27] This is why the most un-Hegelian thing imaginable here would be to present Hegel's idea of the rational state as a vision which is no longer self-contradictory but which, à la Fukuyama, is in its essence the finally found optimal formula that we, Hegel's successors, simply have to gradually improve and reform, rather than attempt to change in its essence. Whatever Hegel stands for politically, however, it is not the gradual improvement of bourgeois society. Hegel's vision of social development is, on the contrary, full of unexpected reversals—the promise of freedom turns into the worst nightmare, and so on. This is why Hegel would have immediately comprehended the logic of the reversal of the emancipatory promise of the October Revolution into the Stalinist nightmare, or, today, of the rise of religious fundamentalism in the midst of consumerist permissiveness. As for reformism, the Hegelian stance would have been: yes, but with a twist—one begins with a modest reform which aims only to make the existing system more just and efficient, and one triggers an avalanche which sweeps away the very order of deliberation which led us to propose the modest reform in the first place.

With regard to Pippin's vision of the gradual progress of bourgeois society, let us also not forget that Hegel concludes his *Philosophy of Right* not with an idealized vision of a modern peaceful corporate state, but with the necessity of war as the moment in which a state is "most supremely its own"—war is a supreme dialectical example of how a negative relation to oneself appears as a contingent external obstacle or threat. The "truth" of the external enemy which, for accidental reasons, poses a threat to a state is the state's self-related negativity, the assertion of the state in its pure essence, in contrast to all its particular moments (individual destinies, property relations, etc.):

---

27   It is in this way that we should read Hegel's last published text, a ferocious polemic against the British Reform Bill which moved in the direction of universal voting rights, by-passing the mediating role of corporate structures: Hegel reacted in such a panic because the Bill clearly signaled the outdated character of his idea of the state.

This negative relation of the state to itself is embodied in the world as the relation of one state to another and as if the negative were something external. In the world of existence, therefore, this negative relation has the shape of a happening and an entanglement with chance events coming from without. But in fact this negative relation is that moment in the state which is most supremely its own, the state's actual infinity as the ideality of everything finite within it. It is the moment wherein the substance of the state—i.e. its absolute power against everything individual and particular, against life, property, and their rights, even against societies and associations—makes the nullity of these finite things an accomplished fact and brings it home to consciousness.[28]

Pippin dismisses my "idea of 'pure' drives (or 'pure' anything)" as something that "belongs in the Hegelian zoo," i.e., something that is definitely superseded, rendered philosophically obsolete, by Hegel's philosophical achievement. But is not war, the way Hegel conceptualizes it, precisely the (re)assertion of the "pure" essence of the state in contrast to its particular content? In this sense, is not the push-towards-war an exemplary case of the "pure" death drive (pure negativity)? One can, of course, argue that war is today more threatening due to the catastrophic potential of new technologies, but this in no way renders Hegel's point outdated; it just compels us to reinvent it for contemporary conditions. For example, today the split between First World and Third World appears, in effect, increasingly like an opposition between leading a long, satisfying life full of material and cultural wealth, and dedicating one's life to some transcendent Cause. Two philosophical references immediately impose themselves apropos this ideological antagonism between the Western consumerist way of life and Islamist radicalism: Hegel and Nietzsche. Is not this antagonism the one between what Nietzsche called "passive" and "active" nihilism? We in the West are the Nietzschean Last Men, immersed in our stupid daily pleasures, while the Muslim radicals are ready to risk everything, engaged in the struggle to the point of their self-destruction. Furthermore, viewing this opposition through the lens of the Hegelian struggle between Master and Servant, one cannot avoid noting the paradox: although we in the West are perceived as the exploitative masters, it is we who occupy the position of the Servant who, in clinging to life and its pleasures, is unable to risk his life (recall Colin Powell's notion of a high-tech war with no human casualties), while the poor Islamist radicals are the Masters ready to risk their lives. But

---

28   Ibid., § 323.

are they really? Deep within themselves, the terrorist fundamentalists lack true conviction—and their violent outbursts are proof of this. How fragile must the belief of a jihadist be if he feels threatened by a stupid caricature in a low-circulation Danish newspaper? Fundamentalist Islamist terror is *not* grounded in the terrorists' conviction of their superiority and desire to safeguard their cultural-religious identity from the onslaught of global consumerist civilization. The fundamentalists' problem is not that we consider them inferior to us, but that *they themselves* secretly consider themselves inferior. This is why our condescending politically correct assurances that we feel no superiority towards them only makes them more furious and feeds their resentment. The problem is not cultural difference (their effort to preserve their identity) but, on the contrary, the fact that they are already like us, that, secretly, they have already internalized our standards and measure themselves by them.

A further reproach might be that Hegel's account of war is too abstract: wars are always the result of concrete social and political conditions. But this also misses Hegel's point: he fully recognizes the external contingency of the causes of conflict, but his point is precisely that, in the case of war, "irrational" contingency and innermost (abstract) notional necessity coincide. A devastating war can explode out of a trifling conflict about some ridiculous point of honor, but this is not what war is really about.

Returning to the topic of bourgeois society: Pippin thinks that, for me, since bourgeois society cannot be reformed to keep its self-destructive tendencies in check, the only way out lies in the imposition of a new ethical order. If this imposition entails radical social change, inclusive of some kind of Cultural Revolution, then I have no problem subscribing to it. But how should this change be brought about? Here again we encounter my abyssal irrational act. Where Pippin totally misses the point is in his reading of my notion of the self-contradictory nature of bourgeois society—the passage is worth quoting again: "Its pretense to being a rational form is undermined by the existence of a merely contingent particular, a figurehead at the top, the monarch. (A better question, it seems to me, is why Hegel bothers, given how purely symbolic and even pointless such a dotter of i's and crosser of t's turns out to be.)" I absolutely in no way claim or imply that having a contingent figurehead limits the rationality of a state—what I claim, following Hegel, is that only through the addition of such a figurehead does the totality of a rational state become actual. The act of the King, his decision, "reabsorbs all particularity into its single self, cuts short the weighing of pros and cons between which it lets itself oscillate perpetually now this way and now that, and by saying 'I will' makes its decision and so inaugurates all activity and actuality." Hegel emphasizes this apartness of the monarch already when he states that the "ultimate self-determination" can "fall within the sphere of human freedom only in so far as it has the position of a pinnacle, explicitly distinct from, and raised above, all that is particular and conditional, for only so is it actual in a way adequate to its concept."[29] This is why "the conception of the monarch" is

> of all conceptions the hardest for ratiocination, i.e. for the method of reflec-
> tion employed by the Understanding. This method refuses to move beyond
> isolated categories and hence here again knows only *raisonnement*, finite points
> of view, and deductive argumentation. Consequently it exhibits the dignity of
> the monarch as something deduced, not only in its form, but in its essence. The
> truth is, however, that to be something not deduced but purely self-originating is
> precisely the conception of monarchy.[30]

The speculative moment that the Understanding cannot grasp is "the transition of the concept of pure self-determination into the immediacy of being and so into the realm of nature." Here politics joins ontology: while the Understanding can well grasp the universal mediation of a living totality, what it cannot grasp is that this totality, in order to actualize itself, has to acquire *actual* existence in the guise of an immediate *contingent* "natural" singularity. The idea of a thoroughly rational totality with no need for such a contingent suturing point is one of the supreme examples of abstract Understanding. This is why, for Hegel, the function of the monarch, while purely symbolic, is definitely not pointless: it is, on the contrary, the point itself, the immediate/contingent element needed to suture or totalize a rational totality. The core of the dialectic of contingency and necessity lies in revealing not a deeper notional necessity expressing itself through contingent empirical reality, but the contingency at the very heart of necessity—not only the necessity of contingency, but the contingency of necessity itself.

---

29   Ibid., Remark to § 279. For a more detailed reading of Hegel's concept of the Monarch, see Interlude 3 in Slavoj Žižek, *Less Than Nothing*, London: Verso 2012.

30   Ibid., Remark to § 279.

THE DISPARITY

The interest of Pippin's reading of Hegel is nonetheless obvious, even if a key dimension of Hegel's thought gets lost along the way: by ditching the ridiculous metaphysical baggage (Spirit as a mega-Subject pulling the strings, manipulating individual subjects in the mode of the "Cunning of Reason"), one produces a Hegel fully compatible with the modern secular post-metaphysical world-view as well as with today's liberal "anti-totalitarian" sensibility. Nevertheless, the ontological problem persists in the background. Pippin seems to imply that the normative structure of recognition and discursive justification can ultimately be incorporated into a global natural history of humanity as a peculiar feature of one animal species, so that, even if the normative dimension remains irreducible to the empirical reality, it somehow emerged out of it de facto. This emergence is, however, never explicitly developed, since this would amount to a full naturalization of the normative-discursive dimension. Although Pippin is critical of Habermas, it would be easy to prove that Habermas' neo-Kantian avoidance of ontological commitment is necessarily ambiguous in a homologous way: while naturalism functions as the obscene secret not to be revealed in public ("of course man developed from nature, of course Darwin was right …"), this obscure secret is a lie, covering up the idealist *form* of thought (the a priori transcendentals of communication which cannot be deduced from natural being). The truth here is in the form: as with Marx's example of royalists in republican form, while the Habermasians secretly think they are really materialists, the truth lies in the idealist form of their thinking.

Ray Brassier confronts this problem head-on when, in his interpretation of Wilfrid Sellars, he defines materialism with the Marxist-sounding notion of "determination in the last instance," which should be opposed to the similar notion of overdetermination: "determination-in-the-last-instance is the causality which renders it universally possible for any object X to determine its own 'real' cognition, but only in the last instance."[31] Overdetermination is transcendental, that is, the point of transcendentalism is that I cannot ever fully "objectivize" myself, reduce myself to a part of the "objective reality" in front of me, since such reality is always already transcendentally constituted by subjectivity: no matter to what extent I succeed in accounting for myself as a phenomenon within the "great chain of being," as a result determined by a network of natural (or supernatural) reasons, this causal image is always already over-determined by the

---

31   Ray Brassier, *Nihil Unbound*, London: Palgrave Macmillan 2007, p. 138.

transcendental horizon which structures my approach to reality. To this transcendental overdetermination Brassier opposes the naturalist determination in the last instance: a serious materialist has to presume that every subjective horizon within which reality appears, every subjective constitution or mediation of reality, has to be ultimately determined by its place in objective reality, that is, it has to be conceived as part of the all-encompassing natural process. The contrast is clear here: overdetermination refers not to the way an all-encompassing whole determines the interplay of its parts, but, on the contrary, to the way a part of the whole emerges as a self-relating One which over-determines the network of its relations with others. In this precise sense, the elementary form of overdetermination is *life*: a living being is part of the world, but it relates to its environs as a function of its self-relating (the simplest example: an organism relates to food because it needs food to survive). Overdetermination is a name for this paradoxical reversal by means of which a moment subsumes under itself the whole out of which it grew (or, in Hegelese, posits its presuppositions). Such a relationship between overdetermination and determination in the last instance is antagonistic, since overdetermination makes any direct conceptualization of determination in the last instance impossible. Alternatively: at the level of temporality, the structure of overdetermination is that of retroactivity, of an effect which retroactively posits (over-determines) the very causes by which it is determined in the last instance; to reduce overdetermination to the determination in the last instance is to succeed in transposing retroactive causality back into the linear causal network. Why, then, does (symbolic-retroactive) overdetermination emerge at all? Is it ultimately an illusion, albeit a spontaneous and necessary one?

The only way to avoid this conclusion is to break the closure of the linear determinist chain and assert the ontological openness of reality: overdetermination is not illusory insofar as it retroactively fills in the gaps in the chain of causality. The solution is thus not to establish a grand evolutionary narrative explaining or describing how higher modes of being emerge out of lower modes (life out of the chemistry of "dead" matter, spirit out of life), but to approach head-on the question of how the pre-human real has to be structured so as to allow for the emergence of the symbolic/normative dimension. It is here that the most radical dimension of Hegel's thought, the dimension overlooked by Pippin, comes into view. In a well-known passage from the Foreword to his *Phenomenology of Spirit* Hegel provides the most elementary formula for what it means to conceive Substance also as Subject:

The disparity which exists in consciousness between the I and the substance which is its object is the distinction between them, the *negative* in general. This can be regarded as the *defect* of both, though it is their soul, or that which moves them. That is why some of the ancients conceived the *void* as the principle of motion, for they rightly saw the moving principle as the *negative*, though they did not as yet grasp that the negative is the self. Now, although this negative appears at first as a disparity between the I and its object, it is just as much a disparity of the substance with itself. Thus what seems to happen outside of it, to be an activity directed against it, is really its own doing, and substance shows itself to be essentially subject.[32]

The final reversal is crucial: the disparity between subject and substance is simultaneously the disparity of substance with itself. This reversal takes place at all levels: subjectivity emerges when substance cannot achieve full identity with itself, when substance is in itself "barred," traversed by an immanent impossibility or antagonism; the subject's epistemological ignorance, its failure to fully grasp the opposed substantial content, simultaneously indicates a limitation, failure, or lack in the substantial content itself; the believer's experience of abandonment by God is simultaneously a gap that separates God from the believer, an indication of the "unfinished" nature of the divine identity, and so on. Applied to Pippin's ontological ambiguity, this means that the gap separating the normative from the factual should be simultaneously conceived as a gap immanent to the factual itself. Or, to put it in a slightly different way, while everything is to be mediated/posited by the self-relating void of subjectivity, *this void itself emerges out of the Substance through its self-alienation*. We thus encounter here the same ambiguity that characterizes the Lacanian Real: everything is subjectively mediated, but the subject does not come first—it emerges through the self-alienation of the Substance. In other words, while we have no direct access to the substantial pre-subjective Real, we also cannot get rid of it.

The subject does not come first: it is a predicate-becoming-subject, a passive screen asserting itself as a First Principle, i.e., something posited which retroactively posits its presuppositions.[33] It is in this sense that, for

---

32 G. W. F. Hegel, *Phenomenology of Spirit*, Oxford: Oxford University Press 1977, p. 21.

33 Does this not hold even for the cognitivist view of subjectivity? Subjective self-awareness emerges late, as a medium registering what goes on in the organism and its environs. But once it is there, it tends to assert itself as the active agent regulating and coordinating the subject's entire action and interaction with its others.

Marx, Capital is a subject: capital is money which becomes a subject, money which not only mediates between commodities as their general equivalent but also becomes the active agent of this mediation, so that the entire movement of the exchange of commodities becomes the self-movement of Capital. And the paradox is that what Hegel was not able to see was this very "Hegelian" dimension of the emerging capitalist order: the limit of the return to Hegel is simply Capital itself, for Hegel was not able to grasp the capitalist dynamic proper. Fredric Jameson is right to draw attention to the fact that "despite his familiarity with Adam Smith and emergent economic doctrine, Hegel's conception of work and labor—I have specifically characterized it as a handicraft ideology—betrays no anticipation of the originalities of industrial production or the factory system."[34]

In short, Hegel's analyses of work and production cannot be "transferred to the new industrial situation."[35] There is a series of interconnected reasons for this limitation, all grounded in the constraints of the historical experience at Hegel's disposal. First, Hegel's notion of industrial revolution was that of Adam Smith-type manufacturing where the work process was still one of combined individuals using tools, not yet the factory system in which the machinery sets the rhythm and individual workers are de facto reduced to organs or appendices serving the machinery. Second, Hegel could not yet imagine the way that abstraction works in developed capitalism: when Marx describes the mad self-enhancing circulation of capital, whose solipsistic path of self-fecundation finds its apogee in today's meta-reflexive speculations on futures, it is far too simplistic to claim that the specter of this self-engendering monster pursuing its ends regardless of any human or environmental concern is an ideological abstraction, and to insist that one should never forget that, behind this abstraction, lie real people and natural objects on whose productive capacities and resources capital's circulation is based and on which it feeds like a gigantic parasite. The problem is that this "abstraction" is not only in our (financial speculator's) misperception of social reality, but is also "real" in the precise sense of determining the structure of very material social processes: the fate of whole swathes of society and sometimes of whole countries can be decided by the speculative dance of Capital, which pursues its goal of profitability with a blessed indifference to how its movements will affect social reality. Therein resides the fundamental systemic violence of capitalism, much

34   Fredric Jameson, *The Hegel Variations*, London: Verso 2010, p. 68.
35   Ibid.

more uncanny than direct pre-capitalist socio-ideological violence: its violence is no longer attributable to concrete individuals with their "evil" intentions, but is purely "objective", systemic, anonymous—quite literally a conceptual violence, the violence of a Concept whose self-deployment rules and regulates social reality. This is why Hegelian references abound in Marx's deployment of the notion of Capital: in capitalism, value is not a mere abstract "mute" universality, a substantial link between the multiplicity of commodities; from being a passive medium of exchange it turns into the "active factor" of the entire process. Instead of merely passively assuming the two different forms of its actual existence (money/commodity), it appears as a subject "endowed with a motion of its own, passing through a life-process of its own": it differentiates itself from itself, positing its otherness, and then again overcomes this difference—the entire movement is *its own* movement. In this precise sense, "instead of simply representing the relations of commodities, it enters ... into private relations with itself": the "truth" of its relating to its otherness is its self-relating, i.e., in its self-movement, capital retroactively "sublates" its own material conditions, turning them into subordinate moments of its own "spontaneous expansion"—in pure Hegelese, it posits its own presuppositions.

The irony is not difficult to miss here: the fact that Marx needed Hegel to formulate the logic of capital (the crucial breakthrough in Marx's work occurred in the mid-1850s, when, after the failure of the 1848 revolutions, he began to read Hegel's *Logic* again) means that what Hegel was not able to see was not some post-Hegelian or post-idealist reality but rather the properly *Hegelian* aspect of the capitalist economy. Here, paradoxically, Hegel was not *idealist enough*, for what he failed to see was the properly *speculative* content of the capitalist speculative economy, the way financial capital functions as a purely virtual notion processing "real people." Which brings us back to the paradox formulated by Ruda: the only way to be a true materialist today is to push idealism to its limit.

This greatest paradox of contemporary materialism was sometimes missed by Lacan himself. In his seminar on anxiety (1962), Lacan boastfully claimed that "if there is anyone, I think, who does not mistake what the *Phenomenology of Spirit* brings us, it is myself."[36] But is it really the case? In his reference to the Hegelian Beautiful Soul, Lacan makes a deeply significant mistake by condensing two different "figures of consciousness": he

---

36   Jacques Lacan, *Le séminaire X, L'angoisse (1962–1962)*, November 14, 1962. All English translations unless otherwise indicated are the author's own.

speaks of the *Beautiful Soul* who, in the name of its *Law of the Heart*, rebels against the injustices of the world.[37] With Hegel, however, the "Beautiful Soul" and the "Law of the Heart" are two quite distinct figures: the first designates the hysterical attitude of deploring the wicked ways of the world while actively participating in their reproduction (Lacan is quite justified in applying it to Dora, Freud's exemplary case of hysteria); the "Law of the Heart and the Frenzy of Self-Conceit," on the other hand, clearly refer to a *psychotic attitude*—that of a self-proclaimed Savior who imagines his inner Law to be the Law for everybody and is therefore compelled, in order to explain why the "world" does not follow his precepts, to resort to paranoid constructions, to the plotting of dark forces (like the Enlightened rebel who blames the reactionary clergy's propagation of superstition for his failure to win the support of the people). Lacan's slip is all the more mysterious for the fact that this difference between Beautiful Soul and Law of the Heart can be perfectly formulated in categories elaborated by Lacan himself: the hysterical Beautiful Soul clearly locates itself within the big Other, and functions as a demand to the Other within an intersubjective field, whereas the psychotic clinging to the Law of the Heart involves precisely a rejection, a suspension, of what Hegel referred to as the "spiritual substance." Similarly, in his key text on the subversion of the subject and the dialectic of desire, Lacan repeats the standard argument against philosophical speculation, and specifically against Hegel, making the old and rather boring point about the "bone" which cannot be dissolved in the circle of dialectical speculation, about the "gap" which all thought has avoided:

> Certainly there is a bone here. Since it is precisely what I am claiming—namely, what structures the subject—it essentially constitutes in the subject the gap that all thought has avoided, skipped over, circumvented, or stopped up whenever thought apparently succeeds in sustaining itself circularly, whether the thought be dialectical or mathematical.[38]

But is not this the very bone mentioned by Hegel in his *Phenomenology*, the bone of the infinite judgment "The Spirit is a bone"? And is not the notion of a "bone-in-the-throat" remainder, which is simultaneously the condition of possibility and the condition of impossibility of the dialectical process, at the very core of the Hegelian dialectic? What happens in the

---

37   See, for example, Jacques Lacan, *Écrits*, New York: Norton 2006, p. 80.
38   Ibid., p. 695.

concluding reversal of that process is not the magical dissolution/reintegration of the "bone" into the circle of dialectical movement, but merely a shift of perspective which makes us see how the "bone" is not merely an obstacle which cannot be sublated but, precisely as such, a positive condition of the movement of sublation—the obstacle retroactively engenders what it is an obstacle to.

Might we not say, then, that *the true "bone" of the philosophical discourse of the last two centuries is Hegel himself*? Is not Hegel's thought the traumatic point which is resisted by the entire post-Hegelian tradition, where this resistance takes the form of all possible negations, from outright psychotic foreclosure (Deleuze) to immanent overcoming (Marx)? In order to see this, however, we should not try simply to return to Hegel "the way he was," but to read Hegel through Freud (as reconceptualized by Lacan).

DIALECTICAL HISTORICITY

A properly Hegelian reading of Freud should not be constrained by the rather obvious objection: "but can we really understand Freud through a Hegelian approach? Does not Hegel's speculative idealism belong to a different epoch in which there is no place for the Freudian unconscious with its contingent mechanisms?" A Hegelian reading of Freud means reading Freud in the same way Hegel approaches great names from the history of philosophy: first isolating Freud's key breakthrough (the unconscious); then "deconstructing" Freud, analyzing his necessary inconsistency to demonstrate how he necessarily missed the key dimension of his own discovery; finally, showing how, in order to do justice to his key breakthrough, one has to move beyond Freud—Lacan achieved this in his "return to Freud," which designates a radical revolutionizing of the entire Freudian edifice. In this sense, Lacan's return to Freud is homologous to Luther's return to Christ, to original Christianity, a return which produced a radically new form of Christianity.

The same goes for a Freudian reading of Hegel: such a reading should not in any sense "psychoanalyze" Hegel, discerning in his system traces of his personal psychopathologies; neither, following some of Freud's own unfortunate remarks, should it denounce Hegel's system as the climax of philosophical paranoia, as a kind of ontologized psychotic conspiracy theory. The point is rather to read Hegel in a Freudian way, the way Freud reads the formations of the unconscious: to focus on the symptoms, the symptomal exceptions in Hegel's text, on what is "repressed" in his theory, and what can only be retroactively reconstructed through its distorted traces in the explicit text. (For example, one might argue that a purely repetitive "death drive" is the repressed focal point of the Hegelian notion of negativity.) And, of course, we should not shrink from applying each approach to its author: to engage in a Hegelian reading of Hegel himself, as well as a Freudian reading of Freud. What characterizes a really great thinker is that they misrecognize the basic dimension of their own breakthrough. (Plato, for instance, misrecognized the evental nature of encountering an Idea.) So the point is not that we can access what remains unthought in Freud through a Hegelian reading, or what remains unthought in Hegel through a Freudian reading; such a procedure should culminate in the self-reflexive move of thinking with Freud against Freud, or with Hegel against Hegel. But is not such an approach too formal—not only in the sense of trying to isolate abstract formal models of the dialectical process, but above all in the sense of missing the ultimate Marxist critical-materialist reversal of Hegel, namely the manner in which dialectical formal models are always mediated by concrete historical content, expressing a certain historical matrix? This case has been made by Peter Osborne:

> As for the "materialist reversal" from Marx back to Hegel, it actually happens within Marx's own texts, specifically in *Capital*, where the ontological peculiarity of the value-form is shown to enact just such a process. However, it is ontologically particular to capital—*that* is its materialism: in Žižek's terms, the contingent historical specificity of its necessity. Such dialectical logical necessity cannot be a feature of a general metaphysics without being precisely what it is in Hegel—idealism—because it lacks the capacity for sufficiently determinate significant (that is, practically relevant) differentiation. Simply calling it "materialism," on the basis of its difference from an ancient philosophical logic of "the One," does not stop it being idealism in a broader sense.[39]

What Osborne proposes here is the old thesis of the Hegel-Capital school (Helmut Reichelt et al.): the Marxian logic of commodities is the contingent historical secret of Hegelian speculation. However, it is not enough to say this. First, there is the fundamental ambiguity of the Marxist reference to Hegel which begins already in Marx himself, and goes on in Lukács and Adorno: is the Hegelian dialectical process the mystified/idealist expression

---

39   Peter Osborne, "More Than Everything," *Radical Philosophy* 177 (January/February 2013), pp. 22–3.

of the process of liberation, or the mystified/idealist expression of capitalist self-reproduction? Second, Marx is not only historicizing universals: he not only analyzes how a universality is always colored by a specific historical context, he also shows how there is a specific epoch in which a universality that is formally valid for all epochs appears as such—for example, the universality of labor only appears, or comes to exist, in capitalist reality. Finally, from Marx to Adorno, there is always a set of propositions which are presented as trans-historical universals. In his 1859 "Preface to the Critique of Political Economy," Marx summarizes "the guiding principle of my studies": "In the social production of their existence, men inevitably enter into definite relations, which are independent of their will, namely relations of production appropriate to a given stage in the development of their material forces of production."[40] These lines are clearly meant as trans-historical social-ontological universals. When, in his *Negative Dialectics*, Adorno talks about the "priority of the objective," when he asserts the non-identical, and so on, such statements are definitely meant to be taken as universal ontological principles whose truth is not limited to specific historical conditions.

Next there is another properly Marxist aspect: not only the historical mediation of universal philosophical categories, but the "practical" status of philosophy itself. As Althusser put it in his *Lenin and Philosophy*, philosophy is "class struggle in theory," by definition it involves taking sides, a practical engagement. The young Lukács said the same thing in a different way when he emphasized that historical materialism is not a new world-view, but a practical engaged stance. Osborne's reproach is that this dimension is lost when I define materialism in formal opposition to the idealist assertion of the One, as the assertion of abyssal multiplicity against the background of the Void, but within the same contemplative world-view.[41] But are things as clear as this? My reading of Hegel is historically located or mediated in a

---

40   Marx, "A Contribution to the Critique of Political Economy," Preface, available at marxists.org.

41   Mladen Dolar (in private conversation) raised a simple question here: did philosophers before Marx really only interpret the world instead of changing it? Did they not all, starting with Plato, propose some project for radically changing the world? Recall Plato's trip to Syracuse, where he tried to convince the local tyrant Dionysius to implement his reforms. It is perhaps only Hegel who was a truly contemplative philosopher, renouncing all projects for a future and limiting his thought to painting "grey on grey" in the present—and the paradox is that it was precisely Hegel's thought which, for that very reason, grounded the most radical attempts to change the world.

very specific way: Hegel is to be repeated today because his and our epochs are both epochs of passage from the Old to the New. A certain epoch is coming to an end (for Hegel premodern society, for us capitalism), but the failure of the Marxist revolutions makes it clear that we can no longer rely on the eschatology of the New-to-come—the future is open.

From the standpoint of emancipatory struggle, it is thus crucial to take into account how, in the process of the actualization of a Notion, the Notion itself changes (into its opposite). And the purer this Notion is, the more brutal the reversal. This is why Marx is "too (pseudo-)Hegelian," he really counts on the "synthesis" of communism as the overcoming of all history hitherto. At a general formal level, let us imagine a dialectical process which points towards its future resolution—the exemplary case would be Marx's vision of history in the *Grundrisse*, where the progress goes from substance to alienated subjectivity, i.e., subjectivity separated from the objective conditions of its labor. This development reaches its apogee in capitalism, in the figure of proletariat as substanceless subjectivity; however, this point of extreme alienation is in itself already a resolution, for it opens up the perspective of its own overcoming, of the collective subjectivity reappropriating its objective conditions—this time not by being substantially immersed in them, but by asserting itself as the subject of the entire process. From a strict Hegelian standpoint, a teleological process like this will always go wrong, and the intended goal will turn into its opposite (as confirmed by the reversal of revolutionary emancipation into Stalinist nightmare). The standard Marxist counter-argument here would have to be that such a reversal is precisely the basic feature of an "alienated" history in which individuals are the playthings of an impenetrable substantial process. For Hegel, however, the self-transformation of the goal during the process of its actualization is not an effect of the "alienated" character of a substantial process in which subjects are caught up—on the contrary, the idea that the process is dominated by a substantial big Other is in itself an ideological illusion. The Hegelian matrix of the dialectical process is thus that one must first fail in reaching the goal, as the intended reconciliation turns into its opposite, and only then, in a second moment, will the true reconciliation come, when one recognizes this failure itself as the form of success.

In this regard, where are we today? Radical historical self-reflection (a philosophy has to account for its own possibility, for how it fits into its own historical constellation) remains a necessity—as Foucault put it, every thought, even a reflection on the ancient past (like his own analysis of

Ancient Greek ethics) is ultimately an "ontology of the present." However, our self-reflection can no longer be that of the revolutionary Marxism exemplified in Lukács's *History and Class Consciousness* (the practical self-awareness of the engaged revolutionary subject). Our moment is more of a Hegelian one: not the moment of highest tension when the teleological (re)solution seems near, but the moment after, when the (re)solution is accomplished, but misses its goal and turns into nightmare. At this moment, the Hegelian problem is that of how to remain faithful to the original goal of the (re)solution and refuse to revert to a conservative position, how to discern the (re)solution in and through the very failure of the first attempt to actualize it. Hegel, of course, refers to the French Revolution, with its attempt to realize freedom that ended in revolutionary Terror, but his entire effort goes into demonstrating how, through this very failure, a new order emerged in which the revolutionary ideals became actuality. Today, we find ourselves in a strictly homologous Hegelian moment: how to actualize the communist project after the failure of its first attempt at realization in the twentieth century? What this impenetrability of the future—this impossibility of the agent's taking into account the consequences of its own act—implies is that, from the Hegelian standpoint, a revolution also has to be repeated: for immanent conceptual reasons, its first strike has to end in fiasco, the outcome must turn out to be the opposite of what was intended, but this fiasco is necessary since it creates the conditions for its overcoming.

Every historical situation harbors its own unique utopian perspective, an immanent vision of what is wrong with it, an ideal representation of how, with the necessary changes, the situation could be rendered much better. When the desire for radical social change emerges, it is thus logical that it should first endeavor to actualize this immanent utopian vision—which is why it has to end in catastrophe. It is here that we can also discern Marx's fundamental mistake: he saw how capitalism had unleashed the breathtaking dynamic of self-enhancing productivity; on the other hand, he also clearly perceived how this dynamic is propelled by its own inner obstacle or antagonism—the ultimate limit of capitalism (of self-propelling productivity) is Capital itself; the very development and revolutionizing of its own material conditions, the mad dance of its unconditional spiral of productivity, is ultimately nothing but a desperate attempt to escape its own debilitating inherent contradiction. Marx's mistake was to conclude that a new, higher social order (communism) was possible, an order that would not only maintain but would raise to an even higher degree the potential of the dynamic of productivity which, in capitalism, on account of its inherent contradiction, is again and again thwarted by socially destructive economic crises. In short, what Marx overlooked was that the inherent antagonism as the "condition of impossibility" of the full deployment of the productive forces is simultaneously its "condition of possibility": if we abolish the obstacle, the inherent contradiction of capitalism, then far from fully unleashing the drive to productivity, we lose precisely this dynamic that seemed to be generated and simultaneously thwarted by capitalism. If we remove the obstacle, the very potential thwarted by the obstacle dissipates (herein would reside a possible Lacanian critique of Marx, focusing on the ambiguous overlap between surplus-value and surplus-enjoyment).

The critics of communism were thus in a sense right when they claimed that Marxian communism is an impossible fantasy. What they did not perceive is that Marxian communism, this notion of a society of unleashed productivity outside the frame of Capital, was a fantasy inherent to capitalism itself, a strictly ideological fantasy of maintaining the thrust of productivity while removing the "obstacles" and antagonisms that are—as the sad experience of "really existing capitalism" demonstrates—the only possible framework for the effective material existence of a society of permanent self-enhancing productivity. This is why a revolution has to be repeated: only the experience of catastrophe can make the revolutionary agent aware of the fateful limitation of the first attempt. Marx, especially in his youthful texts, provides the basic formula of the illusion on which this fatal limitation is based in a series of implicit "instead of" theses which begin with the alleged "normal" state of things, and then go on to describe the alienated inversion of this "normal" state. Here is a long representative passage from his *Economic and Philosophic Manuscripts of 1844*:

> So much does the labor's realization appear as loss of realization that the worker loses realization to the point of starving to death … So much does the appropriation of the object appear as estrangement that the more objects the worker produces the less he can possess and the more he falls under the sway of his product, capital.
>
> All these consequences are implied in the statement that the worker is related to the *product of labor* as to an *alien* object. For on this premise it is clear that the more the worker spends himself, the more powerful becomes the alien world of objects which he creates over and against himself, the poorer he himself—his inner world—becomes, the less belongs to him as his own. It is the same in religion. The more man puts into God, the less he retains in himself. The worker puts his life into the object; but now his life no longer belongs to

him but to the object. Hence, the greater this activity, the more the worker lacks objects. Whatever the product of his labor is, he is not. Therefore, the greater this product, the less is he himself …

(According to the economic laws the estrangement of the worker in his object is expressed thus: the more the worker produces, the less he has to consume; the more value he creates, the more valueless, the more unworthy he becomes; the better formed his product, the more deformed becomes the worker; the more civilized his object, the more barbarous becomes the worker; the more powerful labor becomes, the more powerless becomes the worker; the more ingenious labor becomes, the less ingenious becomes the worker and the more he becomes nature's slave.) …

As a result, therefore, man (the worker) only feels himself freely active in his animal functions—eating, drinking, procreating, or at most in his dwelling and in dressing-up, etc.; and in his human functions he no longer feels himself to be anything but an animal. What is animal becomes human and what is human becomes animal.[42]

It would be easy to rephrase this passage in explicit "instead of" terms: instead of being the realization of the worker, labor appears as the loss of his realization; instead of appearing as what it is, the appropriation of the object through labor appears as its estrangement; instead of possessing what he produces, the more the worker produces the less he possesses; instead of civilizing himself through producing civilized objects, the more civilized his object, the more barbarous the worker becomes; and so on and so forth. Although the mature Marx, returning to Hegel to articulate his critique of political economy, generally leaves this rhetorical figure behind, it returns from time to time, as in the following passage from *Capital*:

This *inversion* (*Verkehrung*) by which the sensibly-concrete counts only as the form of appearance of the abstractly general and not, on the contrary, the abstractly general as property of the concrete, characterizes the expression of value. At the same time, it makes understanding it difficult. If I say: Roman Law and German Law are both laws, that is obvious. But if I say: Law (*Das Recht*), this abstraction (*Abstraktum*), *realizes itself* in Roman Law and in German Law, in these concrete laws, the interconnection becomes mystical.[43]

---

42 Marx, *Economic and Philosophical Manuscripts of 1844*, "Estranged Labour," available at marxists.org.

43 Karl Marx, "The Value Form: Appendix to the First German Edition of *Capital*, Volume 1, 1867," I. § 3(c), available at marxists.org.

In this case, however, we should be careful: Marx is not simply criticizing the "inversion" that characterizes Hegelian idealism (in the style of his youthful writings, especially *The German Ideology*)—his point is not that, while "effectively" Roman Law and German Law are two kinds of law, in idealist dialectics the Law itself is the active agent—the subject of the entire process—which "realizes itself" in Roman Law and German Law. Rather, Marx's thesis is that this "inversion" characterizes capitalist social reality itself. But the crucial point lies elsewhere: *both positions—the alienated inversion as well as the presupposed "normal" state of things—belong to the space of ideological mystification.* That is to say, the "normal" character of the state of things in which Roman Law and German Law are both laws (or in which the worker becomes more powerful the more powerful his labor becomes, or more civilized the more civilized his object becomes, etc.) is effectively the everyday form of appearance of the alienated society, the "normal" form of appearance of its speculative truth. The desire to fully actualize this "normal" state is therefore ideology at its purest and cannot but end in catastrophe.[44] In order to see this, we have to draw another key distinction: between the "alienated" situation in which we, as living subjects, are under the control of a virtual Monster/Master (Capital), and a more elementary "alienated" situation in which, to put it in a somewhat simplified way, *no one* is in control: not only us, but the "objective" process itself is also "decentered," inconsistent—or, to repeat Hegel's formula, the secrets of the Egyptians are also secrets for the Egyptians themselves.

Of what help can Hegel be here? There is definitely more than meets the eye in his famous dismissal of the "desire to teach the world what it ought to be" from the Preface to his *Philosophy of Right*:

---

44   One form this catastrophic reversal can take is the unexpected practical interpretation of the communist ideal which turns its realization into a nightmare. During the Great Leap Forward in the late 1950s, Chinese communists decided that China should by-pass socialism and directly embrace communism. They referred to Marx's famous communist formula: "From everyone according to his abilities, to everyone according to his needs!" The catch was the reading given to this slogan to legitimize the total militarization of life in the agricultural communes: the Party cadre in charge of a commune knows what each farmer is capable of, so he sets the plan and specifies individuals' obligations according to their abilities; he also knows what each farmer really needs for survival and so organizes the distribution of food and other provisions accordingly. The condition of militarized extreme poverty thereby becomes the actualization of communism. It is not sufficient to claim that such a reading falsifies a noble idea—we should rather indicate how it lies dormant in it as a possibility.

For such a purpose philosophy at least always comes too late. Philosophy, as the thought of the world, does not appear until reality has completed its formative process, and made itself ready … When philosophy paints its grey in grey, one form of life has become old, and by means of grey it cannot be rejuvenated, but only known. The owl of Minerva takes its flight only when the shades of night are gathering.[45]

As Pippin notes, if Hegel is minimally consistent, this has to apply also to the notion of the State deployed in his own *Philosophy of Right*: the fact that Hegel was able to deploy this concept means that "the shades of night are gathering" on what readers of Hegel usually take as a normative description of a model rational state. But does this mean that there are no signs from the future in Hegel, no hints about looming prospects? Perhaps we should apply to Hegel the approach advocated by Leo Strauss in his famous *Persecution and the Art of Writing* (1952). Relying on Strauss in his reading of Spinoza, Jean-Claude Milner employs the notion of "brachylogia," referring to formulations of excessive brevity, with words omitted, etc. In such cases, the expression to be decoded has to be read as a fragment, an incomplete phrase whose missing part is the crucial one, although cannot be pronounced publicly—recall Agatha Christie's title *By the Pricking of my Thumbs*, which assumes that an educated reader will recognize it as a fragment of a two-liner from Shakespeare's *Macbeth*: "By the pricking of my thumbs / Something wicked this way comes." Milner decodes in this way Spinoza's motto "*caute*" (I proceed with caution, discreetly, prudently) as part of the old Latin formula "*si non caste, tamen caute*" ("if you cannot be chaste, at least be discreet"), originally a piece of eleventh-century advice to monks and priests on how to act under the conditions of the newly imposed celibacy.[46] The critical edge here is intentional and well deserved since, as Milner points out: "In the same way that, in another time, writing on history was reduced to eulogies to Rome, today it seems that, in certain countries, philosophy reduces itself to a perpetual eulogy to Spinoza. I do not know anything that would have been more infantile."[47]

A variation on the same Straussian procedure is to read two fragments which appear at different places in a work together, as if they were parts of a single sentence. For example, Wagner's musical motif of "renunciation" is first heard in Scene 1 of *Das Rheingold*, when, answering Alberich's query,

45   Hegel, *Philosophy of Right*, Preface, available at marxists.org.
46   Jean-Claude Milner, *Le sage trompeur*, Paris: Verdier 2013, p. 14.
47   Ibid., p. 9.

Woglinde discloses that "*nur wer der Minne Macht versagt*" ("only the one who renounces the power of love") can take possession of the gold; its next most noticeable appearance occurs towards the end of Act 1 of *Walkure*, at the moment of the most triumphant assertion of love between Sieglinde and Siegmund—just prior to his pulling the sword out of the tree trunk, Siegmund sings it to the words: "*Heiligster Minne hoechste Not*" ("holiest love's highest need"). How are we to read these two occurrences together? What if one treats them as two fragments of a complete sentence that has been distorted by "dreamwork," that is, rendered unreadable by being split in two? The solution is then to reconstitute the complete proposition: "Love's highest need is to renounce its own power." This is what Lacan calls "symbolic castration": if one is to remain faithful to one's love, then one should not make it the direct focus of one's life, one must renounce its centrality. And what if we approach Hegel in this way? Let us begin with his account of the "right of distress [*Notrecht*]":[48]

> The particularity of the interests of the natural will, taken in their entirety as a single whole, is personal existence or life. In extreme danger and in conflict with the rightful property of someone else, this life may claim (as a right, not a mercy) a right of distress [*Notrecht*], because in such a situation there is on the one hand an infinite injury to a man's existence and the consequent loss of rights altogether, and on the other hand only an injury to a single restricted embodiment of freedom, and this implies a recognition both of right as such and also of the injured man's capacity for rights, because the injury affects only this property of his.

> *Remark:* The right of distress is the basis of *beneficium competentiae* whereby a debtor is allowed to retain of his tools, farming implements, clothes, or, in short, of his resources, i.e. of his creditor's property, so much as is regarded as indispensable if he is to continue to support life—to support it, of course, on his own social level.

> *Addition:* Life as the sum of ends has a right against abstract right. If for example it is only by stealing bread that the wolf can be kept from the door, the action is of course an encroachment on someone's property, but it would be wrong to

---

48   I owe this reference to Hegel's *Notrecht* to Costas Douzinas, who developed it in his intervention "The Right to Revolution?" at the Hegel colloquium "The Actuality of the Absolute," organized by the Birkbeck School of Law in London, May 10–12, 2013.

treat this action as an ordinary theft. To refuse to allow a man in jeopardy of his life to take such steps for self-preservation would be to stigmatize him as without rights, and since he would be deprived of his life, his freedom would be annulled altogether ...

This distress reveals the finitude and therefore the contingency of both right and welfare of right as the abstract embodiment of freedom without embodying the particular person, and of welfare as the sphere of the particular will without the universality of right.[49]

Hegel does not talk here about humanitarian considerations which should temper our legalistic zeal (if an impoverished father steals bread to feed his starving child, we should show mercy and understanding even though he broke the law ...). The partisans of such an approach, which limits its zeal to combating suffering while leaving intact the economico-legal edifice within which that suffering takes place, "only demonstrate that, for all their bloodthirsty, mock-humanist yelping, they regard the social conditions in which the bourgeoisie is dominant as the final product, the *non plus ultra* of history"[50]—Marx's old complaint which applies perfectly to contemporary humanitarians such as Bill Gates. What Hegel is referring to is a basic legal right, a right which is *as a right* superior to other particular legal rights. In other words, we are dealing not simply with a conflict between the demands of life and the constraints of the legal system of rights, but with a right (to life) that overcomes all formal rights, that is, with *a conflict inherent to the sphere of rights*, a conflict which is unavoidable and *necessary* insofar as it serves as an indication of the finitude, inconsistency, and "abstract" character of the system of legal rights as such. "To refuse to allow a man in jeopardy of his life to take such steps for self-preservation [like stealing the food necessary for his survival] would be to *stigmatize him as without rights*"—so, again, the point is not that the punishment for justified stealing would deprive the subject of his life, but that it would exclude him from the domain of rights, that it would reduce him to bare life outside of the domain of law or the legal order. In other words, this refusal deprives the subject of his very *right to have rights*. Furthermore, the quoted *Remark* applies this logic to the situation of a debtor, claiming that he should be allowed to retain of his resources as much as is indispensable for him to

---

49   Hegel, *Philosophy of Right*, Second Part: Morality, § 127–8.
50   Marx, Letter of March 5, 1852 to Joseph Weydemeyer, MECW Vol. 39, p. 58, available at marxists.org.

continue with his life not just at the level of bare survival, but "on his own social level"—a claim that is today highly relevant to the situation of the impoverished majority in indebted states like Greece.

Here comes the "brachylogical" move: Hegel, of course, does not do this explicitly, but—and it does not matter whether we follow his secret intention here or not—what if we were to read this right of distress together with Hegel's description of the "rabble" as a group or class whose exclusion from the domain of social recognition is *systematic*? "Against nature man can claim no right, but once society is established, poverty immediately takes the form of a wrong done to one class by another."[51] In such a situation, in which a whole class of people is systematically pushed beneath the level of dignified survival, to refuse to allow them to take "steps for self-preservation" (which, in this case, can only mean open rebellion against the established legal order) is to *stigmatize them as without rights*. Are we then not justified in universalizing this "right of distress," extending it to an entire social class and its acts against the property of another class? Although Hegel does not directly address this question, a positive answer imposes itself if, in a Straussian way, we reconstruct Hegel's secret syllogism:

First premise: an individual's "right of distress" to violate the law when his or her life is in danger or his or her normal survival is not possible.

Second premise: there is, in a modern society, a whole class of people, systematically created by the existing social order, whose normal survival is not possible.

Conclusion: so that class, even more so than an individual, should possess the "right of distress" and rebel against the existing legal order.

In short, what we get with such a reading of Hegel is nothing less than a Maoist Hegel, a Hegel who tells us what Mao told the young at the outset of the Cultural Revolution: "*It is right to rebel!*" Therein lies the lesson of a true Master: a true Master is not an agent of discipline and prohibition, his message is not "You cannot!", and not "You have to …!", but a releasing "You can!"—what? Do the impossible, namely what appears impossible within the coordinates of the existing constellation—and today, this means something

---

51   Hegel, *Philosophy of Right*, Third Part: Ethical Life, § 244, Addition.

very precise: you can think beyond capitalism and liberal democracy as the ultimate framework of our lives. A Master is a vanishing mediator who gives you back to yourself, who delivers you to the abyss of your freedom: when we listen to a true leader, we discover what we want (or, rather, what we always already wanted without knowing it). A Master is needed because we cannot accede to our freedom directly—to gain this access we have to be pushed from outside, since our "natural state" is one of inert hedonism, of what Badiou calls the "human animal." The underlying paradox here is that the more we live as "free individuals with no Master," the more we are effectively non-free, caught within the existing frame of possibilities—we have to be impelled or disturbed into freedom by a Master.

This paradox thoroughly pervades the form of subjectivity that characterizes "permissive" liberal society. Since permissiveness and free choice are elevated into a supreme value, social control and domination can no longer appear as infringing on subjects' freedom: they have to appear as (and be sustained by) individuals experiencing themselves as free. There is a multitude of forms of this appearing of un-freedom in the guise of its opposite: in being deprived of universal healthcare, we are told that we are being given a new freedom of choice (to choose our healthcare provider); when we can no longer rely on long-term employment and are compelled to search for a new precarious job every couple of years, we are told that we are being given the opportunity to reinvent ourselves and discover our creative potential; when we have to pay for the education of our children, we are told that we are now able to become "entrepreneurs of the self," acting like a capitalist freely choosing how to invest the resources he possesses (or has borrowed). In education, health, travel … we are constantly bombarded by imposed "free choices"; forced to make decisions for which we are mostly not qualified (or do not possess enough information), we increasingly experience our freedom as a burden that causes unbearable anxiety. Unable to break out of this vicious cycle alone, as isolated individuals—since the more we act freely the more we become enslaved by the system—we need to be "awakened" from this "dogmatic slumber" of fake freedom from outside, by the push of a Master figure.

There was a trace of this authentic Master's call even in Obama's slogan from his first presidential campaign: "Yes, we can!" A new possibility was thereby opened up—but, one might object, did not Hitler also do something formally similar? Was his message to the German people not "Yes, we can …"—kill the Jews, crush democracy, attack other nations? A closer analysis immediately brings out the difference: far from being an authentic

Master, Hitler was a populist demagogue who carefully played upon people's obscure desires. It may seem that in doing so he was following Steve
Jobs' infamous motto: "A lot of times, people don't know what they want
until you show it to them." However, in spite of all there is to criticize about
Jobs, in his own understanding of the motto he was close to the authentic
Master position. When asked how much research Apple undertakes into
what its customers want, he snapped back: "None. It's not the customers'
job to know what they want ... we figure out what we want."[52] Note the
surprising turn of this argumentation: after denying that customers know
what they want, Jobs does not go on with the expected direct reversal "it is
our task (the task of creative capitalists) to figure out what they want and
then 'show it to them' on the market." Instead, he says: "we figure out what
we want"—this is how a true Master works: he does not try to guess what
people want; he simply obeys his own desire and leaves it up to others to
decide if they want to follow him. In other words, his power stems from his
fidelity to his desire, from refusing to compromise on it. Therein lies the
difference between a true Master and, say, the fascist or Stalinist leader who
pretends to know (better than the people themselves) what people really
want (what is really good for them), and is then ready to enforce it on them
even against their will.

In Udi Aloni's documentary *Art/Violence*, a tribute to Juliano Mer-
Khamis, the founder of the Jenin Freedom Theatre, a young Palestinian
actress describes what Juliano meant to her and her colleagues: he gave
them their freedom, he made them aware of what they could do, he opened
up a new possibility for them, homeless kids from a refugee camp. This is
the role of an authentic Master: when we are afraid of something (and fear
of death is the ultimate fear that makes us slaves), a true friend will say
something like: "Don't be afraid, look, I'll do it, this thing you're so afraid
of, and I'll do it for free—not because I have to, but out of my love for you;
I'm not afraid!" In doing so he sets us free, demonstrating *in actu* that it can
be done, and that we can do it too, that we are not slaves. Let us recall, from

---

52   In India, thousands of impoverished intellectual workers are employed in
what are ironically called "like-farms": they are (miserably) paid to spend the whole
day in front of a computer screen endlessly clicking "like" buttons on pages requesting
visitors to "like" or "dislike" a specific product. In this way, a product can be made to
appear very popular and thereby seduce ignorant prospective customers into buying
it (or at least checking it out), following the logic of "there must be something in it if
so many customers are so satisfied!" So much for the reliability of customer reactions
... (I owe this information to Saroj Giri, New Delhi).

Ayn Rand's *The Fountainhead*, the description of the impact Howard Roark makes on the audience in the courtroom where he stands on trial:

> Roark stood before them as each man stands in the innocence of his own mind. But Roark stood like that before a hostile crowd—and they knew suddenly that no hatred was possible to him. For the flash of an instant, they grasped the manner of his consciousness. Each asked himself: do I need anyone's approval?—does it matter?—am I tied?—And for that instant, each man was free—free enough to feel benevolence for every other man in the room. It was only a moment; the moment of silence when Roark was about to speak.[53]

This is the way Christ brings freedom: confronting him, we become aware of our own freedom. Such a Master is not a subject supposed to know, but also not simply a subject supposed to be free—in short, he is not a subject of transference, which is why it is also wrong to see his position as equivalent to that of the analyst in the analytic social link. The obvious question to be raised here is: why does a subject need a Master to assume his or her freedom? Does not such an assumption amount to a kind of pragmatic paradox wherein the very form (a Master gives me freedom) undermines the content (my freedom)? Should we not rather follow the well-known motto of all emancipatory movements: freedom cannot be handed down to us by a benevolent master but has to be won through hard struggle?

---

53   Ayn Rand, *The Fountainhead*, New York: Signet 1992, p. 677.

Part I

BEYOND THE TRANSCENDENTAL

CHAPTER 1

Towards a Materialist Theory of Subjectivity

KANT AVEC ALTHUSSER

The Althusserian theory of ideology fully asserts the gap that separates our ideological sense-experience from the external material apparatuses and practices that sustain that experience. The theory distinguishes two levels of the ideological process: external (following the ritual, ideology as material practice) and internal (recognizing oneself in interpellation, believing). Although Althusser refers to Pascal to account for the passage between them—follow the external rituals and inner belief will come—the two dimensions remain external to each other; their relationship is that of the parallax: we observe ideological practice either from the outside, in bodily gestures, or from the inside, as beliefs, and there is no intermediate space or passage between the two. Nevertheless, (theatrical) comedy seems to provide a kind of intermediate space here, a place for passage in both directions—acting as if one believes and believing that one merely acts. When a character in a comedy feigns to believe or just acts as if he believes, he enacts (in his external behavior) an internal belief, or, vice versa, when he gets caught in his own game, actual belief can arise out of his conviction that he just believes that he acts.[1]

The well-known formula of fetishistic disavowal—*je sais bien, mais quand même ...*—is thus much more complex than it may appear. Recall the murder of the detective Arbogast in Hitchcock's *Psycho*: it comes as a surprise, even more so than the notorious shower murder.[2] The latter is a totally unexpected surprise, but here, although we know something shocking is about to happen, and the whole scene is shot to indicate it, we are still surprised when it does happen. Why? The obvious answer is: because

---

1 I rely here on Mladen Dolar, "Mimesis and Comedy," *Problemi* 5–6 (2012) (in Slovene).

2 We might even suggest that the shower murder explodes out of nothing as a reaction to (the threat of) boredom: when Marion takes the shower, the film could well have ended, if she had avoided the temptation and decided to return to Phoenix and give the stolen money back.

we did not really believe it would. However, we should reduce the formula of fetishistic disavowal to a tautology, that is, replace the standard version "I know very well… (that you don't love me), but I nonetheless believe (that you do)" with "I know very well that you love me, but I nonetheless believe that you do (love me)." The paradox is that this tautological version renders the gap that separates knowledge from belief palpable at its purest: if I already know that you love me, why do I also have to believe that you do? Or, to take Lacan's famous statement that a husband's suspicion that his wife is sleeping with other men remains pathological even if she really is doing so: is not "I know very well that my wife is cheating on me, but I nonetheless believe that she is" much more uncanny than the usual "I know very well that my wife isn't cheating on me, but I nonetheless believe that she is"?[3] Why does knowledge have to be supplemented by belief? Is it that a belief emerges in order to compensate for the failure of knowledge? We believe in God because we cannot know for sure that He exists. The solution is that "even if I know it, I don't really know it": knowledge was not—cannot be—really subjectively assumed, it did not occupy the place of truth (as in Lacan's formula of the analyst's discourse). Belief thus supplements a gap, an immanent split, within knowledge itself, hence we are not dealing here just with a gap between knowledge and belief. The same goes for our stance towards the threat of ecological catastrophe: it is not a simple "I know all about the ecological threat, but I don't really believe in it." It is rather "I know all about … and I nonetheless believe in it," because I do not really assume my knowledge. It is this *immanent* gap that eludes Althusser's theory of the Ideological State Apparatuses (ISAs). According to Althusser, what distinguishes the State from other social apparatuses is that

> everything that operates in it and in its name, whether the political apparatus or the ideological apparatuses, *is silently buttressed by the existence and presence of public, armed physical force.* That it is not fully visible or actively employed, that it very often intervenes only intermittently, or remains hidden and invisible—all this is simply one further form of its existence and action … one had to make a show of one's force so as not to have to make use of it; … it suffices to deploy one's (military) force to achieve, by intimidation, results that would normally have been achieved by sending it into action. We may go further, and say that *one can also not make a show of one's force so as not to have to make use of it.* When

---

3 See Simon Hajdini, *Na kratko o dolgčasu, lenobi in počitku,* Ljubljana: Analecta 2012, pp. 196–9.

threats of brute force, or the force of law, subject the actors in a given situation to obvious pressure, there is no longer any need to make a show of this force; there may be more to be gained from hiding it. The army tanks that were stationed under the trees of Rambouillet Forest in May 1968 are an example. They played, by virtue of their absence, a decisive role in quelling the 1968 riots in Paris.[4]

The first thing to note here is the radical change of terrain that occurs when we pass from the first to the second level of avoiding the use of direct force. First, one makes a show of force so as not to have to use it; then, one does not make a show of force so as not to have to use it. We are effectively dealing here with a kind of negation of negation: first, we "negate" the direct use of force by replacing it with a mere show—say, in a tense situation in which the authorities expect violent demonstrations, they decide to parade columns of tanks through the working-class quarters of the city, expecting that this will dissuade the protestors; then, this "negation" is itself "negated," i.e., there is no show of force, but the authorities expect this to have an even more powerful deterrent effect than an open display of force—since the protestors know there is a police (or military) force ready to confront them, its very absence makes it all the more ominous and omnipotent.[5] The first negation operates at the level of the imaginary: the real of the brutal use of force is substituted by a fascinating spectacle designed to deter protestors. The second negation operates at the level of the symbolic: it is only within the symbolic order of differentiality that "the presence-absence (a presence rendered effective by its very absence)" functions, i.e., that absence can count as a positive feature even more powerful than presence.[6] And it

---

4   Louis Althusser, *Philosophy of the Encounter*, London: Verso 2006, pp. 103–4.
5   This can also be conceptualized as a distinction between two levels of bluffing: 1) at the imaginary level, we bluff with spectacular presence, our public display of force hides the fact that there is no substantial force behind it ready to strike; 2) at the symbolic level, we bluff with absence itself, we create the impression that there is a military force behind the scenes, waiting to intervene—we hide the fact that there is nothing to hide, no hidden force ready to strike. The same distinction could be applied to the digital control exerted by state agencies like the NSA. At the first level, they bluff that they have an abundance of data about our lives, carefully disclosing a little of it to make an impression; at the second level, they bluff by evoking the threat of total control without making any concrete revelations—their knowledge remains invisible and as such even more threatening.
6   Another example: when we do something wrong and expect a figure of authority to explode in fury and shout at us, if they do not explode but remain cold and calm, the effect can be even more threatening, since there is always something

is this properly symbolic dimension that Althusser ignores, as is clear from a footnote attached to the quoted passage, in which Althusser draws attention to how Perry Anderson likened "the presence-absence ... of the state's armed forces to the monetary gold reserves of the Central Banks":

> general circulation in all its forms (which are practically infinite) takes place independently of the presence of the gold stocks on the market. Yet such circulation would be impossible if these reserves did not exist ... they "impinge on the market" simply because they make this market (this market and no other) possible, in exactly the same way as the invisible (should I say "repressed"?—that is indeed the right term as far as most people are concerned, since they "do not care to know" that these reserves exist and play a determinant role) presence of the police or armed forces impinges on a situation.[7]

From this second example, we can see clearly what Althusser misses: the "little piece of the real" (the armed force, gold reserves) that can remain in the background since it can perform its function even without being used, indeed can fulfill that function *even if it does not exist at all*—it is enough that people believe there is an armed force hidden in the background (or gold reserves in an inaccessible bank vault). The real in the background that serves as the ultimate guarantee and support of the public power is thus a spectral entity—not only does it not need to exist in reality, if it did appear and directly intervene in reality, then it would risk losing its power, since, as Lacan made clear, omnipotence (*toute-puissance*) necessarily reverts into "all-in-potency" (*tout en puissance*):[8] a father who is perceived as "omnipotent" can only sustain this position if his power remains forever a "potential," a threat which is never actualized. The full use of force, painful as it might be, makes it part of reality and as such by definition limited. This—and not only the shame at what they had done—was the reason the Chinese authorities turned their crackdown at Tiananmen Square, in which (at least) hundreds died, into a non-event: it was a direct exercise of brute force, but it took place at night, invisibly, like a nightmarish-spectral event of rumor; peace and order were immediately restored, all traces of conflict erased, the appearance of life carrying on as normal resumed. If

---

of a release of tension in the open explosion of fury—OK, this is it, now we've seen it, we can breathe ...

7 Althusser, *Philosophy of the Encounter*, p. 104.
8 Jacques Lacan, *Le séminaire X, L'angoisse (1962–1962)*, June 19, 1963.

a regime gets involved in open warfare against its own population, it risks losing not only the minimum of its legitimacy but the very source of its power.[9]

As already in his classic text on Ideological State Apparatuses, Althusser compulsively repeats the point about the material support of ideology— military, legal, and ideological apparatuses, institutional and educational "machines," etc.—claiming that this material support has been ignored by Marxists from Marx onwards. For traditional Marxists, materialism means that ideology (still conceived in an idealist way, as a form of "social consciousness," a domain of ideas, an inverted ideal mirror of reality) is grounded in the extra-ideological material process of social (re)production ("being determines consciousness"); what they ignore is the proper material existence of ideology in the ISAs, in a complex institutional network of practices and rituals. However, Lacan here goes one step further than Althusser: there is *a specific materiality of ideas themselves*, immanent to the "ideal" symbolic order, insofar as this order cannot be reduced to (an expression of) meaning but functions as a "meaningless" machine, the machine that is the big Other beyond any concrete materialization in institutions or material practices:

> You realize that my intention is not to turn them into "subtle" relations, that my aim is not to confuse letter with spirit ... and that I readily admit that one kills if the other gives life, insofar as the signifier—you are perhaps beginning to catch my drift—materializes the instance of death. But whereas it is first of all the materiality of the signifier that I have emphasized, that materiality is singular in many ways, the first of which is not to allow of partition. Cut a letter into small pieces, and it remains the letter that it is—and this in a completely different sense than *Gestalttheorie* can account for with the latent vitalism in its notion of the whole.[10]

This uncanny "machine in the ghost"—what Lacan called the autonomy of the signifier with regard to the signified—points towards the most difficult and radical sense in which one should assert materialism: not only the "priority of being over consciousness," in the traditional Marxist sense

---

9   And the same goes for gold reserves: imagine they were all poisoned by radiation and thus of no physical use—if people continued to accept them as a point of reference, nothing would actually change.

10   Jacques Lacan, *Écrits*, New York: Norton 2006, p. 16.

that ideas are grounded in the material social and productive process, and not only the material (ideological) apparatuses that sustain ideology, but also the immanent materiality of the ideal order itself. To get a taste of this weird ideal materiality, we can return to Hegel's critique of Kant. The major target of the deservedly famous chapter on the Moral World View in Hegel's *Phenomenology* is the thinking of the Ought-to-be (*das Sollen*)—of positing an inaccessible Ideal which we can only asymptotically approach in an endless effort, but never fully realize. Rebecca Comay has drawn attention to some strange features of this chapter: Hegel's critique of Kant is deployed with a weird passion, almost a rage, brutally mocking a caricature-like image of Kantian ethics in language employing a whole series of terms later appropriated by Freud (repression, displacement, denial …). The point of Hegel's critique is the immanent inconsistency of the moral world-view—briefly, the full realization of the moral Ideal would mean its self-destruction, so that morality has to desire its own ultimate failure as the condition of its infinite self-reproduction. In other words, Hegel's point is that the endless postponement of the arrival of a fully moral universe is not just an effect of the gap between the purity of the Ideal and the empirical circumstances which prevent its full actualization, it is *located in this Ideal itself*, inscribing a contradiction (a self-sabotaging desire) into its very heart.

This implies that there is a distortion immanent to language, a tendency to cheat, lie, engender a false appearance, which cannot be dismissed as a secondary empirical corruption of some original normativity. Habermas' "communicative reason" is emblematic here: communicative action is possible given the human capacity for rationality, but this rationality is no longer of the traditional kind, neither the immanent rational structure of the cosmos (as in the Aristotelian tradition) nor the rational a priori of the Kantian transcendental subject. Aware that today such philosophical "foundationalism" is no longer possible, Habermas conceives rationality as a capacity inherent within language, especially in the form of argumentation. He thus reinterprets the transcendental horizon as a pragmatic a priori of intersubjective speech: all speech acts have the inherent goal of mutual understanding, and human beings possess the communicative competence to bring about such understanding. Argumentative speech relies on an inherent normativity—the absence of coercive force, the mutual search for understanding, the compelling power of the better argument— which makes communication possible. In this way, Habermas endeavors to ground the goals of human emancipation and to maintain a universalist ethical framework: the normativity he talks about is not an external ideal, but is immanent to our participation in linguistic intersubjectivity—when I talk to and with others, I imply that I obey these norms even if I consciously violate them. This pragmatic a priori inherent to language is irreducible ("*unhintergehbares*": one cannot step behind it) in the strict transcendental sense: one cannot ground it in a "deeper" positivity (to explain, say, through evolutionary biology how the human animal developed intersubjective discursive normativity), since in order to provide such an account, one already has to rely on the argumentative normativity of intersubjective space (since every scientific explanation by definition proceeds in such an argumentative way). For Habermas, all other uses of language (to lie and cheat, to pretend, to seduce, etc.) are derivative: secondary empirical distortions of the inherent normativity, conditioned by relations of power and domination or by the pursuit of private interests.

Lacan may seem to say the same thing when he claims that the big Other is the decentered site of Truth which is operative even when we lie—we can lie only against the background of reference to truth. However, Lacan introduces a series of complications. First, his understanding of the big Other as the site of Truth goes beyond the standard notion of truth as correspondence with facts—his favorite example is the old Jewish joke "Why are you telling me you're going to Lemberg when you're really going to Lemberg?" where a lie assumes the form of factual truth: the two friends established have an implicit code that, when you go to Lemberg, you say you are going to Cracow and vice versa, and within this space, telling the literal truth means lying. (The famous Groucho Marx line "He may look like an idiot and talk like an idiot, but don't let that fool you—he really *is* an idiot!" obeys the same logic.) If such cases appear as eccentric exceptions, think about the kind of polite everyday phrases that we don't usually mean, but in response to which, when we *do* mean them, the addressee has the full right to reply: "Why are you saying you're glad to see me when you are actually glad to see me?" or "Why are you asking me how I am when you do actually want to know?" To take a crueler example: I meet an acquaintance who I know to be in the final stages of cancer and tell him (out of politeness, to cheer him up) that he looks much better than the last time I saw him; however, unbeknownst to me, his cancer has been magically reduced since then, and to an attentive gaze he really does look better. In this situation, is not my acquaintance—who of course takes my compliment as mere politeness (i.e., as implying that actually I think he looks ill)—fully justified in replying: "Why are you saying that I'm looking better when I really am looking better?" This is why, far from being mere secondary embellishments, these "empty" gestures of politeness (when I say something without "really meaning it") concern the very core of symbolic exchange, of properly human communication as opposed to the exchange of denotative signs. A bee performs its complex dance in order to signal to other bees where the flowers with the nectar are; if a human being were to do such a dance, the question would pop up: "Why is he doing that? To give me an order, asserting his mastery? To show his love for me? To warn me of danger because there's a lizard crouched there?"

A new terrain thus opens up to our view—a terrain of what are literally "lies," cheats, pretenses, but pretenses that are at the origin of language itself, inscribed into its very essence, not just secondary distortions of its immanent normativity. Even Kant, *the* thinker of transcendental normativity if ever there was one, opened himself up to this uncanny domain of "sincere lies" in his late book on anthropology. This domain compels us to rethink the entire topic of normativity, of an Ideal asymptotically approaching its actualization: what resists this actualization is not just empirical inertia, the resistance is inscribed into the very notion of the Ideal as its immanent inconsistency, inner split, or, to use Hegel's unique term, its "absolute recoil" from itself. The impurity is not just an empirical imperfection, but is itself a priori, transcendental—for example, the fact that language is never directly insincere, that it always has to violate this norm, is an a priori feature constitutive of the very domain of the symbolic order. Although this reinscription of the empirical distortion of a notion into the very heart of that notion, as an immanent self-distortion, is the basic move of Hegel's dialectical reflection, we can find its contours already in Kant, as was pointed out by Michel Foucault.

Foucault's "Introduction to Kant's *Anthropology*" is the introductory essay to his own translation of Kant's last substantial work, *Anthropology from a Pragmatic Point of View*, from 1798. Foucault claims that Kant, in his *Anthropology*, refers the conditions of possibility of experience (transcendental subjectivity) back to the empirical existence of the subject: in an attempt to understand how we experience the world, Kant approaches humans as empirical objects. However, since for Kant the transcendental subject is the starting point of knowledge, the a priori that precedes any empirical knowledge and is constitutive of it, it cannot itself be investigated as an object of that knowledge: if it is an object of empirical knowledge, then it exists as an object of phenomenal reality and is as such already constituted by itself in its transcendental dimension. Foucault thus criticizes Kant for a necessary oscillation between the transcendental and the empirical: all empirical content is transcendentally constituted, but the transcendental subject is itself in need of an empirical grounding.[11]

However, Foucault falls short in this attempt to reduce the tension in Kant's anthropology to the gap between the transcendental and the empirical (the "transcendental-empirical doublet"), that is, to read the pragmatic dimension of which Kant speaks as the dimension of treating humans as empirical worldly beings. Even a quick glance at what Kant does makes it clear that he was aiming at something quite different: neither the subjective (in the sense of transcendental freedom and autonomy) nor the objective (in the sense of the empirical realm of phenomenal causality), but what today we would call the "performative" dimension of social-symbolic interaction, of social role playing, of obeying civilized rules of politeness. Here a weird causality enters—not the causality of hard empirical facts but the causality of polite lies and illusions, of "superficial" manners, of mere pretending—in short, the causality of what Popper called the "Third World" and Lacan the "big Other," the level of sincere lies, of keeping up appearances. In this topsy-turvy world, the deceiver itself is deceived, and the only route to inner moral authenticity goes by way of hypocritical pretense. No wonder, then, that in the subsection "On permissible moral appearance [*Schein*]" in the *Anthropology* we encounter an unexpected Kant, a Kant far from "Kantian" moral rigorism and moralism, a Kant located in a lineage that runs from Pascal to Althusser:

> On the whole, the more civilized human beings are, the more they are actors. They adopt the illusion of affection, of respect for others, of modesty, and of unselfishness without deceiving anyone at all, because it is understood by everyone that nothing is meant sincerely by this. And it is also very good that this happens in the world. For when human beings play these roles, eventually the virtues, whose illusion they have merely affected for a considerable length of time, will gradually really be aroused and merge into the disposition.—But to deceive the deceiver in ourselves, the inclinations, is a return again to obedience under the law of virtue and is not a deception, but rather an innocent illusion [*Tauschung*] of ourselves ...
>
> In order to save virtue, or at least lead the human being to it, nature has wisely implanted in him the tendency to willingly allow himself to be deceived.

11   Michel Foucault, *Introduction to Kant's Anthropology from a Pragmatic Point of View*, Los Angeles: Semiotext(e) 2008. This topic of the "transcendental-empirical doublet" was further developed in Foucault's *The Order of Things: An Archaeology of Human Sciences*, New York: Vintage Books 1994.

Good, honorable *decorum* is an external appearance that instills *respect* in others (so that they do not behave over familiarly with others). It is true that woman would not be content if the male sex did not appear to pay homage to her charms. But *modesty (pudicitia)*, a self-constraint that conceals passion, is nevertheless very beneficial as an illusion that brings about distance between one sex and the other, which is necessary in order that one is not degraded into a mere tool for the other's enjoyment.—In general, everything that is called propriety (decorum) is of this same sort—namely, nothing but *beautiful illusion* [*Schein/* appearance].

Politeness (politesse) is an illusion of affability that inspires love. *Bowing* (compliments) and all *courtly* gallantry together with the warmest verbal assurances of friendship are to be sure not exactly always truthful ("My dear friends: there is no such thing as a friend." *Aristotle*); but this is precisely why they do not *deceive*, because everyone knows how they should be taken, and especially because these signs of benevolence and respect, though empty at first, gradually lead to real dispositions of this sort.

All human virtue in circulation is small change—it is a child who takes it for real gold. But it is still better to have small change in circulation than no funds at all, and eventually they can be converted into genuine gold coin, though at considerable loss ... Even the illusion of good in others must have value for us, for out of this play with pretences, which acquires respect without perhaps earning it, something quite serious can finally develop.—It is only the illusion of good *in ourselves* that must be wiped out without exemption ...[12]

Kant goes even further here than simply praising the "empty" coquetry and gallantry that mask the aim of seduction, offering other surprising details such as celebrating the art of learned conversation in which witty remarks abound during shared meals, and condemning eating alone as barbaric.

This specific dimension of politeness is located between the two extremes of pure inner morality and external legality: while both of these are constructed in a very precise conceptual way (the subject acts morally only if his motive is one of pure duty uncontaminated by pathological considerations; he acts legally if his external acts do not violate any legal prohibitions and regulations), politeness is both more than just obeying external legality and less than pure moral activity—it is the ambiguously imprecise domain of that which one is not strictly obliged to do (in failing

---

12   Immanuel Kant, "Anthropology from a Pragmatic Point of View," in *Anthropology, History, and Education*, Cambridge: Cambridge University Press 2007, pp. 263–4.

to do it one does not break any laws) but which one is nonetheless expected to do. We are dealing here with implicit unspoken regulations, with questions of tact, with something towards which, as a rule, the subject has a non-reflexive relationship: something that is part of our spontaneous sensitivity, a thick texture of customs and expectations that constitutes our inherited substance of mores (*Sitten*). As such, this domain is the domain of ideology *par excellence*, at its purest: it is the air we breathe spontaneously in our daily interactions, in the attitudes we accept as self-evidently given. To put it in Althusserian terms, it is the domain of ideological apparatuses and practices, a domain which, to use Kant's own terms, allows individuals to "schematize" their abstract moral and legal norms, to make them part of their living experience.

To prove the point, it suffices to recall the impasse of political correctness: the need for it arises when unwritten mores are no longer able to regulate everyday interactions effectively—in place of spontaneous customs followed in a non-reflexive way, we have explicit rules ("blacks" become "African Americans," "fat" becomes "weight-challenged," etc.). The main victim of such operations is precisely the order of "sincere lies," of pretense: under the discursive regime of political correctness, it is not enough to follow external rules of politeness, one is expected to be "sincerely" respectful of others, and continually examined on the sincerity of one's innermost convictions. In short, pushed to its extreme, the PC attitude resembles that of a proto-psychotic paranoid about the sincerity of every little politeness: greeting him with a "Hello, nice to meet you!," his reaction is: "Are you really glad to see me or are you just a hypocrite?"

Kant's line of reasoning implies that empirical anthropological knowledge, as well as the practical guidance based on this knowledge, can have an impact on how a free autonomous moral subject acts, that the empirical factors encompassed by culture, civilization and mores can affect moral status, or at least can occasion some form of moral progress. The appearance of virtue in a man playing the role of a virtuous man can gradually become part of his disposition: the pretense of virtue can bring about genuine virtue. Civilized social intercourse, though not yet virtue, is nonetheless a practice and cultivation of virtue: conducting themselves in company in a civilized fashion, people become gentler and more refined, and practice goodness in small matters:

> Although the charms and passions are much exaggerated therein [in books that serve for amusement] they still refine men in their feelings, by turning an object

of animal inclination into one of more refined inclination; a man is thereby made receptive to the motive force of virtue on principles. They also have an indirect use, for in taming their inclinations, men become more civilized. The more we refine cruder elements, the more humanity is purified, and man is rendered capable of feeling the motive force of virtuous principles.[13]

In short, one who loves the illusion of the good is eventually won over to actually loving the good. But how can love of the illusion of the good lead to love of the good itself? If one loves the illusion of the good and enacts this illusion in social intercourse, one might come to appreciate its worth and to love the good itself for its own sake. Correlatively, from the point of view of the spectator, loving the illusion of the good in others may make us act politely in order to become lovable, which leads us to exercise our self-mastery, control our passions, and, eventually, to love the good for its own sake. In this sense, paradoxically, by deceiving others through politeness and social pretence, we in fact deceive ourselves and transform our pragmatic, polite behavior into virtuous behavior: by deceiving others through the pretence of virtue, we foster civil society, and in doing so, deceive ourselves by transforming our pretense of virtue into a disposition for virtue itself. Does not this line of thought recall Pascal's advice to non-believers who would like to believe, but cannot bring themselves to accomplish the leap of faith? "Kneel down, pray, act as if you believe, and belief will come by itself."

Upon a closer look, of course, we soon discover that things are more complicated, and the efficacy of ideological rituals functions in a much more twisted way. Take the case of interpellation, where Althusser's own example contains more than his own theorization gets out of it. Althusser famously imagines an individual who, walking carelessly down the street, is suddenly addressed by a policeman: "Hey, you there!" By answering the call—by stopping and turning round to face the policeman—the individual recognizes-constitutes himself as the subject of Power, of the big Other-Subject:

> [Ideology] "transforms" the individuals into subjects (it transforms them all) by that very precise operation which I have called interpellation or hailing, and which can be imagined along the lines of the most commonplace everyday police (or other) hailing: "Hey, you there!"

---

13   Immanuel Kant, *Lectures on Ethics*, Cambridge: Cambridge University Press 1997, p. 210.

Assuming that the theoretical scene I have imagined takes place in the street, the hailed individual will turn round. By this mere one-hundred-and-eighty-degree physical conversion, he becomes a subject. Why? Because he has recognized that the hail was "really" addressed to him, and that "it was really him who was hailed" (and not someone else). Experience shows that the practical transmission of hailings is such that they hardly ever miss their man: verbal call or whistle, the one hailed always recognizes that it is really him who is being hailed. And yet it is a strange phenomenon, and one which cannot be explained solely by "guilt feelings," despite the large numbers who "have something on their consciences."

Naturally for the convenience and clarity of my little theoretical theatre I have had to present things in the form of a sequence, with a before and an after, and thus in the form of a temporal succession. There are individuals walking along. Somewhere (usually behind them) the hail rings out: "Hey, you there!" One individual (nine times out of ten it is the right one) turns round, believing/suspecting/knowing that it is for him, i.e. recognizing that "it really is he" who is meant by the hailing. But in reality these things happen without any succession. The existence of ideology and the hailing or interpellation of individuals as subjects are one and the same thing.[14]

The first thing to note in this passage is Althusser's implicit reference to Lacan's thesis on the letter that "always arrives at its destination": the interpellatory letter cannot miss its addressee since, on account of its "timeless" character, it is only the addressee's recognition/acceptance of it that constitutes it as a letter. The crucial feature of the quoted passage, however, is the double denial at work in it: the denial of the explanation of interpellative recognition by means of a "guilt feeling," as well as the denial of the temporality of the process of interpellation (strictly speaking, individuals do not "become" subjects, they "always already" are subjects).[15] This double denial can be read in Freudian terms: what the "timeless" character of interpellation renders invisible is a kind of atemporal sequentiality that is far more complex than the "theoretical theatre" staged by Althusser invoking the suspicious alibi of "convenience and clarity." This "repressed" sequence concerns a "guilt feeling" of a purely formal, "non-pathological" (in the

---

14   Louis Althusser, "Ideology and Ideological State Apparatuses," in *Essays on Ideology*, London: Verso 1984, p. 163.

15   I resume here a more detailed critical reading of Althusser's notion of ideology from Chapter 3 of Slavoj Žižek, *The Metastases of Enjoyment*, London: Verso 2006.

Kantian sense) nature, a guilt which, for that very reason, weighs most heavily upon those individuals who "have *nothing* on their consciences." That is to say, the individual's first reaction to the policeman's "Hey, you there!" is an inconsistent mixture of two elements: first, the thought "Why me? What does this policeman want from me? I'm innocent, I was just out for a stroll minding my own business"; second, this perplexed protestation of innocence is always accompanied by an indeterminate Kafkaesque feeling of "abstract" guilt, a feeling that, in the eyes of Power, I am a priori terribly guilty of something, although it is not possible for me to know precisely what, and for that reason I am even more guilty—or, more pointedly, it is in this very ignorance of mine that my true guilt consists.[16]

What we have here is thus the entire Lacanian structure of the subject split between innocence and an abstract, indeterminate guilt, confronted with a non-transparent call emanating from the Other, in which it is not clear to the subject what the Other actually wants from him ("Che vuoi?"). In short, what we encounter here is interpellation prior to identification. Prior to the recognition in the call of the Other by means of which the individual constitutes himself as "always already" subject, we are obliged to acknowledge this "timeless" instant of the impasse in which innocence coincides with indeterminate guilt: the ideological identification by means of which I assume a symbolic mandate and recognize myself as the subject of Power takes place only as an answer to this impasse.

What remains "unthought" in Althusser's theory of interpellation is thus the fact that, prior to ideological recognition, we have an intermediate moment of obscene, impenetrable interpellation without identification, a kind of vanishing mediator that has to become invisible if the subject is to achieve symbolic identity, to accomplish the gesture of subjectivization. In short, the "unthought" of Althusser is that there is already an uncanny subject that precedes the gesture of subjectivization.

It is crucial to recognize that Althusser's two failures—his failure to clearly identify the immaterial "materiality" of the big Other and his failure to grasp the complexity of interpellation—are two sides of the same coin. What escapes Althusser in his description of the process of interpellation is the subject prior to subjectivization, to symbolic identification—this subject which is effectively the answer of the Real to symbolic interpellation but which also stands for the Real that is not simply a product of material

---

16   Here I follow the perspicacious observations of Henry Krips in his excellent unpublished manuscript "The Subject of Althusser and Lacan."

ideological practices but is correlative to the "immaterial" big Other, as its effect in the Real. It is because of the excess of this weird subject that discipline and education are needed—or, to return to Pascal's example of praying, the question to be raised is: *but who will make us pray?* And this brings us to another key question: what is the entity upon which discipline and education work? Kant seems to claim that it is our animal nature:

> Discipline or training changes animal nature into human nature. An animal is already all that it can be because of its instinct; a foreign intelligence has already taken care of everything for it. But the human being needs his own intelligence. He has no instinct and must work out the plan of his conduct for himself. However, since the human being is not immediately in a position to do this, because he is in a raw state when he comes into the world, others must do it for him.[17]

But the need for discipline is not just grounded negatively, in the lack of a firm instinctual base; discipline is also needed because humans display an "unnatural" savagery (*Wildheit*) or passion for freedom specific to human nature:

> Savagery [unruliness, *Wildheit*] is independence from laws. Through discipline the human being is submitted to the laws of humanity and is first made to feel their constraint. Thus, for example, children are sent to school initially not already with the intention that they should learn something there, but rather that they may grow accustomed to sitting still and observing punctually what they are told, so that in the future they may not put into practice actually and instantly each notion that strikes them … Now by nature the human being has such a powerful propensity towards freedom that when he has grown accustomed to it for a while, he will sacrifice everything for it.[18]

The predominant form of appearance of this weird "savagery" is passion, an attachment to a particular choice so strong that it suspends rational comparison with other possible choices. When in the thrall of a passion, we stick to a certain choice whatever it may cost: "Inclination that prevents reason from comparing it with the sum of all inclinations in respect

---

17   Kant, "Lectures on Pedagogy," in *Anthropology, History, and Education*, p. 437.
18   Ibid., p. 438.

to a certain choice is *passion (passio animi)*."[19] As such, passion is morally reprehensible:

> far worse than all those transitory emotions that at least stir up the resolution to be better; instead, passion is an enchantment that also refuses recuperation … Passions are cancerous sores for pure practical reason, and for the most part they are incurable because the sick person does not want to be cured and flees from the dominion of principles, by which alone a cure could occur.[20]

And, as the subsection "On the inclination to freedom as a passion" tells us, "For the natural human being this is the most violent [*heftigste*] inclination of all."[21] Passion is as such purely human: animals have no passions, just instincts. This Kantian savagery is "unnatural" in the precise sense that it seems to break or suspend the causal chain that determines all natural phenomena—it is as if, in its terrifying manifestations, noumenal freedom transpires for a moment in our phenomenal universe.

THE FORCED CHOICE OF FREEDOM

Is this "Althusserian" Kant of the *Anthropology* just the result of Kant applying his ethics to empirical reality, in a kind of "schematization", or does it compel us to change our perception of Kantian ethics itself? Let us begin with an unexpected example of passion from contemporary life. It is all too easy to denounce devotion to computer games as a pathological obsession representing merely a compulsive enslavement to commercialized pop culture. But when one observes teenagers in, say, Seoul engaged in a collective game for several hours or even days, one might rather admire them as an exemplary case of dedicated self-discipline and concentration on an activity which brings joy—something like today's version of the spiritual exercises elaborated by Loyola. Or, to put it in Foucauldian terms, the only real alternative to being controlled and disciplined by anonymous social mechanisms is a no less ruthless self-discipline and training. Such participation is simultaneously a matter of extreme rational self-control and a profoundly ecstatic experience—when I act, the Other acts through me, and in this sense I act "with the grace of God," as Loyola puts it.

---

19   Kant, "Anthropology from a Pragmatic Point of View," p. 367.
20   Ibid., p. 368.
21   Ibid., p. 369.

The aim of the Jesuit spiritual exercises is to enable the subject to develop "discernment" (*discretio*), the ability to discern between good and evil spirits. Our soul is always torn between following the path of Good and succumbing to baseness; through exercises in humility, selflessness, etc., we can discipline ourselves, learning to follow the right path and thereby act with the grace of God. What stands out here is the link between ecstatic contemplation and ethical engagement, between mystical experience and rational practice: the goal is to act with the grace of God, not to drown oneself in a mystical experience of the divine. Acting with the grace of God does not involve a kind of passive surrender in which we allow ourselves to be led by a higher hand; rather, the exercises should be understood as a method of subjective ethical thought, so that in deciding which path will be most to the glory of God we rely on our own discernment. We can recall here Badiou's thesis that an Idea enables us to introduce a pertinent difference, to draw a line of distinction: there is no transcendent guarantee for the rightness of the distinction, since the act of discerning has the self-referential structure of a Pascalian wager that creates the conditions of its own rightness. Divine grace has thus to be precisely located: the point is not that the subject whose knowledge is limited has to guess the right decision and needs divine help in doing so, a hint from God who already knows the answer; the point is rather that there is no right decision prior to the act of deciding, and "grace" is needed if our act is to succeed in creating the conditions for its success. The paradox here is the same as that of predestination in Protestantism,[22] and was also clearly perceived by Descartes when he noted that fatalism and radical freedom go together:

> The idea Descartes articulates is the following. One has to assume that every-thing is already predetermined, although one can never and will never know how. This disposition of mind is the only one that avoids me falling into the idealist position of assuming I could determine everything, that everything is in my power, or that freedom is my capacity. This position suspends my consider-ing freedom to be my capacity, that of which I am able (and this sort of ability is as should have become clear always bodily determined). So, Descartes proposes

---

22   Before we dismiss predestination as an attempt to reduce man to an impo-tent puppet at the mercy of God's inscrutable arbitrary decisions, we should inquire what this notion effectively amounts to: there is no commerce, no tit-for-tat, no exchange between man and God. The moment we think that our salvation depends on our good deeds, these deeds lose their ethical character and become a commercial enterprise ("if I do good deeds, I will be properly rewarded in the afterlife").

to assume the full determinate impact of contingency (God in his terminology) turning into necessity and this is what he calls fatalism. To assume this position, as he claims, one needs courage. Why? Because in the first instance, this might look as if it were the very abolition of freedom. And for Descartes it is the abolition of freedom: of freedom as a capacity. So, what Descartes proposes is to act as if one were not free and this builds the very condition of actual freedom. But why? Because for him any objectifying gesture is problematic—it turns freedom into a capacity, brings subjects into indifference and leads to heteronomous determination (more precisely to a wrong understanding of heteronomy). But by fully assuming that we objectively have nothing in our power and will never know anything about God's power and will, i.e. contingency's plan, this makes it possible to conceive of my actions in a purely subjective way. Acting as if I were not free—being a fatalist—I affirm the very determination that I cannot deduce from my capacities, namely that I am forced to make a choice when I seek to be free. But I thereby do not simply become the instrument of the Other, of God's will (Descartes is not Eichmann); I rather become even more responsible for my deeds as everything is determined but it is fully unclear how (so I should not care). Since even the other—here God—is also determined by contingency (God has no plan about His plan either), I have to assume for Descartes that I am determined (I am forced to be free or to think by something that does not spring from my thought or freedom), and this implies in the heart of the human there thus lies something determining him; the human animal is in its heart an inhuman entity. Assuming this can avoid the type of indifference I outlined; fatalism, the defense of absolute necessity, might be considered to be a tool for a renewal of a true (inhuman) humanism. Or simply put: only a fatalist can be free. His or her slogan, his or her guiding line, should be: act as if you were not free.[23]

This is why radical acts of freedom are possible only under the condition of predestination: in predestination, we know we are predestined, but we don't know how we are predestined, i.e., which of our choices is predetermined, and this terrifying situation in which we have to decide what to do, knowing that our decision is decided in advance, is perhaps the only case of real freedom, of the unbearable burden of a really free choice—we know that what we will do is predestined, but we still have to take a risk and subjectively choose what is predestined.[24]

---

23   Frank Ruda, "How to Act as if One Were Not Free: In Defense of Fatalism" (unpublished manuscript).

24   Postmodern philosophers from Nietzsche onwards expressed their preference for Catholicism over Protestantism: Catholicism is a culture of external playful

From this perspective, the Kantian emphasis on the autonomy of the moral subject should not be read as an expression of "ethical narcissism," but as an acknowledgement of our unsurpassable limitation: since I always act in a situation that is ultimately opaque and thus cannot master the consequences of my acts, all I can do is to act with sincere intentions ... Kant is thus not simply stipulating that the purity of the inner intention is the only criterion of the moral character of my act: he is well aware that, in order for our moral activity to have any sense at all, we have to presuppose a deep affinity or harmony between our moral intentions and the objective structure of reality—therein resides the role of the postulates of pure practical reason. And it is here that the "moral luck" apparently excluded by Kant returns with a vengeance: Kant admits that we cannot effectively practice morality while limiting ourselves to nothing but our inner intention, totally dismissing actual consequences—we are compelled to engage in a kind of "leap of faith" and commit ourselves to a fundamental trust in the friendly structure of reality. One cannot but recall here the wonderful "*Soave sia il vento*" trio from Mozart's *Cosi fan tutte*, with its appeal to the "elements" (of the real) to respond benignly to our desires: "Gentle be the breeze, / calm be the waves, / and every element / respond benignly / to our desires"[25]—an appeal sustained by the suspicion that there is no match between our desires and reality, that their discord is irreducible, that our desires themselves are in no way gentle, that they tend to explode in a violence and thereby provoke an even more violent response from the Real. If we read Kant in this way, focusing on the need to wage a *salto mortale*, then the opposition between autonomy and thrownness or unaccountability loses its edge: the subject's thrownness is the very condition of his autonomy. We can refer here to Lacan's logic of the "non-All": the position of true autonomy is not "I am responsible for everything," but "there is nothing for which I am not responsible," the counterpart of which is "I am

---

rituals in contrast to the inner sense of guilt and the pressure of authenticity that characterize Protestantism; we are allowed just to follow the ritual and ignore the authenticity of our inner belief ... However, this playfulness should not deceive us: Catholicism resorts to such subterfuge to save the divine big Other in his goodness, while the capriciously "irrational" predestination in Protestantism confronts us with a God who is ultimately not good and all-powerful but indelibly stained by the suspicion of His being stupid, arbitrary, even outright evil. The implicit dark lesson of Protestantism is: if you want God, you have to renounce (part of the divine) goodness.

25   "Soave sia il vento, / Tranquilla sia l'onda / Ed ogni elemento / Benigno responda / Ai nostri desir."

not responsible for All": precisely because I cannot have a grasp of All, there is nothing for which I can exempt myself from my responsibility.

Let us imagine a subject in the predicament of having to make a difficult decision which will hurt those close to him; he makes the tough choice and sets about doing what it requires, but just as he is on the way to confronting the consequences a stupid meaningless contingent event intervenes and cancels his act. For example, a Russian psychoanalyst once reported how one of his patients finally decided, after much painful vacillation, to leave his estranged wife and move in with his mistress. His idea was to drive to the nearby town where the mistress lived, and from there to call his wife, letting her know that he was leaving her. However, soon after leaving home, he got caught in a storm and after a couple of minutes the car's windscreen wiper broke off. He managed to get as far as a nearby car repair shop only to discover that it had just closed for the day. Having no other choice, he called the breakdown services and had his car towed back home where he rejoined his wife, telling her nothing about his decision. (The husband admitted to the analyst that, already prior to this incident, he had noticed that the windscreen wiper was a bit rickety—"it works well all the time except when it rains," as he put it.) Such totally contingent events (a machine breaks down, a friend arrives unexpectedly, a storm erupts …)—intervening almost magically at the very last moment, preventing the subject from realizing his decision and allowing him to reverse it and go on with his life as usual—are exemplary cases of the "answer of the Real": a tiny piece of the Real gives body to the subject's psychic resistance to his act, his panic even, a piece which has to appear "objective," that is, independent of his will and intention, so that fate rather than the subject's vacillation can be blamed for his failure to accomplish the act. And the subject should be held fully responsible here: even if not himself responsible for the accident, his reaction to it, and the sense of relief that immediately emerges, signal the falsity of his position.

It is all too easy to oppose a human being as a free autonomous subject and a human being as an object of trade, owned by another human being, deprived of his or her autonomy. The whole point of slavery is that, in some basic sense, the traded human being remains a free subject, no matter how "objectivized" she is. A slave can be angry at his owner, can run away from him, or can even sincerely love him … Therein resides the mystery of the relations of servitude and domination: how can free autonomous subjects nonetheless treat each other as non-free, as "objects"? Is it not that renouncing freedom has to be a minimally free act? In the abstract, there seem to be two extremes between which the social link operates: we either share a space of intersubjectivity as equal participants in communication and cooperation, or we are denied the status of equal communicative partners and reduced to objects dominated and manipulated by those who have appropriated full access to speech. The problem with this abstract opposition, however, is that what it sees as a position somewhere in between the two extremes—neither mutual recognition nor objectivization—is the original position of a participant in the process of symbolic exchange, while the two extremes are mere abstractions which—for reasons of principle, rather than simply as empirical complications—can never occur as actual positions. For example, even a subject deprived of active speech and reduced to an object has to accept this reduction and behave accordingly. This is why the master's pleasure stems from his awareness that his slave is not simply an object but a free being compelled to act as if he were a mere object, a "speaking tool" to use Aristotle's term for slaves. Hegel was well aware of this paradox: the key result of his dialectic of Master and Slave is the insight into how, "in order to keep a speaking being silent, it is not necessary to kill it. At this moment, politics emerges … it suffices to dominate, killing is superfluous, this is the moral of [Hegel's] fable. To keep silent and not to kill, these are the two faces of the same axiom: the initial axiom of politics."[26]

And perhaps the very core of an erotic relationship resides in introducing ambiguity and a hidden reversal into a situation of political domination: while modestly accepting her position, the subordinated woman in an erotic relationship can also play with that subordination, using it as a ploy to effectively dominate and control the situation, sending the message "I will only concede to being subordinated if you …" In politics likewise, is not the figure of the master who plays at being the servant of his subjects the basic gesture of the perverse eroticization of political space? This dimension is, of course, ignored—prohibited, even—by the standpoint of Political Correctness. In order to recognize the limits of the "politically correct" approach to love and seduction, it suffices to note how the ethical injunction to love someone for what he really is, rather than for his status, wealth, etc., is self-defeating: for a priori reasons, it is impossible to draw a clear line of separation between "sincere" love and the "false" love generated by the pressures of status, money, or even brutal coercion (or, in the case of the

---

26   Jean-Claude Milner, *Pour une politique des êtres parlants*, Paris: Verdier 2011, p. 21.

opposite and no less "false" version, the pressures of compassion and sympathy for one's inferior). To attempt to abstract from all these "pathological" features and wait for "pure" love to emerge is to be condemned to wait for ever, since one will never fall in love. The paradox to be accepted is thus that, by definition, love is never "pure": the very features which allegedly stain it, up to and including a future partner's brutal display of power, are what can effectively trigger it. In other words, the choice "Do you love me for myself or for my contingent external features?" presents a false choice, since you can never fall in love with "what I am in myself": what I am in myself is a void filled in precisely by the reflection of my "contingent external features."

The anticipatory subject

What would a materialism look like which fully took into account this traumatic core of subjectivity irreducible to natural processes? In other words, what would a materialism look like which fully assumed the main result of transcendental idealism: the gap in the natural order signaled by the emergence of subjectivity? The answer seems to be provided by Alain Badiou, whose notion of the subject turns around the Althusserian one. Many commentators have noted an homology between Althusserian interpellation and Badiouian subjectivization: in both cases, an external Cause (the big Other in Althusser, the Truth-Event in Badiou) addresses the individual and transforms it into a subject. However, for Althusser, this recognition in the Other's call gives rise to the subject of ideology, while for Badiou, fidelity to the evental Cause gives rise to the subject of Truth. For Althusser, subjectivity is ideological (opposed to scientific knowledge), while for Badiou, Truth itself is subjective (opposed to objective knowledge).

The subtitle of Frank Ruda's book in defense of Badiou, *Idealism without Idealism*,[27] points in the right direction: the predominant philosophical struggle occurs today *within* materialism, between democratic and dialectical materialism—and what characterizes dialectical materialism is precisely that it incorporates the idealist legacy, against vulgar democratic materialism in all its guises, from scientist naturalism to the post-Deleuzian assertion of spiritualized "vibrant" matter. Dialectical materialism is, first,

---

27   See Frank Ruda, *For Badiou: Idealism without Idealism* (unpublished manuscript, from which the following several quotations are taken).

a *materialism without matter*, without the metaphysical notion of matter as a full substantial entity—in dialectical materialism, matter "disappears" in a set of purely formal relations. Second, despite being materialism without matter, it is not idealism without an idea—it is a *materialism with an Idea*, an assertion of the eternal Idea outside the space of idealism. In contrast to idealism, whose problem is how to explain temporal finite reality if our starting point is the eternal order of Ideas, materialism's problem is how to explain the rise of an eternal Idea out of the activity of people caught in a finite historical situation.

Ruda opposes idealist (Hegel's) and materialist (Badiou's) dialectics with regard to the tension between dialectical and non-dialectical aspects of the dialectical process: from the materialist standpoint, the dialectical process "relies upon something that is not itself dialectically deducible": "materialist dialectics has to be understood as a procedure of unfolding consequences, of the attempt to cope with something that due to the logic of retroactivity logically lies before it, is prior to it." Ruda is, of course, not only Hegelian enough to recognize that this priority is retroactive (the event is prior to the unfolding of its consequences, but this can be asserted only once these consequences are here); he even goes to the end and proposes the Hegelian formula of the closed teleological loop between the event and its consequences—the event engenders consequences which constitute the actuality of the event, i.e., which retroactively posit their own cause, so that the event is its own cause, or, rather, its own result:

> the consequences that change the world are engendered by something, the event, *which itself is nothing but what it will have generated* … an event is the creation of the conditions of the possibility of the consequences of an event—i.e. of the event itself. This is why it had the paradoxical structure of naming a multiplicity which belongs to itself … any event is nothing but the ensemble of the consequences it yields—although it is at the same time the enabling cause of these very consequences.

The line that separates idealism from materialism concerns precisely the status of this circle: the "teleological" formula—"a thing is its own result, it becomes what it always already was"—can be read in two opposed ways. It either means that, in the process of its actualization, a Notion deploys or actualizes its immanent potential, so that there are ultimately no contingencies, no contingent encounters, just an immanent self-development in which a Notion merely "plays with itself" (this would be a case of what

Ruda calls "expressive dialectics": in the course of its self-deployment, a Notion expresses its immanent content). Or it means, more literally, that in the course of a contingent process, a Notion *becomes* "what it always already was," for its timelessly past essence is a retroactive illusion. While of course rejecting the idealist "expressive dialectics" of the immanent self-deployment of a Notion, Ruda locates the non-dialectical aspect of a dialectical process in its contingent starting point: its *Anstoss*, to use Fichte's term, the unpredictable event that triggers it. Following Badiou, Ruda describes the stages of the Event illustrated by a love relationship which begins with an unforeseen encounter between two individuals:

> Either, after the encounter, they say "yes" to this unforeseen possibility, draw and unfold consequences from it, that is to say: they change their lives—they become a couple, move in together, buy a dog, etc.—or they remain indifferent. The possibility of this free choice was not given, not present before the vanishing mediator of the encounter emerged. The freedom of this free choice is thus no capacity of the individual as such—it needs something which is able not only to trigger it but rather to produce it. Only retroactively are the lovers able to claim that they voluntarily decided to take it seriously. An eventual encounter therefore generates the very capacity which will retroactively have proven to be that which is able to unfold the consequences of the very conditions of possibility of this unfolding.

So it all begins with the contingent and unpredictable event itself—an encounter between two people that both of them experience as a shattering provocation: their lives are thrown off the rails. The two have to react, and here comes the free decision: will they say *yes* to the event, assume it as their destiny, or will they ignore it? If the latter, life will go on as usual, but if they say *yes* to it, they constitute themselves as a subject, (re)organizing their entire life around the event—in short, out of fidelity to the event, they engage in the long and arduous work of love. A careful reader will not miss the double paradox at work here. According to common sense, the subject precedes free choice: in order for such a choice to take place, there has to be a subject who makes it. For Badiou, on the contrary, the subject is not the agent of a free choice, but the result of a positive free choice—a subject emerges after the choice of fidelity to an event, it is the agent which engages itself in the work of enforcing the consequences of an event. Furthermore, common sense tells us that free choice and forced choice are opposed and mutually exclusive, but for Badiou, a truly free choice is a forced one. A free choice in the ordinary sense of the term (shall I choose chocolate cake or cheese cake?) is a form of indifference, occurring when it doesn't really matter what I choose. A truly free choice only occurs after an evental encounter, when I have to decide whether to engage in the work of fidelity to an event or to ignore the encounter and continue with my life as usual. This choice, however, is an extremely forced one, since the whole weight of ethics exerts a pressure on me to make the positive choice and not to miss the encounter.

Here, though, problems arise—to what precise extent is an event retroactive? If a contingent *Anstoss* is simply ignored, if no subject engages in the work of love for it, is it still an event? Badiou himself has changed his position with regard to this key question. His standard view in *Being and Event* is that an event includes its nomination—it is an event only for those who name it and thereby recognize themselves in it. (The French Revolution is an Event only for its partisans, while for Anglo-Saxon liberals, say, it is just a quirk of French history with no universal dimension.) Later, in *Logics of Worlds*, he holds that an event determines the entire situation whose "symptomal torsion" it is—in short, an event affects all participants in a historical situation, including those who ignore it or say "no" to it. It is only if an event is not self-referential in the sense that it includes its own nomination (there is an Event only for the subjects who are engaged in it, who "believe in it"; there is no Event for a neutral observer) that Badiou can distinguish different modes of subjectivity which are simultaneously the modalities of how the subject relates to the Event. Badiou elaborates four such responses: the faithful subject; the reactive subject; the obscure subject; and resurrection. An Event always occurs within a world, within its transcendental coordinates, and its emergence affects the *entirety* of the world: no one can really ignore it—the post-Evental liberal who tries to prove that there was no Event, that the October Revolution was just a quirk of Russian history, is not the same as the pre-Evental liberal, since he is already mediated by the Event, reacting to it. It is one thing not to know something, it is quite another to act as if one does not know it. So, again, how far does retroactivity reach? If an evental encounter is ignored, is it evental at all? In other words, is it only the free choice of fidelity that retroactively transubstantiates a stupid contingent encounter into an Event?

Once an Event is assumed in a free choice, it constitutes the subject as the agent dedicated to the work of drawing the consequences of the Event in reality: "I have conceived of this power—which Freud perhaps already named with the category of 'working through'—under the name of forcing."[28] The parallel drawn by Badiou between evental (en)forcing (*le forçage*) and Freudian *Durcharbeiten* is interesting in its ambiguity. As a method, "working through" is opposed to hypnosis and refers to the long hard work of undermining resistance to the patient's access to unconscious material. Hypnosis leaves the defensive structure of the ego intact: it circumvents resistance, for in a hypnotic state the ego is simply "put to sleep," so that repressed memories can directly emerge; the problem is that when full conscious awareness returns, the same ego with all its repressive mechanisms also returns in full force—what is missing is the "processes of remodeling the ego." The point of passing from hypnosis to working through is not just that, in the latter, the subject's insight into her unconscious is gained in a more authentic way, through the transformation of her entire subjective structure; the point is a much more subtle and radical one. The unconscious content is not something covered up by resistance, it does not simply pre-exist resistance, it is something that is immanent to resistance, something that can be uncovered by the immanent analysis of resistance.

So enforcing—of what, against what? In Badiou, enforcing works on the pre-evental inertia, it is the work of imposing onto it a truth from outside, while in Freud, resistance is more than such inertia, it is itself contaminated by what it tries to repress, so its analysis in working through is not just a process of dismantling the obstacles in order to gain direct access to truth—here also, *la vérité surgit de la méprise*, truth is immanent to the process of its covering up, or, as Lacan put it, repression equals the return of the repressed. When Lacan writes "I, truth, speak," this does not mean that the substantial "big Other" in me speaks, but, on the contrary, that in the psychoanalytic process truth arises from mistake (or, rather, mis-apprehension: *mé-prise*)—truth says: "Whether you flee from me in deceit or think you can catch me in error, I will catch up with you in the mistake from which you cannot hide."[29] Truth appears in what I hold as least true, most contingent, unworthy of universality—again, truth says: "I wander about in what you regard as least true by its very nature: in dreams, in the way the most far-fetched witticisms and the most grotesque nonsense of jokes defy meaning, and in chance—not in its law, but rather in its contingency."[30] This is why the aspect of repetition in working through also acquires different meanings in Badiou and in psychoanalysis: in Badiou, repetition

28   Alain Badiou, *Conditions*, London: Continuum 2009, p. 138.
29   Lacan, *Écrits*, p. 341.
30   Ibid., p. 342.

amounts to the subject's fidelity to the Event which compels it to engage in the patient arduous interminable work of enforcing; for Freud, repetition is much more, it is the inextricable overlapping between truth and its obfuscation—*truth persists and repeats itself in the very form of its obfuscation*. This difference in the status of repetition also accounts for the difference in their respective notions of subject. Following Badiou, Ruda opposes the (Lacanian) identification of the subject with the void:

> The subject is a process, it is not a point. So the void as the point ... cannot be identified with the subject. The void is an unlocalizable point; the subject is a process which always takes place in a singular and historically specific situation ... The event as localization of the previously unlocalizable and unpresented void is that which enables the subject to come to being, it allows for subjectivization.[31]

We thus have three (logically, if not temporarily) consecutive moments: the primordial unlocalizable void of multiplicity; the event as the localization of the previously unlocalizable void; and the process of subjectivization which emerges out of the free decision to choose fidelity to the event. Like the subject which assumes it, the event "always takes place in a singular and historically specific situation"—in other words, an event takes place at the point of a "symptomal torsion" of a specific situation, i.e., within a transcendentally constituted world, in a space of representation, giving body to its "part of no-part," to its excessive element lacking a place within a situation. What remains unaccounted for here is the passage from ontology (of void and multiplicity) to phenomenology (of specific situations, "states," transcendentally constituted worlds): why, how, in what way does a multiplicity, a part of the order of being, begin to *appear*, to *re-present* itself as a particular world? Furthermore, in what precise sense can an event function as "localization of the previously unlocalizable and unpresented void"? The notion of the localized void as the point of the symptomal torsion of a situation—as the stand-in, within a specific order of representation, of what is unrepresentable within this order—is clear enough; but why exactly is this point the localization of the pre-transcendental ontological void (except in the general sense that the pre-transcendental multiplicity is void, and that what is unrepresentable within an order of representations is the excess of multiplicity)? And, last but not least, if an event localizes the void of a situation, the point of its symptomal torsion, does it not take place

---

31   Ruda, *For Badiou: Idealism without Idealism*.

independently of its assertion-naming? Even more, is it not part (of no part) of any situation? That is to say, is not every specific order of representation structured around its point of impossibility, its immanent exclusion? Within capitalism, for example, the proletariat as the symptomal point of capitalist society is co-substantial with the capitalist order as such. An event proper occurs only when this symptomal point is fully assumed in its truth—say, when the proletariat grasps that its lack of a proper place within the social body signals that it stands for the universality (universal truth) of the society in which there are proletarians. In a strictly homologous way, for Freud, the symptom provides a clue for the entire personality, and that is why the Freudian "enforcing" is different from Badiou's: it is the enforcing of the immanent truth of a situation, not just the enforcing of an Event onto an inert and indifferent situation.

If, then, we have to distinguish between the localization of the void of a situation in its symptomal point (which is constitutive of the situation as such) and the act of assuming the truth announced in this symptomal point, does this not imply that we should extend the scope of subjectivity? In the most basic sense, subjectivity is there in every situation, since there is no symptom without subjectivity—the space of subjectivity is the twisted space of representations which include their point of symptomal torsion, the point of inscription, within the specific field of representations, of their constitutive exclusion or impossibility (or, in Lacanese, every signifying chain includes a signifier which gives body to the very lack of a signifier). If, for Badiou, a subject is an exception to the "normal" run of things, if it emerges only on rare occasions as an affirmative reaction to an Event, what then are we to do—we "human animals" who live (politically, at least) in non-evental times? Well aware of this problem, Ruda addresses it directly in a Cartesian mode, proposing a *morale provisoire* for acting in non-evental times: one should act as

a *hypothetical subject, an anticipated subject* which holds the place open for a new political subject (but the same goes, as should be clear, for any condition in its absence). The philosophical subject is not a subject forcing knowledge into a situation but it produces a forced shift from the objective domain of knowledge into the subjective, or put differently: it takes the position of *the very form of the subject* (in the conditions) ... This is not directly synonymous with choosing but it is rather the *insistence on the very form of a choice*; it is not directly an orientation but it recalls *the very form of subjective orientation* in disoriented times; it is not an anticipation of what will have been the consequences of a truth in a situation, but it clings to the *very form of anticipation*. The operation of philosophical forcing thus can be rendered in one simple formula: There are anticipations, there is orientation, or: there is a choice, *always*.[32]

(Note that this hypothetical subject is identified as a "philosophical subject.") But what if this hypothetical/anticipated subject *is the subject as such*, what if the Hegelian claim that the "subject is not a substance" means precisely that the subject is nothing but its own anticipatory form? In short, what if the subject is something like Malevich's black square on a white background, a pure marking of a difference between inside and outside, a pure frame which paradoxically precedes what it enframes? And, consequently, what if an event is like Duchamp's *urinoir*: a contingent little piece of reality which can provoke an evental reaction from the subject *only if the subject is already there as its own form/anticipation*? This is why Lacan's claim that there is no subject without object is to be strictly distinguished from the standard transcendental correlation between subject and object: the subject is like an empty frame without an object, and it is correlative to an object without a frame, without its proper place. These two can never encounter each other within the same space, not because they are too far away but because they are one, the front side and obverse of the same thing. This object that is the subject, the Lacanian *objet a*, is, however, not the same as the contingent event that triggers subjectivization.

This pure subject, the anticipation of itself, is the Lacanian subject represented by a signifier (of the lack of a signifier) for other signifiers, the subject implied by a structure twisted through a symptomal torsion. It is a subject prior to subjectivization, and, in Badiou's terms, we can define subjectivization as the process through which a subject assumes the truth of its symptomal point. This brings us to a subtle difference between the Lacanian subject and what Ruda conceptualizes as the hypothetical/anticipated subject: the latter is, as its qualification clearly indicates, a deficient mode of the subject proper (the agent of the fidelity to an Event), it is what one can do or be to remain open for the eventuality of an Event in a non-evental time, while for Lacan, the hypothetical/anticipated subject is the subject at its zero-level, and the Badiouian subject is one of its possible derivations or modalities.

In Badiou's affirmative approach, Evil is a defective mode of Good, and the hypothetical subject is a defective mode of the subject as agent of truth,

---

32   Ibid.

while from the Hegelian (and Lacanian, I would claim) perspective, *the negative move comes first*: loss is prior to what it is the loss of, betrayal is prior to what it is the betrayal of, the Fall is prior to what it is the Fall from. This paradoxical reversal (of the common-sense logic which tells us that a positive entity has to precede its lack) defines the space of subjectivity from the Hegelian and Lacanian perspective: a "subject" is something that "is" its own lack, something that emerges out of its own impossibility, something that only persists as "barred."

Perhaps, however, we should employ the distinction between the subject and the process of subjectivization in a different sense, taking into account the fact that, in deconstructionist discourse theory, "subjectivization" has a meaning totally different from Badiou's: "subjectivization" rhymes with assuming subject-positions, referring to modes of subjectivity that hinge on contingent discursive processes. With this meaning in view, we may draw another line of separation between democratic and dialectical materialism: according to democratic materialism, the "subject" is an unstable dynamic entity, a discursive construct, a result of the socio-symbolic process of subjectivization which, through its complex mechanisms of discipline, micro-power, etc., engenders the different subject-positions assumed by individuals. For dialectical materialism, on the contrary, the subject is prior to the process of subjectivization: this process fills in the void (the empty form) that is the pure subject.

This distinction between subject and subjectivization brings us to the heart of the question as to what constitutes ethical engagement and what constitutes its betrayal, or sin, to use the theological term. The seven deadly sins are all defined in opposition to virtues: pride versus humility; avarice versus generosity; envy versus charity; wrath versus kindness; lust versus self-control; gluttony versus temperance; sloth versus zeal. The contrast between the seven sins and the Decalogue is clear: from the legalistic prohibition of precisely defined external acts (murder, theft, worshiping false gods …), we pass to the inner attitudes that cause external evil. This accounts for the structure of the seven sins: first, the three sins of the ego in relation to *itself*, in its lack of self-control, in its excessive, intemperate explosion (lust, gluttony, anger); then, the three sins of the ego in relation to its *object* of desire, i.e., the reflexive internalization of the first three sins (the pride of *having* it, avarice with regard to *getting hold* of it, envy towards the *other* who has it—in symmetry with the lust of consuming it, the gluttony of swallowing it, the anger at the other who has it); finally, sloth as the zero-level sin, as the assertion of the distance from the object of desire, which, according to Agamben,[33] is again secretly structured in three sub-species—the melancholic sadness of not *having* it, "acedia" as the despair at not being able to *get hold* of it, laziness as indifference towards those who have it ("too lazy to bother, even to be envious"), as an ethical attitude: I know what my duty is, but I can't bring myself to do it, I just don't care)… We can also oppose the first six sins along the axis of self and other. Thrift is thus the opposite of envy (the desire to have it versus envying the other who allegedly has it), pride (in one's self) the opposite of wrath (at the other), and lust (experienced by the self) the opposite of gluttony (the insatiable craving for the object). And the three aspects of sloth can also be deployed along this axis: *acedia* is neither thrift nor envy with regard to possession of the Good; melancholy proper is neither masochistic self-indulgent lust nor unsatisfied craving; and, finally, laziness is neither lust nor gluttony but indifference.

This is why the genuine dimension of Christian doubt does not concern the existence of God, for its logic is not "I feel such a need to believe in God, but I cannot be sure that He really exists, that He is not just a chimera of my imagination" (to which the humanist atheist can easily respond: "then dispense with God and simply assume the ideals God stands for as your own"), which is why the Christian believer is indifferent towards the infamous proofs of God's inexistence. What the position of Christian doubt involves is a pragmatic paradox succinctly rendered by Alyosha in Dostoyevsky's *The Brothers Karamazov*: "God exists but I am not sure whether I believe in Him," where "I believe in Him" refers to the believer's readiness to fully assume the existential engagement implied by such a belief:

> the question of the "existence of God" is not really at the heart of Dostoyevsky's labors … Alyosha's uncertainty about whether he "believes in God" is an uncertainty about whether the life he leads and the feelings he has are the life and the feelings that would rightly follow from belief in God.[34]

It is in this sense that every theology is political, confronting us with the question of our social commitment, and this is how we should approach the problem of *acedia* today. Towards the end of *The Little Drummer Girl* (the film based on John le Carré's novel), the Palestinian terrorist (superbly played by Juliano Mer-Khamis) discovers that a remote country house in

---

33   See Giorgio Agamben, *Stanzas*, Minneapolis: University of Minnesota Press 1993, p. 20.

34   Rowan Williams, *Dostoyevsky*, London: Continuum 2008, p. 8.

which he is hiding is surrounded, and instantly realizes that the girl who has spent the night with him has betrayed him; instead of exploding in rage and killing her, he asks her in genuine surprise: "How could you do it? Don't you believe in anything?" He rightly comprehends that the girl is not his ideological enemy, but simply a non-believer, a dis-engaged manipulated individual.[35]

Sloth is not simple (anti-)capitalist laziness but a desperate "sickness unto death," the attitude of knowing one's eternal duty but avoiding it; *acedia* is thus the *tristitia mortifera*, not simple laziness but desperate resignation—I want the object, but not the way to reach it, I accept the gap between desire and its object. In this precise sense, *acedia* is the opposite of zeal. One is even tempted to historicize this last sin: before modernity, it was melancholy (resisting pursuit of the Good); with capitalism, it was reinterpreted as simple laziness (resisting the work ethic); today, in our "post-" society, it is depression (resisting the enjoyment of life, or happiness in consumption).

A short Serb folk song about Kraljević Marko (Prince Marko, the great hero of Serb medieval songs) meeting his warrior companion and competitor Ljutica Bogdan (the Angry Bogdan) offers an unexpected wonderful example of a possible positive role for *acedia* (the prose translation is mine):

> Prince Marko and Ljutica Bogdan, so they say, met on that day. The two grim heroes observe each other for a long time—which of the two will start the fight? They wait one for another. "You know what, my dear Marko, it would be better for both of us if each of us goes his own way—into the vineyard, into the fields? If we were to fight, the world would tremble, and, who knows who would keep his head on." Eagerly awaiting these words, Marko rode off on his horse across the field. Prince Marko and Ljutica Bogdan, so they say, met on that day.

The surprising anti-climactic decision of the two heroes to forgo their duel is not to be read as an indication of cowardice lurking beneath the mask of the fearless warrior, but as offering a momentary insight into the

---

35 Such passive *acedia* is to be opposed to the active version found in de Sade: at its deepest, the Sadean hero is not simply an atheist—he knows God exists, but he dares to challenge Him, to not believe in Him. Perspicuous readers of Sade's work (like Pierre Klossowski) guessed long ago that the compulsion to enjoy driving the Sadean libertine implies a hidden reference to a hidden divinity, to what Lacan called the "Supreme-Being-of-Evil," an obscure God demanding to be fed with the suffering of innocents.

meaninglessness of the pursuit of heroic honor—it is as if their underlying reasoning is: "Why the hell should we risk our lives playing this stupid role of heroes expected to fight whenever they run into each other? Why don't we just step out of it for a moment, disengage and enjoy some peace and quiet?"

We can thus even link *acedia* to Badiou's notion of fidelity to a Truth-Event: animals merely follow their prescribed task, without entering into a reflexive stance towards it, while humans are prone to betrayal—they can choose to disengage themselves, to *not* engage in the "work of love" for the Event. It is not enough to ground this possibility of betrayal in the finitude or mortality of the human being, that is, to reduce it to the gap between the subject defined through its fidelity to an Event and the finite human animal prone to inertia, boredom and laziness (boredom with the Cause, laziness in working for it). The dimension of *acedia* forms the very heart of the subject: the human being is a *lazy* animal, the subject is a lazy subject prone to withdrawal, depression, and melancholic brooding, and this dimension should not be reduced to betrayal, but is also the elementary form of resistance to ideological interpellation. Today, in the crazy late-capitalist social dynamic with its constant demand for workaholic engagement, depression is the new form of *acedia*. (There is also a clear class dimension at work here: precarious workers, low-paid teaching assistants, etc., have to work hard, while top professors can afford be to be lazy. In the ideological perception, the image gets inverted: underprivileged groups, workers, even whole nations [e.g. the Greeks], are accused of laziness and of exploiting the hard-working developed nations.)

It is also interesting to note how this stance of constant engagement is shared by late-capitalist subjectivity as well as by Deleuzian and other grassroots direct democracy movements. Franco Berardi has drawn attention to the accelerating speed of the functioning of the big Other (the symbolic substance of our lives) and the slowness of human reactivity (due to culture, corporeality, disease, etc.): "the long-lasting neoliberal rule has eroded the cultural bases of social civilization, which was the progressive core of modernity. And this is irreversible. We have to face it."[36] What can be done in such a situation? Only withdrawal, passivity, and the abandonment of illusions: "Only self-reliant communities leaving the field of social competition can open a way to a new hope."[37] One cannot but note the cruel

---

36 Franco Bifo Berardi, *After the Future*, Oakland: AK Press 2011, p. 177.
37 Ibid., p. 176.

irony of the contrast between Berardi and Hardt and Negri here. The latter celebrate "cognitive capitalism" as opening up a path towards "absolute democracy," since the object, the "stuff," of immaterial work is increasingly constituted by social relations themselves. Hardt and Negri's wager is that this directly socialized, immaterial production not only renders owners progressively superfluous (who needs them when production is directly social, formally and as to its content?), the producers also master the regulation of social space, since social relations are the essence of their work: economic production directly becomes political production, the production of society itself. The way is thus open for "absolute democracy," with the producers directly regulating their social relations without even the detour of democratic representation. Berardi's conclusion is exactly the opposite: far from bringing out the potential transparency of social life, today's cognitive capitalism makes it more impenetrable than ever, undermining the very conditions for any form of collective solidarity among the "cognitariat." What is symptomatic here is the way the same conceptual apparatus leads to two radically opposed conclusions. For Berardi, if we are unable to avoid the compulsion of the system, the gap between the frantic dynamic it imposes and our corporeal and cognitive limitations sooner or later brings about a fall into depression. Berardi makes the point apropos his friend Félix Guattari, who preached the gospel of hyper-dynamic deterritorialization, while personally suffering from long bouts of depression:

> Actually the problem of depression and of exhaustion is never elaborated in an explicit way by Guattari. I see here a crucial problem of the theory of desire: the denial of the problem of limits in the organic sphere … The notion of the "body without organs" hints at the idea that the organism isn't something that you can define, that the organism is a process of exceeding, of going beyond a threshold, of "becoming other." This is a crucial point, but it's also a dangerous point … What body, what mind is going through transformation and becoming? Which invariant lies under the process of becoming other? If you want to answer this question you have to acknowledge death, finitude, and depression.[38]

When Berardi talks about depression, finitude, exhaustion, and so on, is this with regard to interpellation as such, as a reaction of the human animal to the Cause that addresses it, or does he talk specifically with regard to late-capitalist interpellation? The only proper answer is: both—yes, one has to

---

38   Ibid., pp. 177–8.

step out of the frantic activity imposed by capitalist interpellation, but there is no "natural" harmonious relation between human animals and the socio-symbolic big Other; the gap is constitutive, reaching up to God Himself.

At its most elementary, *acedia* is the disturbance, the perverse reversal, of the most elementary matrix of desire: in contrast to romantic longing in which the subject strives for an impossible object that always eludes his grasp, here the desired object is all too close, intrusively imposing itself, but the subject now no longer desires it, the object gets desublimated, deprived of the *objet a*, of the elusive *je ne sais quoi* which makes it desirable. Laziness, boredom, disgust are all secondary particular forms of this basic disturbance in which all of a sudden we perceive the object outside its fantasmatic frame, in its raw reality, as an intruding foreign body. This is why *acedia* explodes in a permissive superego society, when, for example, one suddenly becomes nauseated by the saturation of objects offering themselves to us with the promise of satisfaction.

Insofar as *acedia* is constitutive of human subjectivity, we should not be surprised to encounter it at the very core of Christianity, the basic message of which is the full incarnation of God, His appearance as a singular human being. As many perspicuous commentators from Chesterton onwards have noted, Christ's desperate call from the Cross "Father, why have you forsaken me?" represents that singular moment when God Himself commits the highest sin of abandoning belief—it is this cry that demonstrates that God really did become human. In other religions, man may betray God, but only in Christianity does God betray Himself and succumb to *acedia*. And the story of divine *acedia* does not end (or even begin) there: before despair comes boredom, the origin of all creativity, including God's creation of the world. This is what Kierkegaard was aiming at when he claimed that boredom is "the root of all evil":

> It is very curious that boredom, which itself has such a calm and sedate nature, can have such a capacity to initiate motion. The effect that boredom brings about is absolutely magical, but this effect is one not of attraction but of repulsion ...
>
> Since boredom advances and boredom is the root of all evil, no wonder, then, that the world goes backwards, that evil spreads. This can be traced back to the very beginning of the world. The gods were bored; therefore they created human beings. Adam was bored because he was alone; therefore Eve was created. Since that moment, boredom entered the world and grew in quantity in exact proportion to the growth of population. Adam was bored alone; then Adam and Eve were bored *en famille*. After that, the population of the world increased and the

nations were bored en masse. To amuse themselves, they hit upon the notion of building a tower so high that it would reach the sky. This notion is just as boring as the tower was high and is a terrible demonstration of how boredom had gained the upper hand. Then they were dispersed around the world, just as people now travel abroad, but they continued to be bored. And what consequences this boredom had: humankind stood tall and fell far, first through Eve, then from the Babylonian tower.[39]

And we can push on here up to our own times: the boredom of living in a closed tribal society pushed humans into engaging in commerce, to develop classes and exploitation; the boredom of medieval stability and inertia pushed them towards capitalist modernization; bored with living on Earth, we built rockets and traveled into space; and today, in the developed consumerist societies, boredom is universalized, pushing us into buying new products over and over again … But is the reasoning here circular? Not at all, since boredom creates the conditions for its own overcoming: boredom is a form of the reflected void, it signals that we have reflexively noted the limitation of what is given, of our situation. Therein also resides the link between boredom and *creatio ex nihilo*: boredom is the *nihil* out of which we create. But the ambiguity here is radical: is boredom evil in the sense of being that which must be overcome through the goodness of creation, or is creation in itself ultimately evil (as some Gnostics claim)? It is against this background that we should reread the passage from Chesterton's famous "Defense of Detective Stories" in which he remarks how the detective story

> keeps in some sense before the mind the fact that civilization itself is the most sensational of departures and the most romantic of rebellions. When the detective in a police romance stands alone, and somewhat fatuously fearless amid the knives and fists of a thief's kitchen, it does certainly serve to make us remember that it is the agent of social justice who is the original and poetic figure, while the burglars and footpads are merely placid old cosmic conservatives, happy in the immemorial respectability of apes and wolves. [The police romance] is based on the fact that morality is the most dark and daring of conspiracies.[40]

---

39   Søren Kierkegaard, *Either/Or, Part 1*, Princeton: Princeton University Press 1987, pp. 285–6.

40   G. K. Chesterton, "A Defense of Detective Stories," in H. Haycraft, ed., *The Art of the Mystery Story*, New York: The Universal Library 1946, p. 6.

Chesterton's aim here is to fight *acedia* in the guise of boredom (the boring nature of fighting for the good) by turning things around: the life of criminals with all its thrills and dangers is boring, while fighting for the law is the true adventure. He repeats the same operation at multiple levels: licentious promiscuity is boring, marriage is true adventure; subversive heresy is boring, orthodoxy is the true adventure; constant novelty is boring and monotonous, repetition of the same is surprising and interesting. And we have to push this line through to the end: if, in the ethical domain, the Fall is primary and opens up the space for what it is the fall from, if *acedia* precedes engagement, then there is a further consequence to be drawn. The *morale provisoire* that Ruda deploys following Descartes is not an exception or a secondary, deficient mode of morals appropriate for non-evental times—it is the rule, the "normal state" of morality, interrupted now and again in political states of exception when social (or personal) life is shattered and reorganized around fidelity to an Event. Which brings us to our own historical moment: we should abandon the predominant "radical" leftist view according to which we live in a non-evental epoch when, since there is no Event on the horizon, we should live like warriors at rest, in a state of suspension. Does such self-awareness, such practical self-understanding, involve an historicist self-relativization? No: in contrast to the classic revolutionary stance that posits the self-consciousness of a revolutionary subject as the universal model and the subject in a non-evental time as its deficient mode, the properly Hegelian approach posits the anticipatory "empty" subject as the universal model, as the zero-level of subjectivity—it is only in the void of anticipation that the universal form of subjectivity appears as such.

This apparently secondary problem of *acedia* thus takes us not only to the very core of subjectivity, but also to the specific status of philosophy with regard to what Badiou calls the four "generic" truth procedures. Ruda follows Badiou's standard line (before Badiou, Althusser developed a similar notion of philosophy in his *Lenin and Philosophy*): since philosophy does not generate new truths, its work is repetitive; philosophical repetition is not Hegelian but Kierkegaardian-Freudian—it does not involve any sublation/idealization. There is no "progress" in philosophy as such—there is progress in the conditions of philosophy with each new evental break in science, politics, art ... but all that philosophy does is to repeat the same gesture of differentiation apropos each new event:

Philosophy has to be repetitive, for if it were not there once could exist something like a last and final articulation of its claim; one could thus think an overcoming of its historical conditioning and something like a final stage of philosophy, a complete revelation after which everything changes and then nothing will ever change again. This radical overcoming of its own historicity one might even call—with reference to traditional renderings of Hegel—the *Hegelian threat to philosophy*.[41]

The authentic Hegelian position (and Ruda is well aware that the idea of Absolute Knowing as a simple end of history is pseudo-Hegelian, which is why he talks about "traditional renderings of Hegel") is the repetition of the very "final articulation," of the very gesture of philosophy "overcoming its own historicity." But, since Ruda nonetheless accepts that, in Hegel's idealism, philosophy "sublates" (in the sense of *Aufhebung*) its specific conditions, abolishing their external materiality, he proceeds at this point to a critique of my (Hegelian) conception of dialectics, raising the question:

is this conception truly post-Hegelian, that is to say is this really a philosophical project that includes the historically specific conditions that philosophy is in here and now? Or does it not rather and again present an ultimate sublation of all forms of practices, of all non-philosophical conditions, into philosophy? Badiou's system is able to avoid this consequence but with Žižek's is there not a danger of suturing philosophy to an (retroactive) ontology that arises out of the dialectical movement (which again is the movement proper to philosophy and in the last instance of a philosophical ontology)? And if this were to be the case, would this not imply that we somehow lose the essential and necessary non-dialectical element of any contemporary materialist dialectics? To put it in more direct terms: One might imagine a situation where Alain Badiou and Slavoj Žižek sit at a coffee table and have a chat about their particular philosophical enterprises. Against the background delineated above, might one not expect Badiou to ask Žižek: My dear Slavoj, are you really post-Hegelian?[42]

To simplify somewhat Ruda's complex line of argumentation, for Hegel, the non-dialectical starting point of the process, its immediate presupposition, is retroactively sublated/mediated and as such posited, the non-dialectical aspect is itself dialecticized, so that the process closes upon itself, erasing

41   Ruda, *For Badiou: Idealism without Idealism.*
42   Ibid.

or internalizing all traces of any external point of reference, like the legend-ary Baron Munchausen who pulled himself out of the swamp by his own hair. Badiou, on the contrary, avoids this idealist closure by conceiving the starting point of the dialectical process, the Event that sets it in motion, as a non-dialectical contingent, unpredictable occurrence "out of nowhere," the real of a materialist miracle, around which the dialectical movement continues to work but which persists as its non-sublatable presupposition or cause.

The answer to this critical point should be that yes, one should look for a non-dialecticizable moment of the dialectical process, but this moment is not to be sought in an external starting point which triggers it: the aspect of the process which cannot be dialecticized is its very motor, the repetitive "death drive" as the basic form of what Hegel calls "negativity." The rela-tionship between Hegel's negativity and Freud's death drive (or compulsion to repeat) is thus a very specific one, well beyond their (hidden) outright identity: what Freud was aiming at with his notion of the death drive— more precisely, the key dimension of this notion to which Freud himself was blind, unaware of what he discovered—is the "non-dialectical" core of Hegelian negativity, the pure drive to repeat without any movement of sublation (idealization). In Kierkegaard-Freudian pure repetition, the dia-lectical movement of sublimation thus encounters itself outside itself, in the guise of a "blind" compulsion-to-repeat. And it is here that we should apply the great Hegelian motto about the internalizing of the external obstacle: in fighting its external opposite, the blind non-sublatable repetition, the dialectical movement is fighting its own abyssal ground, its own core; in other words, the ultimate gesture of reconciliation is to recognize in this threatening excess of negativity the core of the subject itself.[43]

Against the background delineated here, might one not ask Ruda: "My dear Frank, are you really a dialectical materialist, or is your dialectical materialism the mask of an opportunist bourgeois democrat?"

---

43   For a more detailed account of this non-dialectical core of negativity, see Chapter 7 of Slavoj Žižek, *Less Than Nothing*, London: Verso 2012.

CHAPTER 2

From Kant to Hegel

THE ONTIC QUESTION

While the transcendental turn is a specific move that characterizes Kant's philosophical revolution, it is also, at a deeper level, a name—arguably *the* name—for the move that characterizes, constitutes even, philosophy as such, i.e., philosophy in its difference from knowledge of positive reality. Heidegger saw this very clearly when, in *Being and Time*, he proposed a redefinition of hermeneutics as ontology proper, as fundamental ontology, not only as the science of understanding and interpreting texts. Take the example of life: the proper topic of philosophy is not the real nature of life as a natural phenomenon (how did life evolve out of complex chemical processes, what are the minimal characteristics of a living organism, etc.). Philosophy raises a different question: when we encounter living entities, and treat them as such, we already have to possess a certain pre-understanding that enables us to recognize them as alive, and philosophy focuses on this pre-understanding. The same goes for, say, freedom: in what way do we understand "freedom" when we ask the question "Are we free or not?" The basic transcendental-hermeneutic move is the move towards this horizon of pre-understanding which is always already there, and this is what Heidegger means by the Event of the disclosure of being: history at its most radical involves not a change in reality, but a shift in how things appear to us, in our fundamental pre-understanding of reality. Recall the classical topic of the change of frame in our understanding of motion in early modernity:

> Mediaeval physics believed that motion was caused by an impetus. Things are naturally at rest. An impetus makes something move; but then it runs out, leaving the object to slow down and stop. Something that continues moving therefore has to keep being pushed, and pushing is something you can feel. (This was even an argument for the existence of God, since something very big—like God—had to be pushing to keep the heavens going.) So if the Earth is moving, why don't we feel it? Copernicus could not answer that question ... Galileo had

an answer for Copernicus: simple velocity is *not* felt, only acceleration is. So the earth can be moving without our feeling it. Also, velocity does not change until a force changes it. That is the idea of *inertia*, which then replaced the old idea of an impetus.[1]

This shift from impetus to inertia is properly transcendental: it changes the basic mode of our relating to reality. As such, it is an event: at its most elementary, an event is not something that occurs within the world, but just such a change of the frame through which we perceive the world and engage in it. In its response to the cognitivist challenge, neo-Kantian state philosophy (represented today by Habermas) refers to this same dimension: our self-perception as free and responsible agents is not just a necessary illusion, but the transcendental a priori of scientific knowledge itself. Habermas developed his position in response to a manifesto in which eleven distinguished German neuroscientists claimed that our ordinary concept of free will is on the verge of being undone by recent advances in neurobiology: "We stand at the threshold of seeing our image of ourselves considerably shaken in the foreseeable future."[2] For Habermas,

> the attempt to study first-person subjective experience from the third-person, objectifying viewpoint, involves the theorist in a performative contradiction, since objectification presupposes participation in an intersubjectively instituted system of linguistic practices whose normative valence conditions the scientist's cognitive activity.[3]

Habermas characterizes this intersubjective domain of rational validity as the dimension of "objective mind" which cannot be understood in terms of the phenomenological profiles of the community of conscious selves comprised in it: it is the intrinsically intersubjective status of the normative realm that precludes any attempt to account for its operation or genesis in terms of entities or processes simpler than the system itself. (Lacan's term

---

1   Quoted from friesian.com.

2   C. E. Elger, A. D. Friederici, C. Koch, H. Luhmann, C. von der Malsburg, R. Menzel, H. Monyer, F. Rösler, G. Roth, H. Scheich; and W. Singer, "Das Manifest: Elf führende Neurowissenschaftler über Gegenwart und Zukunft der Hirnforschung," *Gehirn und Geist* 6 (2004), p. 37.

3   Jürgen Habermas, "The Language Game of Responsible Agency and the Problem of Free Will: How Can Epistemic Dualism be Reconciled with Ontological Monism?," *Philosophical Explorations* 10:1 (March 2007), p. 31.

for this "objective mind" irreducible to the Real of raw reality as well as to the imaginary of our self-experience is, of course, the big Other.) Neither the phenomenological (imaginary) nor neurobiological (real) profiling of participants can be cited as a constituting condition for this socially "objective mind":

> The resistance to a naturalistic self-description stemming from our self-understanding as persons is explained by the fact that there is no getting round a dualism of epistemic perspectives that must interlock in order to make it possible for the mind, situated as it is within the world, to get an orienting overview of its own situation. Even the gaze of a purportedly absolute observer cannot sever the ties to one standpoint in particular, namely that of a counterfactually extended argumentation community.[4]

Perhaps this transcendental stance is also what ultimately distinguishes Western Marxism from Soviet "dialectical materialism." Dialectical materialism considers historical materialism as a specific ontology, a kind of *metaphysica specialis* of the social being, as the application of the universal laws of dialectics to the social sphere, in contrast to Western Marxism for which collective human *praxis* is the unsurpassable transcendental horizon of our approach to reality, that from which we cannot abstract even in our purest considerations of natural laws. As they used to say, even if humanity is the result of natural evolution, its practical collective engagement with nature always already "frames" our understanding of nature—or, to quote the young Lukács' succinct formula, nature is a historical category.

In this precise sense, Heidegger is the ultimate transcendental philosopher: his achievement is to *historicize* the transcendental dimension. For Heidegger, an Event has nothing to do with ontic processes; it designates the "event" of a new epochal disclosure of Being, the emergence of a new "world" (as the horizon of meaning within which all entities appear). Catastrophe thus occurs before the (f)act: the catastrophe is not the nuclear self-destruction of humanity, but that ontological relation to nature which reduces it to techno-scientific exploitation. The catastrophe is not our ecological ruin, but the loss of our home-roots, thus making possible the ruthless exploitation of the earth.[5] The catastrophe is not that we are

---

4 Ibid., p. 35.

5 Can we then imagine "Heidegger in the Mojave desert"—confronting the inert machinery of this gigantic resting place of old planes, the poignant image of dysfunctional *Gestell*? What is the status of this material inertia?

reduced to automata manipulable by biogenetics, but the very ontological approach that renders this prospect possible. Even in the case of total self-destruction, ontology maintains its priority over the ontic: the possibility of total self-destruction is just an ontic consequence of our relating to nature as a collection of objects for technological exploitation—the catastrophe occurs when nature appears to us within the frame of technology. *Gestell*, Heidegger's name for the essence of technology, is usually translated into English as "enframing." At its most radical, technology designates not the complex network of machines and activities, but the attitude towards reality that we assume when we engage in such activities: technology is the way reality discloses itself to us in modern times, when reality has become a "standing-reserve":

> Enframing means the gathering together of that setting-upon which sets upon man, i.e., challenges him forth, to reveal the real in the mode of ordering, as standing-reserve. Enframing means that way of revealing which holds sway in the essence of modern technology and which is itself nothing technological.[6]

The paradox of technology as the concluding moment of Western metaphysics is that it is a mode of enframing which poses a danger to enframing itself: the human being reduced to an object of technological manipulation is no longer properly human, it loses the very feature of being ecstatically open to reality. However, this danger also contains the potential for salvation: the moment we become aware of and fully embrace the fact that technology itself is, in its essence, a mode of enframing, we overcome it … Giving such priority to the ontological over the ontic dimension leads Heidegger to dismiss gigantic human catastrophes (like the Holocaust) as mere "ontic" events; it leads him to dismiss the differences between, say, democracy and fascism as secondary and ontologically irrelevant (and some critics have hastened to add that this obliteration of ontic differences is not only the consequence but also the hidden cause of his emphasis on the ontological dimension—his own Nazi involvement thus becomes an insignificant error, etc.).

However, even at the immanently philosophical level, what one is tempted to call the "ontic question" continues to lead an underground life in Heidegger's thought: what is the status of ontic reality outside the

---

6   Martin Heidegger, *The Question Concerning Technology and Other Essays*, New York: Harper 1977, p. 20.

ontological horizon, prior to eventual disclosure? Heidegger makes it clear that things "were there" in some sense before the disclosure of Being, they just did not *exist* in the full ontological sense of the term—but *how* were they there? Here is Heidegger's ambiguous formulation of this obscure point: "I often ask myself—this has for a long time been a fundamental question for me—what nature would be without man—must it not resonate through him in order to attain its ownmost potency."[7] This passage recalls Walter Benjamin's *Arcades Project*, where he quotes the French historian André Monglond: "The past has left images of itself in literary texts, images comparable to those which are imprinted by light on a photosensitive plate. The future alone possesses developers active enough to scan such surfaces perfectly."[8] Far from being just a neutral observation on the complex interdependency of literary texts, this notion of past texts pointing towards the future is grounded in Benjamin's basic notion of the revolutionary act as the retroactive redemption of past failed attempts:

> The past carries with it a temporal index by which it is referred to redemption. There is a secret agreement between past generations and the present one. Our coming was expected on earth. Like every generation that preceded us, we have been endowed with a weak Messianic power, a power to which the past has a claim.[9]

The question is how far we should go with this: Do we limit the logic of retroactive redemption to human history, or are we ready to take the risk of applying this logic to nature itself, which calls for humanity, human speech, to redeem it from its mute suffering? More generally, are such speculations about the pain inherent in pre-human nature not simply mythical fables? One of the signals of a transcendental approach is the recourse to myth: after describing a rational structure that goes as far as our thinking can go, thinkers from Plato to Lacan then offer a mythical fable, claiming that we really cannot go beyond the rational structure, and can only speculate about what went on prior to it through the medium of a fable. Classic Lacan thus claims that the fact of the symbolic order, of the *logos*, is the ultimate horizon of our thinking: we cannot go further back, every story about the

---

7   Letter   October   11,   1931,   in   *Martin   Heidegger—Elisabeth   Blochmann. Briefwechsel 1918–1969*, Marbach: Deutsches Literatur-Archiv 1990, p. 44.

8   Walter Benjamin, *The Arcades Project*, Cambridge, MA: Belknap Press 1999, p. 482.

9   Walter Benjamin, *Illuminations*, New York: Schocken Books 2007, p. 254.

"origin of language" is a circular myth which implicitly presupposes what it purports to explain, so all we can do is to concoct amusing fables.

To return to the quoted passage from Heidegger, we should note that it comes from the period immediately after his lectures on *The Fundamental Concepts of Metaphysics* (1929–30), wherein is also formulated a Schellingian hypothesis that perhaps animals are, in a hitherto unknown way, aware of their lack, of the "poorness" of their relating to the world—perhaps, indeed, there is an infinite pain pervading living nature in its entirety: "if deprivation in certain forms is a kind of suffering, and poverty and deprivation of world belongs to the animal's being, then a kind of pain and suffering would have to permeate the whole animal realm and the realm of life in general."[10]

The choice Heidegger is confronting here is the following: according to his basic position, the reproach that the definition of animal as *weltarm* and of stone as *weltlos* implies a reference to the human as opened up to a world is obviously true, but it simply means that we always already understand reality through the way it is disclosed to us, so that we cannot abstract our own position from it. However, as if doubting the sufficiency of this transcendental reply (i.e., admitting that the question of what reality is "in itself," independently of us, persists), Heidegger hints at another position: the deprived-of-world status of things that are simply there in their world-less reality is not just a feature of the way we perceive them from our anthropic position—it is something that characterizes them immanently, in themselves. Heidegger here refers to an old motif of German Romanticism and of Schelling, also taken up by Benjamin, the motif of the "great sorrow of nature": "It is in the hope of requiting that [sorrow], of redemption from that suffering, that humans live and speak in nature."[11] Derrida rejects this Schellingian-Benjaminian-Heideggerian motif, the idea that nature's numbness and muteness signal an infinite pain, as teleologically logocentric: language becomes a *telos* of nature, nature strives towards the Word to release its sadness, to reach its redemption.

But this mystical topos nonetheless raises the right question by inverting the standard perspective: not "What is nature for language? Can we grasp nature adequately in/through language?" but "What is language for nature? How does its emergence affect nature?" Far from belonging to

---

10   Martin Heidegger, *The Fundamental Concepts of Metaphysics*, Bloomington: Indiana University Press 1995, p. 271.

11   Jacques Derrida, *The Animal That Therefore I Am*, New York: Fordham University Press 2008, p. 19.

logocentrism, such a reversal amounts to the strongest suspension of logo-centrism and teleology, in the same way that Marx's thesis on the anatomy of man as the key to the anatomy of ape subverts any teleological evolu-tionism. The moment we raise the question in this way, we move beyond (or rather beneath) the transcendental dimension. The key philosophi-cal problem today is this: is the transcendental dimension the ultimate horizon of our thinking? Is it *unhintergehbares*? If not, then how are we to reach beyond or beneath the transcendental? There seem to be three main options at our disposal:

1) Fichte—the radicalization of the transcendental itself, i.e., the deduction of the entire content, inclusive of empirical multiplicity, from the transcen-dental principle (Fichte, not Hegel, attempts this in his first phase with his notion of the self-positing absolute I).

2) Schelling—the meta-transcendental genesis of the transcendental, that is, the move beyond the transcendental to the arche-transcendental, from late Schelling (with his notion of *Ungrund*, the self-withdrawing abyss out of which everything emerges as the pre-transcendental Real) up to Derrida, whose *différance* names the meta-transcendental conditions of the tran-scendental itself.

3) Return to realism—not primarily to a pre-critical realist ontology, but to a radical scientific program of naturalization that tries to account for the rise of the transcendental horizon itself out of the ontic evolutionary process. However, the vicious cycle between transcendental and empirical ontology remains unsurpassed in this version: scientific naturalization has to rely on an already given transcendental horizon.

THE HEGELIAN MOVE

Where does Hegel stand here? His position is unique: he reinscribes the transcendental frame back into the thing itself. But how? Let us begin with the triad of naive, transcendental, and Hegelian positions: in the naive posi-tion, reality is accepted as simply being out there; the transcendental turn shows how reality is always constituted through a (narrative) frame that is irreducible to its object since it is always already presupposed. How can we move beyond the interplay of these two dimensions, the transcendental and the empirical? Let us take another case of a theory for which the transcendental dimension is always already presupposed: the structuralism of Claude Lévi-Strauss, who designates his position as a transcendentalism without a transcendental subject. The structuralist idea is that one cannot think the genesis of the symbolic (order).[12] The latter, once it is here, is always already here: one cannot step outside of it, all one can do is to construct myths about its genesis (which Lacan engages in occasionally). Recall the wonderful title of Alexei Yurchak's book about the last Soviet generation: *Everything Was Forever, Until It Was No More*—the point we are looking for is the exact inversion of this rupture: nothing of the symbolic order was here, until all of it, all of a sudden, was *always already* here. The problem is that of the emergence of a "closed" self-relating system which has no outside: it cannot be explained from outside because its constitutive act is self-relating, i.e., the system fully emerges only once it starts to cause itself, to posit its own presuppositions in a closed loop. So it is not just that there was nothing and then all of a sudden the symbolic order is here—rather, that there was nothing and then, all of a sudden, it is as if the symbolic order was *always already* here, as if there was never a time without it. (Marx deals with this problem apropos the myth of "primitive accumulation": what he is looking for is not the origins of capitalism but its contingent genealogy sustained by no teleological impetus, which is why "the anatomy of man is the key to the anatomy of ape.") The Hegelian wager is that one *can* account for such emergences: the dialectical reversal is precisely such an emergence of a new order without an outside. So how can we imagine such an emergence within the space of Lévi-Strauss' theory? In a famous passage from *Du miel aux cendres*, Lévi-Strauss tries to define the relationship between his structuralism and history—the passage makes it clear what he means by characterizing his own thought as "Kantianism without the transcendental subject":

> structural analysis does not reject history. On the contrary, it grants it a preeminent place, one owing to the irreducible contingency without which we could not even conceive necessity. For insofar as behind the apparent diversity of human societies, structural analysis claims to go back to fundamental and common

---

12   We can note here, as a curiosity, that in 1866, the Société linguistique de Paris formally prohibited its members from engaging in any research into the origins of language, claiming that it exceeds the cognitive capacities of men: "The society will not admit any communication which concerns the origins of language." Quoted in Étienne Klein, *Discours sur l'origine de l'univers*, Paris: Flammarion 2010, p. 157.

properties, it foregoes explaining not particular differences which it can account for by specifying in each ethnographic context the laws of invariance that govern their production, but rather the fact that these differences given *virtually* as *compossibles* are not all confirmed by experience and that only some of them have been *actualized*. To be viable, an investigation completely focused on structures begins by bowing to the power and inanity of the event.[13]

The basic idea is clear: structural analysis deploys the matrix of all possible variations, and history adds that external contingency on account of which only some variations are realized … But is such a concept enough, and does it fit Lévi-Strauss' own practice? Do we not find in Lévi-Strauss' work indications of a more complex relation between structure and history? His first step was to introduce self-reflexivity into the signifying order: if the identity of a signifier is nothing but the series of its constitutive differences, then every signifying series has to be supplemented—"sutured"—by a reflexive signifier that has no determinate meaning (signified), since it stands only for the presence of meaning as such (as opposed to its absence). Lévi-Strauss was the first to fully articulate the necessity of such a signifier in his famous interpretation of *mana*—his achievement was to demystify *mana*, reducing its irrational connotation of a mythical, magical power to a precise symbolic function. His starting point is that language as a bearer of meaning by definition arises all at once, covering the entire horizon: "Whatever may have been the moment and the circumstances of its appearance in the ascent of animal life, language can only have arisen all at once. Things cannot have begun to signify gradually."[14] This sudden emergence, however, introduces an imbalance between the two orders of the signifier and the signified: since the signifying network is finite, it cannot adequately cover the endless field of the signified in its entirety. In this way,

> a fundamental situation perseveres which arises out of the human condition: namely, that man has from the start had at his disposition a signifier-totality which he is at a loss to know how to allocate to a signified, given as such, but no less unknown for being given. There is always a non-equivalence or "inadequation" between the two, a non-fit and overspill which divine understanding

13   Claude Lévi-Strauss, *Mythologiques, Tome 2: Du miel aux cendres*, Paris: Plon 2009, p. 408.

14   Claude Lévi-Strauss, *Introduction to the Work of Marcel Mauss*, London: Routledge, Kegan & Paul 1987, p. 59.

alone can soak up; this generates a signifier-surfeit relative to the signifieds to which it can be fitted. So, in man's effort to understand the world, he always disposes of a surplus of signification ... That distribution of a supplementary ration ... is absolutely necessary to insure that, in total, the available signifier and the mapped-out signified may remain in the relationship of complementarity which is the very condition of the exercise of symbolic thinking.[15]

Every signifying field thus has to be "sutured" by a supplementary zero-signifier, "a *zero symbolic value*, that is, a sign marking the necessity of a supplementary symbolic content over and above that which the signified already contains."[16] This signifier is "a symbol in its pure state": lacking any determinate meaning, it stands for the presence of meaning *as such* in contrast to its absence (in a further dialectical twist, one should add that the mode of appearance of this supplementary signifier which stands for meaning as such is non-sense—a point developed by Deleuze in his *Logic of Sense*). Notions like *mana* thus "represent nothing more or less than that *floating signifier*."[17] And is not this "floating signifier" precisely that signifier which represents, *within* the symbolic structural matrix of all possible virtualities, its very opposite, the *externality* of pure factual contingency? To put it in Hegelese: in the floating signifier, the universality of the symbolic function encounters itself in its "oppositional determination."

There is a further complication in Lévi-Strauss' procedure which renders problematic the simple opposition of structure and history. His basic thesis is that human history consists in a series of catastrophes or falls: the invention of writing, the "Greek miracle," the rise of monotheism, Descartes and modern industrial-scientific civilization ... Lévi-Strauss insists on the contingency of these falls—there was no necessity to the "Greek miracle," which took place due to a thoroughly contingent intersection of multiple conditions. Such falls are thus not simply variations within an ahistorical structural matrix—they are cuts, contingent explosions of the New. Lévi-Strauss' dream here is the idea of possible virtual alternative histories: not that nothing New would have emerged and that we would have remained in the old universe of *la pensée sauvage*, but that *each new fall is accompanied by (or gives rise to) a virtual shadow of alternative possibilities*: "Indeed, one invariant trait of Lévi-Strauss's catastrophic history is that, at

---

15   Ibid., pp. 62–3.

16   Ibid., p. 64.

17   For a more detailed account of this reflexivity, see Chapter 9 of Slavoj Žižek, *Less Than Nothing*, London: Verso 2012.

each turning point, at each bifurcation, there is the shadow of an alternative history, the phantom of what has never existed, but might have existed."[18] These alternative possibilities are not simply variations within an eternal matrix; the point is rather that each historical event, each emergence of the New, each fall, is always split between what actually happened and its failed alternatives.[19]

The key problem is thus that of the umbilical cord connecting a formal-transcendental structure to its contingent historical content: how is the Real of history inscribed into a structure? Let us approach this problem at its most abstract, apropos historiography itself. Hayden White defines historical work as a verbal structure in the form of a narrative prose discourse that classifies past structures and processes in order to explain them by representing them as models: a historian does not just find history; she takes events that have happened and makes a story out of them, that is, reorganizes them into a narrative prose discourse.[20] She does this by arranging events in a certain order, deciding which to include and exclude, stressing some and subordinating others, all this in order to answer the questions: What happened? When? How? Why? In her answers, the historian relies on three modes of explanation: Emplotment, Argument, and Ideological implication. For each of these three explanations, there are four types from which the historian can choose:

Emplotment—"every history, even the most 'synchronic' of them, will be emplotted in some way."[21] The four types of emplotment are: Romance (the drama of self-identification, including a hero's triumph over evil); Satire (the opposite of romance: people are captives in the world until they die); Comedy (harmony between the natural and the social; causes for celebration); Tragedy (a hero, through a fall or test, learns through resignation to work within the limitations of the world, and the audience learns as well).

Argument—the four types of argument are: Formalist (identification of objects by classifying, labeling, categorizing: "any historiography in

---

18   Christopher Johnson, "All Played Out? Lévi-Strauss's Philosophy of History," *New Left Review* 79 (Jan./Feb. 2013), p. 65.

19   Along these lines, John Millbank proposed an alternate modernity: if, instead of the rise of Protestantism, a Catholic renewal outlined by Meister Eckhart and Nicolaus de Cusa had prevailed, we would have witnessed a much "softer" capitalism, with less individualist competitiveness and more social solidarity.

20   See Hayden White, *Metahistory*, Baltimore: Johns Hopkins University Press 1973.

21   Ibid., p. 8.

which the depiction of the variety, color, and vividness of the historical field is taken as the central aim of the work");[22] Organicist (the whole is more than the sum of its parts; goal-oriented, the principles are not laws but are an integral part of human freedom); Mechanistic (finding laws that govern the operations of human activities); Contextualist (events are explained by their relationships to similar events; threads are traced back to origins).

Ideology—reflects the ethics and assumptions the historian has about life, how past events affect the present, and how we ought to act in the present; claims the authority of "science" or "realism." There are again four types: Conservative (history evolves; we can hope for utopia, but change occurs slowly as part of the natural rhythm); Liberal (progress in social history is the result of changes in law and government); Radical (utopia is imminent and must be effected by revolutionary means); Anarchist (the state is corrupt and therefore must be destroyed and a new community inaugurated).

The historian also "prefigures" the act of writing history by writing within a particular trope—one of four deep poetic structures: metaphor, synecdoche, metonymy, and irony. Tropes "are especially useful for understanding the operations by which the contents of experience which resist description in unambiguous prose representations can be prefiguratively grasped and prepared for conscious apprehension."[23] White glosses the four tropes as follows:

Metaphor—one phenomenon is compared or contrasted to another in the manner of analogy or simile.

Synecdoche—using a part of something to symbolize the quality of the whole; for example, "He is all heart."

Metonymy—substitution of the name of a part for the whole, e.g., "sail" for "ship."

Irony—literal meaning that makes no sense figuratively; examples are paradox (oxymoron) or the "manifestly absurd expression" (catachresis).

Metaphor is representational, metonymy is reductionist, synecdoche is integrative, and irony is negational. The net result is a complex proto-Kantian a priori formal scheme represented in the table below:

---

22   Ibid., p. 14.
23   Ibid., p. 34.

Emplotment	Argument	Ideology	Poetic Structure
Romantic	Formalist	Anarchist	Synecdoche
Tragic	Mechanistic	Radical	Metaphor
Comic	Organicist	Conservative	Metonymy
Satirical	Contextualist	Liberal	Irony

White himself denies being a relativist or postmodernist, asserting that the reality of events in the past is not contradicted by literary portrayals of those events. But he nonetheless remains within a Kantian space, opposing the formal-transcendental a priori of an atemporal scheme or matrix to the contingent reality which actualizes the possibilities prescribed by the scheme—the real for White is the contingent event which affects the scheme from outside. This model can go wrong in two ways: first, reality fails to fit it, to fill in all its places, all the options it allows, so that some remain blank, empty possibilities with no actualization. This is the Lévi-Straussian position, asserting the deficit of reality with regard to the structural matrix. Second, the empiricist shift of perspective: there is too much reality, reality is too rich and will elude any such matrix. This is the common-sense view: every conceptual network will be too rough and abstract to catch the fine texture of the reality out there.

The proper Hegelian path is the third alternative: an immanent structural inconsistency, such that the formal matrix is thwarted immanently, on account of an inherent antagonism rather than an excess of reality. What if the fact that some options remain blank, empty possibilities with no actualization indicates that the matrix proposed by White is an attempt to bring together two different matrixes and obliterate their antagonism? It is *here* that we touch the Real: not as an external reality too rich to be captured by a formal matrix, but as the antagonism causing the formal split of matrixes. We cannot locate it directly in reality but only in the deadlock of the structural formalization of reality. This Real (antagonism) is not relative, it is the "absolute" of a given historical constellation, its fixed impossibility or point of reference. This is how we can avoid relativism even while accepting that historical material is always organized into narratives that are partial and engaged: there is a conflict of narratives, and the Real is touched by this conflict that maintains the distance of the narratives from reality; the Real is inaccessible, and the Real is the very obstacle which makes it inaccessible—this is how the (narrative) form itself falls into its content.

Recall Lévi-Strauss' exemplary analysis, in his *Structural Anthropology*, of the spatial disposition of buildings in the villages of the Winnebago, one of the Great Lake tribes. The tribe is divided into two sub-groups (or "moieties"): "those who are from above" and "those who are from below." If we ask an individual tribesman to draw a ground-plan of his village (the spatial disposition of cottages) the diagram he draws will depend on which sub-group he belongs to. Both sub-groups perceive the village as a circle, but, for one of them, within this circle there is another circle of central houses, so we have two concentric circles, while for the other, the circle is split into two by a clear dividing line. In other words, a member of the first sub-group (let's call it "conservative-corporatist") will see the plan of the village as a ring of houses more or less symmetrically disposed around the central temple, whereas a member of the second ("revolutionary-antagonistic") sub-group sees it as two distinct heaps of houses separated by an invisible frontier.[24] The point Lévi-Strauss wants to make is that this example should in no way entice us into cultural relativism, according to which the perception of social space depends on the observer's group membership: the very split between the two "relative" perceptions implies a hidden reference to a constant—not the objective, "actual" disposition of buildings but a traumatic kernel, a fundamental antagonism that the inhabitants of the village are unable to symbolize, account for, "internalize," or come to terms with, an imbalance in social relations that prevents the community from stabilizing into a harmonious whole. The different perceptions of the ground-plan are simply two mutually exclusive attempts to cope with this traumatic antagonism, to heal the wound with the imposition of a balanced symbolic structure. Here we can see in what precise sense the Real intervenes through anamorphosis. First we have the "objective" arrangement of the houses, and then its two different symbolizations both of which distort that arrangement in an anamorphic way. However, the "Real" here is not the actual arrangement, but the traumatic core of some social antagonism which distorts the individuals' view of the actual arrangement of houses in the village.[25]

At this level, truth is no longer something that depends on the faithful reproduction of facts. We can note here the difference between (factual) truth and truthfulness: what makes a rape victim's report (or any other

24   Claude Lévi-Strauss, "Do Dual Organizations Exist?," in *Structural Anthropology*, New York: Basic Books 1963, pp. 131–63; the drawings are on pp. 133–4.

25   For a more detailed analysis of this example from Lévi-Strauss, see Chapter 3 of Slavoj Žižek, *The Puppet and the Dwarf*, Cambridge, MA: MIT Press 2003.

trauma narrative) truthful is precisely its factual unreliability, confusion, or inconsistency. If the victim were able to report their traumatic and humiliating experience in a clear way, with all the data arranged in a consistent order of exposition, this very fact would make us suspicious. The same holds for the unreliability of the verbal reports given by Holocaust survivors: a witness who was able to offer a crystal-clear narrative of his camp experience would thereby disqualify himself. In an Hegelian way, the problem is here part of the solution: the very weakness of the traumatized subject's report bears witness to its truthfulness, since it signals that the content of the report has contaminated the very form in which it is reported.

The Real thus lies not in what is the same, in the transcendent hard core beyond our narratives, but in the gap between different narratives—why? Because this gap between narrative forms brings out what is *ur-verdraengt* (primordially repressed) from/in the content. Commenting on a short dream related by one of his patients (a woman who at first refused to tell Freud the dream "because it was so indistinct and muddled"), which revealed itself to refer to the fact that the patient was pregnant but unsure who the father was (i.e., the parenthood was "indistinct and muddled"), Freud draws a key dialectical conclusion: "the lack of clarity shown by the dream was a part of the material which instigated the dream: part of this material, that is, was represented in the *form* of the dream. *The form of a dream or the form in which it is dreamt is used with quite surprising frequency for representing its concealed subject-matter.*"[26] The gap between form and content is here properly dialectical, in contrast to the transcendental gap whose point is that every content appears within an a priori formal frame which "constitutes" the content we perceive—or, in structural terms, that we should distinguish between the elements and the formal places these elements occupy. We only attain a proper dialectical analysis of a form when we conceive a certain formal procedure, not as expressing a certain aspect of the (narrative) content, but as signaling that part of the content that is excluded from the explicit narrative line, so that—and herein resides the proper theoretical point—if we want to reconstruct "all" of the narrative content, we must reach beyond the explicit content as such, and include those formal features that act as the stand-in for the "repressed" aspect of the content. In melodramas, for example, the emotional excess that cannot express itself directly in the narrative line finds an outlet in the ridiculously

---

26 Sigmund Freud, *The Interpretation of Dreams*, Harmondsworth: Penguin Books 1976, p. 446.

sentimental musical accompaniment or some other formal feature. In this respect, the standard melodrama can be contrasted with Lars von Trier's *Breaking the Waves*: in both cases, we are dealing with a tension between form and content, but in *Breaking the Waves* the excess is located in the content (the subdued pseudo-documentary form makes the excessive content palpable), while in a melodrama, the excess in the form obfuscates and thus renders palpable the flaw in the content. Therein lies the key consequence of the move from Kant to Hegel: the gap between content and form is to be reflected back into the content itself, as an indication that this content is not all, that something was repressed or excluded from it.[27]

But why does such a reflexive move take us beyond the transcendental dimension? By reflecting the ideological or cognitive antinomy back into reality, does it not simply establish an homology between the inconsistency in ideology and the antagonism in reality, and is it not thereby revealed as just another instance of the ridiculous Marxist-Leninist "theory of reflection"? No, since the parallel here runs between *transcendental* antinomy and—not reality, but—the Real: the distance from reality registers the Real, the Real that is the gap in reality, making it non-All. The solution is thus not to reach into the In-Itself beyond the gap that separates the subject (subjective appearance) from it, but to perceive how this gap is itself In-Itself, how it is a feature of the Real. To clarify this key point, we must leave behind the cognitivist naturalization of language premised on Chomsky's axiom that language is a biological organ, obeying the same evolutionary logic as all other organs. Lacan's axiom, on the contrary, invokes

> the ontological break between language and the living being which speaks. It is the fact that language, far from being a product of spontaneous maturation, falls on the living being which speaks and deregulates it in its enjoyment. It is the fact that the major effect of language is the sexual non-relationship, except if

---

27   The traditional defence of Kant against Hegel's critique is that Hegel brutally simplifies Kant's thought and thereby misses its true point. However, this "true Kant," the Kant missed by Hegel, is as a rule a strangely Hegelian one. In a properly Hegelian reversal, "Hegel" (the Hegelian insight) resides in exactly what we construct as the point which escapes Hegel. For example, defenders of Kant claim that a detailed reading of his text makes it clear that the Thing-in-itself is not simply a positive transcendent entity but a negative category designating a limit of our thought—which is exactly what Hegel claims in his critique of Kant. Typically, one concedes that Kant was often ambiguous, not fully aware of what he effectively did—but what Hegel does in his critique is precisely and only confront Kant with the full scope of what he did.

language is on the contrary the effect of this non-relationship: "Is it the absence of this relationship which exiles humans into the habitat of language? Or is it because humans dwell in language that this relationship can only be half-spoken (*inter-dit*: prohibited)?"[28]

But is the abyss of this circular interdependence the last horizon of our thinking? Is the cognitivist naturalization of language really the only alternative? Should we not take a step further beyond the ontological break between language and the living body and ask: how must the real be structured so that that break can emerge within it? In other words, language colonizing the living body from without cannot be the last word since, in some sense, language itself has to be part of the real. How to think this belonging outside the naturalization of language? There is only one consistent answer: by de-naturalizing nature itself.

Aaron Schuster has drawn attention to how Lacan himself oscillates here between the (predominant) transcendental approach and timid gestures in the direction of its beyond. Lacan's standard topos is the radical discontinuity between (biological) life and the symbolic: the symbolic derails life, subordinating it to a foreign compulsion, depriving it forever of its homeostasis—the move from instinct to drive, from need to desire. Within this perspective, the symbolic order is "always already there" as our unsurpassable horizon, and every account of its genesis amounts to a fantasmatic obfuscation of its constitutive gap. In this Lacanian-structuralist version of the "hermeneutic circle," all we can do is circumscribe the void or impossibility which makes the symbolic non-All and inconsistent, the void in which the external limit coincides with the internal one (the void delimits the symbolic from the Real, but this limitation cuts into the symbolic itself). However, from time to time, and more often in the later Lacan, we find echoes of the Schellingian-Benjaminian-Heideggerian topic of a suffering in nature itself, a pain which comes to be expressed/resolved in human speech—the Freudian *Unbehagen in Der Kultur* is thereby supplemented by an uncanny *Unbehagen in Der Natur* itself:

> imagine all of nature waiting for the gift of speech so it can express how bad it is to be a vegetable or a fish. Is it not the special torment of nature to be deprived of the means of conveying its pent-up aggravation, unable to articulate even the

---

28   Francois Balmès, *Structure, logique, aliénation*, Toulouse: eres 2011, p. 15. The quote within the quote is from Jacques Lacan, "L'étourdit," *Autres écrits*, Paris: Seuil 2001, p. 455.

simplest lament, "Ah me! I am the sea"? And does not the emergence on earth of the speaking being effectively release this terrible organic tension and bring it to a higher level of non-resolution? While there are some intriguing passages in Lacan's seminars where he speculates on the infinite pain of being a plant, raising the possibility of an *Unbehagen in Der Natur*, for the most part he conceives the relationship between nature and culture to be one of radical discontinuity.[29]

In order not to mistake this shift for an outright regression into natural mysticism, it should be read in a strictly Hegelian way: we do not magically overcome the impossibility which cuts across the symbolic—rather, we grasp how this impossibility which seemed to keep us apart from the Real, which rendered the Real impossible, is the very feature which locates the symbolic in the Real. The Real is not beyond the symbolic, it is the impossibility inscribed at its very heart. Hegel's term for this impossibility is the "weakness of nature," the "impotence of nature to obey the concept": nature resists conceptualization not because it is too strong, in excess over every conceptual frame, but because it is too weak:

> The infinite wealth and variety of forms and, what is most irrational, the contingency which enters into the external arrangement of natural things, have been extolled as the sublime freedom of nature, even as the divinity of nature, or at least the divinity present in it. This confusion of contingency, caprice, and disorder, with freedom and rationality is characteristic of sensuous and unphilosophical thinking. This impotence [*Ohnmacht*] of nature sets limits to philosophy ... In the impotence of nature to adhere strictly to the notion in its realization, lies the difficulty and, in many cases, the impossibility of finding fixed distinctions for classes and orders from an empirical consideration of nature. Nature everywhere blurs the essential limits of species and genera by intermediate and defective forms, which continually furnish counter examples to every fixed distinction; this even occurs within a specific genus, that of man, for example, where monstrous births ... must be considered as belonging to the genus.[30]

This is the classic Hegelian reversal: what at first appears as an impotence or limitation in our knowledge, as the impossibility of our grasping the wealth of natural phenomena conceptually, is turned into an impotence in nature itself. And, indeed, do we not find exactly the same constellation in

---

29   Aaron Schuster, *The Third Kind of Complaint* (unpublished manuscript).
30   G. W. F. Hegel, *Philosophy of Nature*, Oxford: Clarendon Press 2004, pp. 23–4.

quantum physics, where indeterminacy (complementarity) points towards a "weakness of nature," in its inability to fully determine itself?

The framed frame

To recapitulate: for the transcendental approach, the a priori ontological frame is irreducible, it can never be inscribed back into reality as an ontic occurrence, since every such occurrence already appears within some transcendental frame. Hegel's way of overcoming the transcendental approach is to introduce a dialectical mediation between the form/frame and its content: the content is in itself "weak," inconsistent, barred, ontologically not fully constituted, and the form fills in this gap, the void of that which is "primordially repressed" from the content. This is why the form is not primarily metonymic with regard to its content: it does not express or mirror it, but fills in its gaps.

Furthermore, since every relation between a frame and its content is necessarily disturbed, there is a need for a supplementary element which will "suture" the entire field. In this element (baptized by Lacan the *objet a*), opposites immediately coincide, i.e., its status is radically amphibolous: it is simultaneously a particular idiosyncratic object which disturbs the frame of reality (the birds in Hitchcock's *The Birds*, say) *and* the frame itself through which we perceive reality (the birds provide the focal point from or through which we read the story). This coincidence of opposites demonstrates Lacan's move beyond transcendental formalism: the fantasy frame is never just a formal frame, it coincides with an object that is constitutively subtracted from reality—or, as Derrida put it, the frame itself is always enframed by a part of its content, by an object that falls within the frame.

Such a disturbance in the "normal" relationship between the frame and its enframed content lies at the very core of modernist art, which is forever split between the two extremes marked at its very beginnings by Malevich and Duchamp: on the one side, the purely formal marking of the Place that confers on an object the status of a work of art (the *Black Square*); on the other side, the display of a common ready-made object (a urinal, a bicycle) as a work of art, as if to prove that what counts as art hinges not on the qualities of the art object, but exclusively on the Place the object occupies, so that anything, even shit, can "be" the work of art if it finds itself in the right Place. In other words, Malevich and Duchamp are like the two sides of a Möbius band, the front side and the obverse of the same artistic event, but for this very reason they cannot ever meet on the same side, within the same space. This is why the definitive kitsch saturation of modernism would have been to combine Malevich and Duchamp in the same exhibit—to put, say, a (painting of a) urinal in a frame (black square). But would this not simply be a return to traditional painting? Yes, which is why, once the modernist break has occurred, one can't pretend that it hasn't happened, and any attempt to ignore it and to go on painting as before will be nostalgic kitsch, in the same way that, after the break introduced by atonality, it would be kitsch to compose romantic music in the old style. Putting a urinal into a frame would, however, remain a modernist gesture since the very obvious gap between form (frame) and content (urinal) would raise the question "Why did the artist put such a common object inside a frame reserved for art objects?" and thereby preserve the gap. That is to say, the only possible answer to that question is: the artist put the urinal in a frame precisely in order to make it palpable that any object can become an art object the moment it occupies the Place of such an object.

Did not something homologous happen in the case of James Hadley Chase, a now half-forgotten hard-boiled writer whose best-known novel is *No Orchids for Miss Blandish*? Chase's books were dismissed as trash in his native England, but treated in France as modern classics, with doctoral theses on, e.g., the notion of fate in his work successfully defended at universities. Is he not like a urinal placed in the Place of modern high art? Even more interesting here would be the opposite case: not to place a urinal (or writer of trash) in the Place of high art, but to treat a high art writer like trash—or, in Duchamp's terms, to urinate into a priceless ancient vase. Maxwell Geismar did precisely this with Henry James, arguing (at a certain level quite convincingly) that we should read him not as an elitist high artist, but as a kitsch author of scandalous commercial plots with ridiculous twists, who covered up his lack of convincing characterizations and failure to understand real life with a confusing overblown pseudo-complex style.[31] Such a reading of James in no way implies that his work should actually be dismissed as kitsch—the point is rather that his true artistic greatness only becomes visible when we take the risk of approaching it through the frame of kitsch, as if it were an exemplary case of sentimental trash. And the same goes for Christianity: its true scope only becomes perceptible when we take

---

31 See Maxwell Geismar, *Henry James and His Cult*, London: Chatto and Windus 1964.

the risk of approaching Christ through the frame of ordinariness, as if he were the lowest dirty beggar or clown with no false dignity. But the supreme example here was provided by Marx who, in his *Class Struggles in France*, notes the imbalance between the formal frame and its content in the sphere of political struggle. His thesis is that, in revolutionary France,

> the petty bourgeois does what normally the industrial bourgeois would have to do; the worker does what normally would be the task of the petty bourgeois; and the task of the worker, who accomplishes that? No one. In France it is not accomplished; in France it is proclaimed. It is not accomplished anywhere within the national boundaries. The class war within French society turns into a world war, in which the nations confront one another.[32]

We have here a systematic displacement between an element and the place (the way to act) prescribed by its position: the petty bourgeoisie is doing what the great industrial bourgeoisie should have been doing; the workers are doing what the petty bourgeoisie should have been doing ... What we would expect at this point is a closure of the circle, i.e., that the highest class (the industrial bourgeoisie, or a class above them) will be doing what the workers should have been doing. But Marx is aware that this all too mechanical logic does not apply here: the summit of the social hierarchy simply disintegrates or is politically immobilized, so that, since there are no elements within the social edifice to do what the workers should be doing, but the class war goes on, the workers' role is externalized, to be played by a foreign agent, which is why in France class struggle assumes the form of war with other nations. What we have then is an overlapping of the inner and the external difference: the external enemy is not simply external, it is a stand-in for the internal enemy—the only way to grasp the French wars adequately is to conceive them as displaced class wars. (Marx later said the same thing when he pointed out that Napoleon continued the French Revolution by turning it into an international war against the other European powers.)

To become aware of these paradoxes, one has to gain a minimal distance from the frame by perceiving it as such, as a frame. Perhaps the most famous case of such an "enframing of the frame" in literature is Saki's classic short story "The Open Window," where the window stands for the frame

---

32   Marx, *The Class Struggles in France, 1848 to 1850*, Part III, available at marxists.org.

of our experience of reality. Framton Nuttel, a nervous young man, has come to stay in the country for the sake of his health. He goes to visit a Mrs. Saprleton, and while waiting for her to come down is entertained by her fifteen-year-old niece who tells him that the French window is kept open, even though it is October, because her aunt's husband and brothers were killed in a shooting accident three years ago, and Mrs. Stapleton believes they will one day come back: "Poor dear aunt, she has often told me how they went out, her husband with his white waterproof coat over his arm, and Ronnie, her youngest brother, singing 'Bertie, why do you bound?'" When Mrs. Saprleton herself appears, she too talks about her husband and brothers, and about how they will soon return from the shoot, and Frampton, of course, takes this as a sign of her deranged mind. But then Mrs. Stapleton suddenly brightens up:

> "Here they are at last!" she cried. "Just in time for tea, and don't they look as if they were muddy up to the eyes!" … In the deepening twilight three figures were walking across the lawn towards the window, they all carried guns under their arms, and one of them was additionally burdened with a white coat hung over his shoulders. A tired brown spaniel kept close at their heels. Noiselessly they neared the house, and then a hoarse young voice chanted out of the dusk: "I said, Bertie, why do you bound?"
>
> Framton grabbed wildly at his stick and hat; the hall door, the gravel drive, and the front gate were dimly noted stages in his headlong retreat.

Framton ran away, of course, because he thought he was seeing ghosts: all that is needed is a frame, and a couple of words can turn it into a fantasy frame, no longer part of reality. Mrs. Saprleton cannot understand why Framton has run away. The niece, who enjoys making up stories about people ("Romance at short notice was her specialty"), explains that Framton ran away because of the spaniel—he's been afraid of dogs ever since being hunted by a pack of pariah dogs in India.

In our most elementary phenomenological experience, the reality we see through a window is always minimally spectral, not as fully real as the enclosed space we inhabit while looking out. The reality outside is perceived in a weirdly de-realized state, as if we were watching a performance on screen. When we open the window, the direct impact of the external reality causes a minimal shock, as we are overwhelmed by its proximity. This is also why we can be surprised when entering the enclosed space of a house: it seems as if the space inside is larger than the outside frame, as if the house is bigger on the inside than the outside. A similar frame, conceived as a window onto another world, appears in Roland Emmerich's 1994 film, *Stargate*. The "stargate" is a large ring-shaped device that functions as a wormhole enabling people to teleport to complementary devices located cosmic distances away. No wonder the world they enter through the stargate resembles Ancient Egypt—itself a kind of "stargate culture" in which the pharaohs organized gigantic public works to secure their passage through the stargate to Orion after their death. And, in science itself, is not the ultimate stargate the idea of a black hole, conceived as the passage into an alternative universe?[33]

At the congress of the Chinese Communist Party, which takes place every eight years or so, the new Standing Committee of the Politburo is presented to the delegates as a mysterious revelation, a *fait accompli*. The selection procedure involves complex, behind-closed-doors negotiations, and the delegates who unanimously approve the list learn about it only when the time comes to vote. As the ferocious factional struggle that goes on behind the scenes is strictly informal, the outcome is experienced as wholly contingent and unfathomable. The effect of the mystery is strictly topological: the podium on which the new members of the Standing Committee present themselves functions as a kind of "stargate"—a frame onto another hidden reality out of which new things emerge into our ordinary world. Of course, there is no alternative reality in fact, and those who have decided the composition of the new Committee are seated in the big hall along with all the others—but the effect is nonetheless magical.

Another version of this kind of frame reversal can be found in Ian McEwan's 2012 novel *Sweet Tooth*, which is structured like Escher's famous image of two hands drawing each other, although the symmetry is not perfect. The novel appears to be the first-person narrative of the main character, Serena, and concludes with a letter she finds on a table in her lover's flat. We read this discovery as if it was "drawn by" (included in) Serena's narrative: she has told us her story and now concludes it with the discovery of the letter. What we learn from the letter, however, is that the author of Serena's first-person narrative was her lover, who, in a tit-for-tat act of revenge, after learning that she was an MI5 agent reporting on him, decided to report on her in the form of a novel describing her life and their

---

33   What if one even reads Plato's cave in this way? I remember seeing a cartoon in a newspaper many years ago depicting a prehistorical family in a cave, sitting together in the evening and observing the events outside—bears and other animals fighting—through the cave opening. The first model of evening cinema entertainment?

relationship in detail. In short, it turns out that the bulk of the novel has been "drawn" by the (author of) the letter that concludes it, so that the only authentic first-person narrator is the letter itself.

When we watch a fictional film, the narrative functions like a frame, and "gaffes" are mistakes which threaten to ruin the effect of reality. But a film can also deliberately play with this gap between its narrative frame and the excess of reality. *Parade*, a short documentary by Dušan Makavejev from the early 1960s, shows the preparations for a military parade in Belgrade (army units getting ready, crowds gathering, children playing, etc.), and when the parade starts, the film ends. In terms of Deleuze's opposition between image-movement and image-time, the film deals exclusively with the "empty time" off stage, limiting itself to image-time and ignoring the narrative image-movement. Welles' *Citizen Kane* here occupies a special place. In her classic study, "Raising Kane," Pauline Kael makes a lucid observation about the true originality of the film:

> One of the games that film students sometimes play is to judge a director on whether you have the illusion that the people on the screen will go on doing what they're doing after the camera leaves them. Directors are rated by how much time you think elapsed before the actors grabbed their coats or ordered a sandwich. The longer the time, the more of a film man the director is said to be; when a director is stage-oriented, you can practically see the actors walking off the set. This game doesn't help in judging a film's content, but it's a fairly reliable test of a director's film technique; one could call it a test of movie believability. However, it isn't applicable to *Citizen Kane*. You're perfectly well aware that the people won't go on doing what they're doing—that they have, indeed, completed their actions on the screen. *Kane* depends not on naturalistic believability but on our enjoyment of the very fact that those actions *are* completed, and that they all fit into place. This bravura is, I think, the picture's only true originality, and it wasn't an intentional challenge to the concept of unobtrusive technique but was (mainly) the result of Welles's discovery of—and his delight in—the fun of making movies.[34]

Welles thus undermines the narrative frame not by showing us bits of off-stage time, but by constructing the narrative action in such a self-consciously spectacular way that the viewer cannot ignore its artificially

---

34   Pauline Kael, "Raising Kane," *New Yorker*, February 21 and 27, 1971, available at paulrossen.com.

staged character. The realist illusion that "the people on the screen will go on doing what they're doing after the camera leaves them" is thus undermined in an immanent way: when the camera leaves them, the people will simply stop acting.[35]

The distance from the narrative frame can also be activated in a more refined form, as in the case of *The Army of Shadows*, a 1969 film by Jean-Pierre Melville, which at the time of its release was not well received (in the aftermath of May '68, it was seen as a glorification of General de Gaulle). Today, however, it is reemerging as one of the great classics of French cinema. The film begins in October 1942 in Vichy France, where Philippe Gerbier, the head of a Resistance network, is arrested. After his escape, Resistance members identify a young agent named Paul Dounat as the informant who has betrayed Gerbier to the Vichy police. They take Dounat to a safe house in order to shoot him, but, finding a family in close proximity next door, they decide to strangle him instead. The story then focuses on Mathilde who, in the guise of a housewife and unbeknownst to her family, is one of the linchpins of Gerbier's network. After a month of solitude, Gerbier receives an unexpected visit from another Resistance leader, Luc Jardie, who has come to seek his advice following the arrest of Mathilde. Despite Gerbier's warning her not to, Mathilde was carrying a photo of her daughter in her wallet when she was caught. The Resistance group receive a coded status report saying that Mathilde has been released and that two Resistance men were picked up that same afternoon. Gerbier orders Mathilde's immediate execution, but another member refuses to carry out the order and swears he will stop Gerbier from killing her. As a fight is about to break out, Jardie emerges from a back room and defuses the tension. He convinces them that the reason Mathilde acted the way she did—betraying only minor agents, and convincing the Gestapo to release her under the pretext of leading them to her network—was to give the Resistance a window of opportunity to kill her, thereby sparing the network and her daughter. They all reluctantly agree to take part in the operation and Jardie announces that he too

---

35   A detail in the famous Chéreau Bayreuth staging of Wagner's *Ring* strangely evoked this logic: at the very end of Act I of *Die Walküre*, we saw Siegmund and Sieglinde in a tight embrace, he lying on top of her, ready to make love (and incept Siegfried). At this point, the curtains closed quickly but a gust of air parted them again for a split second. I remember how I looked attentively, trying to see if the two singers were already getting up, straightening their clothes, etc., or if they were still lying tightly embraced, as if caught in the act and ready to go on (which was indeed the case!).

will be present as a final homage to Mathilde. Soon after, however, Jardie reveals to Gerbier that his argument was purely speculative. A few days later, Mathilde is walking the streets of Paris when Jardie and his men pull up next to her in a stolen German car; seeing them, Mathilde freezes and keeps her eyes locked on Jardie's as she is shot. As the film comes to an end, silent captions reveal the eventual fate of the four members of the group: they all die, and Jardie, who is tortured to death, betrays no other name than his own.[36]

The same gap between the Real and the fable is palpable in the two liquidation scenes: in each case, the fable that legitimizes the killing creates the window, but this window is disturbed by the raw Real of the act of killing.[37] In the first case, the justification is obvious: the man was a traitor. In the second case, when Jardie provides the fable (Mathilde requires us to kill her, it's the only way out for her), he admits immediately afterwards that it is just a hypothesis—but the act of killing remains no less necessary. The film thus avoids the twin traps of pacifism and simple heroic identification: there is no doubt that the gruesome task has to be undertaken, and there is no easy skeptical way out (in the style of "killing never solves anything; if we do that, we become like our enemies; the experience of war is deeply traumatic and repellent"); nonetheless, the *necessary* act remains *impossible* and traumatic, it loses its heroic transparency and acquires a terrifying impenetrable density.

---

36   The figure of Jardie is based on Jean Cavaillès, the legendary philosopher and mathematician who specialized in philosophy of science, took part in the Resistance, and was tortured and shot by the Gestapo on February 17, 1944. His main work, *Transfinite and Continuous*, written in Montpellier prison in 1942, was published posthumously in 1947.

37   Along the same lines, one should always bear in mind that, for psychoanalysis, "castration" is not a fact but a fable, a fantasy, a cultural scenario, in answer to the enigma of the deadlock of *jouissance*. (This is why the feminine "penis-envy" is also an attempt to renormalize the excess of sexuality.)

CHAPTER 3

The Wound

What we confront with late Heidegger is the problem of historicity at its most radical: a historicity which goes "all the way down" and cannot be reduced to the deployment or revelation in history of a non-historical Absolute. In a way, the true *Kehre* from *Being and Time* to the late Heidegger is the shift from ahistorical formal-transcendental analysis to radical historicity. To put it in (the not quite appropriate) terms of German Idealism, Heidegger's achievement is to elaborate a radically historicized transcendentalism: Heideggerian historicity is the historicity of transcendental horizons themselves, of the different modes of the disclosure of being, with no agent regulating the process—historicity happens as an *es gibt* (*il y a*), the radically contingent abyss of a world-game.[1] This radical historicity reaches its definitive formulation with the shift from Being to *Ereignis*. This shift thoroughly undermines the idea of Being as a kind of super-subject of history, sending its messages/epochs to man. *Ereignis* means that Being is *nothing but* the *chiaroscuro* of these messages, *nothing but* the way it relates to man. Man is finite, and *Ereignis* also: it names the very structure of finitude, the play of Clearing/Concealment with nothing behind. "It" is just the impersonal it, a "there is." There is an un-historical dimension at work here, but what is un-historical is the formal structure of historicity itself. It is this radical historicity that forever separates Heidegger from so-called Oriental thought: despite the similarity of *Gelassenheit* to nirvana, etc., the attainment of zero-level of nirvana is meaningless within the horizon of Heidegger's thought—it would mean something like doing away with all shadow of concealment. Like Kafka's man from the country who learns that

---

1 This is also why there is no place for the Lacanian Real in Heidegger's thought. The most concise definition of the Real is that it is a *given without givenness*: it is just given, without the possibility of accounting for its being-given by any agency of giving, even the impersonal *"es gibt / il y a,"* without a phenomenological horizon opening the space for it to appear. It is the impossible point of the ontic without the ontological.

the Door of the Law is there for him only, *Dasein* has to experience how Being needs us, how our strife with Being is Being's strife with itself.

There is, however, a weird overlapping between Heidegger and Buddhism. In his reading of the fragment of Anaximander on order and disorder, Heidegger considers the possibility that an entity

> may even insist [*bestehen*] upon its while, solely to remain more present, in the sense of perduring [*Bestaendigen*].That which lingers persists [*beharrt*] in its presencing. In this way it extricates itself from its transitory while. It strikes the willful pose of persistence, no longer concerning itself with whatever else is present. It stiffens—as if this were the only way to linger—and aims solely for continuance and subsistence.[2]

Is not this line of thought homologous to the Buddhist idea that suffering originates from excessive attachment to a worldly entity? A third player enters the scene here: the difference between Buddhism (plus Heidegger) and Lacan is crucial. It concerns not only the fact that while Buddhism strives for eternal peace, Lacan focuses on what Buddhism perceives as the Fall (the fixation on a particular feature which starts to matter more than anything and thus derails the cosmic balance). Lacan's point is a much more precise one: only the "getting stuck," the fixation on a particular feature, opens up the space for the possible withdrawal into eternal inner peace. That is to say, prior to fixation, the subject does not dwell in inner peace but remains fully caught up in the flow of things, their generation and degeneration, the circle of life. What if *stricto sensu* there is no world, no disclosure of being, prior to this "stuckness," and it is this very excess of willing that opens up the space for *Gelassenheit*? What if it is only against the background of this stuckness that a human being can experience itself as mortal, in contrast to an animal which simply is mortal?

The primordial fact is thus not the fugue of Being (or the inner peace of *Gelassenheit*), which may then be disturbed or perverted by the rise of ur-willing; the primordial fact is this ur-willing itself, its disturbance of the "natural" fugue. To put it another way: for a human being to be able to withdraw from full immersion in its environs into the inner peace of *Gelassenheit*, this immersion has first to be broken by the excessive "stuckness" of the drive. What this means is that we never have a direct choice

---

2   Martin Heidegger, *Gesamtausgabe, Band 5: Holzwege*, Frankfurt: Klostermann 1977, p. 355.

between immersion in the natural circle of life and withdrawal into nirvana: the first choice is rather that between immersion and excessive attachment ("stuckness"), and only after choosing "stuckness" can we withdraw from it into nirvana. The Fall thus never happens, since it has always already happened. If we accept the primacy of the Fall over what it is the Fall from (that is, if we accept the primacy of "stuckness") as the axiom of human life, then the consequences are tremendous, especially in matters of religion. Original Sin, as the Fall from innocence, can only be explained if what precedes it is not simply the immediacy of innocence—that is, if innocence is already permeated by anxiety (dread). This is brilliantly articulated by Kierkegaard in §5 of *The Concept of Dread*:

> Innocence is ignorance. In his innocence man is not determined as spirit but is psychically determined in immediate unity with his natural condition. This view is in perfect accord with that of the Bible, and by refusing to ascribe to man in the state of innocence a knowledge of the difference between good and evil it condemns all the notions of merit Catholicism has imagined.
>
> In this state there is peace and repose: but at the same time there is something different, which is not dissension and strife, for there is nothing to strive with. What is it then? Nothing. But what effect does nothing produce? It begets dread. This is the profound secret of innocence, that at the same time it is dread. Dreamily the spirit projects its own reality, but this reality is nothing, but innocence constantly sees this nothing outside itself ... Innocence still *is*, but one word suffices, and with that ignorance is concentrated. Innocence of course cannot understand this word; but dread has as it were obtained its first prey; instead of nothing, innocence gets an enigmatic word. So when it is related in Genesis that God said to Adam, "Only of the tree of the knowledge of good and evil thou shalt not eat," it is a matter of course that Adam did not really understand this word. For how could he have understood the difference between good and evil, seeing that this distinction was in fact consequent upon the enjoyment of the fruit?
>
> When one assumes that the prohibition awakens desire, one posits knowledge instead of ignorance; for Adam would have had to have the knowledge of freedom, since his desire was to use it. The explanation therefore anticipates what was subsequent. The prohibition alarms Adam (induces a state of dread) because the prohibition awakens in him the possibility of freedom ... After the word of prohibition follows the word of judgment: "Thou shalt surely die." What it means to die, Adam of course cannot conceive; but if one assumes that these words were said to him, there is nothing to prevent his having a notion of the

terrible. Indeed even the beast is able to understand the mimic expression and movement in the speaker's voice, without understanding the word. In case one lets the prohibition awaken desire, one may also let the word about punishment awaken a deterring conception.[3]

We have here a precise succession of steps, beginning with a state of innocence which is not the same as immediacy: innocence is "peace and repose," there is no knowledge and no sin (in short, no knowledge of sin, of the difference between good and evil, or, even shorter, no knowledge at all, since knowledge as such is sinful), but there is already "something different," something that disturbs the peace of innocence and gives rise to dread. Kierkegaard struggles with how to define this externality that does not yet involve differentiality, negation, opposition, or mutual exclusion. Innocence is not good and its externality is not evil, there is no limit separating innocence from "something different," innocence forms a closed circle with no limit, just the feeling (of those inside the circle) that there is an indeterminate something outside, that they are moving within a closed circle.[4]

This state of things fits perfectly with the notion of the non-All in Lacan's feminine formula of sexuation: there is no limit, no exception, and yet we are nonetheless somehow aware that the circle in which we dwell is not "all," and this emptiness, this shapeless void, triggers the most elementary dread. The feminine character of this constellation seems further confirmed by Lacan's claim that Don Giovanni is a feminine fantasy: he takes women one by one, never as a whole (as all), jumping from one to the next as if to postpone falling into an abyss that threatens to swallow him up the moment he stops his frantic pursuit. No wonder that, in his famous analysis of Mozart's *Don Giovanni* from *Either-Or*, Kierkegaard characterizes Don Giovanni's subjective stance as a type of innocence. Might one even say: demonic innocence? Here is Kierkegaard's (deservedly) famous description of Mozart's overture to *Don Giovanni*:

---

3   Quoted from Walter Kaufman, ed., *Existentialism from Dostoevsky to Sartre*, New York: Meridian 1975, pp. 101–5.

4   Things are similar, but not the same, with the hermeneutic circle of understanding: we cannot step outside our horizon of understanding, every outside is already interpreted from inside, and although the circle is finite, it forms a loop, so that we can never reach its limit and take a peek at its outside. However, this very absence of a visible limit makes our experience claustrophobic, since we are well aware that our horizon is not the only one, that there are other horizons.

The overture begins with a few deep, earnest, even notes; then for the first time we hear infinitely far away an intimation that is nevertheless instantly recalled, as if it were premature, until later we hear again and again, bolder and bolder, more and more clamorous, that voice which at first subtly, demurely, and yet seemingly in anxiety, slipped in but could not press through. So it is in nature that one sometimes sees the horizon dark and clouded; too heavy to support itself, it rests upon the earth and hides everything in its obscure night; a few hollow sounds are heard, not yet in motion but like a deep mumbling to itself. Then in the most distant heavens, far off on the horizon, one sees a flash; it speeds away swiftly along the earth, is gone in an instant. But soon it appears again; it gathers strength; it momentarily illuminates the entire heaven with its flame. The next second, the horizon seems even darker, but it flares up more swiftly, even more brilliantly; it seems as if the darkness itself has lost its composure and is starting to move. Just as the eye in this first flash has a presentiment of a great fire, so the ear has a presentiment of the total passion in that dwindling stroke of the violin bow. There is an anxiety in that flash; it is as if in that deep darkness it were born in anxiety—just so is Don Giovanni's life. There is an anxiety in him, but this anxiety is his energy. In him, it is not a subjectively reflected anxiety; it is a substantial anxiety. In the overture there is not what is commonly called—without knowing what one is saying—despair. Don Giovanni's life is not despair; it is, however, the full force of the sensuous, which is born in anxiety; and Don Giovanni himself is this anxiety, but this anxiety is precisely the demonic zest for life. After Mozart has had Don Giovanni come into existence this way, his life now develops for us in the dancing strains of the violin, in which he lightly, fleetingly speeds on over the abyss. When one throws a pebble in such a way that it skims the surface of the water, it can for a time skip over the water in light hops, but it sinks down to the bottom as soon as it stops skipping; in the same way he dances over the abyss, jubilating during his brief span.[5]

Don Giovanni's anxiety is thus not in some kind of dialectical tension with his erotic energy, his anxiety *is* his erotic energy: in his demonic zest for life, his jumping from one woman to the next, he is like a pebble skipping over the water before it sinks to the bottom, in a frantic effort to postpone falling into the Void. In this precise sense, Don Giovanni's demonic zest is innocent: it is not sustained by knowledge of the difference between Good and Evil, it is just an endless repetitive movement

5   Søren Kierkegaard, *Either/Or, Part 1*, Princeton: Princeton University Press 1987, pp. 129–30.

of postponing the fall into a shapeless "something other" that generates anxiety.

So we begin with a closed loop of innocence turning around a shapeless Void that generates dread—how can this deadlock be resolved? Kierkegaard's answer: with the intervention of a Word of Prohibition. In the Bible this is, of course, God's "Don't eat from the tree of knowledge!"; in the case of Don Giovanni, the word belongs to the statue of the Commendatore which, at the opera's end, calls on Don Giovanni to repent. As Kierkegaard emphasizes, this word which disturbs innocence is "enigmatic," the subject to whom it is addressed cannot understand it, it is what Lacan would have called an empty Master-Signifier, a signifier without a signified. It cannot be understood for the simple reason that the innocent subject cannot yet know what knowledge is, or the difference between Good and Evil—he knows no Evil, just the formless Void outside the limitless loop of his pleasurable innocence, and the first Word materializes, condenses, or "concentrates" this Void: "Innocence still *is*, but one word suffices, and with that ignorance is concentrated." "Concentrating ignorance" here means condensing the shapeless Void into its signifying representative, an empty signifier.

A further explanation is needed here: it is not that we need words to designate objects, to symbolize reality, and that there is some excess of reality, a traumatic core that resists symbolization, which is then "concentrated" in an enigmatic signifier. We have reality in front of our eyes well before language, and what language does, in its most fundamental gesture, is the very opposite of designating reality: as Lacan put it, it *digs a hole in reality*, opening up the visible/present reality to the dimension of the immaterial/unseen. When I see you, I just see you—but by naming you I indicate the abyss in you beyond what I see. The enigmatic "empty signifier" thus in a sense comes first, its emergence is the founding gesture of language. Let us explain this through another example.

Jonathan Lear has demonstrated how Freud's "pre-Socratic" turn to Eros and Thanatos as the two basic polar forces of the universe is a false escape, a pseudo-explanation generated by his inability to properly conceptualize the dimension "beyond the pleasure principle" he encountered in his clinics. After establishing the pleasure principle as the "swerve" which defines the functioning of our psychic apparatus, Freud is compelled to take note of the phenomena (primarily repetitions of traumatic experiences) which disrupt this functioning: they form an exception which cannot be accounted for in terms of the pleasure principle. It was "at this point that Freud covers over the crucial nugget of his own insight: that the mind can disrupt its own functioning."[6] Instead of trying to conceptualize this break (negativity) as such in its modalities, he wants to ground it in another "deeper" positivity. In philosophical terms, the mistake here is the same as that made by Kant (according to Hegel): after Kant discovers the inner inconsistency of our experiential reality, instead of accepting that inconsistency, he feels compelled to posit the existence of another, inaccessible, true reality of Things-in-themselves: "Freud is not in the process of discovering a new life force, he is in the process of trying to cover over a trauma to psychoanalytic theory. In this way, invoking Plato and the ancients gives a false sense of legitimacy and security."[7] One can only fully agree with Lear: far from being the name of an unbearable traumatic fact unacceptable to most of us (the fact that we "strive towards death" ...), the introduction of Thanatos as a cosmic principle (and the retroactive elevation of libido into Eros) is *an attempt to cover up the true trauma*. The apparent "radicalization" is effectively a philosophical domestication: the break that disrupts the functioning of the universe, its ontological fault as it were, is transformed into one of two positive cosmic principles, thus reestablishing a pacifying harmonious vision of the universe as a battlefield of two opposing principles. (The theological implications are here also crucial: instead of thinking through to the end the subversive deadlock of monotheism, Freud regresses to a pagan wisdom.)

Lear introduces here the notion of "enigmatic terms," terms which seem to designate a determinate entity, but effectively just stand for a failure of our understanding: when he mentions Thanatos, Freud "takes himself to be naming a real thing in the world but he is in fact injecting an enigmatic term into our discourse. There is no naming, for nothing has genuinely been isolated for him to name. His hope is to provide an explanation, in fact all we have is the illusion of one."[8] But is this not too dismissive of "enigmatic terms"? Are they really just indexes of our failure and ignorance, or do they play a key structural role? "Enigmatic term" fits exactly what Lacan calls the Master-Signifier (the phallus as signifier), the "empty" signifier without a signified. This signifier (the paternal metaphor) is the substitute for the mother's desire, and the encounter with that desire, with its enigma (*Che Vuoi?*, what do you want?), is the primordial encounter with the opacity of

---

6   Jonathan Lear, "Give Dora a Break! A Tale of Eros and Emotional Disruption," in Shadi Bartsch and Thomas Bartscherer, eds., *Erotikon: Essays on Eros, Ancient and Modern*, Chicago: Chicago University Press 2006, p. 198.

7   Ibid., p. 199.

8   Ibid.

the Other. The fact that the phallus is a *signifier*, not the signified, plays a pivotal role here: the phallic signifier does not explain the enigma of the mother's desire, it is not its signified (i.e., it does not tell us "what mother really wants"), it just designates the impenetrable space of her desire.

The homology with Lacan goes even further: is not Lear's point that the Freudian pleasure principle is "non-All"? There is nothing outside it, no external limit, and yet it is not all, it can break down. How, then, does a break occur? How does our mind, which follows the pleasure principle, disrupt its functioning? As Deleuze pointed out in his *Difference and Repetition*, reading Freud in a way which meets Lear's critique, Eros and Thanatos are not two opposite drives that both compete and combine forces (as in eroticized masochism): there is only one drive, the libido, striving for enjoyment, and the "death drive" is the curved space of its formal structure:

> It plays the role of a transcendental principle, whereas the pleasure principle is only psychological. For this reason, it is above all silent (not given in experience), whereas the pleasure principle is noisy. The first question, then, is: How is it that the theme of death, which appears to draw together the most negative elements of psychological life, can be in itself the most positive element, transcendentally positive, to the point of affirming repetition?...
>
> Eros and Thanatos are distinguished in that Eros must be repeated, can be experienced only through repetition, whereas Thanatos (as transcendental principle) is that which gives repetition to Eros, that which submits Eros to repetition.[9]

We have thus three movements of repetition: downward repetition (repetition as decay, as a mere copy); the standard Hegelian upward repetition (repetition as idealization, as the passage from contingency to notional necessity); and pure repetition (mechanical reproduction of the same, which ends up repeating the very impossibility of purely repeating). The notion of pure repetition can be nicely illustrated by a weird thing that happened to the front page of *Pravda*, the official Soviet daily newspaper. Before the public rejection of Stalin in 1962, the title "PRAVDA" was accompanied by drawings of two profiles, Lenin's and Stalin's, side by side; what happened after was not what one would have expected, i.e., just the one profile of Lenin—instead, there were two identical profiles of Lenin printed side

9   Gilles Deleuze, *Difference and Repetition*, New York: Columbia University Press 1994, pp. 16 and 18.

by side. In this weird repetition, Stalin was in a way more present than ever in his absence, since his shadowy presence was the answer to the obvious question "why Lenin twice, why not just one Lenin?"

This is how Don Giovanni works: his "death drive" is the transcendental frame of his pursuit of pleasure, his compulsion to repeat his conquests again and again to defer the fall into the Void. The emergence of a Word interrupts this mad circular dance by "concentrating" the shapeless Void that causes dread into a signifier, and since this signifier refers to the Void, it has to be an "enigmatic" signifier naming the unnameable. The first Word thus has no determinate content, it is an empty "Don't!" whose object can only be the Void of the impossible Real—in short, the first prohibition can only prohibit what is already in itself impossible. The advantage of this operation is that the impossible becomes something prohibited, with the accompanying illusion that, if we violate the prohibition, we can thereby reach the impossible. It is in this sense that, as Kierkegaard puts it, the prohibition awakens the possibility of freedom—the freedom to violate the prohibition, i.e., to eat from the tree of knowledge.

In the Genesis story, God engages in a perverse strategy: in pronouncing the prohibitive Word, He pushes man into violating the prohibition and thereby into becoming human. As St. Augustine put it long ago (in his *Enchiridion*, xxvii): "God judged it better to bring good out of evil, than to allow no evil to exist." Or as Hegel, Kierkegaard's great opponent, would have it, knowledge is not just the possibility of choosing evil or good, "it is the consideration or the cognition that *makes* people evil, so that consideration and cognition [themselves] are what is evil, and that [therefore] such cognition is what ought not to exist [because it] is the *source* of evil."[10] In short, prohibition precedes what it prohibits, or as Kierkegaard puts it, the explanation anticipates what is subsequent.

THE FALL

The knowledge gained by Adam and Eve is nonetheless not simply empty— here is what happens after they eat from the tree:

> Then the eyes of both of them were opened, and they realized they were naked; so they sewed fig leaves together and made coverings for themselves. Then the

---

10   G. W. F. Hegel, *Vorlesungen über die Philosophie der Religion II*, Frankfurt: Suhrkamp Verlag 1969, p. 205.

man and his wife heard the sound of the Lord God as he was walking in the garden in the cool of the day, and they hid from the Lord God among the trees of the garden. But the Lord God called to the man, "Where are you?" The man answered, "I heard you in the garden, and I was afraid because I was naked; so I hid." And he said, "Who told you that you were naked? Have you eaten from the tree that I commanded you not to eat from?" (Genesis 3:7–11)

Before eating from the tree, the two were already naked, they just didn't know that they were—one can imagine them doing a "double take." The shift involved in the Fall is thus purely subjective, it involves Adam and Eve adopting a different attitude towards themselves: they merely realize (register, take note of) what they are, as in the famous passage from Molière in which a guy, when told that he is speaking prose—a newly learned word for him—asserts with pleasure that he knows how to speak prose. What betrayed them to God was not their brash display of nakedness, but their feeling of shame at realizing that they were naked—one can thus say that it was the moral feeling of shame that itself made them guilty. Recall Alphonse Allais' old joke, pointing to a woman walking along the street and shouting: "Look at her! Beneath her clothes, she's totally naked!" In exactly the same way, a human being is guilty only under the cover of his or her shame.

And is it not similar with the punishment that befalls them—that they are no longer immortal? In the same way that they were already naked, they were also already mortal, they just did not relate to their mortality—as Heidegger would have put it, animals die, but only man relates to his death as his innermost (im)possibility. So when God announces the punishment, he just spells out what Adam and Eve have already realized in noticing that they were naked, namely, their misery as two weak mortal beings.

This is why, in Christianity, the true Event is the Fall itself. As was made clear by Kierkegaard, Christianity is the first and only religion of the Event: our only access to the Absolute is through our acceptance of the unique event of Incarnation as a singular historical occurrence. This is why Kierkegaard insists it is a matter of Christ versus Socrates: Socrates stands for remembrance, for rediscovering the substantial higher reality of Ideas that are always already in us, while Christ announces the "good news" of a radical break. The event proper is "Christ has risen," and the Christian belief is a belief in this miracle. However, we should not take resurrection as something that happens *after* Christ's death, but as the obverse of the death itself—Christ is alive as the Holy Ghost, as the love that binds the community of believers. In short, *"Christ has risen" means that Christ has fallen:*

in other religions, man falls away from God (into sinful terrestrial life or whatever), only in Christianity does God Himself fall—how, from where? The only possibility is: from Himself, into His own creation.[11]

We can arrive at the same result through a close reading of the Paulinian passage from Law to love.[12] In both cases (Law and love), we are dealing with division, with a "divided subject"; however, in each case the modality of the division is quite different. The subject of the Law is "decentered" in the sense that it is caught up in the self-destructive vicious cycle of sin and Law in which each pole engenders its opposite. Paul provided the unsurpassable description of this entanglement in Romans 7:

> We know that the law is spiritual; but I am carnal, sold into slavery to sin. What I do, I do not understand. For I do not do what I want, but I do what I hate. Now if I do what I do not want, I concur that the law is good. So now it is no longer I who do it, but sin that dwells in me. For I know that good does not dwell in me, that is, in my flesh. The willing is ready at hand, but doing the good is not. For I do not do the good I want, but I do the evil I do not want. Now if I do what I do not want, it is no longer I who do it, but sin that dwells in me. So, then, I discover the principle that when I want to do right, evil is at hand. For I take delight in the law of God, in my inner self, but I see in my members another principle at war with the law of my mind, taking me captive to the law of sin that dwells in my members. Miserable one that I am! (Romans 7:14–24)

It is thus not that I am merely torn between two opposites, Law and sin; the problem is that I cannot even clearly distinguish them: I want to follow the Law, and I end up in sin. This vicious cycle is (not so much overcome as) broken, one breaks out of it, with the experience of love, more precisely: with the experience of the radical gap that separates love from the Law. Therein lies the radical difference between the couple Law/sin and the couple Law/love. The gap that separates Law and sin is not a real difference: their truth is their mutual implication or confusion—Law generates sin and feeds on it. Only with the couple Law/love do we attain a real difference: these two moments are radically separated, not "mediated," one is not the

---

11   Christianity thus enjoins us to reverse the terms of the "king's two bodies": God Himself has two bodies, but in the crucifixion it is not that the terrestrial body dies while the sublime body remains as the Holy Spirit; what dies on the Cross is the sublime body of Christ.

12   See Alain Badiou, *Saint Paul: The Foundation of Universalism*, Stanford: Stanford University Press 2003.

form of appearance of its opposite. It is therefore wrong to ask: "Are we then forever condemned to suffer the split between Law and love? What about the synthesis between Law and love?" The split between Law and love is of a radically different nature than the split between Law and sin: instead of the vicious cycle of mutual reinforcement, we get a clear distinction of two different domains. Once we become fully aware of the dimension of love in its radical difference from the Law, love has in a way already won, since this difference is visible only when one already dwells in love, adopts the standpoint of love. This is why Paul's negative appreciation of the Law is clear and unambiguous: "For no human being will be justified in his sight by deeds prescribed by the law, for through the law comes the knowledge of sin" (Romans 3:20); "The sting of death is sin, and the power of sin is the law" (1 Corinthians 15:56); and, consequently, "Christ redeemed us from the curse of the law" (Galatians 3:13). The strongest proponents of this radical opposition between the Law and divine love are Lutheran theologians like Bultmann, for whom

> the way of works of the Law and the way of grace and faith are mutually exclusive opposites … man's effort to achieve his salvation by keeping the Law only leads him into sin, *indeed this effort itself in the end is already sin* … the Law brings to light that man is sinful, whether it be that his sinful desire leads him to transgression of the Law or that *that desire disguises itself in zeal for keeping the Law.*[13]

But if "the power of sin is the law," why did God proclaim Law in the first place? According to the standard reading of Paul, God gave the Law to men in order to make them conscious of their sin, even to make them sin all the more, and thus make them aware of their need for salvation which can come only through divine grace. But does not this reading involve a somewhat perverse notion of God? The only way to avoid such a reading is to insist on the absolute *identity* of the two gestures: God does not *first* push us into sin in order to create the need for salvation, and *then* offer Himself as Redeemer from the trouble He got us into in the first place—it is not that the Fall is followed by Redemption; rather, the Fall is *identical* to Redemption, it is "in itself" already Redemption. After all, what *is* "Redemption"? It is the explosion of freedom, the breaking of our natural chains—*and this, precisely, is what happens in the Fall.* One should bear in mind here the central tension in the Christian notion of the Fall: conceived

---

13   Rudolf Bultmann, *Theology of the New Testament*, Vol. 1, London: SCM 1952, pp. 264–5.

as a "regression" to the natural state of enslavement to the passions, it is *stricto sensu* identical with the dimension *from which* we fall, i.e., it is the very movement of the Fall that creates, or opens up, what is lost in it.

To put it in mystical terms, the Christian Event is the exact opposite of any "return to innocence": it is Original Sin itself, the abyssal disturbance of the primeval Peace, the primordial "pathological" choice of an unconditional attachment to some singular object (like falling in love with a singular person who thereafter matters to us more than everything else). In Buddhist terms, the Christian Event is the exact structural obverse of enlightenment or nirvana: it is the very gesture by which the Void is disturbed and Difference (and, with it, false appearance and suffering) emerges in the world. Is Eve not thus the only true partner of God in the affair of the Fall? The act, the catastrophic decision, is hers: it is she who opens up the path towards the knowledge of good and evil (which is the consequence of the Fall) and towards the shame of being naked—in short, the path towards the properly human universe. To grasp the true situation we should bear in mind Hegel's (rather obvious) point: the innocence of "paradise" is another name for animal life, so that what the Bible calls the "Fall" is nothing but the passage from animal life to a properly human existence. It is thus, once again, the Fall itself which creates the dimension from which it is the Fall—with such considerations we enter the obscure domain of what Kierkegaard called the religious suspension of the ethical, and we must proceed carefully here in order to avoid perverse traps. Here is how one fundamentalist commentator justifies God's command to the Israelites to kill all the Canaanites, children included, dwelling in the land that God had promised to the Jews:

> So the problem isn't that God ended the Canaanites' lives. The problem is that He commanded the Israeli soldiers to end them. Isn't that like commanding someone to commit murder? No, it's not. Rather, since our moral duties are determined by God's commands, it is commanding someone to do something which, in the absence of a divine command, *would have been* murder. The act was morally obligatory for the Israeli soldiers in virtue of God's command, even though, had they undertaken it on their own initiative, it would have been wrong. On divine command theory, then, God has the right to command an act, which, in the absence of a divine command, would have been sin, but which is now morally obligatory in virtue of that command.[14]

---

14   "Slaughter of the Canaanites," from reasonablefaith.org.

Does every religious suspension of the ethical rely on such an obscenity? No—in the quoted passage, the ethical is not suspended, but simply directly incorporated into God: God is the origin of our morality, so whatever He enjoins us to do is by definition moral, even if it appears to be a terrifying act of genocide. The authentic suspension of the ethical is something quite different: in it, I step out of the ethical in the sense that I have to assume full responsibility for deciding what my ethical duty is—in Kierkegaard's terms, I regress from an already constituted ethical edifice to an ethics-in-becoming.

So one has to be careful here not to succumb to a perverse reading of the priority of the Fall. The most radical case of such a reading was that given by Nicolas Malebranche, the great Cartesian Catholic, excommunicated after his death for his excessive orthodoxy (Lacan probably had figures like Malebranche in his mind when he claimed that theologians are the only true atheists). In the best Pascalian tradition, Malebranche laid the cards on the table and "revealed the secret" (the perverse core) of Christianity: his Christology is based on an original proto-Hegelian answer to the question "Why did God create the world?"—so that He could bask in the glory of being celebrated by His creation. God wanted recognition, and since recognition requires another subject to do the recognizing, He created the world out of pure selfish vanity. Consequently, it was not that Christ came down to Earth in order to deliver people from sin, the legacy of Adam's Fall; on the contrary, *Adam had to fall in order to enable Christ to come down to Earth and dispense salvation*. Here Malebranche applies to God Himself the "psychological" insight according to which the saintly figure who sacrifices himself for the benefit of others, to deliver them from their misery, secretly *wants* them to be miserable *so that he will be able to help them*—like the proverbial husband who works all day for his poor crippled wife, yet would probably abandon her were she to regain her health and turn into a successful career woman. It is much more satisfying to sacrifice oneself for the poor victim than to help the other overcome their victim status and perhaps become even more successful than oneself.

Malebranche pushed this parallel to its conclusion, to the horror of the Jesuits who organized his excommunication: in the same way that the saintly person exploits the suffering of others to ensure his own narcissistic satisfaction, God also ultimately *loves only Himself*, and merely uses man to promulgate His own glory. From this reversal, Malebranche draws a consequence worthy of Lacan's reversal of Dostoyevsky ("If God doesn't exist, then nothing is permitted"): it is not true that, if Christ had not come to

Earth to deliver humanity, everyone would have been lost—quite the con-trary, *nobody* would have been lost. In other words, *every* human being had to fall so that Christ could come and deliver *some* of them. Malebranche's conclusion is shattering: since the death of Christ is the key step in realizing the goal of creation, at no time was God (the Father) happier than when observing His son suffering and dying on the Cross.

The only way to truly avoid this perversion, rather than merely obfus-cate it, is to fully accept the Fall as the starting point that creates the conditions of salvation: there is nothing prior to the Fall from which we fall, the Fall itself creates that from which it is a fall—or, in theological terms, God is not the Beginning. If this sounds like yet another typical Hegelian dialectical tangle, then we should disentangle it by drawing a line of separa-tion between the true Hegelian dialectical process and its caricature. In the caricature, we have an inner Essence externalizing itself in the domain of contingent appearances, and then gradually reappropriating its alienated content, recognizing itself in its Otherness—"we must first lose God in order to find Him," we must fall in order to be saved. Such a position opens up the space for the justification of Evil: if, as agents of historical Reason, we know that Evil is just a necessary detour on the path towards the final triumph of the Good, then of course we are justified in engaging in Evil as a means of achieving the Good. In true Hegelian spirit, however, we should insist that such a justification is always and a priori retroactive: there is no Reason in History whose divine plan can justify Evil; the Good that may come out of Evil is a contingent by-product. We can say that one result of Nazi Germany and its defeat was the institution of much higher ethical standards of human rights and international justice; but to claim that this result in any sense "justifies" Nazism would be an obscenity. Only in this way can we truly avoid the perverse logic of religious fundamentalism. Among Christian theologians, it was—as usual—G. K. Chesterton who was unafraid to draw out the consequences of this paradox, locating precisely at this point the break between the Ancient world and Christianity:

> The Greeks, the great guides and pioneers of pagan antiquity, started out with the idea of something splendidly obvious and direct; the idea that if man walked straight ahead on the high road of reason and nature, he would come to no harm … And the case of the Greeks themselves is alone enough to illustrate the strange but certain fatality that attends upon this fallacy. No sooner did the Greeks themselves begin to follow their own noses and their own notion of being natural, than the queerest thing in history seems to have happened to them …

The wisest men in the world set out to be natural; and the most unnatural thing in the world was the very first thing they did. The immediate effect of saluting the sun and the sunny sanity of nature was a perversion spreading like a pestilence. The greatest and even the purest philosophers could not apparently avoid this law sort of lunacy. Why? ... When Man goes straight he goes crooked. When he follows his nose he manages somehow to put his nose out of joint, or even to cut off his nose to spite his face; and that in accordance with something much deeper in human nature than nature-worshippers could ever understand. It was the discovery of that deeper thing, humanly speaking, that constituted the conversion to Christianity. There is a bias in a man like the bias on a bowl; and Christianity was the discovery of how to correct the bias and therefore hit the mark. There are many who will smile at the saying; but it is profoundly true to say that the glad good news brought by the Gospel was the news of original sin.[15]

The Greeks lost their moral compass precisely because they believed in the spontaneous and basic uprightness of the human being, and thus neglected the "bias" towards Evil at the very core of humanity: true Good does not arise when we follow our nature, but when we fight it.[16]

THE ANTI-COLONIAL RECOIL

We are not talking here about abstract theoretical issues, but about a very concrete historical experience. According to some Indian cultural theorists, the fact that they are compelled to use the English language is a form of cultural colonialism that suppresses their true identity: "Since we have to speak in an imposed foreign language to express our innermost identity, does this not put us in a position of radical alienation, so that even our resistance to colonization has to be formulated in the language of the colonizer?" The answer to this is: yes—but this imposition of a foreign language itself created the very X which is "oppressed" by it; that is, what is oppressed is not the actual pre-colonial India, but the authentic dream of a new universalistic and democratic India. It is crucial to note that this role of the English language was clearly perceived by many intellectuals among the

---

15   G. K. Chesterton, *Saint Francis of Assisi*, New York: Empire Books 2012, pp. 11–12.

16   Schelling made the same point when he emphasized how, in the Ancient Roman empire, the rise of Christianity was preceded by the rise of decadence and corruption.

Dalits (the "untouchables"): a large number of Dalits welcomed the English language and indeed even the colonial encounter. For Ambedkar (the main political figure of the Dalits) and his legatees, British colonialism—at least incidentally—created the conditions for the so-called rule of law and the formal equality of all Indians. Prior to this, Indians had only caste laws, which gave the Dalits many duties and almost no rights.[17]

Was not Malcolm X following the same insight when he adopted X as his family name, thereby signaling that the slave traders who had brought his ancestors from their homeland had deprived them of their family and ethnic roots, of their entire cultural life world? The point was not to mobilize the blacks to fight for a return to their primordial African roots, but precisely to seize the opening provided by the X—an unknown new (lack of) identity engendered by the very process of enslavement that had ensured those roots were forever lost. The idea was that this X which had deprived the blacks of their particular traditions offered them a unique chance to reinvent themselves, to form a new identity more universal than the professed universality of the whites. (As is well known, Malcolm X himself found this new identity in the universalism of Islam.) The same experience of an unintended liberating dimension opened up by enslavement is beautifully related in Frederick Douglass' narrative of his life, in which he reports on the radical change that occurred when he went to live as a slave with the family of Mr. and Mrs. Auld:[18]

> [Mrs. Auld] had never had a slave under her control previously to myself, and prior to her marriage she had been dependent upon her own industry for a living. She was by trade a weaver; and by constant application to her business, she had been in a good degree preserved from the blighting and dehumanizing effects of slavery. I was utterly astonished at her goodness. I scarcely knew how to behave towards her … My early instruction was all out of place. The crouching servility, usually so acceptable a quality in a slave, did not answer when manifested toward her. Her favor was not gained by it; she seemed to be disturbed by it. She did not deem it impudent or unmannerly for a slave to look her in the face.[19]

---

17   Chandra Bhan Prasad, a leading Dalit intellectual, celebrated English by anointing the "Dalit Goddess, English." See S. Anand, "Jai Angrezi Devi Maiyya Ki," available at openthemagazine.com. I owe this reference to my good friend S. Anand (New Delhi).

18   I owe this example to Ed Cadava, Princeton.

19   Frederick Douglass, *Narrative of the Life of Frederick Douglass*, Chapter 6, available at http://classiclit.about.com.

Mrs. Auld's attitude was not primarily an expression of her personal good-ness—she simply did not really know about slavery or how it functioned, and looked upon the young Frederick with a prelapsarian innocence, per-ceiving him as just another human being. When she became aware that the boy didn't know how to read and write, she "very kindly commenced to teach me the A, B, C. After I had learned this, she assisted me in learn-ing to spell words of three or four letters." This in itself, however, was not enough to put Frederick on the path of liberation—crucial for that was Mr. Auld's violent reaction to his wife's effort to teach the young slave. From Mr. Auld's perspective, his wife's prelapsarian innocence was in reality the very opposite of what it appeared to be—in his eyes, she was unwittingly playing the role of the snake, seducing the young Frederick into eating from the prohibited tree of knowledge:

> Just at this point of my progress, Mr. Auld found out what was going on, and at once forbade Mrs. Auld to instruct me further, telling her, among other things, that it was unlawful, as well as unsafe, to teach a slave to read. To use his own words, further, he said, "If you give a nigger an inch, he will take an ell. A nigger should know nothing but to obey his master—to do as he is told to do. Learning would spoil the best nigger in the world. Now," said he, "if you teach that nigger (speaking of myself) how to read, there would be no keeping him. It would forever unfit him to be a slave. He would at once become unmanageable, and of no value to his master. As to himself, it could do him no good, but a great deal of harm. It would make him discontented and unhappy." These words sank deep into my heart, stirred up sentiments within that lay slumbering, and called into existence an entirely new train of thought. It was a new and special revelation, explaining dark and mysterious things, with which my youthful understanding had struggled, but struggled in vain. I now understood what had been to me a most perplexing difficulty—to wit, the white man's power to enslave the black man. It was a grand achievement, and I prized it highly. From that moment, I understood the pathway from slavery to freedom. It was just what I wanted, and I got it at a time when I the least expected it. Whilst I was saddened by the thought of losing the aid of my kind mistress, I was gladdened by the invaluable instruction which, by the merest accident, I had gained from my master. Though conscious of the difficulty of learning without a teacher, I set out with high hope, and a fixed purpose, at whatever cost of trouble, to learn how to read. The very decided manner with which he spoke, and strove to impress his wife with the evil consequences of giving me instruction, served to convince me that he was deeply sensible of the truths he was uttering. It gave me the best assurance that I

might rely with the utmost confidence on the results which, he said, would flow from teaching me to read. What he most dreaded, that I most desired. What he most loved, that I most hated. That which to him was a great evil, to be carefully shunned, was to me a great good, to be diligently sought; and the argument which he so warmly urged, against my learning to read, only served to inspire me with a desire and determination to learn. In learning to read, I owe almost as much to the bitter opposition of my master, as to the kindly aid of my mistress. I acknowledge the benefit of both.[20]

Note the quasi-humanitarian accent of Mr. Auld's argumentation—the young boy should not learn to read and write not only because it would make him unfit as a slave and thus of no use to his master, but also *for his own good*: "As to himself, it could do him no good, but a great deal of harm. It would make him discontented and unhappy." This last sentence should not be dismissed as total hypocrisy (although undoubtedly it is deeply hypocritical): compared with the life of an uneducated slave who has the luck to be owned by relatively kind masters, engaging in the struggle for emancipation will at first bring only discontent and unhappiness. The magnificent and precise conclusion of the quoted passage should therefore be taken literally: "In learning to read, I owe almost as much to the bitter opposition of my master, as to the kindly aid of my mistress. I acknowledge the benefit of both." Mrs. Auld did not want to liberate Frederick from slavery—how could she when she was not even fully aware of what it was? Her reaction, in short, was moralistic, not political: a reaction of spontaneous decency and kindness. It was only through the husband's explicitly racist-paternalist reaction that Frederick became aware of the political-emancipatory (and even properly revolutionary) dimension of what it means to know how to read and write. Without that brutal intervention, Frederick would have become an educated household slave loving and respecting his owners, not the emancipatory symbol he is now.

Today, more than ever, one should insist on this properly Hegelian ambiguity of colonialism. The colonial powers did indeed brutally intrude into traditional societies all around the world, derailing their customs and destroying their social fabric—not to mention the economic exploitation. It is therefore hypocritical of Westerners to complain about immigration— when immigrants from poor countries try to enter rich Western states, the latter are simply reaping the harvest of their own past acts. It is precisely

20   Ibid.

apropos the wound of colonialism that the final message of Richard Wagner's *Parsifal* holds: "The wound can be healed only by the spear that smote it [*Die Wunde schliesst der Speer nur der Sie schlug*]." In other words, the very disintegration of traditional forms opens up the space of liberation. As was clear to Nelson Mandela and the ANC, white supremacy and the temptation of a return to tribal roots were two sides of the same coin.

There is a vulgar joke about Christ of some relevance here: the night before he was to be arrested and crucified, his followers started to worry— Christ was still a virgin, wouldn't it be nice for him to experience a little bit of pleasure before he dies? So they asked Mary Magdalene to go into the tent where Christ was resting and seduce him. Mary gladly agreed and went in, but five minutes later she ran out screaming, terrified and furious. The disciples asked her what had gone wrong, and she explained: "I slowly undressed, spread my legs and showed Christ my vagina; he took one look and said 'What a terrible wound! It should be healed!', then gently put his palm on it ..." The moral, then, is that we should be wary of people too intent on healing other people's wounds—what if one enjoys one's wound? In the same way, attempting to heal the wound of colonialism directly (by returning to pre-colonial reality) would have been a nightmare: if today's Indians were to find themselves back in pre-colonial reality, they would undoubtedly let out the same terrified scream as Mary Magdalene.

THE VIOLENCE OF THE BEGINNING

The point all these examples illustrate is not that there was nothing prior to the loss. Of course there was—in the case of India, a vast and complex civilization; but this was a heterogeneous mess that has nothing to do with what the later national revival wants to return to. This holds in general for all processes of lost and regained national identity. In the process of its revival, a nation-in-becoming experiences its present constellation in terms of a loss of precious origins, which it then strives to regain. In reality, however, there were no origins that were subsequently lost, for the origins are constituted through the very experience of their loss and the striving to return to them. (Maybe Foucault has a point here: the discovery of what went on before the loss is a topic for genealogy, which, precisely, has nothing to do with the historicist topic of origins.) This holds for every return to origins: when, from the nineteenth century onwards, new nation-states popped up across Central and Eastern Europe, their returning to "old ethnic roots" generated these very roots, producing what the Marxist historian Eric Hobsbawm calls "invented traditions." Hegel was fully aware of the violence of this cut with tradition—here is his surprising description of the Ancient Greek miracle:

> They certainly received the substantial beginnings of their religion, culture, and social relations more or less from Asia, Syria, and Egypt; but they have so very much obliterated [getilgt] the foreign aspect of this origin, transformed, elaborated, reversed, and made it so thoroughly different, that what they (as we) value, recognize and love in it is essentially their own ... They have, so to speak, ungratefully [undankbar] forgotten the foreign origin, put it in the background, perhaps burying it in the darkness of the mysteries which they have kept secret [geheim] from even themselves ... They have not only done this, have not only used and enjoyed what they have brought before themselves and made from out of themselves, but they have become conscious of, and gratefully [dankbar] and joyfully represented to themselves this at-homeness [Heimatlichkeit] of their whole existence, their very own beginning and origin.[21]

So there is nothing new for Hegel in the "Black Athena" thesis—as Rebecca Comay has noted, he even describes the way Greek art relates to its predecessors in terms of a "conquering" (siegen), "repression" (zurückdrängen), "abolition" (fortfallen), "expunging" (tilgen), "annihilation" (vertilgen), "effacement" (Auslöschung), "erasure" (Verwischung), "stripping away" (Abstreifung), "excision" (abschneiden), "concealment" (verstricken)—of what? Of the "Orient or its equivalents—animal, bodily, ugly, stupid ..."[22] The notion of the Greek miracle as an outcome of organic spontaneous self-generation is thus an illusion grounded on brutal repression—and, as always with Hegel, the repressed origins return in the fatal flaw of classical Greek art which is the obverse of its highest achievement. The classical Greek statue captures the perfect human form, the optimal balance of body and spirit—however, as such, it has to be without a gaze: its eyes are flat, pure surfaces, rather than punctual windows into the depths of the soul, since such a crack in the bodily surface would disturb its unity, its harmonious beauty. (This is also why Greek statues do not yet display subjectivity proper.) However, in Greek art itself, this excluded (foreclosed

---

21   G. W. F. Hegel, *Vorlesungen über die Philosophie der Geschichte*, Frankfurt: Suhrkamp 1970, p. 174.

22   Rebecca Comay, "Defaced Statues: Idealism and Iconoclasm in Hegel's Aesthetics" (unpublished manuscript).

even) excess of gaze returns as a disturbing multitude: the whole body of a Greek statue becomes a surface with hundreds of eyes. Exemplary here is the case of Argus, a monster with a hundred eyes who protects the nymph Io: in this vulgar over-ripe figure whose surface is punctuated by obscene cracks and protuberances, the standard metonymic relationship of the *pars pro toto* "slides into the preemptive fiction of the *totum pro parte*. The body as a whole becomes a substitute for its own missing organ [the excluded gaze]. Becoming the very thing it lacks, the body itself takes on the character of a fetish."[23] Only in later Romantic art is this excess "renormalized" in the gazing eye of subjectivity—modern subjectivity is the return of the monstrous dimension excluded from the harmonious art of classical Greece.

According to the standard liberal myth, the universality of human rights establishes the conditions for peaceful coexistence between the multiplicity of particular cultures. The reproach from the standpoint of the colonized is that such liberal universality is false, that in practice it merely facilitates the violent intrusion of a foreign culture that dissolves indigenous roots. Even if she admits there may be some truth in this, a liberal would continue to strive for a "universality without wounds," for a universal frame that would not impinge violently on particular cultures. From a properly dialectical perspective, we should strive for (or endorse the necessity of) the exact reverse of this approach: the wound as such is liberating—or rather, contains a liberatory potential. So while we should definitely problematize the positive content of the imposed universality (i.e., the particular content it secretly privileges), we should also fully endorse the liberating aspect of the wound (to our particular identity) as such.

Back in ancient China, the first to accomplish such a reversal was the king of Qin, who ruthlessly united the country and in 221 BC proclaimed himself its First Emperor. This arch-model of "totalitarian" rule relied so heavily on the advice of the "Legalist" philosophers that one can see in him the first case of a conscious and well-planned decision to break with past traditions and impose on society a new order conceived in theory:

> The king of Qin was not necessarily the brains of the outfit—his advisers, free of the strictures of courtly life, were the ones who had masterminded his rise to power. The plan to install him as the ruler of the world had commenced before he was even born, with the contention of long-dead scholars that the world

---

23   Ibid.

required an enlightened prince. It had proceeded with … an alliance of scholars in search of a patron who might allow them to secure their own political ends. Ying Zheng, the king of Qin, became the First Emperor with the help of great minds.[24]

The Legalists—first among them Han Fei and the great Li Si—emerged out of the crisis of Confucianism. During the fifth to third centuries BC, when China went through the period of the "Warring States," the Confucians located the ultimate cause of the chaos in the betrayal of the old traditions and customs. The Legalists changed the very coordinates of the perception of the situation. For the Confucians, states like Qin with their centralized military organization and ignorance of the old ways were seen as the embodiment of what had gone wrong. However, in contrast to his teacher Xunzi, who regarded nations like Qin as a threat to peace, Han Fei "proposed the unthinkable, that maybe the way of the Qin government was not an anomaly to be addressed, but a practice to be emulated."[25] The solution thus resided in what had appeared to be the problem: the true cause of the troubles was not the abandonment of the old traditions, but *these traditions themselves*, which daily demonstrated their inability to serve as guiding principles for social life. As Hegel put it in the Foreword to his *Phenomenology of Spirit*, the standard by means of which we measure the situation and establish that it is problematic is itself part of the problem and should be abandoned. Han Fei applied the same logic to the fact that (the majority of) men are evil by nature: instead of bemoaning the fact, he saw it as something that a power enlightened by the right theory (a theory "beyond good and evil") might be able to steer with the help of the proper mechanisms. "Where Xunzi saw an unfortunate observation, that men were evil by nature, Han Fei saw a challenge for the institution of stern laws to control this nature and use it to the benefit of the state."[26]

In similar fashion, one of the great achievements of contemporary leftist political theory (Althusser, Balibar, Negri) has been to rehabilitate Machiavelli, rescuing him from the standard "Machiavellian" reading. Since the Legalists are often presented as ur-Machiavellians, one should do the same with them, extricating the radical-emancipatory kernel from the predominant image of them as proto-"totalitarians." The great insight of

---

24   Jonathan Clements, *The First Emperor of China*, Chalford: Sutton Publishing 2006, p. 16.

25   Ibid., p. 34.

26   Ibid., p. 77.

the Legalists was to see the wound to the social body, the disintegration of the old habits, as the opportunity for a new order.[27]

This brings us back to Wagner's "*Die Wunde schliesst der Speer nur der Sie schlug.*" Hegel says the same thing, although with the accent shifted in the opposite direction: the Spirit is itself the wound it tries to heal, that is, the wound is self-inflicted. "Spirit" at its most elementary is the "wound" of nature. The subject is the immense—absolute—power of negativity, the power of introducing a gap or cut into the given-immediate substantial unity, the power of differentiating, of "abstracting," of tearing apart and treating as self-standing what in reality is part of an organic unity. This is why the notion of the "self-alienation" of Spirit is more paradoxical than it may appear: it should be read together with Hegel's assertion of the thoroughly non-substantial character of Spirit: there is no *res cogitans*, no thing which also thinks, Spirit is nothing but the process of overcoming natural immediacy, of the cultivation of this immediacy, of withdrawing-into-itself or "taking off" from it, of—why not?—alienating itself from it. The paradox is thus that there is no Self that precedes the Spirit's "self-alienation": the very process of alienation generates the "Self" from which Spirit is alienated and to which it then returns. (Hegel here inverts the standard notion that a failed version of X presupposes this X as its norm or measure: X is created, its space is outlined, only through the repeated failure to reach it.) Spirit's self-alienation is the same as, fully coincides with, its alienation from its Other (nature), because it constitutes itself through its "return-to-itself" from its immersion in natural Otherness. Spirit's return-to-itself creates the very dimension to which it returns. What this means is that the "negation of the negation," the "return-to-oneself" from alienation, does not occur where it seems to: in the negation of the negation, Spirit's negativity is not relativized, subsumed under an encompassing positivity; it is, on the contrary, the "simple negation" which remains attached to the presupposed positivity it has negated, the presupposed Otherness from which it alienates itself, and the negation of the negation is nothing but the negation of the substantial character of this Otherness itself, the full acceptance of the abyss of Spirit's self-relating which retroactively posits all its presuppositions. In other words, once we are in negativity, we can never leave it

---

27 The topic of the Fall also resonates outside the religious field and can be given a totally anti-religious twist—recall the anti-holistic notion of something emerging when the balance of the Whole is disturbed. At the most elementary level, something happens when something else goes wrong, when a symmetry is broken, when a one-sided decision ruins the preceding peace.

and regain the lost innocence of the origins; in the "negation of the negation" the origins are truly lost, their very loss is lost, they are deprived of
the substantial status of that which has been lost. Spirit heals its wound not
directly, but by getting rid of the full and sane Body into which the wound
was cut. It is in this precise sense that, according to Hegel, "the wounds of
the Spirit heal, and leave no scars behind."[28] His point is not that Spirit heals
its wounds so perfectly that, in a magical gesture of retroactive sublation,
even the scars disappear; the point is rather that, in the course of the dialectical process, a shift of perspective occurs which makes the wound itself
appear as its opposite—the wound itself is its own healing when seen from
another standpoint. At its sharpest, this coincidence of opposites appears
apropos self-consciousness, i.e., the thinking subject as the agent of rational
consideration, and its relation towards evil:

> Abstractly, being evil means singularizing myself in a way that cuts me off from
> the universal (which is the rational, the laws, the determinations of spirit). But
> along with this separation there arises being-for-itself and for the first time the
> universally spiritual, laws—what ought to be. So it is not the case that [rational]
> consideration has an external relationship to evil: it is itself what is evil.[29]

Does not the Bible say exactly the same thing? The serpent promises Adam
and Eve that, by eating the fruit of the tree of knowledge, they will become
like God, and after they do so, God says: "Behold, Adam has become like
one of us" (Genesis 3:22). Hegel's comment is: "So the serpent did not lie,
for God confirms what it said." He then goes on to reject the claim that
what God says is meant ironically: "Cognition is the principle of spirituality, and this ... is also the principle by which the injury of the separation is
healed. It is in this principle of cognition that the principle of 'divinity' is
also posited."[30] Subjective knowledge is not just the possibility of choosing
evil or good, "it is the consideration or the cognition that *makes* people
evil, so that consideration and cognition [themselves] are what is evil, and
that [therefore] such cognition is what ought not to exist [because it] is the
source of evil."[31] This is how we should understand Hegel's dictum from his
Phenomenology that Evil is the gaze itself which perceives Evil everywhere

---

28   G. W. F. Hegel, *Phenomenology of Spirit*, Oxford: Oxford University Press
1977, p. 129.
29   Ibid., p. 206.
30   Ibid., p. 207.
31   Hegel, *Vorlesungen über die Philosophie der Religion II*, p. 205.

around it: the gaze that sees Evil everywhere excludes itself from the social Whole it criticizes, and this exclusion is the formal characteristic of Evil. Hegel's point is that the Good emerges as a possibility and duty only through this primordial, constitutive choice of Evil: we experience the Good when, after choosing Evil, we become aware of the utter inadequacy of our situation.

In the tradition of Kabbala, this primordial wound appears in the guise of a "broken vessel." According to the so-called Lurianic Kabbala (named after Isaac Luria [1534–72]),[32] Ein Sof created the world in order to understand itself better. Because it was infinite, Ein Sof was also formless and without purpose—it existed as pure energy. Ein Sof therefore resolved to create something with both form and purpose—human beings. Because Ein Sof's energy had filled the entire universe prior to the creation of human beings, Ein Sof's first action had to be *tsimtsum*, "withdrawal." In order to make room for creation, Ein Sof had to first create a void inside itself, a space in which to make *yesh* (something) from *ayin* (nothing). However, as Ein Sof attempted to fill the vessel it had created with its light, catastrophe struck, the light was too intense to be contained within the vessel and the vessel shattered. The breaking of the vessel destroyed the ordered universe that Ein Sof had begun to create: tiny pieces of the vessel, like shards of glass, scattered and brought chaos to the universe. When the shards began to fall, they brought with them sparks of Ein Sof's light; together, the shards and the sparks fell into what would become material reality, or the human world. In place of a harmonious world, human beings entered a broken world filled with "husks," scattered sparks of divine light. Every human being is required to liberate the sparks of light from these husks through the righteous study of the Kabbala—only when all the sparks are freed will Ein Sof become whole again, ushering in the perfect world that Ein Sof designed at the moment of creation.

What this implies is that Ein Sof is not an all-knowing God but a dependent God who needs human beings to restore it to wholeness. God is here a *becoming*, not a *being*: as the world develops, sparks are liberated, people are born, and Ein Sof evolves to become more and more true to itself. The creation of the world was thus an act of God's self-sacrifice, but also a disaster, a catastrophic descent into chaos—the world and human beings were formed not according to God's perfect plan, but as a result of

---

32   I rely here shamelessly on the Spark Notes guide to the Kaballah, available at sparknotes.com.

destruction. Yet because human beings can liberate the sparks from the material world and help restore God to wholeness, the universe becomes filled with good deeds and the hope for redemption.

How should this myth be modified to produce a "materialist" version? The solution seems obvious: there was no vessel, and so no original breaking, the universe is just a contingent collection of fragments that we can tinker with to produce new assemblages ... What gets lost in this solution is the immanent antagonism/tension/blockage (the barred/impeded "Whileness") that underlies and sets in motion the movement of fragmentation. The consequences of such an approach were spelled out by Walter Benjamin who, in his "The Task of the Translator," used the Lurianic notion of the broken vessel to explore the inner workings of the process of translation:

> Just as fragments of a vessel, in order to be articulated together, must follow one another in the smallest detail but need not resemble one another, so, instead of making itself similar to the meaning of the original, the translation must rather, lovingly and in detail, in its own language, form itself according to the way of signifying [*Art des Meinens*] of the original, to make both recognizable as the broken parts of a greater language, just as fragments are the broken parts of a vessel.[33]

The movement described here by Benjamin is a kind of transposition of metaphor into metonymy: instead of conceiving translation as a metaphoric substitute of the original, as a process of rendering its meaning as faithfully as possible, both the original and its translation are posited as belonging on the same level, as parts of the same field (in the same way that for Lévi-Strauss the main interpretations of the Oedipus myth are themselves new versions of the myth). The gap that, in the traditional view, separates the original from its (always imperfect) translation is thus transposed back into the original itself: the original itself is already a fragment of a broken vessel, so that the goal of the translation is not to achieve fidelity to the original but to supplement it, to treat it as a fragment of the broken vessel and produce another fragment that, rather than imitating the original, will fit it as one fragment of a broken Whole may fit with another. A good translation will thus destroy the myth of the original's organic Wholeness,

---

33   Walter Benjamin, "The Task of the Translator," in *Illuminations*, London: Collins 1973, pp. 69–82.

rendering this Wholeness visible as a fake. One can even say that, far from being an attempt to restore the broken vessel, translation is the very act of breaking: once the translation sets in, the original organic vessel appears as a fragment that has to be supplemented—the breaking of the vessel *is* the opening to its restoration.

In the world of storytelling, a gesture homologous to translation would be to change the plot of the original narrative in a way that makes us think "only now do we really understand what the story is about." This is how we should approach the numerous recent stagings of classical operas that not only transpose the action into a different (usually contemporary) era, but also change some basic elements of the narrative itself. There is no a priori abstract criterion that would allow us to judge the success or failure of such an approach: each intervention is a risky act and must be judged by its own immanent standards. Such experiments often misfire badly—*but not always*, and as there is no way to tell in advance, one has to take the risk. In fact, the *only* way to be faithful to a classical work is to take just such a risk—avoiding it, sticking to the traditional letter, is the safest way to betray the spirit of the classic. In other words, the only way to keep a classical work alive is to treat it as "open," as pointing towards the future, or, to use the metaphor evoked by Benjamin, to act as if the classic work is a reel of film for which the appropriate chemicals needed to develop it are invented only later, so that only today does it become possible to see the full picture.

Two stagings of Wagner's operas stand out as examples of such successful changes: Jean-Pierre Ponelle's Bayreuth version of *Tristan*, in which Tristan dies alone (Isolde has stayed with her husband, King Marke, and her appearance at the end is merely the dying Tristan's hallucination), and Hans-Juergen Syberberg's film version of *Parsifal* (in which Amfortas' wound is treated as a partial object, a kind of continually bleeding vagina carried on a pillow outside his body; also, at the moment of his insight into Amfortas' suffering, the boy who has played Parsifal is replaced by a cold young girl). In both cases, the changes have a tremendous power of revelation: one cannot resist the strong impression that "this is how it really should be."

Can we imagine a similar change in the staging of *Antigone*, one of the founding narratives of the Western tradition? What if we were to rewrite *Antigone* along the lines of Brecht's *Jasager*, *Neinsager*, and *Jasager 2*: three versions of the same story in which, at a crucial point, the plot takes a different turn? In the case of *Antigone*, the starting point would remain the same, and it would be only at the crucial point in the middle of the play—the big confrontation between Antigone and Creon—that the three versions would diverge:

The first version follows Sophocles' narrative, and the concluding chorus praises Antigone's unconditional adherence to her principles—*fiat justitia pereat mundus* ...

The second version shows what would have happened if Antigone had won, convincing Creon to allow Polynices a proper burial, i.e., if her principled attitude had prevailed. Insisting on revenge against the traitor Polynices, the patriotic-populist crowd rebels, a mob enters the palace and lynches Creon, and chaos reigns in the city. In the final scene, a half-crazed Antigone stumbles around in a trance among the ruins, fires burning all around her, crying "But I was created for love, not for war" ... In this version, the concluding chorus offers a Brechtian eulogy to pragmatism: the ruling class can afford to be honorable and stick to their rigid principles, while the ordinary people pay the price.

In the third version, the Chorus is no longer the peddler of commonplace wisdoms, but becomes an active agent. At the climactic moment of the ferocious debate between Antigone and Creon, the Chorus steps forward, castigating both of them for their stupid conflict which threatens the survival of the entire city. Acting like a kind of *comité de salut public*, the Chorus takes over as a collective organ and imposes a new rule of law, installing people's democracy in Thebes. Creon is deposed, both he and Antigone are arrested, put on trial, swiftly condemned to death and liquidated. Before her execution, Antigone pleads her innocence, claiming that in demanding a proper burial for Polynices she was giving voice to all those who are excluded, without a voice, leading a shadowy existence at the margins of the city-state. The Chorus replies that the excluded do not need sympathy from the privileged, that they do not want others to speak *for* them, and that they themselves should speak and articulate their own plight. In conclusion, the Chorus extends its famous statement about man ("There are many uncanny/demonic things in the world, but nothing more uncanny/demonic than man") into a praise of democracy: since man is an uncanny being, no single man is fit to rule alone, they should rule themselves collectively and control each other to prevent demonic outbursts which can lead to catastrophe.

Such a staging would be a true *Antigone* for our times, ruthlessly abandoning our sympathy and compassion for the play's heroine, making her part of the problem, and proposing a way out which shatters our humanitarian complacency. And, in the spirit of Benjamin's idea of translation, the task of such a rewriting would be to make all three versions of *Antigone* recognizable as the broken parts of a greater Play, a virtual/impossible ur-*Antigone*. Therein also resides the redeeming quality of Zachary Mason's *The Lost Books of the Odyssey*,[34] which contains a series of variations on Homer's "official" story presented as fragments from the (recently discovered) vast chaotic mess of legends from which Homer cut out and fashioned his epic poem: Odysseus returns home to Ithaca and finds that, following the ancient custom, Penelope married another man who is a good king; Polyphemus was really a quiet farmer who found Odysseus and his men in his cave, stuffing their faces with his provisions; the old Odysseus visits the ruins of Troy and finds it has become a market town, in which actors are working the crowd, "aping famous Greeks and Trojans"; etc. These (imagined) variations should not be read as distortions of some lost primordial original, but as fragments of a totality which would have consisted of the matrix of all possible permutations (in the sense in which Lévi-Strauss claims that all interpretations of the Oedipus myth, inclusive of Freud's, are part of the myth). Should we then endeavor to reconstruct the full matrix? What we should rather do is locate the traumatic point, the antagonism, that remains untold and around which all the variations and fragments circulate.

Is not the supreme case of a "broken vessel" the Seven Last Words of Christ? 1) *Father forgive them, for they know not what they do* (Luke 23:34); 2) *Truly, I say to you, today you will be with me in paradise* (Luke 23:43); 3) *Woman, behold your son: behold your mother* (John 19:26–27); 4) *My God, My God, why have you forsaken me?* (Matthew 27:46 and Mark 15:34); 5) *I thirst* (John 19:28); 6) *It is finished* (John 19:30); 7) *Father, into your hands I commit my spirit* (Luke 23:46). The most stupid thing imaginable to do with them is what Franco Zeffirelli and Mel Gibson did in their kitsch cinematic versions: using all of them, with Christ pronouncing one after the other while dying on the Cross—the effect is one of a ridiculous and suffocating excess, there is just too much of it, as in some Hollywood films or classic operas where the dying hero miraculously goes on talking, delivering his final message in its entirety when he should have dropped dead long ago. Along these lines, one could play an obscene game of trying to construct a single linear narrative that would encompass all the last words—for example, Christ prolongs his complaint "*My God, why have you forsaken*

---

34   Zachary Mason, *The Lost Books of the Odyssey*, New York: Farrar, Straus & Giroux 2010.

me?" with *"I thirst, so at least get me a drink!"*; after his thirst is satisfied, he adds: *"OK, now I feel better, I am calm and ready to die, so it is finished and I commit my spirit into your hands, Father."* But instead of striving for this kind of unification, we should treat the Seven Last Words as a case of what is called in quantum physics the superposition of multiple quantum states—as synchronous alternate versions which are in a way "all true." Their truth does not reside in a single narrative or in conceiving the seven versions as fragmentary remainders of a consistent single original; it resides in the way the seven versions resonate among themselves, interpreting each other. This, perhaps, is also the ultimate lesson of Christianity: Judaism conceives our universe as a broken vessel, the result of a cosmic catastrophe, giving us the endless task of gathering the broken pieces and reconstructing the universe as a harmonious Whole, while Christianity, at its most radical, conceives the act of breaking itself as the instance of divine creativity. Once again, it was G. K. Chesterton who made this point clearly, and with explicit reference to the broken vessel:

> It is the instinct of Christianity to be glad that God has broken the universe into little pieces ... all modern philosophies are chains which connect and fetter; Christianity is a sword which separates and sets free. No other philosophy makes God actually rejoice in the separation of the universe into living souls.[35]

What if we apply Benjamin's notion of translation to the very relationship between God and man, to the notion that man was made in the likeness of God? Instead of making himself similar to God, man must rather, lovingly and in detail, in his own way, form himself according to the way of God, to make both recognizable as the broken parts of a greater vessel. The gap that, in the traditional view, separates the perfect God from His (always imperfect) human image is thus transposed back into God: God Himself is imperfect, already a fragment of a broken vessel, so that He needs man to supplement His imperfection. The goal of humanity is then not to achieve fidelity or likeness to God but to supplement God, to treat Him as a fragment of the "broken vessel" and to make itself into another fragment which will fit it as one fragment of a broken Whole may fit another. The topic of the divine Trinity, of Christ's doubt on the Cross, and other similar motifs, clearly indicate that in Christianity the "broken vessel" is not only the created reality which fell from God and lost its perfection—*the ultimate*

---

35   G. K. Chesterton, *Orthodoxy*, San Francisco: Ignatius Press 1995, p. 139.

broken vessel is God himself. Father, Son, and Holy Spirit should thus be conceived as three fragments of the vessel whose unity is forever lost.

THE ABSOLUTE RECOIL

At a more formal level of his logic of reflection, Hegel uses the unique term "*absoluter Gegenstoss*" (recoil, counter-push, counter-thrust, or, why not, simply counter-punch): a withdrawal that creates what it withdraws from:

> Reflection therefore *finds before it* an immediate which it transcends and from which it is the return. But this return is only the presupposing of what reflection finds before it. What is thus found only *comes to be* through being *left behind* … the reflective movement is to be taken as an *absolute recoil* [*absoluter Gegenstoss*] upon itself. For the presupposition of the return-into-self—that from which essence *comes*, and *is* only as this return—is only in the return itself.[36]

Absoluter Gegenstoss thus stands for the radical coincidence of opposites in which the action appears as its own counter-action, or, more precisely, in which the negative move (loss, withdrawal) itself generates what it "negates." "What is found only *comes to be* through being *left behind*," and its inversion (it is "only in the return itself" that what we return to emerges, like nations who constitute themselves by way of "returning to their lost roots") are the two sides of what Hegel calls "absolute reflection": a reflection which is no longer external to its object, presupposing it as given, but which, as it were, closes the loop and posits its own presupposition. To put it in Derridean terms, the condition of possibility is here radically and simultaneously the condition of impossibility: the very obstacle to the full assertion of our identity opens up the space for it. Another exemplary case: the Hungarian ruling class "had long 'possessed' (i.e., patronized and cultivated) a distinctive music, the so-called *magyar nota* ('Hungarian tune') which in educated Hungarian circles was regarded as a stylistic emblem of the national identity,"[37] and predictably, in the nineteenth century, with the great nationalist revival, this style exploded in operas and symphonies. When, at the beginning of the twentieth century, modernist composers

---

36   G. W. F. Hegel, *Science of Logic*, Atlantic Highlands: Humanities Press 1969, p. 402.
37   Richard Taruskin, *Music in the Early Twentieth Century*, Oxford: Oxford University Press 2010, p. 367.

like Bartók and Kodalyi started to collect authentic popular music and discovered that it "was of an altogether different style and character from the
magyar nota,"[38] and, even worse, that it consisted of an inextricable mixture
of "all the peoples who inhabited 'greater Hungary'—Romanians, Slovaks,
Bulgars, Croats, and Serbs—and even ethnically remoter people like the
Turks ... or the Arabs of North Africa."[39] For this, predictably, Bartók was
reviled by the nationalists and felt compelled to leave Hungary.

This, then, is the dialectical process: an inconsistent mess (first phase,
the starting point) which is negated and, through negation, the Origin is
projected or posited backwards, so that a tension is created between the
present and the lost Origin (second phase). In the third phase, the Origin
is perceived as inaccessible, relativized—we are in external reflection, that
is, our reflection is external to the posited Origin which is experienced as a
transcendent presupposition. In the fourth phase of absolute reflection, our
external reflexive movement is transposed back into the Origin itself, as its
own self-withdrawal or decentering. We thus reach the triad of positing,
external reflection, and absolute reflection.[40]

In his critical reading of Hegel, Badiou proposes his own materialist
rendering of the quadruple structure of the dialectical process: "indifferent
multiplicities, or ontological unbinding; worlds of appearing, or the logical
link; truth-procedure, or subjective eternity," plus the Event itself, the additional "vanishing cause, which is the exact opposite of the Whole."[41] As we
have just seen, we can find this materialist version of the dialectical process
already in Hegel—apropos the British colonization of India, first there is
the "indifferent multiplicity" of pre-colonial India; then the British colonizers brutally intervene, imposing the transcendental structure of a colonial
order, justified in terms of Western universalism; then Indian resistance
to colonization develops, pointing out how, in colonizing India, the West
is betraying its own legacy of egalitarian emancipation. The anti-colonial
struggle thus refers to the Idea of India as a secular democratic state, an
Idea which originated in the West. The Indian version of this Idea, however,
is not a "synthesis" of the Western secular-egalitarian spirit and the Indian
tradition, but a full assertion of the egalitarian spirit by way of cutting
the roots that ground it in the Western tradition and affirming its actual

---

38   Ibid., p. 375.
39   Ibid., p. 378.
40   For a more detailed description of Hegel's triad of reflection, see Chapter 6
of Slavoj Žižek, *The Sublime Object of Ideology*, London: Verso 1989.
41   Alain Badiou, *Logics of Worlds*, London: Continuum 2009, p. 144.

universality. In short, only when the Western Idea is "ex-apted" by India does it achieve actual universality: when Indians embrace the European democratic-egalitarian Idea, they become more European than the Europeans themselves.

The ultimate case here is, of course, that of the subject itself: the priority of the Fall means that we should drop all the standard "Hegelian" talk about the subject's externalization in its own product in which it no longer recognizes itself, and then its reappropriation of this alienated content as its own product: there is no subject which is the agent of the process and suffers a loss, for the subject is the outcome of a loss. This is what Lacan indicates with his notion of a "barred" or crossed-out subject ($): the subject is not just thwarted, blocked, impeded, stigmatized by a constitutive impossibility; the subject is the result of its own failure, of the failure of its symbolic representation—a subject endeavors to express itself in a signifier, it fails, and the subject *is* this failure. This is what Lacan means by his deceptively simple claim that, ultimately, a subject is what is not an object—every hysteric knows this well, since the hysterical question is: What object am I for the Other? What does the Other desire in me? In other words, the primordial lost object of desire is *the subject itself*.

And, insofar as subjectivity is at its most basic feminine, the same priority of the void over what fills it in determines the opposition between the feminine hysterical mask (the confusing oscillation between multiple identifications) and the presupposed deeper or true substantial personality, the Real Woman. The idea is that the hysterical mask, this inconsistent mixture of provocation and desire for submission, of aggression and pity, is the result of patriarchal oppression that has distorted women's true identity, so that a woman should learn to drop the mask and assert her true personality. Lacan suggests that we should invert things here: the very idea that, beneath the hysterical mask, there is the Real Woman is a male myth—the Woman does not exist, it is a fantasmatic entity filling in the gap that lurks beneath the hysterical mask.

The only full case of absolute recoil, of a thing emerging through its very loss, is thus that of the subject itself, as the outcome of its own impossibility. In this precise Hegelian sense, the subject is the truth of substance: the truth of every substantial thing is that it is the retroactive effect of its own loss. The subject as $ does not pre-exist its loss, it emerges from its loss as a return to itself. When one reaches the absolute standpoint (in disalienation) what one sees is that not only is the subject co-substantial with its loss (in the sense that it is always barred, curtailed), but that the subject *is* the loss. It is this speculative insight that enables us to resist the temptation of returning to the innocence before the Fall: there is no such thing as a lost innocence, only the choice of Evil makes us aware of the Good as that which was lost in making this choice. The choice is thus a forced one, since it is in its form itself the choice of Evil:

> Human beings must consider themselves as [being initially the way] they ought not to be. From this separation an infinite need arises. In this cognition [of self], in this separation and rupture, the subject ... here defines itself, grasping itself as the extreme of abstract being-for-self, or abstract freedom; the soul plunges into its depths, right down into its abyss. This soul is the undeveloped monad, the naked monad, the empty soul lacking fulfillment.[42]

What Hegel here calls the "naked monad," subjectivity plunged into its abyss, found its first formulation in his *Jenaer Realphilosophie*, where he writes about the "Night of the World"—why, then, is the passage through the abyssal "Night of the World" necessary? Hegel provides a precise answer:

> [because] the universal posited as universal is found only in the subjectivity of consciousness, [and in fact is] only this infinite inward movement in which all determinatedness of existence is simultaneously resolved and [posited] in the most finite existence. Only in the latter as subjectivity [is there found] an intuition of infinite universality, i.e. of thinking that is for itself.[43]

Or, to put it in Hegel's standard terms: it is only in subjectivity that the Universal moves beyond the "in-itself" of the abstract "mute universality" and becomes "for-itself." Subjectivity is by definition, in its very notion, singular, which is why God has only *one* son, and why Hegel adds a unique remark: "*Once is always.* The subject must have recourse to a subject, without option."[44]

This is why Catherine Malabou was right to note that, in spite of the precise logical deduction of the plurality of subjects out of the notion of life, there is an irreducible *scandal*, something traumatic and unexpected,

---

42 Hegel, *Vorlesungen über die Philosophie der Religion II*, pp. 209–10.
43 Ibid., pp. 113–14.
44 Ibid., p. 115. In the German original: "'*Einmal*' ist im Begriff '*allemal*,' und das Subjekt muss sich ohne Wahl an eine Subjektivitaet wenden" Literally translated: "'Once' is in notion 'always,' and the subject has no choice but to have recourse to one subjectivity."

in the encounter with *another* subject, in the fact that the subject (a self-consciousness) encounters outside itself, in front of it, another living being there in the world, among things, which also claims to be a subject (a self-consciousness).[45] As a subject, I am by definition alone, a singularity opposed to the entire world of things, a punctuality to which all the world appears, and all phenomenological descriptions of my being always "together-with" others cannot ultimately cover up the scandal of there being another such singularity. In the guise of a living being in front of me which also claims to be a self-consciousness, infinity assumes a determinate form, and this coincidence of opposites (the infinity of the self-relating consciousness is this particular living being) points towards the infinite judgment "spirit is a bone" which concludes the section on the observing reason in Hegel's *Phenomenology*. The shape of the singular human being "is the one and only sensible shape of spirit—it is *the appearance of God in the flesh*. This is the monstrous reality [*das Ungeheure*] whose necessity we have seen."[46] Here, Hegel explicitly raises the obvious humanist-materialist question:

> Cannot the subject bring about this reconciliation by itself, through its own efforts, its own activity … And further, is this not within the capability [not merely] of a single subject but of all people who genuinely wish to take up the divine law within themselves, so that heaven would exist on earth and the Spirit would be present in reality and dwell in its community?[47]

His answer, while it may appear abstractly scholastic, is absolutely crucial: "This positing must essentially be a *presupposing*, in such a way that what is posited is also something implicit. The unity of subjectivity and objectivity—this divine unity—must be a presupposition for my positing. For only then does the latter have a content."[48] In short: subjects posit the substantial content, but they can only do so if they presuppose a Substance as the ground of their activity. We work for a common Cause which is alive only through us, but we have to presuppose it. So, again, why can we not recognize ourselves as the collective authors of this substance? In other words, are we not dealing here with a simple necessary illusion: we, the subject, generate and keep alive the substance, but, in a necessary reversal, we have

---

45   See Judith Butler and Catherine Malabou, *Sois mon corps. Une lecture contemporaine de la domination et de la servitude chez Hegel*, Paris: Bayard 2010.

46   Hegel, *Vorlesungen über die Philosophie der Religion II*, p. 214.

47   Ibid., p. 212.

48   Ibid.

to treat it as if it is already there, presupposed? This solution, although obvious, is too facile: it is precisely "subjectivist," that is, it presupposes the subject as the always already given generative power; it does not take into account how the subject itself emerges through the self-splitting of the substance.[49] "Absolute reflection" thus reaches much further than the standard (and rather boring) "dialectical" claim that every immediacy is already "mediated," grounded in and generated by a complex network of mediations, so that we should "de-fetishize" anything that appears to be an immediate Given: *what is really presupposed is reflective positing itself*, or, in Wendell Kisner's concise formulation, *seeming seems to seem*:

> Essence is not different from seeming—it is the seeming in itself. But this seeming is not mere immediacy in so far as essence, the sheer negativity which being has become, cannot just immediately *be* what it is. Essence cannot just be semblance—it only *seems* to be semblance. Essence has its being in so far as it only seems to be merely seeming—it is a semblance that is reflected negatively into itself ... Essence has no immediacy of its own—it is just the move from not to not. Semblance refers to what is not it, essence, which as something other than semblance is only a semblance, that is, itself. Seeming seems to seem. Being is thought within the sphere of reflection as the reflexivity of seeming itself. This brings us finally to the aforementioned absolute reflection. Hegel writes:
>
> > "The becoming into essence, its reflecting movement, is accordingly the *movement from nothing to nothing and so back to itself*. The transition or becoming supersedes itself in its transition; the other that comes to be in this transition, is not the not-being of a being, but the nothing of a nothing, and this, to be the negation of a nothing, constitutes being—being is only as the movement of nothing to nothing, thus it is essence."
>
> This is the movement Hegel calls absolute reflection. There is nothing that is immediately "there," subsequently to be negated—this was a determination of essence that only seemed to be essence. Here the movement of reflection that is essence is spelling itself out. The immediacy of essence only *is* as *Ruckkehr*, as a turning back from a negative. One could say that essence only is as withdrawal, where there is no immediacy that predates the withdrawing movement. Thus

---

49   At a theological level, therein resides the necessity of Christ: not of a substance before the subject, but of a *subject before the subject*: Christ stands for the self-alienation of substance itself—our distance from substance is the distance of substance from itself.

absolute reflection resists any presentation, if presentation means to present it in its immediacy or "thereness"—it is not "there" at all; it only is in the turning back. But this itself constitutes its immediacy ... from which it withdraws.[50]

This brings us back to the anecdote, repeatedly evoked by Lacan, about Zeuxis and Parrhasius, two painters from Ancient Greece who compete to determine who can paint a more convincing illusion.[51] First, Zeuxis produced such a realistic picture of grapes that the birds tried to eat them. But Parrhasius won by painting a curtain on the wall of his room, so that Zeuxis, when Parrhasius showed him the painting, said: "OK, now please pull the aside curtain and show me what you've done!" In Zeuxis' painting, the illusion was so convincing that the image was taken for the real thing. In Parrhasius' painting, the illusion resides in the very notion that what the viewer sees in front of him is just a veil covering up the hidden truth. Does not Parrhasius' painting literally *seem to seem*?

The beginning of Hegel's logic as well as the beginning of his "logic of essence" which deals with the notion of reflection are just two, though crucial, examples that demonstrate how misleading, even outright wrong, is the standard notion of the dialectical process which begins with a positive entity, then negates it, and finally negates this negation itself, returning at a higher level to the positive starting point. Here we see a quite different logic: we begin with nothing, and it is only through the self-negation of nothing that something appears. A key detail not to be missed here is that, in both cases, Hegel uses the same expression: "always already." Being and Nothing have *always already* passed into Something; in the movement of reflection, the Immediate/the Origin is *always already* lost, withdrawn, since it is constituted in this withdrawal. (No wonder Hegel defines Essence as "*zeitlos-gewesene Sein*," a timelessly past being, i.e., a past which was not present and then passed, but was passed from the very beginning.)

The passage of Being to Nothing is *not* the same as other (later) passages; it is rather the impossibility of a passage: we look closely at Being to see what it is, to determine it further, but we find nothing, *and this nothing, the absence of determination, is the only determination of Being*. The ultimate good news/bad news doctor joke reaches the dark limit of humor; it

---

50   Wendell Kisner, "Erinnerung, Retrait, Absolute Reflection: Hegel and Derrida," available at http://athabascau.academia.edu.

51   See Jacques Lacan, *The Four Fundamental Concepts of Psychoanalysis*, New York: Norton 1998, p. 103.

starts with the good news, but since this is so ominous no further bad news is needed: Doctor: "First the good news—we have definitively established that you are not a hypochondriac." No need for a counter-point here ... Another version: Doctor: "I have some good news and some bad news." Patient: "What's the good news?" Doctor: "The good news is that you will soon be a household name around the world—they're naming a disease after you!" Is this a non-dialectical short-circuit? Or is it rather the proper dialectical beginning which immediately negates itself? Something like this joke happens at the beginning of Hegel's logic, not a passage to the opposite side, but the immediate self-sabotage of the beginning. In his *The Opposing Shore*, Julien Gracq describes the weird relationship between Orsenna and Farghestan—the two countries have been formally at war for 300 years, but for centuries nothing has happened, the two sides have just ignored each other:

> Equally reluctant to make the first overture to a peaceful settlement, both nations immured themselves in a touchy and arrogant stagnation and henceforth, by tacit agreement, made sure to avoid contact ... As the years of so indulgent a war accumulated, Orsenna gradually reached the undeclared conclusion that even a peaceful diplomatic overture would be regarded as an impolite gesture, involving something too specific, too intense, and likely to disturb in its grave this corpse of a war long since laid to rest for good.[52]

We are dealing with a subtle paradox of symbolization here: sometimes, an undeclared de facto peace is sustained and protected by the formal continuation of war, so that, the moment one tries to formalize peace, one risks opening the old wounds and triggering a renewed war. The same can happen with a friendship: if it is formally declared, it can be ruined. A similar dialectic of form and content is sometimes at work in marriage: promiscuity can be silently tolerated, but when one of the partners tries to turn this de facto situation into an explicit symbolic rule, everything breaks down. Even love affairs often work the same way: they can go on happily as long as neither partner wants to clarify its status—Are we just having a brief affair? Shall we move in together permanently? Declare our relationship publicly? No solution works here, even the easy opportunist one ("For now, let's just treat it as a short affair, and we'll see if anything more substantial develops!")—the pre-reflexive innocence is ruined, the

---

52 Julien Gracq, *The Opposing Shore*, New York: Columbia University Press 1986, p. 7.

Word was spoken, the big Other is present. There are things that can only occur if they remain unnamed. Does this not hold also and especially for happiness, which can only exist as a by-product, not as a directly intended result? Aristophanes had a point with his cruel mockery of Socrates: we go on leading our lives normally, and then some Socratic philosopher comes along and ruins everything by bothering us with questions like: "Do you know what happiness is? Can you define it? Are you really happy?"[53] And perhaps this is what Freud had in mind in characterizing governing, teaching, and psychoanalyzing as "impossible professions": in each case, we have to teach something that cannot directly be taught since it can only emerge as a by-product.

---

53   See Jonathan Lear, *Happiness, Death, and the Remainder of Life*, Cambridge, MA: Harvard University Press 2002.

Staging Feminine Hysteria

When Anton Webern proposed to Arnold Schoenberg that he write the music for a concert in Barcelona, Schoenberg replied: "I have made many friends here who have never heard my works but who play tennis with me. What will they think of me when they hear my horrible dissonances?"[1] All Schoenberg is here: awareness of his radical breakthrough, but mixed up with irony and kindness. There was no envy in him; Schoenberg was friends with Gershwin and enjoyed meeting US commercial composers. And he was right: his work was unbearably shattering, a key part of the modernist breakthrough—the only true artistic Event of the twentieth century (whatever it is, postmodernism is not an Event).

In his *Philosophy of History*, Hegel gives a wonderful characterization of Thucydides' book on the Peloponnesian war: "his immortal work is the absolute gain which humanity has derived from that contest."[2] One should read this judgment in all its naivety: in a way, from the standpoint of world history, the Peloponnesian war took place so that Thucydides could write a book about it. What if something similar holds for the relationship between the explosion of modernism and World War I, but in the opposite direction? The Great War was not the traumatic break that shattered late nineteenth-century progressivism, but a reaction to the *true* threat to the established order: the explosion of vanguard art, science and politics that was undermining the established world-view (artistic modernism in literature—from Kafka to Joyce; in music—Schoenberg and Stravinsky; in painting—Picasso, Malevich, Kandinsky; psychoanalysis; relativity theory and quantum physics; the rise of Social Democracy ...). This rupture—condensed in 1913, the *annus mirabilis* of the artistic vanguard—was so radical in its opening up of new spaces that, in our speculative historiography, it is tempting to claim that the outbreak of the Great War in 1914

---

1 Quoted from Richard Taruskin, *Music in the Early Twentieth Century*, Oxford: Oxford University Press 2010, p. 45.

2 G. W. F. Hegel, *Philosophy of History*, Part II, Section II, Chapter III, "The Peloponnesian War," available at http://socserv.mcmaster.ca.

was, from the "spiritual" standpoint, a reaction to this Event. Or, to para-phrase Hegel, the horror of World War I was the price humanity had to pay for the immortal artistic revolution of the years just prior to the war. In other words, we must invert the pseudo-profound insight according to which Schoenberg et al. prefigured the horrors of twentieth-century war: what if the true Event was 1913? It is crucial to focus on this intermediate explosive moment, between the complacency of the late nineteenth century and the catastrophe of World War I—1914 was not an awakening, but the forceful and violent return of a patriotic slumber destined to block the true awakening. The fact that the fascists and other patriots hated the vanguard *entartete Kunst* is not a marginal detail but a key feature of fascism.

Nothing encapsulates more forcefully the violent impact of the vanguard rupture than the (in)famous *Skandalkonzert* of March 31, 1913, a concert of the *Wiener Konzertverein* conducted by Schoenberg. Here is the program: Webern's *Six Pieces for Orchestra*, Zemlinsky's *Four Orchestral Songs on Poems by Maeterlinck*, Schoenberg's *Chamber Symphony* No. 1, Berg's *Five Orchestral Songs on Postcard Texts of Peter Altenberg*, and Mahler's "Now the Sun Wants to Rise as Brightly" (No. 1 from the *Kindertotenlieder*). However, Mahler's song was not performed because the concert ended prematurely: it was during Berg's *Songs* that the fighting began, with the audience calling for both poet and composer to be committed to the asylum.

Schoenberg's *Chamber Symphony* No. 1 was composed seven years earlier, in 1906, but the work which stands for his musical revolution is *Erwartung* (Op. 17, composed in 1909). *Erwartung* is a double Event, maximal and minimal. First, it was a turning point in the history of music: nothing remained the same after *Erwartung*, the coordinates of the entire musical landscape were transformed. However, one should not forget that *Erwartung* simultaneously renders a minimal Event—a barely per-ceptive subjective shift in the depicted "inner life" of its protagonist. This thirty-minute one-act opera—or, rather, monologue for solo soprano accompanied by a large orchestra—to a libretto by Marie Pappenheim was premiered in 1924 in Prague, conducted by Alexander Zemlinsky. Pappenheim studied medicine, but both her brother and her future husband were psychoanalysts; furthermore, her second cousin, Bertha Pappenheim, was treated for hysteria by Joseph Breuer—she is the famous "Anna O.," the subject of the first case study presented in Breuer and Freud's *Studies on Hysteria*.

ART AND THE UNCONSCIOUS

Although there is a great tradition of portraying hysterical women in late nineteenth- and early twentieth-century music—starting with Kundry from Wagner's *Parsifal* and continuing in Strauss' *Salome* and *Electra*, as well as the Chosen One in Stravinsky's *The Rite of Spring*—in all these cases the theme of the hysterical madwoman is "camouflaged with the exotic trappings of antiquity (classical, biblical, primitive) … distancing it from its uncomfortable contemporary relevance. Schoenberg and Pappenheim gave it a raw, unvarnished treatment that laid its social and psychological message bare."[3] This brings us back to the tension between Pappenheim's original libretto (a Freudian case rooted in social reality) and Schoenberg's version of it (rendering a pure inner delirium with no social roots). The trap to be avoided here is to privilege either of the two versions: either to claim that Schoenberg's version is an aesthetic-irrationalist mystification of Pappenheim's socially situated case of hysteria, or to dismiss Pappenheim's libretto as a boring realist report that only becomes a work of art thanks to Schoenberg's purification.

The linking of *Erwartung* with feminine hysteria is a commonplace— but how exactly are we to define it? Behind the reference to hysteria, there are two different, although connected, phenomena. First, there is the artistic line from the mid-nineteenth century (Wagner, the Pre-Raphaelites, Strindberg). Second, there is Freudian psychoanalysis, which developed out of the treatment of hysterical patients ("Anna O" but also "Dora," Freud's first great case study). Lacan rendered the division that characterizes the hysterical feminine subject in a concise formula: "I demand that you refuse my demand, since this is not that." When, for example, Wagner's Kundry seduces Parsifal, she actually wants him to resist her advances—does not this obstruction, this sabotage of her own intent, testify to a dimension in her which resists the domination of the Phallus? The male dread of woman, which so deeply branded the Zeitgeist at the turn of the twentieth century, from Edvard Munch and August Strindberg up to Franz Kafka, thus reveals itself as the dread of feminine inconsistency: feminine hysteria confronted these men with an inconsistent multitude of masks (all of a sudden the hysterical woman moves from desperate pleas to cruel, vulgar derision, etc.); leaving them traumatized. What causes such uneasiness is the impossibility of discerning a consistent subject behind the masks: behind the layers of masks there is nothing; or, at most, nothing but the shapeless, mucous stuff

---

3   Taruskin, *Music in the Early Twentieth Century*, p. 327.

of the life-substance. Suffice it to mention Edvard Munch's encounter with hysteria, which left such a deep mark upon him:

> In 1893 Munch was in love with the beautiful daughter of an Oslo wine merchant. She clung to him, but he was afraid of such a tie and anxious about his work, so he left her. One stormy night a sailing-boat came to fetch him: the report was that the young woman was on the point of death and wanted to speak to him for the last time. Munch was deeply moved and, without question, went to her home, where he found her lying on a bed between two lighted candles. But when he approached her bed, she rose and started to laugh: the whole scene was nothing but a hoax. Munch turned and began to leave; at that point, she threatened to shoot herself if he left her; and drawing a revolver, she pointed it at her breast. When Munch bent to wrench the weapon away, convinced that this too was only part of the game, the gun went off and wounded him in the hand.[4]

Here we encounter hysterical theatre at its purest: the subject is caught up in a masquerade in which what appears to be deadly serious (her imminent death) reveals itself as fraud, and what appears to be an empty gesture reveals itself as deadly serious (the threat of suicide). The panic that seizes the (male) subject confronting this theatre expresses a dread that behind the many masks there is nothing, no ultimate feminine Secret. *This* is what makes hysteria so unbearable: neither the primordially unconscious "irrationality" of the woman (on which Schoenberg's music focuses) nor the feminine confusion as a reaction to the pressure exerted by the patriarchal order (on which Pappenheim's libretto focuses).

The narrative content of the *Erwartung* libretto is minimal. In the first three shorter scenes, nothing happens other than the Woman's incomprehensible rambling. Only at the beginning of Scene 4 do elements of narrative content emerge—indications of her lover's infidelity; an accident on her journey to a house; a woman who will prevent her from entering it: "And they won't let me in there ... The unknown woman will drive me away ... And with him so ill ..." When she stumbles upon the corpse of her lover, she struggles with disbelief, shocked by the discovery. But it later becomes clear that she herself was the killer:

---

4   J. P. Hodin, *Edvard Munch*, London: Thames & Hudson 1972, pp. 88–9.

No, that isn't the shadow of the bench ... Someone is there ... He isn't breathing ... Moist ... something is flowing here ... It shines red ... Oh, it's my hands, they are torn and bleeding ... No, it's still wet, it's from there ... [*She tries with great exertion to drag the object forward.*] I can't do it ... It's him ...

Her inability to grasp the reality of her lover's murder predictably indicates her hysterical condition; only after she finds the strength to accept and integrate the knowledge of her lover's infidelity do her thoughts become more focused and her emotions less malleable—she forgives and expresses compassion for his infidelity, arriving at a full awareness of her self-deceit:

My dear ... my only darling ... did you kiss her often? ... while I was dying with longing. Did you love her very much? Don't say yes ... You smile painfully ... Maybe you too have suffered ... maybe your heart called out for her ... Is it your fault? ... Oh, I cursed you ... but your compassion made me happy ... I believed ... I was happy ...

It is true that the Woman does not achieve the complete resolution of her psychic deadlock: at the end of the opera, she again becomes dissociated, resuming her search. There is, however, a minimal event—a subjective reversal—just before the end, in her acceptance of the crime. One should note here the difference between Pappenheim's original libretto and the version used by Schoenberg. The original is basically a realistic narrative that locates the hysterical woman in a clear social context: abandoned by her lover, she kills him, and the horror of the act causes her to lose contact with reality and suffer hallucinations; only gradually does she become aware of what she has done and reconnect with reality. Through numerous deletions of references to actual events and circumstances, Schoenberg transformed a coherent realistic narrative with a clear feminist subtext into an illogical nightmarish hallucination unconstrained by external reality.

Two questions have to be raised here: why this link between atonal music and psychoanalysis, and why does Schoenberg attempt to transform a clinical case into a self-contained portrait of hysterical hallucination? The answer to the first question seems obvious:

Freud's findings held particular promise for Expressionist artists seeking to eradicate ornamentation, superficial obedience to established forms, and surface prettiness from their works. The revelation that there existed an unconscious mind, replete with images, feelings, and desires, obeying only its own labyrinthine logic ... It is not surprising that Schoenberg found *Erwartung*'s hysterical Woman an ideal subject for his leap into the world of the unconscious mind. The quest to access subliminal realms of thought and experience had augmented a widespread fascination with hysterics, for whom the barriers between conscious and unconscious mind had fractured.[5]

The answer to the second question is that Schoenberg's reworking of the libretto was a result of his drive to liberate music from imitating external reality: "Kandinsky viewed line and color as emotional effects and removed them from their descriptive function. Schoenberg does similar things with his music, which mirrors the extremely expressive content of the text."[6] In other words, we remain within the space of mimesis, and what changes is simply the object imitated. In contrast to traditional figurative art, which aims at a mimesis of external reality, authentic modern art attempts to by-pass the detour through external reality and achieve a direct mimesis of spiritual-affective life, a "representation of inner occurrences."[7] Here enters psychoanalysis: this inner life, as yet uncontaminated by external reality, is unconscious: "art must express the instinctive and the inborn, the part of ourselves that is wholly unconscious and uncorrupted by convention."[8]

In a famous letter to Kandinsky, Schoenberg emphatically asserted that "art belongs to the *unconscious*."[9] This is the irrational hallucinatory unconscious of the psychic "inner life," the confused and incoherent flow of ideas, passions, affects—in short, the psychological unconscious of the absolute immanence of psychic life which is, as such, de facto indistinguishable from the stream of consciousness itself. But is this the Freudian unconscious? Did not Lacan demonstrate that the latter is not psychological—the unconscious of the irrational inner flow—but, on the contrary, quite literally meta-psychological: a symbolic structure? Lacan began his "return to Freud" with a linguistic reading of the entire psychoanalytic edifice, encapsulated in what is perhaps his single best-known formula: "the unconscious is structured as a language." The standard view of the unconscious is that it

---

5   Claudia L. Friedlander, "Man sieht den Weg nicht ... Musical, Cultural and Psychoanalytic Signposts Along the Dark Path of Schoenberg's *Erwartung* Op. 17," unpublished manuscript (1999), available at http://liberatedvoice.typepad.com.

6   Rory Braddell, "Schoenberg and Atonality," available at http://homepage.eircom.net.

7   Taruskin, *Music in the Early Twentieth Century*, p. 306.

8   Ibid., p. 330.

9   Ibid., p. 307.

is the domain of irrational drives, something opposed to the rational conscious self. For Lacan, this notion of the unconscious belongs to Romantic
Lebensphilosophie and has nothing to do with Freud. The Freudian unconscious caused such a scandal not because of the claim that the rational self
is subordinate to a much vaster domain of blind irrational instincts, but
because it demonstrated how the unconscious itself obeys its own grammar
and logic—the unconscious talks and thinks. The unconscious is not a res-
ervoir of wild drives that has to be conquered by the ego, but the site from
which a traumatic truth speaks. Therein resides Lacan's version of Freud's
motto *wo es war, soll ich werden* ("where it was, I shall become"): not "the
ego should conquer the id," the site of the unconscious drives, but "I should
dare to approach the site of my truth." What awaits me "there" is not a
deep Truth I have to identify with, but an unbearable truth I have to learn
to live with:

> The unconscious is neither the primordial nor the instinctual, and what it knows
> of the elemental is no more than the elements of the signifier … The intolerable
> scandal when Freudian sexuality was not yet holy was that it was so "intellec-
> tual." It was in this respect that it showed itself to be the worthy stooge of all
> those terrorists whose plots were going to ruin society.[10]

Unconscious Reason is, of course, not like the coherent structures of
conscious thought processes, but a complex network of particular links
organized along the lines of condensation, displacement, etc., full of pragmatic and opportunistic compromises—something is rejected, but not
quite, since it returns in an encrypted mode; it is rationally accepted, but
isolated or neutralized in its full symbolic weight; and so on and so forth.
We thus get a mad dance of distortions which follow no clear univocal
logic, but form a patchwork of improvised connections.

How does the unconscious that Schoenberg refers to relate to the
"oceanic" unconscious of aesthetic self-obliteration prevalent in the great
tradition of the nineteenth century which begins with Schopenhauer, reaches
its peak in Wagner's *Tristan*, and whose last great expression is Thomas
Mann's *Death in Venice*? Let us proceed step by step. Jacques Rancière—
who has developed the opposition between the Freudian unconscious
(which, as we have just seen, is thoroughly "rational," as the articulation
of a strategy to deal with specific traumatic experiences) and the aesthetic

10   Jacques Lacan, *Écrits*, New York: Norton 2006, pp. 434–5.

unconscious—perspicuously notes that Freud's rejection of the latter also accounts for the psychologically realistic character of his interpretations of works of art, interpretations which are sometimes embarrassingly naive. Freud is not interested in textual details that might subvert the narrative or the content of a work; what he does is either treat a character from literary fiction as a real clinical case, or interpret the artwork as a symptom of the artist's pathology.

Rancière's thesis needs to be supplemented on three counts. He writes that the discovery of the death drive is "an episode in Freud's long and often disguised confrontation with the great obsessive theme of the epoch in which psychoanalysis was formed, the unconscious of the Schopenhauerian thing-in-itself and the great literary fictions of return to this unconscious."[11] Freud's numerous literary and art analyses were thus "so many ways of resisting the nihilist entropy that Freud detects and rejects in the works of the aesthetic regime of art, but that he will also legitimize in his theorization of the death drive."[12] But one can easily show (as Lacan did in a very convincing way) that the Freudian death drive is not his term for the Schopenhauerian striving for self-annihilation, the descent into the primordial abyss, etc., but, quite the contrary, names a radical compulsion-to-repeat which persists "beyond life and death." Freud invented the "death drive" in order to posit a libidinal force which, precisely, runs against "nihilist entropy."

This point is linked to the second correction: Rancière is too quick to identify today's predominant "textual" psychoanalytic dealing with art and literature as a continuation of the Schopenhauerian self-dissolution in the primordial abyss. In fact, one can demonstrate how modernism proper enacts a break with precisely this late Romantic topic. Although both the Romantic poetry of the "eternal Night" and modernist formalism oppose the traditional representational narrative logic, they undermine it from opposite directions: Romanticism asserts the force of "nihilist entropy" which dissolves the structures of narrative representation, while modernism insists on formal details that display a structure of their own, at a distance from narrative representation, but also from self-annihilation in the "eternal sea." These formal details which insist independently of narrative representation are more like the Freudian death drive, an insistence

---

11   Jacques Rancière, *The Aesthetic Unconscious*, Cambridge: Polity Press 2009, p. 82.

12   Ibid., p. 83.

beyond the cycle of "life and death" rendered by the narrative—only in this way can Freudian theory be linked to modern art.

Third and final point: can Wagner's Romanticism really be reduced to nihilist entropy? With Romanticism, music changes its role: no longer a mere accompaniment to the message delivered in speech, it contains/ renders a message of its own, "deeper" than the one delivered in words. It was Rousseau who first clearly articulated this expressive potential of music as such, when he claimed that, instead of merely imitating the affective features of verbal speech, music should be given the right to "speak for itself": in contrast to deceptive verbal speech, in music it is, to paraphrase Lacan, the truth itself which speaks. As Schopenhauer put it, music directly expresses the noumenal Will, while speech remains limited to the level of phenomenal representation. Music is the substance that renders the true heart of the subject, the abyss of radical negativity: music becomes the bearer of the true message beyond words with the shift from the Enlightenment subject of rational *logos* to the Romantic subject of the "Night of the World," i.e., with the shift of the metaphor for the kernel of the subject from Day to Night. Here we encounter the Uncanny: no longer external transcendence, but, following Kant's transcendental turn, the excess of the Night in the very heart of the subject (the dimension of the Undead), what Gary Tomlinson has called the "internal otherworldliness that marks the Kantian subject."[13] What music renders is no longer the "semantics of the soul," but the underlying "noumenal" flux of *jouissance* beyond linguistic meaningfulness. This noumenal is radically different from the pre-Kantian transcendent divine Truth: it is the inaccessible excess which forms the very core of the subject.

After such a celebration of musicality, one can only agree with Vladimir Nabokov when he characterized the ideal state as one in which there is "no torture, no executions, and no music."[14] Effectively, the line of separation between the sublime and the ridiculous, between a noble act and a pathetic empty gesture, is ultimately untraceable. Take the beginning of the first movement of Beethoven's Ninth Symphony: was there ever a more succinct declaration of the resolute stance, of the uncompromising will to enact one's decision? However, with merely the slightest shift of perspective, the same gesture can appear ridiculous, a hysterical waving of hands which betrays the fact that we are effectively dealing with an imposture.

---

13   Gary Tomlinson, *Metaphysical Song*, Princeton: Princeton University Press 1999, p. 94.

14   Vladimir Nabokov, *Strong Opinions*, New York: McGraw-Hill 1973, p. 35.

But what if we read the stance of the first movement not in terms of dignity, but as the *obstinacy* of the "undead" drive? What this oscillation of ours suggests is that there is no kitsch in itself: what Bartók achieves in his *Concerto for Orchestra* is to *redeem* the ultimate kitsch melody from Lehar's *The Merry Widow*—the quoting of Lehar is in no way meant ironically, since, by quoting it in a different context, he de-fetishizes it, providing us with a proper musical environment out of which this beautiful melody emerges "organically." Luckily, however, the problem with this expressive potential of music is that, taken to the end, it cancels itself. When we progress to the very core of the subject, we encounter the fantasmatic kernel of enjoyment which can no longer be subjectivized, affectively assumed by the subject—the subject can only stare, with a cold, transfixed gaze, at this kernel, unable to fully recognize itself in it. Recall "Der Laienmann," the last song from Schubert's *Winterreise*: at the very high point of despair, all emotions are frozen, we are back with the non-expressive mechanism, the subject is reduced to the utter despair of mimicking the automatism of mechanical music.

THE IMPASSES OF ATONALITY

This clarification of the Freudian unconscious brings us back to *Erwartung*, more precisely, to the passage from atonality to dodecaphony. *Erwartung* was written in 1909—after the leap into pure atonality, but before Schoenberg had begun to work out his twelve-tone ideas in a systematic way. The commonplace observation is that the passage from atonality to dodecaphony is the shift from extreme expressionism (abandoning all pre-established formal constraints in order to render as directly as possible the innermost unconscious subjective truth) to its opposite extreme: to "a haven for technical research and compositional tours de force ... twelve-tone composers went further than any others in ordering the content of their work according to rational structural principles, making content in effect tantamount to form."[15] Even Adorno agrees with this commonplace, reading the passage from atonality to dodecaphony as a dialectical reversal of expression into external mechanical order. Here, however, Lacan's notion of the unconscious as "structured like language" regains its pertinence: the passage from atonality to dodecaphony is not a passage from the depths of the irrational

---

15   Taruskin, *Music in the Early Twentieth Century*, p. 704.

unconscious to a new form of consciously planned rationality, but a passage from the chaotic flux of consciousness to the real unconscious. Tonality—atonality—dodecaphony thus form a good old Hegelian triad, but not only in the simplistic sense that atonality negates tonality and then dodecaphony negates the negation to introduce a new positive order; they do this in a much more precise and interesting way. Tonality is first negated in the terms of the old musical order, due to its mimetic inadequacy: the reproach is that it does not render faithfully the inner psychic reality of man, and the shift to atonality is justified in the terms of extreme expressionism, as the only way to follow the inner stream. Only then is the mimetic principle itself abandoned, and the new radical de-psychologized formal order (dodecaphony) imposed—or, in Lacan's terms, Schoenberg finally learned that the Unconscious is outside, not in the depths of our soul.

What ordinary listeners usually perceive in atonal music is a lack of melody. The situation is more complex, however, since the predominance of melody in the nineteenth century was already a sign of the decline of harmonic relationships: "It is certainly true that melody was the principal basis of form in all nineteenth-century music after the death of Beethoven, but that was because harmonic relationships no longer possessed the force and influence they had throughout the eighteenth century."[16] The composer whose work bears testimony to this decline in an exemplary way is Tchaikovsky, an indisputable melodic talent who was well aware of his weakness in deploying the texture of a large musical form.

For a European classical music elitist educated in the tradition of Adorno, the name "Tchaikovsky" cannot but provoke a Goebbels-style gun-toting reaction—Tchaikovsky stands for the lowest of low kitsch, comparable only to Sibelius or Rachmaninov. However, as Daniel Gregory Mason has succinctly put it, Tchaikovsky "has the merits of his defects": not only was he aware of his limitations and weak points, his (few) truly great moments paradoxically grew out of these defects. Tchaikovsky admitted that he could "seldom sustain a whole movement at the height of its greatest passages"—a problem not only for him, but for most Romantics up to Elgar. Berlioz made the well-known vicious quip that Mendelssohn's melodies usually begin well but finish badly, losing their drive and ending in a "mechanical" resolution (see his *Fingal's Cave* overture, or the first movement of the Violin Concerto). But far from being a sign of Mendelssohn's weakness as a composer, this failure of the melodic line rather bears witness

16   Charles Rosen, *Schoenberg*, London: Fontana Collins 1975, p. 42.

to his sensitivity towards historical change: those still able to write "beau-tiful melodies" were kitsch composers like Tchaikovsky. Tchaikovsky approaches true art not in his numerous "beautiful melodies," but when a melodic line is thwarted. At the very beginning of *Onegin*, in the brief orchestral prelude, the short melodic motif ("Tatyana's theme") is not properly developed, but merely repeated in different modes, fully retain-ing its isolated character of a melodic fragment, not even a full melodic line. There is a genuine melancholic flavor in such a repetition which registers and displays the underlying impotence, the failure of proper development.

Maybe Schoenberg was too dismissive of pseudo-atonal composers in whose predominantly tonal works one can discern echoes and traces of the atonal revolution—here are two surprising examples from none other than Shostakovich (maybe the fourth in the series of Those Whose Name Should Not Be Pronounced In Public). In his key symphonies (Fifth, Eighth, and Tenth), the longest movement is always the first, whose inner logic follows something quite different than the sonata form: the movement begins with a strong Thesis, a proud Beethovenesque assertion of strength in pain, which is then gradually morphed into a withdrawal towards another spiritual/ethereal dimension—it is, paradoxically, this very withdrawal that generates an unbearable tension. Furthermore, there is an opposite move-ment in Shostakovich's work: David Hurwitz noted as one of Shostakovich's procedures that he learned from Mahler the "technique of brutalizing a former lyrical melody"[17]—say, in the development of the first movement of his Fifth Symphony, its principal theme, a lyric descending phrase on violins over a string accompaniment, is repeated as a grotesque, goose-stepping march, with cymbals, trumpets, snare drum, and timpani.

Schoenberg's passage from pure atonality to dodecaphony was thus necessitated by the immanent deadlock of atonality. *Erwartung* is praised by Charles Rosen as "the quintessential Expressionist work"—Schoenberg himself wrote: "In *Erwartung* the aim is to represent in slow motion every-thing that occurs during a single second of maximum spiritual excitement, stretching it out to half an hour." However, such a radical approach soon reveals its immanent limitations. With the rise of atonality,

---

17   David Hurwitz, *Shostakovich Symphonies and Concertos*, Milwaukee: Amadeus Press 2006, p. 25.

it seemed as if music now had to be written note by note; only chains of chromatic or whole-tone scales were possible, and these only sparingly. The renunciation of the symmetrical use of blocks of elements in working out musical proportions placed the weight on the smallest units, single intervals, short motifs. The expressive values of these tiny elements therefore took on an inordinate significance: they replaced syntax. ... And since they took a preponderant role in composition it was obvious that a composer would choose elements with the most powerful, even the most violent values, as these small elements now had to do the work of much larger groups. The relation between the violence and morbidity of emotional expression and the formal changes of style is therefore not fortuitous.[18]

In a truly materialist formalism, one should thus invert the relationship between form and content, following Fredric Jameson's famous analysis of Hemingway in which he pointed out that Hemingway did not write short terse sentences in order to render the isolated heroic individuality of his heroes—form comes first, he invented the isolated heroic individuality to be able to write in a certain way. And the same goes for Schoenberg: he did not take the fateful step into atonality in order to express in music the extremes of morbid hysterical violence; he chose the topic of hysteria because it fitted atonal music.

Philip Friedheim has described *Erwartung* as Schoenberg's "only lengthy work in an athematic style," where no musical material returns once stated over the course of 426 measures. As such, as a case of pure atonality, *Erwartung* is a *hapax*, like the Malevich square, something that can really be done only once, the only specimen of its genre. *Erwartung* thus stands for "the extremity of the principle of non-repetition" and, as such, it confronts us with the obvious problem of pure atonality, insoluble within its space, which is, predictably: the problem of large musical forms. On what to base the coherence of a large form when large-scale repetitions and similarities are prohibited? Schoenberg endeavored to resolve this problem through a series of strategies. His first, obvious, option was that, if an atonal work cannot achieve "a purely musical form drawn from the logic of a purely musical material," then the principle of unity has to be sought in "extra-musical material, poetical texts, inner feelings, as if these feelings could in the final result be distinguished from their extraordinary

---

18   Rosen, *Schoenberg*, pp. 29–30.

musical incarnation."[19] The problem with this solution is that, when the "extra-musical material" is composed exclusively of inner feelings, these feelings, rendered in their chaotic immanence, are a dispersed inconsistent flow with no organic unity.

Schoenberg resolved a particular sub-aspect of this problem—how to conclude a work when final harmonies are prohibited—with "the filling out of the chromatic space which brought about a saturation of the musical space, his substitute for the tonic chord—instead of absolute consonance, we get a state of chromatic plenitude in which every note in the range of the orchestra is played in a kind of glissando."[20] This solution points forwards towards dodecaphony, in which all twelve notes of the chromatic scale are used as often as one another in a piece of music while preventing the emphasis of any one note through the use of tone rows; all twelve notes are thus given more or less equal importance, and the music avoids being in a key. (Schoenberg himself described the system as a "method of composing with twelve tones which are related only with one another"—echoing Saussure's notion of differentiality: each tone is only its difference towards the others, so there are only differences with no positive terms.[21] For this reason, Schoenberg did not like the term "atonality," much preferring "pantonality": while the first term is merely negative, the second suggests how the tonal focus shifts from one to another tone, so that every tone gets its moment of hegemony.) The saturation of the chromatic space thus condenses into a final moment what dodecaphony deploys as—or expands into—a system. While atonality and dodecaphony are both "egalitarian," rejecting any Master-Tone, dodecaphony is an attempt to solve the problem of how to transform the atonal "egalitarianism" into a new order. In other

---

19   Ibid., pp. 95–6.

20   Ibid., p. 66.

21   The problem of serialism, of the equality of all variations and the hidden focus of the entire matrix, can be illustrated through a stupid incident that happened in a Slovenian hippy commune at the end of 1960s, at the high point of the sexual revolution. A "coordinator" of the commune (its de facto master, although masters were prohibited) proposed that, in order to break out of bourgeois individualism in matters of sex, a complex matrix for varying sexual partners should be introduced, so that, over a specified period of time, every man in the group would have sex with every woman. The group soon discovered that the coordinator had proposed this complex matrix for one purpose only: he wanted to sleep with a particular young woman who was the partner of another commune member, and the matrix appeared to him as the only way to do so without admitting his individual preference and possessive desire.

words, while atonality is the hysterical Event, dodecaphony is the result of the "work of love" in fidelity to the Event.[22]

Richard Taruskin remarks with acerbic irony that Schoenberg's formula of the "emancipation of dissonances" "has excellent political 'vibes'";[23] it immediately evokes freedom from an oppressive regime which has tried to suppress its own inner antagonisms—in other words, it is as if the admission of musical dissonances somehow mirrors the admission of social antagonisms. Taruskin is right to point out that the crucial result of the "emancipation of dissonances" was not the capacity of music to express catastrophic emotions—this was merely the by-product (or collateral damage, as we say today) of "the achievement of a fully integrated musical space in which the 'horizontal' and the 'vertical' dimensions were at last equivalent": as long as composing was constrained by rules of harmony, "'horizontal' ideas like melodies could not always be 'vertically' represented."[24]

There is, however, another option, which Schoenberg does not shirk from using: playing with the absent tonality itself. For example, he observed that when "a resolution of the two upper notes into consonances according to the rules of tonal harmony appears to be implied by the structure of the chord ... this allusion to older forms seems to have a satisfying effect even though the resolution does not actually occur."[25] Did not Mallarmé do something homologous with his virtual rhymes: the preceding lines imply that the verse in question will finish with a rhyme, but it does not, making the missing word even more present in its absence (like "After my wife dropped dead, I went straight to bed, and decided that until tomorrow, I will not give way to my joy" [instead of the expected 'sorrow']).

---

22   Another procedure with a similar function is, of course, the use of *Klangfarbenmelodie* (color-of-the-sound-melody), a technique that involves splitting a musical line or melody between several instruments rather than assigning it to just one instrument (or set of instruments), thereby adding color (timbre) and texture to the melodic line. The term was coined by Schoenberg in his *Harmonielehre* from 1911.

23   Taruskin, *Music in the Early Twentieth Century*, p. 310.

24   Ibid., p. 340.

25   Rosen, *Schoenberg*, p. 53.

THE "DREAM-THOUGHT" OF *ERWARTUNG*

This brings us to the uniqueness of Schoenberg's *Gurre-Lieder*, a cantata for five vocal soloists, narrator, chorus and large orchestra, based on poems by Jens Peter Jacobsen. The title refers to Gurre Castle in Denmark, scene of the Danish national legend about the love of King Valdemar for his mistress Tove, and her subsequent murder by Valdemar's jealous Queen Helvig. At the first performance in Vienna on February 23, 1913, Schoenberg was churlishly dismissive of its positive reception, saying "I was rather indifferent, if not even a little angry." Perhaps, however, his dismissal was misdirected.

   Gurre-Lieder is one of the strangest pieces in the entire history of music. Schoenberg's preference for chamber music is well known: in a nice swipe at American vulgarity, he said that everything in music can be performed with a maximum of five or six instruments—we only need orchestras so that the Americans can get it ... How, then, to account for *Gurre-Lieder*, which demands soloists, a full orchestra and three choruses? In the notes to his recording, Simon Rattle proposed a wonderful formula: *Gurre-Lieder* is a chamber piece for orchestra and chorus—this, indeed, is how one should approach it. Any average composer can write a chamber piece for three or four performers—only a genius like Schoenberg can write one for 600 performers. The work is marked by a double split: its melodic line was composed in 1901-2, when Schoenberg was still a late Romanticist, and instrumentalized in 1910, after his atonal break; this discord between the late Romantic melodic line and the atonal orchestration accounts for the piece's uncanny effect on the listener. But what makes *Gurre-Lieder* really unique is the mirroring between its musical line and the history of music itself: the shift from a heavy late-Romantic Wagnerian pathos to atonal *Sprechgesang* is rendered in the very progress of the piece.

   Gurre-Lieder starts with an unbearably beautiful dialogue between King Valdemar and Tove, his secret love. When the dove's song tells the king of Tove's death, Schoenberg out-Wagners Wagner himself with the intensity of the music. (If, as the saying goes, Wagner's *Rienzi* is Meyerbeer's best opera, then Schoenberg's *Gurre-Lieder* is Wagner's.) Totally shattered, Valdemar rises against God himself, and is punished for this blasphemy by being condemned to return as an undead specter along with his band of soldiers. At this point, the singing begins to shift from late-Romantic pathos to the atonal *Sprechgesang* that announces the regeneration of Life; the nightly spectral roaming of the "undead" knights gives way to a celebration of the new daylight in a reawakened, now "sane" nature. But what kind of daylight is this? Definitely not the old, pre-Romantic daylight of a serene Classicist Reason. True, the Romantic passion, melancholy and uprising against God is replaced by a renewed optimist beatitude—but, again, what kind of beatitude? Is it not uncannily close to the kind caricatured in the archetypal cartoon scene in which, after the cat or dog is hit on the head with a heavy object, it begins to laugh blissfully and see birds twittering and dancing all around it?

Part III of *Gurre-Lieder* is subdivided into three parts in each of which an eccentric carnivalesque character acts as focus—a naive frightened peasant, Klaus the Jester, and the Speaker.[26] Is not this triad like that of the notorious doctor friends from the second part of Freud's dream about Irma's injection? And does this not reflect the overall homology of *Gurre-Lieder* with Freud's dream: in both cases, the descent into ultimate trauma changes into a strange, sublime and simultaneously ridiculous irreal beatific scene. There is certainly something terrifyingly obscene about the excessively pathetic declamation of the Speaker's *Sprechgesang* which concludes the work, suggesting an utterly denaturalized nature, a kind of perverted, mocking innocence, not unlike the corrupt debauchee who, to add spice to his games, mimics a young innocent girl. The daybreak with which *Gurre-Lieder* concludes thus represents the moment when Romanticist infinite longing and pain break down in utter insensitivity, so that the subject is in a way de-subjectivized, reduced to the level of a blessed idiot able to utter only meaningless babble. The entire "theater of the absurd" is already there, in the finale of *Gurre-Lieder*.

To return to *Erwartung*: the key application of this procedure of gradually building up a motif from its sketchy fragments—themselves like distorted signals coming from the future (the future of the fully formed motif)—is a motif which emerges in fully realized form only in the concluding moments of *Erwartung*, at measure 410. The surprising fact is that this motif, which serves "as a *Grundgestalt*, a fundamental musical idea or 'basic shape' that gave coherence to the harmonically nonfunctional ('atonal') musical texture"[27] of *Erwartung*, comes from Schoenberg's

---

26   The position of court jester is already mentioned at the end of Part II, when, after issuing a terrifying curse of God, Waldemar plans to assume this role. The fact that God allowed the murder of Tove proves that he is "a tyrant, not a king," and as such he needs someone to rebuke him, a court jester telling him the truth—"Let me, Lord, wear your jester's cap!"

27   Taruskin, *Music in the Early Twentieth Century*, p. 353.

earlier *tonal* song "Am Wegrand" (Opus 6), where it is part of the opening phrase.[28] A commonplace psychoanalytic interpretation would be that it is as if, through free association, the earlier, repressed melody has returned to consciousness—here, psychoanalysis not only provides the topic (feminine hysteria), it affects the musical form itself.[29] However, the enigmatic fact is that it looks as though Schoenberg was pursued by the specter of tonality as he set about the creation of his first atonal works:

> The internalized languages of the past, "something familiar and old established in the mind that has been estranged only by the process of repression," come back to haunt the new emerging language. This process is particularly vivid in music. The ghosts of the past become particularly haunting if we live with them on a day to day basis. Transposing Freud's thoughts onto a musical sphere, I would say that tonality, the most "Heimlich" of musical groundings, becomes increasingly estranged and repressed as Schoenberg and others struggle to surmount it. The glimmerings of tonality that emerge here and there, in varying degrees and in varying intensities throughout Schoenberg's compositional life, can well be understood as "unheimlich." The sonorities of tonality have not fully disappeared, they have become estranged, evanescent specters.[30]

It is difficult to miss the irony at work here: the repressed "dream-thought" is *tonal*—so which is the unconscious desire that operates in the song? The

---

28   The first to draw attention to Schoenberg's recycling of the material from "Am Wegrand" was Herbert Buchanan, in his "A Key to Schoenberg's *Erwartung* Opus 17" (1967).

29   We find something similar in the TV series *24*. Almost one-third of each episode is taken up by the commercials that interrupt the show. The way the commercials break the continuity of the narrative is in itself unique and contributes to the sense of urgency: a single installment, commercials included, lasts exactly one hour, so the breaks are part of the temporal continuity of the series. Say we see the on-screen digital clock showing "7.46" and then there is a commercial break. When the program returns, we see the same digital clock signaling that it is now "7.51"—the length of the break in the viewers' real time is exactly the same as the temporal gap in the on-screen narrative. It is as if the commercial breaks fit miraculously into the real-time unfolding of the events in the narrative; as if we take a break from events that nonetheless *go on* while we are watching commercials; as if a live transmission has been temporarily interrupted. The continuity of the ongoing action thus appears so pressing and urgent, spilling over into the real time of the viewers themselves, that it cannot be interrupted even for the commercial breaks.

30   Michael Cherlin, "Schoenberg and Das Unheimliche: Spectres of Tonality," *Journal of Musicology* (1993), p. 362, quoted in Friedlander, "Man sieht den Weg nicht …"

amorphous continuity of atonal music was often designated as a kind of stream of consciousness—but where is the unconscious here? The atonal flow should function as a direct rendering of the unconscious, freed from the constraints of rational conscious speech or tonality—but this unconscious flow itself relates to a *tonal* fragment as its own unconscious. The atonal flow is rather like the flow of free associations—not primordial, but the conscious chaotic flow out of which interpretation should dig the unconscious kernel. But, again, is the tonal motif the unconscious moment? Freud's analysis of dreams provides a precious key here.

The Freudian unconscious also has a formal aspect and is not merely a matter of content: recall the cases where Freud interprets a dream so that what is repressed/excluded from its content returns as a feature of the form of the dream; furthermore, Freud emphasizes that the true secret of the dream is not its content (the "dream-thoughts"), but the form itself:

> The latent dream-thoughts are the material which the dream-work transforms into the manifest dream … The only essential thing about dreams is the dream-work that has influenced the thought-material. We have no right to ignore it in our theory, even though we may disregard it in certain practical situations. Analytic observation shows further that the dream-work never restricts itself to translating these thoughts into the archaic or regressive mode of expression that is familiar to you. In addition, it regularly takes possession of something else, which is not part of the latent thoughts of the previous day, but which is the true motif force for the construction of the dream. This indispensable addition [*unentbehrliche Zutat*] is the equally unconscious wish for the fulfillment of which the content of the dream is given its new form. A dream may thus be any sort of thing in so far as you are only taking into account the thoughts it represents—a warning, an intention, a preparation, and so on; but it is always also the fulfillment of an unconscious wish and, if you are considering it as a product of the dream-work, it is only that. A dream is therefore never simply an intention, or a warning, but always an intention, etc., translated into the archaic mode of thought by the help of an unconscious wish and transformed to fulfill that wish. The one characteristic, the wish-fulfillment, is the invariable one; the other may vary. It may for its part once more be a wish, in which case the dream will, with the help of an unconscious wish, represent as fulfilled a latent wish of the previous day.[31]

---

31   Sigmund Freud, *Introductory Lectures on Psychoanalysis*, Harmondsworth: Penguin 1973, pp. 261–2.

Every detail is worth analyzing in this brilliant passage, from its implicit opening motto "what is good enough for practice—namely the search for the meaning of dreams—is not good enough for theory," to its concluding redoubling of the wish. Its key insight is, of course, the "triangulation" of latent dream-thought, manifest dream-content, and the unconscious wish, which limits the scope of—or, rather, directly undermines—the hermeneutic model of the interpretation of dreams (the path from the manifest dream-content to its hidden meaning, the latent dream-thought), which reverses the path of the formation of a dream (the transposition of the latent dream-thought into the manifest dream-content by the dream-work). The paradox is that the dream-work is not merely a process of masking the dream's "true message": the dream's true core, its unconscious wish, inscribes itself only through and in this very process of masking, so that the moment we re-translate the dream-content back into the dream-thought expressed in it we lose the "true motif force" of the dream—in short, it is the process of masking itself which inscribes into the dream its true secret. One should therefore invert the standard notion of an ever-deeper penetration to the core of the dream: it is not that we first move from the manifest dream-content to the first-level secret, the latent dream-thought, and then penetrate deeper, into the dream's unconscious wish. This "deeper" wish is located in the very gap between the latent dream-thought and the manifest dream-content.

So, in a strictly homologous way, in *Erwartung* the *Wegrand* motif is not the unconscious element, but the "dream-thought" of the piece. The actual Unconscious dwells elsewhere—where, exactly? In the music itself, in the form of the music. The gap between form and content is here properly dialectical, rather than transcendental. Herein lies the key difference between melodrama and *Erwartung*. In melodrama, as noted earlier, the emotional excess that cannot express itself directly in the narrative finds its outlet in the sentimental musical accompaniment or some other formal feature. In *Erwartung*, by contrast, the very gap between content and form is to be reflected back into the content itself, as an indication that the content is not all, that something was repressed/excluded from it—this exclusion which establishes the form is itself the "primordial repression" (*Ur-Verdrängung*), and no matter how much we bring out all the repressed content, this primordial repression persists. In other words, what is repressed in a cheap melodrama (and then returns in the music) is simply the sentimental excess of its content, while what is repressed in *Erwartung*, its Unconscious, is not some determinate content but the void of subjectivity itself that eludes the musical form and is as such constituted by it, as its remainder.

Part II

THE HEGELIAN EVENT

CHAPTER 4

Evental Truth, Evental Sex

THE THREE EVENTS OF PHILOSOPHY

"I don't much like hearing that we have *gone beyond* Hegel, the way one hears we have *gone beyond* Descartes. We go beyond everything and always end up in the same place."[1] This *aperçu* by Lacan can serve as our guiding principle: beware of all too easy attempts to "overcome" metaphysics! There are three (and only three) key philosophers in the history of (Western) metaphysics: Plato, Descartes, Hegel. The proof of their privileged status is their extra-ordinary position in the series of philosophers: each of them not only designates a clear break with the past, but also casts a long shadow over the thinkers who follow him—they can all be conceived as a series of negations of or oppositions to his position. Foucault already noted that the entire history of Western philosophy can be defined as a history of rejections of Platonism: in an homologous way, the whole of modern philosophy can be conceived as a history of rejections of Cartesianism, from subtle corrections (Malebranche, Spinoza) to outright dismissals. With Hegel things are, if anything, even more obvious: what unites all that comes after Hegel is the opposition to the specter of his "panlogicism."[2]

The notion of the Event seems especially incompatible with the philosophy of Plato, for whom our constantly changing reality is grounded in the eternal order of Ideas. But things are not so simple. Plato is the first in a series of philosophers who fell out of favor in the twentieth century, being blamed for all our misfortunes. Alain Badiou has enumerated six main (partially intertwined) forms of twentieth-century anti-Platonism: vitalist, empiricist-analytic, Marxist, Existentialist, Heideggerian, and "democratic."[3] "Plato" is thus the negative point of reference which unites otherwise irreconcilable enemies: Marxists and anti-communist liberals,

---

1 Jacques Lacan, *Seminar, Book II*, New York: Norton 1991, p. 71.
2 For a more condensed version of the same line of thought see Slavoj Žižek, *Event*, London: Penguin Books 2014.
3 For an extended discussion, see Slavoj Žižek, *Less Than Nothing*, London: Verso 2013, Chapter 1.

existentialists and analytic empiricists, Heideggerians and vitalists ... Does not something similar hold for Descartes? Here are the main versions of anti-Cartesianism:

1) The *Heideggerian* notion of Cartesian subjectivity as the radical step in metaphysical nihilism which finds its fulfillment in modern technology.

2) The *ecological* rejection of Cartesian dualism as opening up the path to the ruthless exploitation of nature. Here is Al Gore's version: the Judeo-Christian tradition, in establishing mankind's "dominion" over the earth, also charged mankind with environmental stewardship; Descartes remembered "dominion," but breezed past the idea of stewardship, thereby yielding to the "great temptation of the West" and placing the idealized world of rational thought on a higher plane than nature.[4]

3) The *cognitivist* rejection of Descartes' privileging of the rational mind over the emotions (see Antonio Damasio's *Descartes' Error*), as well as his notion of the Self as a single autonomous agent which controls psychic life in a transparent way (see Daniel Dennett's critique of the "Cartesian theatre").

4) The *feminist* claim that the Cartesian *cogito*, while appearing gender-neutral, effectively privileges the male subject (only the masculine mind deals with clear and distinct thought, while the feminine mind is under the spell of confused sensual impressions and affects).

5) The *linguistic turn*, whose proponents deplore the "monological" character of the Cartesian subject for whom intersubjectivity comes afterwards, as a secondary feature; Descartes fails to see how human subjectivity is always embedded in an intersubjective linguistic context.

6) *Vitalists* point out that, in the Cartesian dualism of *res cogitans* and *res extensa*, there is no place for life in its full sense, a life that cannot be reduced to the interaction of mechanical nuts and bolts; this is why Descartes claims that, since animals do not have souls, they don't really suffer—their cries have the status of mechanical squeaks coming from a malfunctioning machine.

---

4   See "Plato, Aristotle, and the 2000 Election," from slate.com.

Which brings us to Hegel, the ultimate *bête noire* of the last two centuries of philosophy:

1) Proponents of the *"philosophy of life"* (*Lebensphilosophie*) claim that the life of the Hegelian dialectical process is not actual organic life, but an artificial shadowy realm of arbitrary intellectual gymnastics: when Hegel says that a notion passes into its opposite, he should have said that a living, thinking being passes from one thought to another.

2) *Existentialists* from Kierkegaard onwards deplore Hegel's subordination of the individual, singular existence to the universality of a notion: in this way, concrete and unique individuals are reduced to mere dispensable paraphernalia of the movement of the abstract Notion.

3) *Materialists* predictably reject Hegel's idea that external material nature is just a moment in the self-deployment of Spirit: in an unexplained way, the Idea posits nature as its free self-externalization.

4) *Historicists* reject Hegel's metaphysical teleology: instead of opening up to the plurality and contingency of the historical process, Hegel reduces actual history to the external face of notional progress—for him, a single and all-encompassing Reason rules in history.

5) *Analytic philosophers* and *empiricists* make fun of Hegel as the hyperbolic exemplar of speculative madness, playing conceptual games which can in no way be experimentally tested: Hegel moves in a self-relating loop.

6) *Marxists* advocate the (in)famous inversion of the Hegelian dialectical process—standing on its head, it must be set back on its feet: ideas and notions are just the ideological superstructure of the material process of production which overdetermines all social life.

7) For traditional *liberals*, Hegel's "divinization" of the State as the "material existence of God" makes him (together with Plato) one of the main forerunners of the "closed society"—there is a straight line from Hegelian totality to political totalitarianism.

8) For some *religious moralists*, the Hegelian "coincidence of opposites" as well as his historicism lead to a nihilistic vision of society and history in

which there are no transcendent or stable moral values and in which a murderer is perceived as equal to his victim.

9) For (most of) the *deconstructionists*, the Hegelian "sublation" (*Aufhebung*) is the very model of how metaphysics, while acknowledging difference, dispersal, and otherness, again subsumes it into the One of the self-mediating Idea—it is against *Aufhebung* that deconstructionists assert an irreducible excess or remainder which can never be reintegrated into the One.

10) For the *Deleuzian* thought of productive difference, Hegel cannot think difference outside the frame of negativity—and negativity is the very operator of subsuming difference under the One; the Deleuzian formula is thus that Hegel should not even be criticized but simply forgotten.

Each of the three philosophers stands not only for an Event—the shattering encounter of an Idea; the emergence of a purely evental *cogito*, a crack in the great chain of being; the Absolute itself as an evental self-deployment, as the result of its own activity—they also stand for a moment of negativity or a cut—the normal flow of things is interrupted, another dimension breaks in. And they also stand for a moment of madness: the madness of being captivated by an Idea (like falling in love, or Socrates under the spell of his *daimon*), the madness at the heart of cogito (the "Night of the World"), and, of course, the ultimate "madness" of the Hegelian System, this Bacchanalian dance of concepts. So one can say that the philosophies which come after Plato, Descartes, or Hegel are all attempts to contain or control this excess, to renormalize it, inscribe it back into the normal flow of things.

If we stick to the textbook version of Plato's idealism as positing an immutable eternal order of Ideas, then indeed he can only appear to be denying the event as something that belongs to our unstable material reality and does not concern Ideas—but another reading is possible: to conceive the "Idea" as the event of the appearing of the suprasensible. Recall the well-known descriptions of Socrates caught in a hysterical seizure when struck by an Idea, standing frozen for hours, oblivious to the world around him—is this not an evental encounter *par excellence*? This same "madness" assumes a new dimension with Descartes: what one should always bear in mind when talking about the *cogito* is that we are dealing not with silly or extreme logical games ("imagine that you alone exist" …), but with the description of a very precise existential experience of radical self-withdrawal, or the reduction of all external reality to a vanishing illusion—an experience well known in psychoanalysis (as psychotic withdrawal) and in religious mysticism (under the name of the so-called "Night of the World").[5] After Descartes, this idea was deployed by Schelling in his basic insight that, prior to its assertion as the medium of the rational Word, the subject is the "infinite lack of being" (*unendliche Mangel an Sein*), the violent gesture of contraction that negates every being outside itself. The same idea also forms the core of Hegel's notion of madness: when Hegel determines madness to be a withdrawal from the actual world, the closing of the soul upon itself, its "contraction," cutting off of its links with external reality, he all too quickly conceives of this as a "regression" to the level of the "animal soul" still embedded in its natural environs and determined by the rhythm of nature (night and day, etc.). But does not this withdrawal, on the contrary, designate the severing of all links with the *Umwelt*, the end of the subject's immersion in its immediate natural environs, and, as such, is it not the founding gesture of "humanization"? Was not this withdrawal-into-self accomplished by Descartes with his universal doubt and reduction to the *cogito*, which also involves a passage through the moment of radical madness? We are thus back at the passage from the "Jenaer Realphilosophie" in which Hegel characterizes the experience of pure Self, of the contraction-into-self of the subject, as the "Night of the World," the eclipse of (constituted) reality. The symbolic order, the universe of the Word, logos, can only emerge from the experience of this abyss: as Hegel puts it, this inwardness of the pure self "must enter also into existence, become an object, oppose itself to this

---

5   The *cogito* as Descartes' starting point may appear as the very model of asserting the primacy of thinking subjectivity; however, the first thing that should draw our attention is the echo that Descartes' thought found from the very beginning among women—the "*cogito* has no sex" was the reaction of an early female reader. The first to deploy this feminist potential of Cartesianism was François Poullain de la Barre, a follower of Descartes who, after becoming a priest, converted to Protestantism. When the Edict of Fontainebleau revoked the Edict of Nantes, he was exiled in Geneva, where he applied Cartesian principles to the question of women and denounced injustice against women and championed social equality between women and men. In 1673, he published anonymously *De l'égalité des deux sexes, discours physique et moral où l'on voit l'importance de se défaire des préjugés*, showing that the inequality and the treatment that women undergo do not have a natural base, but proceed from cultural prejudice. He recommends that women receive a true education and also says all careers should be open to them, including scientific ones. One should add that a couple of years later, de la Barre systematically refuted his own argument and advocated the excellence of men.

innerness to be external; return to being. This is language as name-giving power ... Through the name the object as individual entity is born out of the I."[6] What we must be careful not to miss here is how Hegel's break with the Enlightenment tradition can be discerned in the reversal of the very metaphor for the subject: the subject is no longer the Light of Reason opposed to the non-transparent, impenetrable stuff of Nature, Tradition ... On the contrary, for Hegel, the gesture that opens up the space for the Light of Logos is absolute negativity, the "Night of the World," the point of utter madness in which fantasmatic apparitions of "partial objects" float around. Consequently, there is no subjectivity without this gesture of withdrawal; which is why Hegel is fully justified in inverting the standard question of how the fall or regression into madness is possible: the true question is rather how the subject is able to climb out of madness and reach "normality." That is to say, the withdrawal-into-self, the cutting-off of links to the environs, is followed by the construction of a symbolic universe which the subject projects onto reality as a kind of substitute-formation, destined to recompense us for the loss of the immediate, pre-symbolic real. However, as Freud himself asserted in his analysis of Daniel Paul Schreber's paranoia, the manufacturing of a substitute-formation that recompenses the subject for the loss of reality is the most succinct definition of the paranoid construction as an attempt to cure the subject of the disintegration of his universe. In short, the ontological necessity of "madness" resides in the fact that it is not possible to pass directly from the purely "animal soul," immersed in its natural environs, to "normal" subjectivity, dwelling in its symbolic virtual environs—the "vanishing mediator" between the two is the "mad" gesture of radical withdrawal from reality, which opens up the space for its symbolic (re)constitution. This brings us back to Schelling: following Kant, Schelling deployed the notion of the primordial decision-differentiation (*Ent-Scheidung*), the unconscious atemporal deed by means of which the subject chooses his eternal character which, afterwards, in his conscious-temporal life, he experiences as the inexorable necessity, as "the way he always was":

> The deed, once accomplished, sinks immediately into the unfathomable depth, thereby acquiring its lasting character. It is the same with the will which, once posited at the beginning and led into the outside, immediately has to sink into

---

6   G. W. F. Hegel, "Jenaer Realphilosophie," in *Fruehe politische Systeme*, Frankfurt: Ullstein 1974, p. 204.

the unconscious. This is the only way the beginning, the beginning that does not cease to be one, the truly eternal beginning, is possible. For here also it holds that the beginning should not know itself. Once done, the deed is eternally done. The decision that is in any way the true beginning should not appear before consciousness, it should not be recalled to mind, since this, precisely, would amount to its recall. He who, apropos of a decision, reserves for himself the right to drag it again to light, will never accomplish the beginning.[7]

With this abyssal act of freedom, the subject breaks up the rotary movement of the drives, the abyss of the Unnameable—in short, this deed is the very founding gesture of naming. Therein resides Schelling's philosophical revolution: he does not simply oppose the dark domain of the pre-ontological drives, the unnameable Real which can never be totally symbolized, to the domain of Logos, of the articulated Word which can never totally "force" it (like Badiou, Schelling insists that there is always a remainder of the unnameable Real—the "indivisible remainder"—which eludes symbolization). Rather, at its most radical, the unnameable Unconscious is not external to Logos, not its obscure background, but *the very act of Naming, the very founding gesture of Logos*. The greatest contingency, the ultimate act of abyssal madness, is the act of imposing a rational Necessity on the pre-rational chaos of the Real. The true point of "madness" is thus not the pure excess of the Night of the World, but the madness of the passage to the symbolic itself, of imposing a symbolic order onto the chaos of the Real.[8] If madness is constitutive, then *every* system of meaning is minimally paranoid, or "mad." Therein lies the lesson of David Lynch's *Straight Story*: what is the ridiculously pathetic perversity of figures like Bobby Peru in *Wild at Heart* or Frank in *Blue Velvet* compared to Alvin Straight's decision to cross the US Midwest on a lawnmower to visit a dying relative? Measured against this, Frank's and Bobby's enraged outbursts look like the impotent theatrics of old and sedate conservatives. In the same way,

---

7   F. W. J. von Schelling, *Ages of the World*, Ann Arbor: University of Michigan Press 1997, pp. 181–2. For a more detailed reading of this notion, see Chapter 1 of Slavoj Žižek, *The Indivisible Remainder*, London: Verso 1997.

8   Recall Freud who, in his analysis of the paranoid Judge Schreber, points out how the paranoiac's "system" is not madness, but a desperate attempt to *escape* madness—the disintegration of the symbolic universe—through an ersatz universe of meaning. See Sigmund Freud, "Psychoanalytic Notes Upon an Autobiographical Account of a Case of Paranoia," in *Three Case Histories*, New York: Touchstone 1996.

we might ask: what is the madness caused by the loss of reason compared to the madness of reason itself?

This step is the properly "Hegelian" one—which is why Hegel, the philosopher who made the most radical attempt to think the abyss of madness at the core of subjectivity, is also the philosopher who brought to its "mad" climax the philosophical System as the totality of meaning. This is also why, for very good reasons, "Hegel" stands in the eyes of common sense for the moment at which philosophy goes mad, exploding in a crazy pretense at "absolute knowledge."

"LA VÉRITÉ SURGIT DE LA MÉPRISE"

So what did Hegel intend with his notion of "absolute knowing"? It can only be grasped against the background of the immanence of false appearance to truth: take away the illusion and you lose the truth itself—a truth needs time to make a journey through illusions in order to form itself. We must put Hegel back into the series Plato–Descartes–Hegel which corresponds to the triad of Objective–Subjective–Absolute: Plato's Ideas are objective, Truth embodied; the Cartesian subject stands for the unconditional certainty of subjective self-awareness ... and Hegel, what does he add? If "subjective" is what is relative to our subjective limitations, and if "objective" is the way things really are, what does "absolute" add? Hegel's answer: the "absolute" does not add some deeper, more substantial, dimension—all it does is include (subjective) illusion in (objective) truth itself. The "absolute" standpoint makes us see how reality includes fiction (or fantasy), how the right choice only emerges after the wrong one:

> absolute knowing is the point at which consciousness reflexively assumes the fact that the share of illusion or fantasy is constitutive of the progress of truth. The truth is not located outside fantasy, since fantasy is the key element of its deployment. This insight compels us to conceive of absolute knowing as the point of traversing the fantasy ... absolute knowing is to be seen as the point at which fantasy acquires its place in philosophy ... If fantasy first appeared as a *negativum*, i.e., as the point of failure of a specific philosophical wager, it is now conceived as a positive moment of the deployment of truth.[9]

---

9   Jela Krečič, *Philosophy, Fantasy, Film*, doctoral thesis (in Slovene), University of Ljubljana 2008.

Hegel thus enjoins us to invert the entire history of philosophy, which constitutes a series of efforts to clearly differentiate *doxa* from true knowledge: for Hegel, *doxa* is a constitutive part of knowledge, and this is what makes truth temporal and evental. This evental character of truth involves a logical paradox deployed by Jean-Pierre Dupuy in his admirable text on Hitchcock's *Vertigo*:

> An object possesses a property x until the time t; after t, it is not only that the object no longer has the property x; it is that it is not true that it possessed x at any time. The truth-value of the proposition "the object O has the property x at the moment t" therefore depends on the moment when this proposition is enunciated.[10]

Note the precise formulation here: it is not that the truth-value of the proposition "the object O has the property x" depends on the time to which the proposition refers—*even when the time is specified, the truth-value depends on the time at which the proposition itself is enunciated*. Or, to quote the title of Dupuy's text, "When I die, nothing of our love will ever have existed." Think about marriage and divorce: the most intelligent argument for the right to divorce (proposed, among others, by none other than the young Marx) does not invoke vulgar claims such as "like all things, love attachments are not eternal, they too change over the course of time," etc.; rather, it concedes that indissolubility is part of the very notion of marriage. The argument is that divorce always has a retroactive scope: this means not only that the marriage is now annulled, but also something much more radical—the marriage should be annulled because *it never was a true marriage*. The same holds for Soviet communism: it is clearly insufficient to say that, in the years of "stagnation" under Brezhnev, it "exhausted its potential, failing to keep up with the times"; what its miserable end demonstrates is that it was in an historical deadlock *from its very beginning*.

This is why the properly Hegelian view is fundamentally *static*: things become what they always already are, what constantly changes are static totalities. What historicist-evolutionary "mobilism" fails to grasp is the (properly dialectical) point, made long ago by (among others) T. S. Eliot, regarding the fact that each truly new artistic phenomenon not only

---

10   Jean-Pierre Dupuy, "Quand je mourrai, rien de notre amour n'aura jamais éxisté," unpublished typescript of an intervention at the colloquium *Vertigo et la philosophie*, Ecole Normale Supérieure, Paris, October 14, 2005.

represents a break with the entire past, but retroactively changes the past itself. At every historical conjuncture, the present is not only the present, but also encompasses a perspective on the past immanent to it—after the disintegration of the Soviet Union in 1991, say, the October Revolution is no longer the same historical event, it is (for the triumphant liberal-capitalist view) no longer the beginning of a new progressive epoch in the history of humanity, but the beginning of a catastrophic deviation in that history, a deviation that came to an end in 1991. This is the ultimate lesson of Hegel's anti-"mobilism": dialectics has nothing whatsoever to do with a certain politics or practice being justified in or for a certain stage of development and then losing this justification in a later "higher" stage. Reacting to the revelations about Stalin's crimes at the twentieth congress of the Soviet Communist Party, Brecht noted that the same political agent who earlier played an important role in the revolutionary process (Stalin) now became an obstacle to it, and praised this as a proper "dialectical" insight. But we should thoroughly reject this logic. In the dialectical analysis of history, on the contrary, each new stage "rewrites the past" and retroactively de-legitimizes the previous one.[11]

Such retroactive de-legitimization makes "vanishing mediators" of past phenomena: although a past phenomenon can be a necessary moment in the emergence of a new form, its role becomes invisible once the New has arrived. Let us take an unlikely example: Ayn Rand's first novel written in English, *We the Living*, set in Petrograd between 1922 and 1925. Kira Argounova, the young daughter of a bourgeois family and a strong-willed independent spirit, manages to enroll in the Technological Institute where she aspires to fulfill her dream of becoming an engineer. At the Institute, Kira meets Andrei Taganov, an idealistic communist and high-ranking officer in the GPU (the secret police); the two share a mutual respect and admiration for each other in spite of their differing political beliefs. Kira finds Andrei to be the one person she can trust, and with whom she can discuss her most intimate thoughts and views. Not even her passionate lover, Leo Kovalensky—a handsome member of the nobility with a free spirit to match Kira's own—can fulfill this role for her. When Leo contracts tuberculosis and cannot get State help for his stay at the sanatorium, Kira feigns love for Andrei and agrees to become his mistress in order to secure his help in getting medical treatment for Leo. Months later, after Leo has been cured, he gets involved in black market speculation. Andrei is tipped

---

11   I resume here the line of thought from Chapter 4 of *Less Than Nothing*.

off about this venture and, unaware of Kira's love for Leo, arrests him for crimes against the State. Eventually he finds out about Kira's relationship with Leo, and the ensuing confrontation between Andrei and Kira is the most poignant scene in the story. When Kira tells Andrei that she has faked her love for him just to get support for Leo, her true love, his reaction is not the expected one of rage and vengeance, but one of regret at the suffering he has unknowingly caused Kira, and understanding of the depth of her love for Leo for whom she was sacrificing herself. In order to redress the situation, Andrei promises to bring Leo back to her; after Leo's release from the prison, Andrei loses his position in the Party and commits suicide.

Although staunchly anti-communist, the novel remains ambiguous: what is surprising is not only the highly ethical reaction of the Bolshevik hero Andrei when he learns that Kira did not love him; even more surprising is the fact that this ethical reaction seems to be part of his communist *persona*. What is evil here is not simply the Bolshevik revolution as such, but its betrayal, which culminates in the pact between the revolutionaries who have betrayed their vocation and the old corrupt bourgeoisie. It is as if, although the revolution was flawed in its very essence and its corruption was unavoidable, the only path to truth leads *through* revolution: it is Andrei, a communist (and even a GPU officer) who, confronted with a tribunal, gives the original version of the staple Randian speech praising the individual spirit and rejecting collectivism, a speech whose later versions are Howard Roark's in front of the jury in *Fountainhead* and John Galt's long radio speech in *Atlas Shrugged*. Andrei is thus a kind of vanishing mediator: the proto-figure of the Randian hero whose communist roots, still visible here, disappear in her late "mature" anti-communism. The first step in an effective critique of ideology is to render such vanishing mediators visible again—in the case of Rand, to show how even an extreme anti-communist stance was secretly based on communist premises. (At a different level, the same holds for *The Fountainhead*: is not the architecture of Howard Roark, the novel's hero modeled on Frank Lloyd Wright, also uncannily similar to the Soviet modernism of the 1920s?)

Not the least irony of such retroactive de-legitimization of communism in Rand's work is that the same procedure was widely practiced by the target of her criticism, Stalinism itself. This is why, in contrast to Leninism, Stalinism had no use for the category of the renegade: for Lenin, Kautsky was a "renegade," which meant that he was once one of us, but then betrayed the Cause; in Stalinism, however, there are no renegades, only traitors. When Stalin moved against Trotsky in the mid-1920s, it did not mean that he considered Trotsky a "renegade," someone who had served the revolution in the past but then lost his way—on the contrary, Trotsky became a "vanishing mediator" of the revolutionary process, and the Stalinists claimed that he had sabotaged the revolutionary struggle from the very beginning, totally ignoring his role in organizing the Red Army.

This is why Hegelian dialectics is not a vulgar evolutionism according to which a phenomenon may be justified in its own time, but deserves to disappear when its time passes: the "eternity" of dialectics means that the de-legitimization is always retroactive, what disappears "in itself" always deserved to disappear. This brings us to the crux of the matter, the crux which is, as expected, the subject itself. *The Hegelian-Lacanian subject is the ultimate "vanishing mediator"*: it is never present here-and-now, in every present constellation it already vanishes in its symbolic representation. In other words, the "subject" is an X which always already vanishes in its representations, and this is what makes this concept an eminently dialectical one.

How is this circle of changing the past possible without recourse to time travel? The solution was already proposed by Henri Bergson: of course one cannot change the past reality, but what one can change is the virtual dimension of the past—when something radically New emerges, this New retroactively creates its own possibility, its own causes or conditions.[12] A potentiality can be inserted into (or withdrawn from) past reality. Falling in love, for example, changes the past: it is as if I *always already* loved you, our love was destined, an "answer of the Real." My present love thus causes the past which gave birth to it. The same temporal paradox characterizes all events proper, including political ones—Rosa Luxemburg was well aware of this when, in her polemic against Eduard Bernstein, she proffered two arguments against the revisionist fear that the proletariat would take power prematurely, before the circumstances were ripe:

> In the first place, it is impossible to imagine that a transformation as formidable as the passage from capitalist society to socialist society can be realized in one happy act ... The socialist transformation supposes a long and stubborn struggle, in the course of which, it is quite probable the proletariat will be repulsed more than once so that for the first time, from the viewpoint of the final outcome of the struggle, it will have necessarily come to power "too early."

---

12   For a more detailed elaboration of this Bergsonian line of thought, see Chapter 9 of Slavoj Žižek, *In Defense of Lost Causes*, London: Verso 2007.

In the second place, it will be impossible to avoid the "premature" conquest of State power by the proletariat precisely because these "premature" attacks of the proletariat constitute a factor and indeed a very important factor, creating the political conditions of the final victory. In the course of the political crisis accompanying its seizure of power, in the course of the long and stubborn struggles, the proletariat will acquire the degree of political maturity permitting it to obtain in time a definitive victory of the revolution. Thus these "premature" attacks of the proletariat against the State power are in themselves important historic factors helping to provoke and determine the *point* of the definite victory. Considered from this viewpoint, the idea of a "premature" conquest of political power by the labouring class appears to be a polemic absurdity derived from a mechanical conception of the development of society, and positing for the victory of the class struggle a point fixed *outside* and *independent of* the class struggle.

Since the proletariat is not in the position to seize power in any other way than "prematurely," since the proletariat is absolutely obliged to seize power once or several times "too early" before it can maintain itself in power for good, the objection to the "premature" conquest of power is at bottom nothing more than a *general opposition to the aspiration of the proletariat to possess itself of State power.*[13]

There is no meta-language: no outside-position from which the agent can calculate how many "premature" attempts are needed to get at the right moment—why? Because this is a case of truth which arises out of misrecognition (*la vérité surgit de la méprise*, as Lacan put it) where the "premature" attempts transform the very space or measure of temporality: the subject "jumps ahead" and takes a risk in making a move before its conditions are fully met.[14] The subject's engagement in the symbolic order coils the linear flow of time in both directions: it involves precipitation as well as

---

13 Rosa Luxemburg, *Reform or Revolution*, Chapter VIII, available at marxists.org.

14 This, perhaps, is what makes the practice of the short session introduced by Lacan problematic. The idea is clear: Lacan noticed that, in the standard 50-minute session, the patient prattles on, and only in the final minutes, when the shadow of the end, of being cut off by the analyst, draws closer, does the patient start to panic and produce some valuable material. So the idea was to simply skip the long period of lost time and limit the session to the final minutes when, under pressure, something actually happens. The question is whether those first forty-five minutes of lost time function as a gestation period necessary for the content of the final minutes to explode.

retroactivity (things retroactively become what they are, the identity of a thing only emerges when the thing is in delay with regard to itself)—in short, every act is by definition too early and, simultaneously, too late. One has to know how to wait, and not lose one's nerves: if one acts too fast, the act turns into a *passage à l'acte*, a violent forward-flight to avoid deadlock. If one misses the moment and acts too late, the act loses its quality as an act—as a radical intervention after which "nothing remains the way it was"—and becomes just a local change within the order of being, part of the normal flow of things. The problem is, of course, that an act always occurs simultaneously too fast (the conditions are never fully ripe, one has to succumb to the urgency to intervene) and too late (the very urgency of the act signals that we come too late, that we always already should have acted). In short, *there is no right moment to act*—if we wait for the right moment, the act is reduced to an occurrence in the order of being.

THE CIRCLE OF BECOMING

It is because of this temporal complication that, in Hegel, everything becomes eventful: a thing is the result of the process (event) of its own becoming, and this processuality de-substantializes it. Spirit itself is thus radically de-substantialized: it is not a positive counter-force to nature, a different substance which gradually breaks and shines through the inert natural stuff, it is *nothing but* this process of freeing-itself-from. Hegel directly disowns the notion of Spirit as some kind of positive Agent which underlies the process:

> Spirit is usually spoken of as subject, as doing something, and apart from what it does, as this motion, this process, as still something particular, its activity being more or less contingent ... it is of the very nature of spirit to be this absolute liveliness, this process, to proceed forth from naturality, immediacy, to sublate, to quit its naturality, and to come to itself, and *to free itself*, it being itself only as it comes to itself as such a product of itself; *its actuality being merely that it has made itself into what it is.*[15]

The materialist reversal of Hegel in Ludwig Feuerbach and young Marx rejects this self-referential circularity, dismissing it as a case of idealist

---

15   G. W. F. Hegel, *Philosophie des subjektiven Geistes*, Dordrecht: Riedel 1978, pp. 6–7.

mystification, and returns to the Aristotelian ontology of substantial entities endowed with essential qualities: for Marx, man is a *Gattungswesen*
(being-of-genus) which asserts its life by realizing its "essential forces."
Robert Pippin exemplifies in what sense the Hegelian Spirit is "its own
result" by referring to the finale of Proust's *Recherche*: how does Marcel
finally "become what he is"? By way of breaking with the Platonic illusion
that his Self can be "secured by anything, any value or reality that transcends the wholly temporal human world":

> It was ... by failing to become "what a writer is," to realize his inner "writer's
> essence"—as if that role must be some transcendentally important or even a defi-
> nite, substantial role—that Marcel realizes that such a becoming is important
> by *not* being secured by the transcendent, *by* being wholly temporal and finite,
> always and everywhere in suspense, and yet nonetheless capable of some illumi-
> nation ... If Marcel has become who he is, and this somehow continuous with
> and a product of the experience of his own past, it is unlikely that we will be able
> to understand that by appeal to a substantial or underlying self, now discovered,
> or even by appeal to successor substantial selves, each one linked to the future
> and past by some sort of self-regard.[16]

It is thus only by fully accepting this abyssal circularity, in which the search
itself creates what it is looking for, that the Spirit "finds itself." This is why
the verb "failing" used by Pippin is to be given full weight: the failure to
achieve the (immediate) goal is absolutely crucial to, constitutive of, this
process—or, again, as Lacan put it: *la vérité surgit de la méprise*. If, then,
"it is *only* as a result of itself that it is spirit,"[17] this means that the standard
talk about the Hegelian Spirit alienating itself from itself and then recognizing itself in its otherness and thus reappropriating its content, is deeply
misleading: the Self to which spirit returns is produced in the very movement of this return; or, that to which the process of return is returning is
produced by the very process of returning. Which brings us to the specific temporality of the symbolic event: the abrupt reversal of "not yet" into
"always already." There is always a gap between formal and material change:
things gradually change at the material level, and this change is subterranean, like the work of a mole; when the struggle erupts into the open, the
mole has already completed its job and the battle is de facto over—all one

---

16   Robert Pippin, *The Persistence of Subjectivity*, Cambridge: Cambridge
University Press 2005, pp. 332–4.
17   Hegel, *Philosophie des subjektiven Geistes*, p. 7.

has to do is to remind those in power to look down and see that there is no longer any ground under their feet, and the whole edifice collapses like a house of cards. Famously, when Margaret Thatcher was asked what her greatest achievement was, she snapped back: "New Labour." And she was right: her triumph was that even her political enemies had adopted her basic economic policies—the true triumph is not the victory over the enemy but occurs when the enemy itself starts to use your language, so that your ideas form the foundation for the entire field. The same holds for the great polemics between John Locke and Robert Filmer: against the Enlightenment notion that all men are created equal in the state of nature by God, and that as such they possess a series of natural rights, Filmer claimed that the government of a family by the father is the true origin and model of all government. In the beginning God gave authority to Adam; from Adam this authority was inherited by Noah, and so on, so that the patriarchs inherited the absolute power that they exercised over their families and servants. It is from these patriarchs, Filmer argued, that all kings and governors derive their authority, which is therefore absolute and founded upon divine right. The problem was that, in engaging in this kind of rational argumentation, Filmer was already moving onto the terrain determined by his opponent, the terrain of the natural history of society.

This brings us back to the topic of (falling in) love, which is characterized by the same temporal gap. In one of Henry James's stories, the hero says about a woman close to him: "She already loves him, she just doesn't know it yet." Here we have a kind of Freudian counterpart of Benjamin Libet's famous experiment concerning free will: even before we consciously decide (say, to move a finger), the appropriate neuronal processes are already under way—which means that our conscious decision merely takes note of what is already going on (adding its superfluous authorization to what is in fact a *fait accompli*). With Freud too, decision is prior to consciousness—but the decision is unconscious rather than a purely objective process. Freud here rejoins Schelling for whom a truly free decision is also unconscious, which is why we never fall in love in the present (time): after a (usually long) process of subterranean gestation, we all of a sudden become aware that we (already) *are* in love. The Fall (into love) never *happens*—at a certain moment, it has *always already happened*.

In the general economy of Wagner's work, the long narratives that interrupt the flow of events—where the singer recapitulates what went on before the opera, or in the previous opera or act—cannot but appear as a symptom of the inherent failure of the *Gesamtkunstwerk* project: instead

of the organic *Darstellung*, the direct rendering of events, we get the artificial *Vorstellung*, their representation.[18] What if, however, they obey a very
precise performative logic of the "declarative"? One does something, one
declares oneself as the one who did it, and, on the basis of this declaration,
one does something new—here the proper moment of subjective transformation occurs at the moment of declaration, not at the moment of the act.
In other words, the truly New emerges through the narrative, the apparently purely reproductive retelling of what happened—it is this retelling
that opens up the space (the possibility) of acting in a new way. Furious
about his condition, a worker explodes against his master (participates
in a wildcat strike, etc.); however, it is only in the aftermath of the explosion, when he recounts it as an act of class struggle, that he subjectively
transforms himself into a revolutionary subject, and on the basis of that
transformation he can then go on acting as a true revolutionary. Nowhere
is this "performative" role of retelling more palpable than in what fools
consider the most boring passages in Wagner's musical dramas—the long
narratives in which the hero recapitulates what has gone on up to that point.
As Alain Badiou has pointed out,[19] these long narratives are the true sites of
dramatic shift—in the course of them, we witness the narrator's profound
subjective transformation. Exemplary is here Wotan's great monologue in
Act II of *Die Walküre*: the Wotan who emerges from his own narrative is
not the same Wotan as the one who embarked upon it, but a Wotan determined to act in a new way—Wotan sees and accepts his ultimate failure,
and decides to desire his own end. And, as Badiou has also noted, the role
of the musical texture is crucial here: it is the music that changes (what may
sound like) a report on the events and state of the world into the deployment of the subjective metamorphosis of the narrator himself. One can also
see how right Wagner was to reduce the actual act (a battle, usually) to an
insignificant occurrence to be disposed of quickly, preferably even off stage
(as is the case at the beginning of Act II of *Parsifal*): it is impossible not to
note how strangely the brevity of the actual fights in Wagner's works—e.g.,
the brief duel between Lohengrin and Telramund in Act III of *Lohengrin*,
or the duel between Tristan and Melot at the end of Act III of *Tristan*—
contrasts with the long duration of the narratives and declarations.

---

18   For this idea, see David J. Levin, *Richard Wagner, Fritz Lang, and the
Nibelungen*, Princeton: Princeton University Press 1998.

19   In his seminar on Wagner at the *École Normale Supérieure*, May 14, 2005.

Das Unbehagen in der Sexualität

This, finally, brings us to the Freudian revolution, which can also be formulated as an insight into the evental character of sexuality, or the immanence of false appearance to truth in sexuality. The story begins with the strange case of infantile sexuality, one of Freud's key discoveries—as Gérard Wajcman has perspicuously observed, in our era, which presents itself as permissive, as violating all sexual taboos and repressions, thereby making psychoanalysis obsolete, Freud's fundamental insight into the sexuality of the child is strangely ignored:

> The sole remaining prohibition, the one sacred value in our society that seems to remain, is to do with children. It is forbidden to touch a hair on their little blond heads, as if children had rediscovered that angelic purity on which Freud managed to cast some doubt. And it is undoubtedly the diabolical figure of Freud that we condemn today, seeing him as the one who, by uncovering the relationship of childhood to sexuality, quite simply depraved our virginal childhoods. In an age when sexuality is exhibited on every street corner, the image of the innocent child has, strangely, returned with a vengeance.[20]

What, then, is so scandalous about infantile sexuality? It is not the simple fact that even children, presumed innocent, are already sexualized. The scandal lies in two features (which, of course, are the two sides of the same coin). First, infantile sexuality is a weird phenomenon which is neither biological, nor biologically grounded, nor part of symbolic/cultural norms. This weirdness, however, is not sublated in adult or "normal" sexuality, which is itself also always distorted, displaced:

> when it comes to sexuality, man is subject to the greatest of paradoxes: what is acquired through the drives precedes what is innate and instinctual, in such a way that, at the time it emerges, instinctual sexuality, which is adaptive, finds the seat already taken, as it were, by infantile drives, already and always present in the unconscious.[21]

---

20   Gérard Wajcman, "Intimate Extorted, Intimate Exposed," *Umbr(a)* (2007), p. 47.

21   Jean Laplanche, "Sexuality and Attachment in Metapsychology," in D. Widlöcher, ed., *Infantile Sexuality and Attachment*, New York: Other Press 2002, p. 49.

And the reason for this strange excess is the link between sexuality and cognition. Against the standard idea of sexuality as some kind of instinctual vital force which must be repressed/sublimated through the work of culture since, in its raw state, it poses a threat to the latter, one should assert a link between sexuality and cognition which also throws a new light on sexuality and politics. The old motto of the 1960s, "the personal is political," should be thoroughly rethought:[22] the point is no longer that even the intimate sphere of sexual relations is pervaded by power relations of servitude and domination. The point, rather, is to refocus on the most elementary feature of the political: the universe of politics is by definition ontologically open, and political decisions are by definition made "without sufficient reason," or, more precisely, in politics, we always move in a minimal vicious cycle where a decision retroactively posits its own reasons. This is why political disputes can never be settled through rational debate and the comparison of arguments: the same argument counts differently within a different position. In a typical political debate, one person proposes an argument that, according to their opponent, contains a fatal flaw ("Don't you see that what you are claiming means ..."), but the interlocutor replies: "But that's precisely why I am for it!" Politics is not applied pre-existing neutral knowledge, since all knowledge is already partial, "colored" by one's commitment. There is no ultimate neutral Norm to which both sides could refer ("human rights," "freedom" ...), because their struggle is precisely a struggle about what this Norm is (what freedom or a human right consists in—for a conservative liberal, freedom and equality are antagonistic, while for a leftist, they are the two facets of the same *égaliberté*). In other words, politics is structured around a "missing link," it presupposes a kind of ontological openness, a gap or antagonism, and this same gap or ontological openness is at work also in sexuality—in both cases, a relationship is never guaranteed by an encompassing universal Signifier. In the same way that there is no political relationship (between parties engaged in a struggle), there is also no sexual relationship.

It is the search for this "missing link" that sustains the link between sexuality and knowledge, that makes cognitive probing an irreducible component of human sexuality. Such cognitive probing and questioning go against the grain of the predominant attitude today, which either reduces sexuality to a particular problem of functional satisfaction (Can the man

---

22   In what follows, I rely extensively on Alenka Zupančič, "Die Sexualität innerhalb der Grenzen der bloßen Vernunft" (unpublished manuscript).

get a full erection? Can the woman relax enough to get a full orgasm?), or—again in a reductionist way—treats it as an expression of deeper emotional or existential problems (a couple's sex life is unsatisfactory because they live alienated lives, are caught up in consumerist perfectionism, are harboring repressed emotional traumas, etc.).

However, a further step has to be taken here in order to avoid the last and perhaps most dangerous trap. It is not enough to reassert infantile sexuality as a plural multitude of polymorphously perverse drives which are then totalized by the Oedipal genital norm. Infantile sexuality is not a truth or base (or some kind of original productive site) of sexuality which is subsequently oppressed/totalized/regulated by the genital norm. In other words, one should absolutely not apply to sexuality the standard Deleuzian topos of the productive molecular multitude on which the higher molar order parasitizes. Sexuality is defined by the fact that *there is no sexual relationship*, all polymorphously perverse play of partial drives takes place against the background of this impossibility/antagonism. The sexual act (copulation) thus has two sides: the obverse of the orgasmic culminating moment of sexuality is the deadlock of impossibility—it is in performing the act of copulation that the subject experiences the impossibility, the immanent blockage, that saps sexuality, which is why copulation cannot stand on its own, but needs support from partial drives (from caressing and kissing to other "minor" erotic practices like slapping and squeezing), as well as from the web of fantasies. The act of copulation is thus a little bit like the Castle from Kafka's novel of the same name: viewed up close, it is a heap of old dirty cottages, so one has to withdraw to a proper distance to see it in its fascinating presence. Viewed in its immediate materiality, the act of copulation is a rather vulgar set of stupid repetitive movements; viewed through the mist of fantasies, it is the height of intense pleasure. In Lacanian terms, if the front side of the act of copulation is S_1, the Master-Signifier which totalizes the series of sexual activities, its obverse is $S(\cancel{A})$, the signifier of the "barred Other," of the antagonism/blockage of the order of sexuality.

The original site of fantasy is that of the small child overhearing or witnessing parental coitus and unable to make sense of it: what does this all *mean*, the intense whispers, the strange sounds in the bedroom, etc.? So the child fantasizes a scene that would account for these strangely intense fragments—recall the best-known scene in David Lynch's *Blue Velvet*, in which Kyle MacLachlan, hidden in the closet, witnesses the weird sexual interplay between Isabella Rossellini and Dennis Hopper. What he sees can be read as a fantasmatic supplement conjured up to account for what he hears: hearing the intense breathing accompanying sexual activity, he fantasizes seeing Hopper putting on the mask and taking deep breaths. And the fundamental paradox of the fantasy is that the subject never really "grows up," that one never arrives at the moment when one can say "OK, now I fully understand it—my parents were having sex, so I no longer need a fantasy!"—*this*, among other things, is what Lacan meant with his *il n'y a pas de rapport sexuel*. The comical effect of fantasizing occurs when the knowledge about the role of copulation gets combined with infantile speculation—for example, a friend of mine once told me that, after learning that copulation plays a role in making children, he concocted a myth to combine this knowledge with his belief that children were delivered by storks: while a couple is making love, they are secretly observed by a stork, and if the stork likes how their bodies dance and move, it brings them a child as a reward ...

According to the common view, psychoanalysis tells us that whatever we are doing, we are secretly "thinking about *that*"—sexuality is the universal hidden reference of every activity. However, the true Freudian question is: what are we thinking when we *are* "doing that"? It is sex itself which, in order to be palatable, has to be sustained by a fantasy. The logic here is the same as that of a native American tribe who have discovered that all dreams have some hidden sexual meaning—all, that is, *except the overtly sexual ones*: here, precisely, one has to look for another meaning. Any contact with a "real," flesh-and-blood other, any sexual pleasure that we find in touching *another* human being, is not something self-evident, but is inherently traumatic, and can be sustained only insofar as this other enters the subject's fantasy frame. This role of fantasy hinges on the fact that "there is no sexual relationship," no universal formula or matrix guaranteeing harmonious sexual relations with one's partner: every subject has to invent a fantasy of his own, a "private" formula for the sexual relationship—for a man, his relationship with a woman is possible only insofar as she fits his formula. This, then, is why adults also need sexual education—perhaps even more than children. What they have to learn is not the technique of the act, but what to fantasize while they are doing it. Each couple has to invent their specific formula. Indeed, to paraphrase Dogberry's advice to Seacoal from Shakespeare's *Much Ado About Nothing*, to which Marx already referred in *Capital*: "To be able to enjoy sex is the gift of fortune; but reading and writing comes by nature."

This means that we should also reject the dominant view according to which hegemonic ideology in all its aspects (social, legal, economic, ethical, religious) privileges "natural" sexuality (standard reproductive copulation) and tries to repress or suppress the polymorphously perverse sexuality of partial drives which is considered asocial and dangerous, and is tolerated only as a subordinate preparatory moment of "normal" sexual activity (fondling and kissing as a foreplay, etc.). The best argument against this predominant view is to be found in the history of its greatest advocate, Christianity:

> Christ, even when resurrected from the dead, is valued for his body, and his body is the means by which communion in his presence is incorporation—oral drive—with which Christ's wife, the Church as it is called, contents itself very well, having nothing to expect from copulation.
>
> In everything that followed from the effects of Christianity, particularly in art—and it's in this respect that I coincide with the "baroquism" with which I accept to be clothed—everything is exhibition of the body evoking *jouissance*—and you can lend credence to the testimony of someone who has just come back from an orgy of churches in Italy—but without copulation.[23]

Lacan is very clear here: one should reject the endlessly repeated "critical" thesis that Catholic sexual morality imposes a "normative heterosexuality" on the subversive and destabilizing "polymorphous sexuality" of humans. In contrast to the idea that partial drives are masturbatory, asocial, and so on, while genital sexuality grounds the social bond (the family as elementary social form), one should insist that there is nothing necessarily asocial in partial drives: they function as the glue of society, the very *stuff of communion*, in contrast to the heterosexual couple which is—as Freud emphasizes in *Group Psychology and the Analysis of the Ego*—effectively asocial, isolating itself from the community, and is therefore distrusted by the church and the army, Freud's two models of the social bond (recall the implicit military rule: yes to rape, no to permanent couples):

> directly sexual tendencies are unfavorable to the formation of groups ... Two people coming together for the purpose of sexual satisfaction, in so far as they seek for solitude, are making a demonstration against the herd instinct, the group feeling. The more they are in love, the more completely they suffice for each other ... In the great artificial groups, the church and the army, there is no

---

23   Jacques Lacan, *On Feminine Sexuality, the Limits of Love and Knowledge (Seminar XX)*, New York: Norton 1999, p. 113.

room for woman as a sexual object. The love relation between men and women remains outside these organizations. Even where groups are formed which are composed of both men and women the distinction between the sexes plays no part.[24]

And, to quote the concise comment on these lines by Alenka Zupančič:

So there is something profoundly disruptive at stake in copulation. For the kind of (social) bond it proposes, Christianity doesn't need the latter, which functions as the superfluous element, something on top of what would be (ideally) needed, and hence as disturbing. Indeed, "natural" copulation is utterly banned from the religious imaginary, whereas the latter doesn't recede from, for example, images of canonized saints eating the excrement of another person. If looked at from this perspective, Christianity is indeed all about "*jouissance* of the body," about the body (of God) as constituting another person's *jouissance*. Partial drives and the satisfaction they procure are rather abundantly present, and in this sense one would be justified in claiming that in its libidinal aspect the Christian religion massively relies on what belongs to the register of "infantile sexuality": satisfaction and bonding by way of partial objects, with the exclusion of sexual coupling. Pure enjoyment, "enjoyment for the sake of enjoyment," is not exactly what is banned here; what is banned, or repressed, is its link with sexuality, particularly in the form of "copulation."[25]

Christianity thus acknowledges the polymorphously perverse satisfactions of drives, but it *desexualizes* them, desexualizes the pleasures they provide. Pleasures as such are not problematic: Christian literature abounds with descriptions of the ecstatic heavenly pleasures provided by meditation, prayers, and rituals, but it cuts them off thoroughly from sexuality. The irony here is that the greatest analyst and critic of the Christian mode of subjectivization, Michel Foucault, does exactly the same as Christianity did inasmuch as he endeavors to assert pleasure beyond the domain of sexuality. The next question is, of course: *what* does the church repress in repressing copulation? It is not sexual pleasure as such ("the lust of animal copulation") which isolates the couple from its community, it is not raw natural pleasure that has to be cultivated if a human being is to deploy its

---

24   Sigmund Freud, *Group Psychology and the Analysis of the Ego*, Chapter XII, Postscript, available at bartleby.com.
25   Zupančič, "Die Sexualität."

spiritual potential, but the very metaphysical dimension of sexuality. That is to say, far from being the natural foundation of human lives, sexuality is the very terrain on which humans detach themselves from nature: the idea of sexual perversion or of a deadly sexual passion is totally foreign to the animal universe. Here, Hegel himself commits an error by his own standards: he notes how, by way of culture, the natural substance of sexuality is cultivated, sublated, mediated—as humans we no longer just engage in sex for procreation, we become involved in complex processes of seduction and marriage by means of which sexuality becomes an expression of the spiritual bond between a man and a woman, etc. However, what Hegel misses is how, within the human condition, sexuality is not only transformed or civilized, but, much more radically, *changed in its very substance*: it is no longer the instinctual drive to reproduce, but a drive that is now thwarted as to its natural goal (reproduction) and thereby explodes into an infinite, properly metaphysical, passion. The becoming-cultural of sexuality is thus not the becoming-cultural of nature, but the attempt to domesticate a properly unnatural excess of the metaphysical sexual passion. This excess of negativity discernible in sex, and apropos the rabble, is the very dimension of "unruliness" identified by Kant as the violent freedom on account of which man, in contrast to animals, needs a master. So it is not just that sexuality is the animal substance which is "sublated" into civilized modes and rituals, gentrified, disciplined, etc.—the excess of sexuality which threatens to explode "civilized" constraints, sexuality as unconditional Passion, is itself the result of Culture. In the terms of Wagner's *Tristan*: civilization is not only the universe of the Day, of the rituals and codes of honor that bind us, but is the Night itself, the infinite passion in which the two lovers want to dissolve their ordinary daily existence. Animals know no such passion. In this way, civilization retroactively posits or transforms its own natural presupposition: Culture retroactively "denaturalizes" nature itself, and this is what Freud called the Id, the libido. This is how, here also, in opposing its natural obstacle, natural substance, Spirit fights itself, its own essence.

Is humanity then the exception, the curve of the drive which breaks out of the instinctual animal balance? Is the ultimate horizon of our thought this excess/disturbance that brings about the transformation or denaturalization of instinct into drive? If so, then we remain in the standard opposition between nature and the human excess. But we should take a step further here: pre-human reality is itself "exceptional," incomplete, unbalanced, and this ontological gap or incompleteness emerges "as such" with humanity. (This path was outlined by Schelling, Benjamin, and quantum physics.) Man is thus more literally the exception of nature: in humanity, the exception constitutive of nature appears as such. It is as if the logic of the constitutive exception is at work here in a different version, that of the "part of no-part": precisely as the disturbance of nature, humanity gives body to nature as such, in its universality.

At this crucial point we thus encounter the ultimate temptation to be avoided: the temptation to account for ontological negativity, for the rupture introduced by sexuality, in terms of the contrast between animal and human sexuality. Lacan himself was not immune to this standard topos: throughout his work, he repeatedly varies the motif of negativity and rupture introduced into the world of natural copulation by human sexuality. The very distinction between instinct and drive can be read in this way: animals possess instinctual knowledge which tells them when and how to copulate, for them copulation is simply part of the natural circuit of life, while we humans are radically disoriented, lacking the instinctual coordinates for sexual life, which is why we have to learn how to do it, relying on culturally structured scenarios: "there is sexual instinct in nature, but not in human beings (who are the point of exception in respect to nature). Humanity, at its most fundamental level, is a deviation from Nature."[26] It is along these lines that Gérard Wajcman explains why we find watching wildlife documentaries on TV so endlessly pleasurable: they provide a glimpse into a utopian world in which no language and training are needed, a "harmonious society" (as they would say today in China) in which everyone spontaneously knows their role:

> Man is a denatured animal. We are animals sick with language. And how sometimes we long for a cure. But just shutting up won't do it. You can't just wish your way into animality. So it is then, as a matter of consolation, that we watch the animal channels and marvel at a world untamed by language. The animals get us to hear a voice of pure silence. Nostalgia for the fish life. Humanity seems to have been hit by Cousteau syndrome.[27]

There is however another, more radical and properly Hegelian, way to understand the dislocation of sexuality: what if balanced "natural" sexuality is a human myth, a retroactive projection? What if this image of nature is the ultimate human myth, the ultimate "invented tradition"? Lacan himself

26   Zupančič, "Die Sexualität."
27   Gérard Wajcman, "The Animals that Treat Us Badly," *lacanian ink* 33, p. 131.

is divided here: sometimes he claims that "animals know," that they possess instinctual knowledge about sexuality; sometimes (apropos the *lamella*, for example) he claims that there is a lack already in natural sexual difference: the *lamella* is "what is subtracted from the living being by virtue of the fact that it is subject to the cycle of sexed reproduction,"[28] so already in natural sex there is a loss or a deadlock, some kind of dislocation or negativity is already at work in nature itself, in the very heart of sexual reproduction:

> There seems to be something in nature itself that is dramatically wrong at this point. The problem is not that nature is "always already cultural," but rather that nature lacks something to be Nature (our Other) in the first place. One way of putting it is to say that there is no sexual instinct, that is to say no knowledge ("law") inherent in sexuality which would be able to guide it.[29]

Human sexuality is thus not an exception with regard to nature, a pathological dislocation of natural instinctual sexuality, but *the point at which the dislocation/impossibility that pertains to sexual copulation appears as such.* In what precise form? Both humans and sexed animals "don't know," that is, both lack a firm and stable instinctual foundation of their sexuality; the difference is that animals do not know that they do not know, they are simply disoriented, at a loss, while humans know that they do not know—they *register* their not-knowing and go in search of knowing (this search is what "infantile sexuality" is about). In Hegelese, we could say that, in the passage from sexed animals to humans, not-knowing passes from the In-itself to the For-itself, to its reflexive registration; but we are not talking here about consciousness, about "becoming aware of" our not-knowing. This registration is precisely unconscious: "What distinguishes the human animal is not that it is conscious, or aware of this natural lack of knowledge (the lack of sexual knowledge in nature), but that it is 'unconscious of it.'"[30]

Over a decade ago, Donald Rumsfeld famously engaged in a little bit of amateur philosophizing about the relationship between the known and the unknown: "There are known knowns. These are things we know that we know. There are known unknowns. That is to say, there are things that we know we don't know. But there are also unknown unknowns. There are things we don't know we don't know." What he forgot to add was the

---

28   Jacques Lacan, *The Four Fundamental Concepts of Psychoanalysis*, New York: Norton 1998, p. 198.

29   Zupančič, "Die Sexualität."

30   Ibid.

crucial fourth term: the "unknown knowns," things we do not know that we know—which is precisely the Freudian unconscious, the "knowledge which doesn't know itself," as Lacan used to say. Here enters a further complication, however: if we say just this, the way is still open for some kind of Jungian or New Age notion of the Unconscious as the secret treasury of a profound knowledge about ourselves, of our innermost truth, so that the goal of a treatment is to make the "voyage inside" and discover the hidden treasure of a wisdom buried deep in us. The Freudian unconscious, on the contrary, is not simply unknown knowledge, but an *unknown knowledge about not-knowing*: what we unconsciously know is that we lack knowledge about sexuality, the traumatic fact that we obfuscate with myths and fantasies about the sexual relationship.

Animal sexuality may appear to be stable and instinctually regulated because sexed animals are like the proverbial cartoon cat above the precipice—they don't fall, they think their sexuality works, because they don't look down and register the abyss beneath them, because they are not "unconscious of" the deadlock of sexuality. Here, however, we reach another key point: is their not-knowing like plain coffee, or is it like coffee without x ...—are the animal's "unknown unknowns" simply a direct absence of knowing, a pure innocent not-knowing, or is there already at work in them a kind of obscure longing for knowing, for registering the lack or abyss?[31] The answer is that animals do not know they do not know, but this should not deceive us: *they still do not know.* Even animal not-knowing is thus not the same as an absolutely external not-knowing: animal not-knowing concerns their own mess or lack. In other words, yes, man is a wound of nature, but literally and radically: a wound of nature itself—in man, the innermost feature of nature is registered.

The Bible is thus on the right track when it links sexuality to knowledge: humans become sexed after Adam eats from the tree of knowledge, the biblical term for having sex with a woman is to "know her," etc. Recall the motif of an older experienced woman who introduces a younger man to sex—in Robert Siodmak's 1949 *noir, Criss Cross,* when a son defends his mistress, the *femme fatale,* against his mother's reproaches, claiming she is just a poor and uneducated girl, his mother warns him: "In some ways she

31   What we should bear in mind here is the fact that the distinction Nature/Culture is a distinction *within* nature, so that every gesture of opposing culture to nature has to fetishize nature minimally: the only consistent naturalism is to see the specifically human dimension as part of nature. However, once we are within the horizon of meaning, the distinction Nature/Culture becomes a cultural one.

knows more than Einstein." The catch here is that, precisely, it is not possible to arrive at this knowledge—the ultimate knowledge about sexuality
is a fantasy. And thus we come back to polymorphously perverse infantile
sexuality: the term "perverse" has to be taken here in its strict psychoana-
lytical meaning. In contrast to the hysterical subject who does not know
and bombards the Other with questions ("Why am I what you are saying
I am? What do you want from me? What do I really want?"), the pervert
knows. This is why partial drives constitute a domain of multiple happy
pleasures, each of them grounded in some specific knowledge: the subject
knows what to do (how to suck and squeeze, how to shit, how to look at,
how to destroy ...) so that it brings pleasure. But, as Lacan points out, *there
is no genital drive*, no drive that would push the subject towards satisfaction in the act of copulation—knowledge is here by definition lacking, and
the subject needs fantasies to find its way in this mess. So when genital
copulation is imposed as the sexual norm, it is imposed not to repress the
multiplicity of partial drives, but to obfuscate the negativity/impossibility
at its very heart.

Partial drives are thus not simply happy self-enclosed circular movements that generate pleasure; their circular movement is a repeated failure,
a repeated attempt to encircle some central void. What this means is that
the drive is not a primordial fact, that it has to be deduced from a previous
constellation: what logically precedes the drive is the ontological failure—
the thwarted movement towards a goal, some form of radical ontological
negativity—and the basic operation of the drive is to find enjoyment in the
very failure to reach full enjoyment. We should thus distinguish between
the drives with their partial satisfactions (oral, anal, scopic), and the disruptive negativity this circular movement of the drives tries to cope with.
So what name should we give to this radical negativity that forms the silent
background of the drives? Should we simply distinguish between drives
stuck on partial objects, drives whose repetitive circular movement generates satisfaction, and the "pure" death drive, the impossible "total" will to
(self-)destruction, the ecstatic self-annihilation in which the subject rejoins
the fullness of the maternal Thing? What makes this distinction problematic is that it retranslates the death drive into the terms of desire and its lost
object: it is in desire that the positive object is a metonymic stand-in for the
void of the impossible Thing; it is in desire that the aspiration to fullness
is transferred to partial objects—this is what Lacan called the metonymy
of desire. Here it is crucial not to confuse desire and drive: the drive is
not an infinite longing for the Thing which becomes fixated on a partial

object—the *"drive"* is *this fixation itself in which resides the "death" dimension of every drive*. The drive is not a universal thrust towards the incestuous Thing, which finds itself halted or held back, it *is* this brake itself, a brake on instinct. Its basic movement is not that of transcending all particular objects towards the void of the Thing, but that of our libido getting "stuck" on a particular object, condemned to circle around it forever. The concept of the "pure death drive" is thus ultimately a pseudo-concept: an attempt to think the beyond of drives within the horizon of the drives. Rather than defining the void of negativity around which the drives circulate as the "pure" death drive, it would be more appropriate to posit a negativity/impossibility that precedes the very distinction between drive and desire, and to conceive of the drive and desire as the two modes of coping with this ontological impasse.

CHAPTER 5

Being, Not-Knowing, Absolute Knowing

What if only a God who does not see and know all, who cannot read my mind and needs my confession, a God who has to rely on a big Other outside Himself—what if only such a God can be said to exist? What if total knowledge entails inexistence and existence as such implies a certain non-knowledge? Such a paradoxical relation between being and knowing introduces a third term into the standard opposition between ordinary materialism, for which things exist independently of our knowledge of them, and subjectivist idealism, for which things exist only insofar as they are known or perceived by a mind—things exist insofar as they are *not* known.

This is why the critique of ideology has to contain a theory of con-structed ignorance: one of the main lessons of the critique of ideology is that it is not only knowledge that is socially constructed but also ignorance—in all its fifty shades from simply not knowing that we don't know to a polite ignoring of what we know very well, and covering all intermediate levels, in particular the institutional Unconscious.[1] Recall the liberal appropriation of Martin Luther King, in itself an exemplary case of un-learning. Henry Louis Taylor recently remarked: "Everyone knows—even the smallest kid knows about Martin Luther King—can say his most famous moment was that 'I have a dream' speech. No one can go further than one sentence. All we know is that this guy had a dream. We don't know what that dream was."[2] King had come a long way from the crowds who cheered him at the 1963 March on Washington, when he was introduced as "the moral leader of our nation": by taking on issues beyond segregation, he had lost much public support, and was increasingly considered to be a pariah. As Harvard Sitkoff

---

1 See Robert Proctor and Londa Schiebinger, eds., *Agnotology: The Making and Unmaking of Ignorance*, Stanford: Stanford University Press 2008.

2 This quote and the two following two (Sitkoff and Harris-Lacewell) are taken from http://wcbstv.com.

put it, he took on issues of poverty and militarism because he considered them vital "to make equality something real and not just racial brother-hood but equality in fact." In Badiou's terms, King followed the "axiom of equality" well beyond the topic of racial segregation. He had spoken out against the Vietnam War and was supporting striking sanitation workers in Memphis when he was assassinated in April 1968. As Melissa Harris-Lacewell noted, "Following King meant following the unpopular road, not the popular one." In short, elevating King into a moral icon involved a sys-tematic erasure of a lot of what was known about him.

One could go on citing innumerable similar cases, from the virtual disappearance of the key Freudian topic of infantile sexuality in our "per-missive" era, up to the systematic unlearning of facts about colonized peoples imposed by the colonizers—such unlearning concerns not only the facts, but even more so the ideological space that establishes the coor-dinates for our understanding of "primitives." (For example, when early ethnologists encountered a tribe whose totem was a bird, they automati-cally attributed to the tribe members the ridiculous belief that they were descended from this bird.) However, there is also a positive aspect to this process of unlearning. In the final pages of his monumental history of World War II, Winston Churchill ponders the enigma of military decision making: after the specialists (the economic and military analysts, psycholo-gists, meteorologists …) have offered their multiple, elaborated and refined analyses, someone has to assume the simple and for that very reason most difficult act of reducing this complex multiplicity of views, where for every reason for there are two reasons against, into a resolute "Yes" or "No"—we shall attack, we shall continue to wait. In this sense, a decision to act involves unlearning the complexity of a situation. This is why what Hegel calls "negativity" can also be put in terms of insight and blindness—as the "positive" power of blindness, of ignoring parts of reality. But the most uncanny case of this type of not-knowing is to be found in one of the best-known Freudian dreams, the one about the apparition of the "father who didn't know he was dead":

> a man who had nursed his father during his last illness, and who felt his death very keenly, dreamed some time afterwards the following senseless dream: *His father was again living, and conversing with him as usual, but* (and this was the remarkable thing) *he had nevertheless died, though he did not know it.* This dream is intelligible if, after "he had nevertheless died," we insert *in consequence of the dreamer's wish,* and if after "but he did not know it," we add *that the dreamer*

had entertained this wish. While nursing him, the son had often wished that his father was dead; that is, he had had the really compassionate thought that it would be a good thing if death would at last put an end to his sufferings. While he was mourning his father's death, even this compassionate wish became an unconscious reproach, as though it had really contributed to shortening the sick man's life.[3]

The formula of the dream is thus: "Father doesn't know *(that I wish)* that he is dead." This provides the standard explanation—the elision of the signifier *(that I wish)* which registers the dreamer's desire. However, what gets lost in this reading is the uncanny effect of the scene of the father who does not know he is dead—of an entity which is alive only because it is not aware of being dead. What if—following Lacan's rereading of the Freudian dream about the dead son who appears to his father, uttering a terrifying reproach: "Father, can't you see that I am burning?"—in this dream we interpret the wish for the father to be dead not as a repressed unconscious wish, but as the preconscious problem that bothered the dreamer? The dynamic of the dream is then the following: the dreamer invents the dream to quell his (preconscious) guilt-feeling at wishing his father dead while he was nursing him; but what he encounters in the dream is something much more traumatic than his preconscious death-wish—the figure of a father who is still alive because he does not know that he is dead, the obscene specter of the undead father. This is the direction in which Lacan points when he reads the dream of the father who does not know he is dead against the background of "the imperative Freud raised to the sublime stature of a pre-Socratic gnome in his formulation, *Wo Es war, soll Ich werden*":

> "where it was … [*là où ça fut* …]"—what does that mean? If it were but this [*ça*] that might have been (to use the aoristic form), how to come to the same place in order to make myself be there, by stating it now? But the French translation says: "*Là où c'était* …" Let us take advantage of the distinct imperfect it provides. Where it was just now, where it was for a short while, between an extinction that is still glowing and an opening up that stumbles, I can come into being by disappearing from my statement. An enunciation that denounces itself, a statement that renounces itself, an ignorance that sweeps itself away, an opportunity that self-destructs—what remains here if not the trace of what really must be in order to fall away from being?

---

3   Sigmund Freud, *The Interpretation of Dreams*, Chapter 6, Section G, Dream 2, available at http://books.eserver.org.

A dream related by Freud in his article, "Formulations on the Two Principles of Mental Functioning," gives us a sentence, related to the pathos with which the figure of a dead father returning as a ghost would be invested: "He did not know he was dead." I have already used this sentence to illustrate the subject's relation to the signifier—through an enunciation that makes a human being tremble due to the vacillation that comes back to him from his own statement. If this figure of the dead father subsists only by virtue of the fact that one does not tell him the truth of which he is unaware, what then is the status of the one on which this subsistence depends? He did not know ... He was to know a bit later. Oh! may that never happen!

May I die rather than have him know. Yes, that's how I get there, where it was (to be): who knew, thus, that I was dead?[4]

Note how Lacan shifts the focus from the fascinating figure of the father who "does not know he is dead" to the question that lurks in the background: to the *other* subject (the dreamer to whom the father appears, in this case) who *does* know that the father is dead, and, paradoxically, in this way *keeps him alive by not telling him that he is dead*. The father's death is, of course, experienced by the dreamer as the ultimate catastrophe, so his entire strategy is directed at protecting the other/father from knowledge—a protection that includes self-sacrifice: "Oh! may that never happen! May I die rather than have him know." The political implications of such a subjective attitude are crucial, as it is clear from a dream had by Trotsky, who, on the night of June 25, 1935, while in exile, dreamt that the dead Lenin was questioning him anxiously about his illness:

Last night, or rather early this morning, I dreamed I had a conversation with Lenin. Judging by the surroundings, it was on a ship, on the third-class deck. Lenin was lying in a bunk; I was either standing or sitting near him, I am not sure which. He was questioning me anxiously about my illness. "You seem to have accumulated nervous fatigue, you must rest ..." I answered that I had always recovered from fatigue quickly, thanks to my native *Schwungkraft*, but that this time the trouble seemed to lie in some deeper processes ... "Then you should seriously (he emphasized the word) consult the doctors (several names) ..." I answered that I had already had many consultations and began to tell him about my trip to Berlin; but looking at Lenin I recalled that he was dead. I immediately tried to drive away this thought, so as to finish the conversation. When I had

---

4   Jacques Lacan, *Écrits*, New York: Norton 2006, pp. 678–9.

finished telling him about my therapeutic trip to Berlin in 1926, I wanted to add, "This was after your death"; but I checked myself and said, "After you fell ill …"[5]

In his interpretation of this dream, Lacan focuses on the obvious link with the Freudian dream of the father who does not know that he is dead.[6] So what does it mean that Lenin does not know he is dead? There are two radically opposed ways to read Trotsky's dream. According to the first reading, the terrifyingly ridiculous figure of the undead Lenin

> doesn't know that the immense social experiment he single-handedly brought into being (and which we call soviet communism) has come to an end. He remains full of energy, although dead, and the vituperation expended on him by the living—that he was the originator of the Stalinist terror, that he was an aggressive personality full of hatred, an authoritarian in love with power and totalitarianism, even (worst of all) the rediscoverer of the market in his NEP— none of those insults manage to confer a death, or even a second death, upon him. How is it, how can it be, that he still thinks he is alive? And what is our own position here—which would be that of Trotsky in the dream, no doubt—what is our own non-knowledge, what is the death from which Lenin shields us?[7]

The dead Lenin who does not know that he is dead here stands for our own obstinate refusal to renounce our grandiose utopian projects and accept the limitations of our situation: there is no big Other, Lenin was mortal and made errors like everyone else, so it is time for us to let him die, put this obscene ghost who haunts our political imaginary to rest, and approach our problems in a non-ideological, pragmatic way. There is, however, another sense in which Lenin is still alive: he is so insofar as he embodies what Badiou calls the "eternal Idea" of universal emancipation, the immortal striving for justice that no insults or catastrophes will manage to kill off.

A couple of pages later, Lacan returns to this topic when he writes about the square root of -1 (the *objet a* as the object which cannot be positivized):

5   Leon Trotsky, *Diary in Exile 1935*, Cambridge, MA: Harvard University Press 1976, pp. 145–6.

6   The dream is analyzed by Lacan in his Seminar VI on *Le désir et son interprétation*, the session of January 7, 1959 (unpublished).

7   Fredric Jameson, "Lenin and Revisionism," in Sebastian Budgen, Stathis Kouvelakis and Slavoj Žižek, eds., *Lenin Reloaded*, SIC series, Vol. 7, Durham, NC: Duke University Press 2007, p. 59.

This is what the subject is missing in thinking he is exhaustively accounted for by his *cogito*—he is missing what is unthinkable about him. But where does this being, which appears in some way missing from the sea of proper names, come from? We cannot ask this question of the subject *qua* I. He is missing everything he needs in order to know the answer, since if this subject, I, was dead [*moi jĕtais mort*], he would not know it, as I said earlier. Thus he does not know I'm alive. How, therefore, will I prove it to myself? For I can, at most, prove to the Other that he exists, not, of course, with the proofs of the existence of God with which the centuries have killed him, but by loving him, a solution introduced by the Christian *kerygma*. It is, in any case, too precarious a solution for us to even think of using to circumvent our problem, namely: What am I? I am in the place from which "the universe is a flaw in the purity of Non-Being" is vociferated.[8]

The first thing to note in this passage is the temporality of the subject: the subject is never in the present, since, if present, it would be a pure object-less self-consciousness, able to say in the first person singular "I am dead," and then dissolve into mucous filth, as happens in Poe's "The Facts of M. Valdemar's Case":

"M. Valdemar, can you explain to us what are your feelings or wishes now?" There was an instant return of the hectic circles on the cheeks: the tongue quivered, or rather rolled violently in the mouth (although the jaws and lips remained rigid as before), and at length the same hideous voice which I have already described, broke forth: "For God's sake!—quick!—quick!—put me to sleep—or, quick!—waken me!—quick!—I say to you that I am dead!" I was thoroughly unnerved, and for an instant remained undecided what to do. At first I made an endeavor to recompose the patient; but, failing in this through total abeyance of the will, I retraced my steps and as earnestly struggled to awaken him. In this attempt I soon saw that I should be successful—or at least I soon fancied that my success would be complete—and I am sure that all in the room were prepared to see the patient awaken.

For what really occurred, however, it is quite impossible that any human being could have been prepared. As I rapidly made the mesmeric passes, amid ejaculations of "dead! dead!" absolutely bursting from the tongue and not from

---

8   Lacan, *Écrits*, p. 694. Note how the last sentence echoes quantum cosmology: the universe, our material universe, is a flaw in the purity of the Void, i.e., it emerged from this Void as the result of a broken symmetry.

the lips of the sufferer, his whole frame at once—within the space of a single minute, or less, shrunk—crumbled—absolutely rotted away beneath my hands. Upon the bed, before the whole company, there lay a nearly liquid mass of loathsome—of detestable putrescence.[9]

This "detestable putrescence" is not the *objet a* but its exact opposite—what remains of the body when the *objet a* is subtracted from it, a kind of desublimated body.[10] The point is, of course, that such a subjective position—the position of an enunciator who clearly assumes that he is dead—is structurally impossible for a human subject. Is it the case then that only a god can know he is dead? Lacan claims the opposite: the same paradox holds for God, who was always already dead, but just didn't know it—He learns it in Christianity. And, in the case of God, it is us, the believers, on whom God's subsistence depends. As believers, we can well imagine us telling ourselves: "God did not know that he is dead … He was to learn it a bit later. Oh! may that never happen! May I die rather than have him know. Yes, that's how I get there, where it was (to be): who knew, thus, that I was dead?"

The answer to the last question is, of course: *nobody* knows that I am dead—which is why I am still alive. The intersubjective status of knowledge, of "cognizance being taken," is crucial here: what we are dealing with is not simply knowledge, but *knowledge about the Other's knowledge*. Recall the final reversal of Edith Wharton's *Age of Innocence* in which the husband who for many years has harbored an illicit passion for Countess Olenska is, after his wife's early death, free to join his love; however, when, on the way to her, he learns from his son that his young wife *knew* all along about his secret passion, his relationship with the Countess becomes impossible for him. Therein lies the enigma of knowledge: how is it possible that the whole psychic economy of a situation radically changes not when the hero directly learns something (some long-repressed secret), but when he *gets to know that the other* (whom he mistook for ignorant) *also knew it all the time* and just pretended not to know for the sake of appearances—is there anything more humiliating than the situation of a husband who, after a long secret affair, all of a sudden learns that his wife had known about it all along, but said nothing out of politeness or, even worse, out of love for him?

---

9   Edgar Allen Poe, "The Facts of M. Valdemar's Case," available at eapoe.org.

10   The New York–based Alliance of Women Film Journalists hands out an award for the "Movie You Wanted to Love but Just Couldn't" (*Cloud Atlas* got it for 2012)—it is simply a movie lacking *objet a*, a movie that has all the proper ingredients but is just missing that *je ne sais quoi* which would unite them into a magic whole.

The husband is alive as long as (he does not know that) the Other (his wife) knows (about his affair)—in a sense, he dies the moment he learns about her knowledge, his entire libidinal life collapses.

This brings us to one of the fundamental functions of sacrifice: one sacrifices oneself to prevent the Other from knowing. Is this not what Roberto Benigni's film *Life Is Beautiful* is about? The father sacrifices himself in order for his son not to know (that they are in a death camp), indeed the father's reasoning can be rendered again by Lacan's words: "May I die rather than have him know [that we are in a death camp]!" This is why all we have to do to see what is wrong with the film is carry out a simple thought experiment: to imagine the same film with one change—at the end, the father learns that his son knew all along he was in a death camp, and was just pretending he believed his father's story to make him happy.

In his short story "Le Horla," Guy de Maupassant describes a man who suddenly sees his own back in the mirror: it is his back, but since it appears in a position from which the man himself definitely ought not to be able to see it in the mirror, it appears as a strange object—strange not because of its immanent uncanniness, but because it implies the point of view of an impossible gaze. Perhaps such an experience provides the most elementary example of the Freudian Uncanny: we see something that is thoroughly familiar, "homely," but what makes it uncanny is simply the implied gaze, as if one were looking at oneself (one's body) from the outside—such a gaze reduces one (as the subject of this gaze) to a pure bodiless gaze, in short, to a dead gaze. An encounter with one's double would be the extreme case here: I see myself outside myself, in an object (another human body), which implies that if I am outside myself as a living body, then I myself must already be dead—which is why Maupassant is quite right in concluding his story with the line: "No—no—there is no doubt about it—He is not dead. Then—then—I suppose I must kill myself!"

But we should introduce a further distinction here: for Lacan, perverse sacrifice has two modes. First, a sacrifice enacts the disavowal of the impotence of the big Other: at its most elementary, the subject does not offer his sacrifice to profit from it himself, but to fill in the lack *in the Other*, to sustain the appearance of the Other's omnipotence or, at least, consistency. In *Beau Geste*, the classic Hollywood adventure melodrama from 1938, the eldest of the three brothers who live with their benevolent aunt steals the enormously expensive diamond necklace which is the pride of the aunt's family, and disappears with it, knowing that he will be forever despised as the ungracious embezzler of his benefactress. So why did he do it? At the end of the film, we learn that he did so in order to prevent the embarrassing disclosure that the necklace was a fake. He had discovered that, years earlier, the aunt had been forced to sell the necklace to a rich maharaja in order to save the family from bankruptcy, and had replaced it with a worthless imitation. Just prior to his "theft," he learned that a distant uncle who co-owned the necklace wanted it to be sold off for financial gain—if the necklace were to be sold, its fakeness would have been exposed, so the only way to retain the aunt's and thus the family's honor was to stage its theft. This is the proper deception of the crime of stealing: to hide the fact that, ultimately, *there is nothing to steal*—in this way, the constitutive lack of the Other is concealed, the illusion is maintained that the Other possessed what was stolen from it. If, in love, one gives what one does not possess, in a crime of love, one steals from the beloved Other what the Other does not possess. This is the "beau geste" to which the film's title alludes. And therein resides also the meaning of sacrifice: one sacrifices oneself (one's honor and future in respectable society) to maintain the appearance of the Other's honor, to save the beloved Other from shame.

There is yet another, much more uncanny, dimension of sacrifice. Let me take another example from cinema, Jeannot Szwarc's *Enigma* (1981), the story of an East German dissident journalist who emigrates to the West and is then recruited by the CIA and sent back to East Germany to get hold of a scrambler computer chip that gives the user access to all communications between KGB headquarters and its outposts. When it becomes clear that the East Germans and Russians had been informed about his arrival, the spy begins to suspect that something is badly wrong with his mission and that the communists have a mole in the CIA. However, as we learn towards the film's end, the solution is much more ingenious: the CIA in fact *already possesses* the scrambler chip, but the Russians, suspecting as much, have temporarily stopped using it for their secret communications. The real aim of the operation is thus to convince the Russians that the CIA do not possess the chip by sending an agent to get hold of it and, at the same time, leaking his mission to the Russians, counting on the likelihood that they will arrest him. The tragic aspect of the story, of course, is that the CIA *wants* the mission to fail: the agent is sacrificed in advance for the sake of the higher goal of convincing the enemy that one does not possess his secret.[11]

---

11   In Slavoj Žižek, *On Belief*, London: Routledge 2001, I deal with these two examples of sacrifice from a different standpoint.

The strategy here is that of staging a search operation in order to convince the Other that one does not already possess what one is looking for—one feigns a lack, a want, to conceal from the Other that one already possesses the *agalma*, the Other's innermost secret. Is not this structure somehow connected with the basic paradox of symbolic castration as constitutive of desire, in which the object has to be lost in order to be regained on the inverse ladder of desire regulated by the Law? Symbolic castration is usually defined as the loss of something one never possessed, i.e., the object-cause of desire is an object which emerges through the very gesture of its withdrawal; however, what we encounter here is the obverse structure of feigning a loss. Insofar as the Other of the symbolic Law prohibits *jouissance*, the only way for the subject to enjoy is to feign that he lacks the object that provides *jouissance*, concealing the fact of possession from the Other's gaze by staging the spectacle of a desperate search for it.

Surprisingly, we can discern a homologous feigning in Christian theology. In his *Summa Theologica*, Thomas Aquinas reaches the conclusion that the blessed in the Kingdom of Heaven will be allowed to see the damned being punished so that their own bliss will be that much more delightful (St. John Bosco drew the same conclusion in the opposite direction: the damned in Hell will also be able to see the joy of those in Heaven, which will add to their suffering). Here are Aquinas' two formulations of this claim:

> Nothing should be denied the blessed that belongs to the perfection of their beatitude ... Wherefore in order that the happiness of the saints may be more delightful to them and that they may render more copious thanks to God for it, they are allowed to see perfectly the sufferings of the damned ...
>
> That the saints may enjoy their beatitude more thoroughly, and give more abundant thanks for it to God, a perfect sight of the punishment of the damned is granted them.[12]

Aquinas, of course, takes care to avoid the obscene implication that the good souls in Heaven might take some pleasure in observing the terrible suffering of other souls. He proceeds along two lines. First, he proposes the thesis that, in Heaven, the blessed will enjoy the full illumination of their minds, since knowledge is also a blessing and a perfection that should not

---

12   Thomas Aquinas, *The Summa Theologica*, Supplementum Tertia Partis, Question 94, Article 1.

be denied to the saints. If the saints in Heaven were to be ignorant of the damned, this would be a denial of the blessing of knowledge. Consequently, the saints will possess greater knowledge, including a greater knowledge of Hell, including being allowed to see it in action. Next problem: good Christians should feel pity when they see suffering—so will the blessed in Heaven also feel pity for the torments of the damned? Aquinas' "no" is grounded in a rather flimsy hair-splitting argument: "Seeing the punishment of the wicked, the righteous have no pity: Whoever pities another shares somewhat in his unhappiness. But the blessed cannot share in any unhappiness. Therefore they do not pity the afflictions of the damned."[13]

Aquinas' second line of argumentation tries to refute the notion that the blessed in Heaven will derive joy from witnessing the punishment of the damned in an explicitly obscene way. He does so by introducing a distinction between two modes of enjoying a thing:

> A thing may be a matter of rejoicing in two ways. First directly, when one rejoices in a thing as such: and thus the saints will not rejoice in the punishment of the wicked. Secondly, indirectly, by reason namely of something annexed to it: and in this way the saints will rejoice in the punishment of the wicked, by considering therein the order of Divine justice and their own deliverance, which will fill them with joy. And thus the Divine justice and their own deliverance will be the direct cause of the joy of the blessed: while the punishment of the damned will cause it indirectly.[14]

The problem with this last explanation is, of course, that the relationship between the two levels will actually be inverted: the enjoyment of Divine Justice functions as a rationalization, a moral cover-up, for the sadistic enjoyment of the eternal suffering of one's neighbor. What makes Aquinas' formulation suspicious is the surplus-enjoyment it introduces: as if the simple pleasure of living in Heavenly bliss is not quite enough, and has to be supplemented by the additional pleasure of being allowed to take a look at another's suffering—only in this way may the blessed souls "enjoy their beatitude more thoroughly." We can imagine the appropriate scene in Heaven: when some blessed soul complains that the nectar on the table today is not quite as tasty as yesterday's, and that in fact living in bliss is becoming mildly boring, the angels serving the blessed soul will snap

---

13   Ibid., Question 94, Article 2.
14   Ibid., Question 92, Article 3.

back: "You don't like it here? Well take a look at how life is down there, then maybe you'll realize how lucky you are to be here!" The corresponding scene in Hell should also be imagined somewhat differently from the vision of St. John Bosco: far away from the Divine gaze, the damned souls are enjoying an intense and pleasurable life in Hell—only when the Devil's administrators learn that a party of blessed souls from Heaven are to be allowed a brief glimpse of life in Hell do they kindly implore the damned souls to stage a performance of terrible suffering in order to impress the fools from Heaven. In short, the sight of the other's suffering is the *objet a*, the obscure cause of desire which sustains our own happiness—take it away, and our bliss appears in all its sterile stupidity.[15]

What such paradoxes reveal is that symbolic castration is not just the gap between my symbolic identity and the misery of my empirical existence (no father is really a Father, even Hell is not really hellish, etc.)—due to the reflexivity of the symbolic order, this gap has to be reflected back into the symbolic itself, becoming internal to the symbolic function, designating its inconsistency, namely the fact that no (particular) determination of what it is to be a Father can fully fit the universal dimension of Father. With regard to bureaucracy, this is why the perfect administrator who clings to the letter of the Law, meticulously meeting all its particular demands, is simultaneously the most obscene and ridiculous one, displaying a filthy *jouissance* that undermines his universal symbolic function.[16] This is also why the real undermining of symbolic authority occurs not when a stupid little piece of the real intervenes (the bureaucrat trips up, lets out a fart, etc.), but precisely when the bureaucrat fully identifies with his role. Towards the end of Lars von Trier's early masterpiece *Zentropa*, set in Germany in the summer of 1946, there is a scene which exemplifies this bureaucratic *jouissance* at

---

15   This is why we should not be too shocked by excessive indifference towards suffering, even and especially when this suffering is widely reported and condemned in the media, as if it is our very outrage at suffering that turns us into its immobilized fascinated spectators. Recall, in the early 1990s, the three-year-long siege of Sarajevo, with its starving population exposed to constant shelling and sniper fire. The enigma here was that although the media were full of terrible pictures and reports, neither UN forces, NATO, nor the US made even the slightest effort to break the siege, such as establishing a corridor through which provisions could be delivered. It would have cost nothing, and with a little bit of serious pressure on the Serb forces, the prolonged spectacle of an encircled city exposed to a daily dose of terror would have been over. Clearly, the suffering in Sarajevo sustained the happiness of Western observers.

16   See Simon Hajdini, *Na kratko o dolgčasu, lenobi in počitku*, Ljubljana: Analecta 2012, p. 210.

its most obscene. On a night train in which the hero is expecting a bomb to explode at any moment, he is subjected to an exam for the job of night porter on a sleeping car; while all our attention is focused on the bomb threat, the examiner calmly and with obvious self-satisfaction proceeds with his work, insisting with absurd punctiliousness on the most nonsensical details, asking where one should put the passenger's pajamas, and so on.

Quantum knowing

This paradoxical status of the knowledge of the Other enables us to draw out another feature of the distinction between what Badiou calls (hedonist) "democratic" materialism and dialectical materialism. For standard materialism, things exist independently of our knowledge of them; for subjectivist idealism, *esse = percipi*, i.e., things exist only insofar as they are known or perceived by a mind, as perfectly formulated in the famous Berkeleyan limerick on "God in the Quad" (a courtyard on a campus):

> There was a young man who said, "God
> Must find it exceedingly odd
> To think that the tree
> Should continue to be
> When there's no one about in the quad."

To which God replies:

> Dear Sir: Your astonishment's odd;
> I am always about in the quad.
> And that's why the tree
> Will continue to be
> Since observed by, Yours faithfully, God.

Note here the formal similarity with quantum physics, in which some kind of perception (or registration) is needed to bring about the collapse of the wave function, i.e., the emergence of reality.[17] However, this similarity masks the fundamental difference: the agency which registers the collapse of the wave function is not in any sense "creating" the observed reality, it

---

17   I resume here the line of thought from Chapter 14 of Slavoj Žižek, *Less Than Nothing*, London: Verso Books 2012.

is registering an outcome that remains fully contingent. Furthermore, the whole point of quantum physics is that many things go on before registration: in this shadowy space, the "normal" laws of nature are continuously suspended. The theological implications of this gap between virtual proto-reality and the fully constituted form are of special interest. Insofar as "God" is the agent who creates things by observing them, quantum indeterminacy compels us to posit a god who is *omnipotent, but not omniscient*: "If God collapses the wave functions of large things to reality by His observation, quantum experiments indicate that He is not observing the small."[18] The ontological cheating with virtual particles (an electron can create a proton and thereby violate the principle of constant energy, on condition that it reabsorbs it before its environs "take note" of the discrepancy) is a way to cheat God Himself, the ultimate agency taking note of everything that goes on: God Himself does not control the quantum processes; therein resides the atheist lesson of quantum physics. Einstein was right with his famous claim "God doesn't cheat"—but what he forgot to add is that He can Himself be cheated. Insofar as the materialist thesis is that "God is unconscious" (God does not know), quantum physics is indeed materialist: there are micro-processes (quantum oscillations) which are not registered by the God-system.

The idea that knowing changes reality is what quantum physics shares with both psychoanalysis (for which interpretation has effects in the real) and historical materialism (in his *History and Class Consciousness*, Georg Lukács describes how the proletariat's acquiring of self-consciousness—its becoming aware of its historical mission—changes its object; through this awareness, the proletariat in its very social reality turns into a revolutionary subject). And we should not be afraid to push this logic to its extreme: there is reality because everything is not/cannot be symbolized. In Arthur C. Clarke's short story "The Nine Billion Names of God" (1953), the monks in a Tibetan lamasery are convinced that the universe was created in order to note down all the names of God—once this naming is completed, God will bring the universe to an end. The monks have created an alphabet in which they calculate they could encode all the possible names of God, numbering about nine billion, each name having no more than nine characters. Writing the names out by hand will take thousands of years, so the monks rent a computer capable of printing out all the possible permutations. The two Western experts hired to install and program the machine are skeptical

---

18   Brian Greene, *The Elegant Universe*, New York: Norton 1999, p. 171.

about the outcome; as the job nears completion, they fear that the monks will blame them when nothing happens. To avoid this, they delay the operation so that the computer will complete its final print run just after their planned departure. Leaving as scheduled on ponies, they pause on the mountain path on their way back to the airfield, where a plane is waiting to take them back to civilization. Under a clear night sky they estimate that it must be just about now that the monks will be pasting the final printed names into their holy books. Then they notice that "overhead, without any fuss, the stars were going out."

The psychoanalytic notion of the symptom designates such a reality which subsists only insofar as something remains unsaid, insofar as its truth is not articulated in the symbolic order—which is why the proper psychoanalytic interpretation has effects in the Real, for it can dissolve the symptom. On this reading, the premise of Clarke's story would thus be that our universe, reality itself, is a symptom, that it only subsists insofar as something (here: God's name) is not said. While such a notion of reality may appear to be an exemplary case of idealist madness, we should not miss its materialist core: reality is not simply external to thought/speech, to the symbolic space, reality thwarts this space from within, making it incomplete and inconsistent—the limit that separates the Real from the symbolic is simultaneously external and internal to the symbolic.

At this point, a reply can be formulated to Ed Pluth's perspicuous critique of my approach to quantum physics.[19] His starting point is the gap between nature-in-itself (as thematized by the natural sciences, this nature is "incomprehensible" in the sense of being meaningless in terms of the categories of our life world—for example, the universe described by quantum physics cannot be translated back into our life-world experience of reality) and the life world itself whose structure is inherently dialectical in the Marxian sense of social *praxis* or in the Hegelian sense of the mediation between being and thought (where the change in our comprehension of an object changes the object itself since it is already in itself subjectively mediated). How are we to deal with this gap? Is it possible to overcome it? Naturalist scientism has a clear and simple reductionist answer: since humans are part of nature and emerged out of nature, in principle at least we should be able to describe how humanity developed out of animal life (and the brain sciences are already providing concrete descriptions of this

---

19   See Ed Pluth, "On Transcendental Materialism and the Natural Real," in *Filozofski vestnik: Science and Thought*, Ljubljana: Slovene Academy of Sciences 2012.

process). Pluth's point here is that, of course, materialism should be in some sense reductionist; however, if it is also to be dialectical, it should simultaneously assert the (relative) autonomy of each level or sphere of reality. Genesis does not fully encompass its outcome: yes, our symbolic universe emerged from nature, but its functioning has to be described in its own terms. With regard to Lacan, this means that, while there is a scientific "natural" Real (articulated in the formalized sciences), there is also a different "symbolic" Real, the deadlock at the very heart of the symbolic universe, its constitutive impossibility. If we do not take into account this "symbolic" Real in its uniqueness, then we end up "de-realizing" the human symbolic universe characteristic of scientific naturalism: the only thing that is "really real" is nature and its processes, while our life world (consciousness, meaning) is only an appearance, something to be accounted for in the terms of those natural processes.

Here enters Pluth's critique: according to him, I take a series of steps, some of which are problematic, in my dealing with quantum physics. My starting point is the homology between the paradoxes of the "symbolic Real" (non-All, lack and impossibility, antagonism, etc.) and the "natural Real" (the paradoxes articulated by quantum physics): quantum physics discovers in non-human nature features that were hitherto thought to be specific to the symbolic universe (retroactivity, etc.), indeed it is as if we discover the core of our humanity out there in a state of nature. On the basis of this homology I posit a kind of transcendental structure which is the same Real at work in nature as well as in symbolic-dialectical human reality. Next step: since I am not simply an Hegelian idealist, I do not claim that one can directly deploy the entire structure and being of reality (natural and symbolic) out of the Real; in other words, my Real is a kind of Kantian a priori structure which, in order to actualize itself, needs to be applied to, or encounter, some positive reality (natural, human)—therein resides my "transcendental materialism" (incidentally, a term of Adrian Johnston's which I never use). Since, however, as a materialist, I have to admit the priority of (non-human) nature, this means that I nonetheless end up in my own version of naturalist reductionism: nature itself, outside and independently of the specific dialectics of human *praxis*, forms the order of Being *qua* Being which also already displays the innermost structure of the human universe, so that this latter becomes just a special case of the universal structure of Being.

My counter-argument here is that Pluth misses the point of my reference to quantum physics: one precisely cannot say that quantum physics talks about reality the way it is independently of human practice—insofar as our human reality is characterized by the irreducible gap between imaginary-symbolic experience and the Real, where the two levels are inextricably mediated (i.e., the "symbolic Real" is the Real of this human reality), *it is this very gap which is present in the quantum universe*, in the guise of the gap between the virtual pre-ontological quantum universe and ordinary physical reality that emerges through the collapse of the wave function, and this collapse has to be mediated (if not by subjectivity proper then) by some kind of perceptive/registering agency. In other words, what quantum physics discovers "in nature" is another version of the very gap between "objective mechanisms" and "subjective experience" that we usually take as specifically human. In this precise sense, quantum physics is not simply and directly "reductionist": its lesson is not that there is a natural "real Real" independent of our experience, reducing this experience to a mere appearance, but that this very gap between the Real and its appearing is already out there, "in nature." Or, to put it in yet another way, the lesson of quantum physics is that "nature itself" is already "non-reductionist": *already "in nature," appearance matters, is constitutive of reality.*[20]

A similar (although opposed) critique with regard to the same topic has been proposed by Adrian Johnston, concerning the status of negativity.[21] What Johnston rejects is the notion of negativity as a primordial unanalyzable Void which disturbs the homeostatic cycle of natural reproduction, throwing it off its rails and introducing the dimension of subjectivity. In Badiou, an evental encounter quasi-magically cuts into the flow of human-animal life; in Lacan, the negativity proper to the symbolic interrupts animal life out of nowhere, invading it like a parasite—and likewise with my notion of negativity as the core of subject. Against this exemption of negativity from concrete analysis, against this elevation of negativity (or its synonyms: void, lack, gap ...) into an *unhintergehbares* fact, Johnston points out how, even in Lacan, we often find hypotheses about the concrete biological (pre)conditions of the rise of negativity. The main ones concern the premature birth of the human individual, its primordial situation of a *corps morcelé*, its helplessness, its inability to coordinate its bodily movements,

---

20   This is why, incidentally, Pluth is also wrong to describe the "natural real" as the order of Being qua Being: as Lacan emphasized again and again, the Real is a pre-ontological category, an obstacle/impossibility which undermines every project of ontology.

21   See Adrian Johnston, "Reflections of a Rotten Nature: Hegel, Lacan, and Material Negativity," *Filozofski vestnik* 32:2 (2013).

and so on. It is this "denaturalization" of natural life which opens up the space for symbolic activity as an attempt to supplement the deficiency. In short, one cannot jump directly from the inertia of animal life to the glorious abyss of negativity: the latter emerges out of a very precise biological deadlock.

My counter-argument here is that this line of thought should nonetheless be further developed in (at least) two directions. While "rotten nature," the failure and dysfunctionality of animal life, opens up the space for the symbolic, the entry of the symbolic still cannot be causally explained in this way—it does indeed occur as a "miracle," *ex nihilo*. In other words, there is no teleology here, the symbolic only retroactively renders its natural (pre)conditions readable as such, as its (pre)conditions. But how is this "miraculous" entry *ex nihilo* possible? How should the "pre-human Real" be structured so that the symbolic can explode in its midst? A possible answer is indicated by speculations in quantum physics about the virtual Void out of which (particular) reality emerges through the collapse of the wave function: negativity materialized in the symbolic process is not something that magically cuts into positive nature; it rather (re)actualizes at the specific level a negativity immanent to the "pre-human Real" as such. So while it is true that the emergence of (human) negativity can take place only against the background of certain biological (pre)conditions, the pre-human Real itself *does* emerge *ex nihilo*. (Stephen Hawking makes this point nicely when he claims that, although within an established order of things, nothing—no particular element—can emerge *ex nihilo* without violating the laws of nature, an entire universe paradoxically *can* emerge *ex nihilo*.)

Is Absolute Knowing Hegel's *Docta Ignorantia*?

What happens to the link between being and not-knowing at the unique point of what Hegel calls "Absolute Knowing"? Does all being dissolve here? One has to proceed very carefully, beginning with the passage from the end of logic (absolute Idea) to the beginning of the philosophy of nature (total self-externality of the Idea, the immediacy of space) which confronts us with a kind of philosophical enigma: is this passage—the notion of the Idea "setting itself free" into the externality of nature—legitimate or just a cheap trick, a pseudo-"deduction" pretending to engender what is always already here? What makes this passage even more enigmatic is that it seems to imply an act of absolute forgetting, as if, at the end of the logic, Spirit is somehow able to forget the extraordinarily complex network of notional articulations that culminates in the absolute Idea, and begin again with nature at its most elementary and external. Rebecca Comay speaks here of a case of "feigned amnesia regulated by the analogical, Kantian-style, subjunctive of the 'as if'," quoting Hegel: "Spirit has to start afresh *as if* for it all that preceded were lost and as if it had learned nothing from past experience."[22]

We should nonetheless add two things here. First, as Hegel repeatedly makes clear, the deployment of his system does not imply temporal succession: Hegel knows full well that his logic describes a "realm of shadows," and that the passage from logic to nature does not "generate" nature but does something entirely different—namely, it answers the question "how can the thinking process break out of its closed circle and open itself up to externality, to its radical otherness?" That is to say, how does this opening occur *immanently*, rather than as the result of an accidental stumbling upon "external reality"? Second, for Hegel, "forgetting" (in the sense of erasing all the empirical pseudo-"wealth" of properties that obfuscate the immanent determination of a notion) is for Hegel the key aspect of the absolute power of thinking. Directly contradicting the standard opposition between the mortifying rigidity of the Understanding and the life of Reason, Hegel directly praises the Understanding and emphasizes that the properly dialectical re-animation is to be sought in this very medium of "grey" notional determinations: "The understanding, through the form of abstract universality, does give [the varieties of the sensuous], so to speak, a *rigidity* of being ... but, at the same time through this simplification it *spiritually animates* them and so sharpens them."[23] This "simplification" is precisely what Lacan, referring to Freud, deployed as the reduction of a thing to *le trait unaire* (*der einzige Zug*, the unary feature): we are dealing with a kind of epitomization by means of which the multitude of properties is reduced to a single dominant characteristic, so that we get "a concrete shape in which one determination predominates, the others being present only in blurred outline": "the content is already the actuality reduced to a possibility [*zur Moeglichkeit getilgte Wirklichkeit*], its immediacy overcome, the embodied shape reduced to abbreviated, simple determinations of thought."[24]

22   Rebecca Comay, "Hegel's Last Words," in A. E. Swiffen, ed., *The End of History*, London: Routledge 2012, p. 229; G. W. F. Hegel, *Science of Logic*, London and New York: Humanities Press 1976, p. 808.

23   Hegel, *Science of Logic*, p. 611.

24   G. W. F. Hegel, *Phenomenology of Spirit*, Oxford: Oxford University Press 1977, p. 17.

The dialectical approach is usually seen as trying to locate the phenom-enon-to-be-analyzed in the totality to which it belongs, to bring the wealth of its links to light, and thus to break the spell of fetishizing abstraction: from a dialectical perspective, one should see not just the thing in front of one, but this thing as it is embedded in all the wealth of its concrete his-torical context. This, however, is the most dangerous trap to be avoided: for Hegel, the true problem is the opposite one, the fact that, when we observe a thing, we see *too much* in it, we fall under the spell of the wealth of empirical detail, which prevents us from clearly perceiving the notional determination that forms the core of the thing. The problem is thus not that of how to grasp the wealth of determinations, but, precisely, how to *abstract* from them, how to constrain our gaze and teach it to grasp only the notional determination. We should thus totally reject the pseudo-Hegelian commonplace according to which the Understanding deals with simplified abstractions, while Reason understands things in all their complexity, in the endless intricacy of their mutual relations which only makes them what they are.

Another commonplace tells us that, when engaged in a struggle, we automatically adopt a partial or particular standpoint, while the universal standpoint has to be elevated above the mêlée of passionate commitments. Hegel's authentic position inverts both these commonplaces: it is the Understanding that insists on the endless complexity of a situation, always pointing out that things are more complicated than they appear ("on the other hand …"), while Reason is the power to simplify, to isolate the essential feature, the one which really matters in a complex situation. Furthermore, this isolation does not emerge out of a distanced "objective" analysis, but through our engaged ("partial") approach to reality. It was Heidegger who elaborated this feature apropos language when, in his reading of "essence or *Wesen*" as a verb ("essencing"), he provided a de-essentialized notion of essence. Traditionally, "essence" refers to a stable core that guarantees the identity of a thing. For Heidegger, "essence" is something that depends on the historical context, on the epochal disclosure of being that occurs in and through language, the "house of being." His expression "*Wesen der Sprache*" does not mean "the essence of language," but the "essencing," the making of essences that is the work of language,

> language bringing things into their essence, language "moving us" so that things matter to us in a particular kind of way, so that paths are made within which we can move among entities, and so that entities can bear on each other as the

entities they are ... We share an originary language when the world is articulated in the same style for us, when we "listen to language," when we "let it say its saying to us."[25]

For a medieval Christian, say, the "essence" of gold resides in its incorruptibility and sheen, which make it a "divine" metal. For us, it is either a flexible resource to be used for industrial purposes or a metal appropriate for aesthetic purposes. For Catholics, similarly, the castrato voice was once the very voice of the angels prior to the Fall. For us today, it is a monstrosity. This change in our sensitivity is sustained by language, hinging on a shift in our symbolic universe. A fundamental violence inhabits this "essencing" ability of language: our world is given a partial twist, it loses its balanced innocence, one partial color gives the tone of the Whole.

Hegel's formulation is very precise here: the reduction to the signifying "unary feature" contracts actuality to possibility, in the precise Platonic sense in which the notion (Idea) of a thing always has a deontological dimension to it, designating *what the thing should become in order to be fully what it is.* "Potentiality" is thus not simply the name for the essence of a thing as actualized in the multitude of empirical things of this genre (the Idea of a chair as a potentiality actualized in empirical chairs). The multitude of the actual properties of a thing is not simply reduced to the inner core of this thing's "true reality"; what is more important is that it accentuates (profiles) the thing's inner potential. When I call someone "my teacher," I thereby outline the horizon of what I expect from him; when I refer to a thing as "a chair," I profile the way I intend to use it. When I observe the world around me through the lenses of a language, I perceive its actuality through the lenses of the potentialities hidden, latently present, within it. In other words, potentiality appears "as such," becomes actual *as potentiality,* only through language: it is the appellation of a thing that brings to light ("posits") its potentials. In short, impartial observation gets caught up in the "bad infinity" of complex features, without being able to decide on the essentials, and the only way to arrive at true universality is by way of a reasoning that is sustained by a practical engagement.[26]

Hegelian forgetting is thus not a weakness to be feigned, but the expression of Spirit's highest, "absolute," power—the absence of this power of forgetting (which is effectively a specific aspect of negativity) causes a

---

25   Mark Wrathall, *How to Read Heidegger*, London: Granta 2005, pp. 94–5.
26   For a more detailed analysis of this aspect of language, see Chapter 2 of Slavoj Žižek, *Violence*, London: Profile Books 2008.

debilitating indecision, as is made clear in Alexander Luria's classic *The Mind of a Mnemonist*, a brilliant short case study of an individual who was unable to forget anything: although he made a living as a circus freak answering encyclopedic questions, his subjective life was a mess since he was unable to make even the most simple decision (which requires the ability to brutally simplify a complex network of pros and cons). As a result, his entire life was organized as a waiting—waiting for some big act or event which would happen in the near future (but which never in fact did).[27] This notion of forgetting as being not a weakness but a supreme power also explains the passage from the absolute Idea to Nature, which is precisely the extreme point of forgetting, of self-negation.

However, does this forgetting not rely on the circular logic of self-mediation? That is, the Idea can afford even this extreme self-externalization since it is merely playing a game with itself, knowing full well that, at the end, it will safely return to itself, reappropriating its otherness—and this, precisely, is why the amnesia is feigned. But does this (standard) objection hold? To clarify this point, let us take a look at the very end of the Hegelian system, the entry of the (in)famous figure of Absolute Knowing. Comay is right to discern at this point an even more radical overlapping of recollection and forgetting: "The truth of absolute knowing as recollection is thus the fiction of an absolute forgetting."[28] In what precise sense does this overlapping function? Comay endeavors to unravel this sense in her close reading of the conclusion of Hegel's *Phenomenology*, in which a dense description of Absolute Knowing is "sutured" by a quote from Schiller:

> The goal, absolute knowing, or Spirit that knows itself as Spirit, has for its path the recollection of the Spirits as they are in themselves and as they accomplish the organization of their realm. Their preservation, seen from the side of their free existence appearing in the form of contingency, is history; but regarded from the side of their comprehended organization, it is the science of knowing in the sphere of appearance: the two together, comprehended history [*begriffene Geschichte*], form alike the inwardizing [*Erinnerung*] and the Calvary of absolute Spirit, the actuality, truth, and certainty of its throne, without which it would be lifeless and alone; only—

---

27   See Alexander Luria, *The Mind of a Mnemonist*, Cambridge, MA: Harvard University Press 1987.

28   Comay, "Hegel's Last Words," p. 232.

from the chalice of this realm of spirits
foams forth for Him his infinitude.

[aus dem Kelche dieses Geisterreiches
schäumt ihm seine Unendlichkeit][29]

The last two lines are a (subtly transformed) quote from Friedrich Schiller's "Die Freundschaft" (the original version of 1782):[30]

Friendless was the great world-master
Felt a *lack*—and so created spirits,
Blessed mirrors of his *own* blessedness
But the highest being still could find no equal.
From the chalice of the whole realm of souls
Foams up to *him*—infinitude.

[Freundlos war der grose Weltenmeister
Fühlte *Mangel*—darum schuf er Geister,
Sel'ge Spiegel *seiner* Seligkeit!—
Fand das höchste Wesen schon kein gleiches,
Aus dem Kelch des ganzen Seelenreiches
Schäumt *ihm*—die Unendlichkeit.]

Schiller describes a lonely Creator who cannot overcome the gap that separates Him from his creation: the spirits He creates remain his own mirror images, shadowy insubstantial others, so He remains alone, caught in his own narcissistic game. So what does Hegel achieve with his subtle changes in the last two lines he quotes? Focusing on the erasure of the dash, an erasure that indicates an imposed continuity, a covering up of the break, Comay reads Hegel's paraphrase as

---

29   Hegel, *Phenomenology of Spirit*, pp. 492–3.

30   The choice of Schiller is also politically evocative—Schiller is at the origin of the aestheticization of politics which should protect us from the revolutionary terror in which the French Revolution culminated, i.e., he "expresses the wager of an entire generation: we don't need that kind of revolution. Only through *aesthetic* revolution can we forestall the short-circuit of politics into terror. Only through beauty do we inch our way towards freedom" (Comay, "Hegel's Last Words," p. 234). This is how fascism begins—in contrast to Hegel whose point is not to forestall the short-circuit of terror but to accept the necessity of passing through it.

a typographical suture of the ontological fissure separating God from world. In Schiller the transition from lack to satisfaction, from loneliness to friendship, is as precipitous as the dash that announces it. Hegel smooths over this transition. Both traumatic lack and its correlative on the battlefield of enjoyment—friendlessness, on the one hand, the foaming surplus of *jouissance*, on the other—are absorbed in the philosophical rewriting that erases context, grammar, and punctuation. Between Schiller's last word and Hegel's lies the almost imperceptible difference between the bad infinite of lack, finitude, or indeterminacy and its philosophical homonym.[31]

Comay adds two further specifications of Hegel's covering up of the break acknowledged by Schiller. At the formal level, Hegel's general goal is the sublation (*Aufhebung*) of the "poetry of representation (*Vorstellung*)" into the "prose of thinking"—however, at the very end of the text of the *Phenomenology*, poetry returns, providing the two exit lines. At the level of libidinal economy, Comay raises a brutally simple but highly pertinent question: "Is Hegel a mourner or a melancholic?"[32] Hegel's official position is that of a mourner: the sublation of poetic representations in pure notional content is a successful work of mourning by means of which we accept the loss of the wealth of poetic representations; however, the return of poetic representation in the last two lines of the book signals the failure of this work of mourning: the loss is not effectively cancelled, it persists, and the subject is not ready to let go poetic representation. Beneath Hegel the Mourner, there is thus Hegel the Melancholic forced to enact again and again the failure of the sublation through the work of mourning ...

But what if we read Hegel's sudden insertion of the Schiller fragment not as a strange case in need of explanation, but as standard fundamental dialectical procedure? Take the case of the state as a totality sublating its own particular elements into moments of a rational Whole: the process can be brought to a conclusion, the state can establish itself as an actually existing rational totality, only when the process reaches its peak in an additional element in which the sublated natural immediacy returns at its most brutal—in the person of the king, whose right to rule is determined

---

31   Comay, "Hegel's Last Words," p. 237. And, we may add, the erased dash returns with a vengeance not only at the end of Hegel's own text, announcing the abrupt passage to Schiller ("only—"), but also at the very beginning of Hegel's logic: "Being, pure being—without any further determination" (*Sein, reines Sein,—ohne alle weitere Bestimmung*).

32   Comay, "Hegel's Last Words," p. 234.

by the most stupid natural contingency, the fact of biological descendance. Only this "irrational" element actualizes the state as a rational totality, and in an exactly homologous way, the process of the conceptual sublation of the "poetry of *Vorstellung*" in the prose of thinking—the entire process of the *Phenomenology of Spirit*—can only reach its end with the final punctual supplement in which, in a fragment of poetry, the non-conceptual domain of representation and of historical contingency returns with a vengeance. Or, to put it even more pointedly, in order for all citizens of a state to function like autonomous subjects who through the effort of work have to create what they are, one needs at the summit of the state a person who, precisely, does not need to produce what he is through the effort of work, but who is what he is (who gains the right to its symbolic title) simply by virtue of his natural birth, merely by being what he is.

When Hegel quotes the same two lines from Schiller in his *Philosophy of Religion*,[33] he supplements them with another poetic quote—the two lines from Goethe's "An Suleika" (from *West-Oestlicher Divan*) where, apropos the torment of the endless striving of love, Goethe writes: "Ought such torment to afflict us, / since it enhances our desire?"[34] The link between the two quotes is clear: what appears in the "chalice of this realm of spirits" is, as Hegel says two lines before, the "Calvary of absolute Spirit," and insofar as the Spirit is able to recognize in this path of torment his own infinitude, traversing this path brings joy, i.e., pleasure in pain itself. This also echoes in the famous line from the Preface to the *Philosophy of Right*: "To recognize reason as the rose in the cross of the present, and to find delight in it, is a rational insight which implies reconciliation with reality."[35] Which position is then occupied by the Hegelian philosopher as the observer of this "Calvary of absolute Spirit"? Is the regard of the philosopher the lifeless regard of old age, when all battles are already won or lost? This may appear to be the case:

> The old man lives without any definite interest, for he has abandoned the hope of realizing the ideals which he cherished when he was young and the future seems to hold no promise of anything new at all; on the contrary, he believes that he already knows what is universal and substantial in anything he may yet encounter ... But in thus dwelling in the memory of the past and of the

---

33   G. W. F. Hegel, *Lectures on the Philosophy of Religion, III: The Consummate Religion*, Oxford: Clarendon Press 2007, p. 111.
34   Ibid., p. 112.
35   G. W. F. Hegel, *Philosophy of Right*, Preface, available at marxists.org.

substantial element, he loses his memory for details of the present and for the arbitrary things, names, for example, in the same measure that, conversely, he firmly retains in his mind the maxims of experience and feels obliged to preach to those younger than himself. But this wisdom, this lifeless, complete coincidence of the subject's activity with the world, leads back to the childhood in which there is no opposition.[36]

And, as we saw earlier, does not Hegel conclude his Preface to the *Philosophy of Right* in the same vein, with a remark concerning "the desire to teach the world what it ought to be"?

For such a purpose philosophy at least always comes too late. Philosophy, as the thought of the world, does not appear until reality has completed its formative process, and made itself ready. History thus corroborates the teaching of the conception that only in the maturity of reality does the ideal appear as counterpart to the real, apprehends the real world in its substance, and shapes it into an intellectual kingdom. When philosophy paints its grey in grey, one form of life has become old, and by means of grey it cannot be rejuvenated, but only known. The owl of Minerva, takes its flight only when the shades of night are gathering.[37]

No wonder, then, that there are no proper names in the text of the *Phenomenology*: proper names stand for living individuals, while the *Phenomenology* apprehends reality in its lifeless spiritual substance. But, again, is this the standpoint of Absolute Knowing? What is a dialectical analysis of, say, a past event, of a revolutionary break? Does it really amount to identifying the underlying necessity that regulated the apparent confusion of prior events? What if the opposite is true, and the dialectical analysis *reinserts possibility back into the necessary past*? There is something of an unpredictable miraculous emergence in every turn from "negation" to "negation of negation," in every rise of a new Order out of the chaos of disintegration—which is why dialectical analysis is for Hegel always the analysis of *past* events.[38] No deduction will bring us from chaos to order,

---

36   G. W. F. Hegel, *Philosophy of Mind*, Oxford: Clarendon Press 1992, p. 64.

37   Hegel, *Philosophy of Right*, Preface, available at marxists.org.

38   One of the paradoxes of this properly dialectical tension between possibility and actuality is that, in a situation of ultimate choice (to kill oneself or to go on living and struggling), the choice of suicide can help the subject to postpone actual suicide: "Now that I've decided to kill myself, I know an escape from my desperate situation is open to me, so until that moment, I can take life more easily since I'm rid

and locating this moment of the magic turn, this unpredictable reversal of chaos into Order, is the true aim of dialectical analysis. For example, the aim of the analysis of the French Revolution is not to unearth the "historical necessity" of the passage from 1789 to the Jacobin Terror and then to Thermidor and Empire, but *to reconstruct this succession as a series of (to use this anachronistic term) existential decisions made by agents who, caught in the whirlpool of action, had to invent a way out of the deadlock* (in the same way that Lacan reconceptualizes the succession of oral, anal, and phallic phases as a series of dialectical reversals).

Absolute Knowing is thus not simply the concluding point of re-collection that sublates the preceding life in the form of notional necessity —an additional "push" or move is needed to bring the movement to a conclusion. But is this additional move really the return of melancholia? To answer this question properly, one has first to specify the nature of melancholy. At its most radical, melancholy is not the failure of the work of mourning, a persisting attachment to the lost object, but its very opposite: "melancholy offers the paradox of an intention to mourn that precedes and anticipates the loss of the object."[39] Therein resides the melancholic's stratagem: the only way to possess an object we never had, which was lost from the very outset, is to treat an object that we still fully possess as if it is already lost. This is what gives a melancholic love relationship its unique flavor (like that already mentioned between Newland and Countess Olenska in Wharton's *The Age of Innocence*): although the partners are still together, desperately in love, and enjoying each other's presence, the shadow of their future separation already colors their relationship, so they perceive their current pleasures under the aegis of the catastrophe to come. How are we to unravel this paradox of mourning an object that is not yet lost, that is still here? The key to this enigma lies in Freud's precise formulation according to which the melancholic is not aware of *what he has lost* in the lost object[40]—one has to introduce here the Lacanian distinction between the object and the (object-)cause of desire: while the object of desire is simply the desired object, the cause of desire is the feature on account of which we desire the desired object (some detail or tic which we are usually unaware

---

of the unbearable pressure to choose ...")—in this way, I gain time to reconsider my decision and go on living.

39   Giorgio Agamben, *Stanzas*, Minneapolis: University of Minnesota Press 1993, p. 20.

40   Sigmund Freud, "Trauer und Melancholie," in *Psychologie des Unbewussten*, Frankfurt: Fischer Verlag 1975, p. 199.

of, and sometimes even misperceive as the obstacle, as that in spite of which we desire the object). From this perspective, the melancholic is not primarily the subject fixated on the lost object, unable to perform the work of mourning in relation to it, but rather the subject who possesses the object but has lost his desire for it, because the cause which made him desire it has withdrawn, lost its efficacy. Far from accentuating to an extreme the situation of frustrated desire, of desire deprived of its object, melancholy rather stands for the presence of the object itself deprived of our desire for it—melancholy occurs when we finally get the desired object, but are disappointed with it.[41] In this precise sense, melancholy effectively is the beginning of philosophy—but is such melancholic disappointment also its end (in Hegel)? It may seem so: with Hegel, philosophy claims to reach its goal, Absolute Knowing, and once it gets there, once we reach Absolute Knowing, there is nowhere else to go, we can only turn backwards and long for the lost universe of loss. Comay's own characterization of the concluding gesture is, however, at odds with such a melancholic stance:

> It's the Saturnine aspect of the operation that fascinates me. Sluggish, torpid, "sunk into the night of its own self-consciousness," Absolute Knowing digests what it encounters and secretes what it has assimilated as its own excrescence. The subject simultaneously reaps and lays waste to the harvest of its history in a kind of philosophical potlatch or Saturnalia—a moment of kenotic expenditure in which the speculative reversal from loss to gain is in turn reversed ... Could such an undecidable figure—the very figure of indecision—make its comeback as the final figure of the dialectic?[42]

Does not this (highly pertinent) description point in the direction of what, in Freudian terms, is called *drive* (in its opposition to desire)? That is to say, what it describes is a joyous repetitive movement in which gain and loss are inextricably intertwined and which enjoys its own repetition. The *objet a* is here not lost (as in melancholy proper), but located in the very "moment of kenotic expenditure in which the speculative reversal from loss to gain is in turn reversed."[43] In other words, what pushes the drive is not the

---

41   For a more detailed account of melancholy, see Chapter 1 of Slavoj Žižek, *Did Somebody Say Totalitarianism?*, London: Verso Books 2011.

42   Comay, "Hegel's Last Words," pp. 232–3.

43   Hegel ends his *Encyclopaedia* in a similar vein, evoking the Idea which enjoys repeatedly going through its path: "the eternal idea which is for itself eternally sets itself to work, engenders and enjoys itself as absolute spirit" (*"die ewige an und*

persisting attachment to the lost object, but the repeated enacting of the loss as such—*the object of the drive is not a lost object, but loss itself as an object*. To get this key point, we should make clear the radical ambiguity of the *objet a*: when we define the *objet a* as the object which overlaps with its loss, which emerges at the very moment of its loss (so that all its fantasmatic incarnations, from breast to voice to gaze, are metonymic figurations of the void, of nothing), we remain within the horizon of *desire*—the true object-cause of desire is the void filled in by its fantasmatic incarnations. While, as Lacan emphasizes, the *objet a* is also the object of the drive, the relationship is here thoroughly different: although, in both cases, the link between object and loss is crucial, in the case of the *objet a* as the object-cause of *desire*, we have an object which is originally lost, which coincides with its own loss, which emerges as lost, while, in the case of the *objet a* as the object of drive, the "object" *is directly the loss itself*—in the shift from desire to drive, we pass from the *lost object* to *loss itself as an object*. That is to say, the weird movement called "drive" is not driven by the "impossible" quest for the lost object; it is *a push to directly enact the "loss"—the gap, cut, distance—itself*. The (death) drive which emerges at the concluding moment of the dialectical process, in its shift from the idealizing progress of sublation to pure repetition, does not intervene only at this point; its traces are discernible all over Hegel's edifice, from the status of madness in "Anthropology" to the necessity of war in the *Philosophy of Right*.[44]

Furthermore, if we read the infinite "foaming forth" from the chalice of spirits in this way, as the repetitive movement of the drive, then it also becomes clear how we can read it in a non-narcissistic way, not as the philosophical covering up of the gap (conceded by Schiller) that separates the divine Absolute from the realm of finite spirits. In Hegel's version, God is not just playing a game with Himself, pretending to lose Himself in externality while fully aware that He remains its master and creator: infinity is *out there*, and this "out there" is not a mere shadowy reflection of God's infinite power. In short, the divine Absolute is itself caught up in a process it cannot control—the Calvary of the last paragraph of the *Phenomenology* is not the Calvary of finite beings who pay the price for the Absolute's progress, but *the Calvary of the Absolute itself*. One should note how Hegel says here the exact opposite of the famous passage on the Cunning of Reason in his *Philosophy of History*:

---

für sich seiende Idee sich ewig als absoluter Geist betätigt, erzeugt und genießt") (§ 577).
44   See Chapter 7 of Žižek, *Less Than Nothing.*

The special interest of passion is thus inseparable from the active development of a general principle: for it is from the special and determinate and from its negation, that the Universal results. Particularity contends with its like, and some loss is involved in the issue. It is not the general idea that is implicated in opposition and combat, and that is exposed to danger. It remains in the background, untouched and uninjured. This may be called the *cunning of reason*,—that it sets the passions to work for itself, while that which develops its existence through such impulsion pays the penalty and suffers loss. For it is *phenomenal* being that is so treated, and of this, part is of no value, part is positive and real. The particular is for the most part of too trifling value as compared with the general: individuals are sacrificed and abandoned. The Idea pays the penalty of determinate existence and of corruptibility, not from itself, but from the passions of individuals.[45]

Here we get what we expect the "textbook Hegel" to say: Reason works as a hidden substantial power that realizes its goal by deftly exploiting individual passions; engaged individuals fight each other, and through their struggle the universal Idea actualizes itself. The conflict is thus limited to the domain of the particular, while the Idea "remains in the background, untouched and uninjured," at peace with itself, as the calm of the true universality. This standard teleology is, however, totally rejected by what Hegel sees as the fundamental lesson of Christianity: far from remaining "in the background, untouched and uninjured," *the Absolute itself pays the price, irretrievably sacrificing itself.*

We should remember here that Schiller was the main proponent of the German aesthetic reaction to the French Revolution: his message was that, in order to avoid the destructive fury of the Terror, the revolution should occur with the rise of a new aesthetic sensibility, through the transformation of the state into an organic and beautiful Whole (Lacoue-Labarthe located the beginnings of fascism in this aesthetic rejection of the Jacobin Terror[46]). Since Hegel clearly saw the necessity of the Terror, his reference to Schiller could be paraphrased as: "*only from the chalice of this revolutionary Terror foams forth the infinitude of spiritual freedom.*" And, taking a step further, we can even propose a paraphrase concerning the relationship

---

45   G. W. F. Hegel, *Philosophy of History, III*, Philosophic History, § 36, available at marxists.org.

46   See Philippe Lacoue-Labarthe, *Heidegger, Art and Politics*, London: Blackwell 1990.

between Phenomenology and Logic: "*only from the chalice of phenomenology, which contains the Calvary of the Absolute Spirit, foams forth the infinitude of logic, pure logic.*" The relationship between Hegel's Logic and Phenomenology should thus be conceived along the lines of Walter Benjamin's early essay "On Language in General and Human Language in Particular"—the point here is not that human language is a species of some universal language "as such," which also comprises other species (the languages of gods and angels, of animals, aliens, computers, DNA?): there is no actually existing language other than human language—but, in order to comprehend this "particular" language, one *has* to introduce a minimal difference, conceiving it with regard to the gap that separates it from language "as such" (the pure structure of language deprived of the insignia of human finitude, of erotic passions and mortality, of struggles for domination and the obscenity of power). In a strictly homologous way, one could say "On Logic in General and Phenomenology in Particular": in order to comprehend the logic of historical phenomena, one has to introduce the gap which separates it from logic "as such."

Furthermore, one should insist here on the ambiguity of Hegel's basic claim that the subject "recognizes itself in the Other": we can read it as the formula of the narcissistic reappropriation of the Other (the subject swallows the Other, depriving it of its apparent autonomy), but also in a more literal way as that of recognizing oneself as "decentered," as a moment of the self-mediation of an irreducible Otherness. Read this way, Hegel implicitly answers here the critique formulated by Habermas and others according to which the Hegelian Absolute remains "monological," playing with itself and admitting no intersubjectivity proper. The subject not only has to share the central space with other subjects, it is in itself "decentered" in the sense that its rise is an effect of the inconsistency/antagonism of the substantial Other. But how? François Balmès pointed out the path when he claimed that

> *structure is what allows us to think the subject's constitution*, since, in the real, the subject is a structure's effect. It follows that this question of the subject's constitution is, for sure, subversive with regard to the philosophical tradition concerning the subject. In that tradition, this question has no sense, since the subject is its ultimate condition, so that one cannot derive it from anything else—although it is possible for the subject to emerge to itself in a history, as is the case with Hegel and in Hegelianizing readings of *wo es war*.[47]

---

47   François Balmès, *Structure, logique, aliénation*, Toulouse: eres 2011, p. 44.

What this means is that we should leave behind the stale old topic of "structure versus the subject": Lacan rejects the Sartrean notion of structure as the "reified" residue of the living subject's productive activity, as well as the contrary Lévi-Straussian notion of subjective experience as an illusory surface effectively regulated by objective structural networks. The question nonetheless remains: how are we to think the structure so that the subject emerges from it? Lacan's answer is: as an inconsistent, non-All, symbolic structure articulated around a constitutive void/impossibility. More precisely, the subject emerges through the structure's own reflective self-relating which inscribes into the structure itself its constitutive lack—this inscription *within* the structure of what is constitutively *excluded* from it is "the signifier which represents the subject for other signifiers."

Lacan once quipped that the best way to read Hamlet's famous "to be or not to be" is to see it as a bungled attempt to fill in a gap by means of recourse to tautology. The natural form of Hamlet's line would have been "to be or not ..."—let us say, a Danish prince, so we can imagine Hamlet unable to decide whether he should assume his title or not: "To be or not to be the Prince of Denmark, that is the question for me now, the dilemma I am not able to resolve ..." But Hamlet got stuck just prior to pronouncing the title he is called on to assume: "To be or not ..."; so to avoid getting caught up in a stuttering repetition ("To be or not ... to be or not ..."), he makes a desperate move to fill in the gap with the only means at his disposal, tautology: "To be or not ... to be!" This is why Graham Priest's answer to Shakespeare's question—"TO BE *AND* NOT TO BE—THAT IS THE ANSWER"[48]—somehow falls flat, offering a "synthesis" of being and non-being that obliterates the concrete existential tension of Shakespeare's question: it is better not to be, but even this attempt at radical negation can fail, perhaps it cannot even be achieved, so that we are condemned as undead. In other words, what Hamlet discovers in the "To be or not to be" soliloquy is that annihilation may be impossible—a dimension beyond Heidegger's being-towards-death. The awareness that nothingness is a screen covering up the horror of interminable existence deprives suicide, which appears as the final mastery one can exercise over being, of its function of mastery. Here we should deploy the distinction between being-towards-death and the death drive, Freud's name for the ultimate immortality.

---

48 See Graham Priest, *Doubt Truth to Be a Liar*, Oxford: Oxford University Press 2008, p. 208.

Man is uncanny because he not merely *has* but *is* the 'audacity ... to overwhelm the appearing sway by withholding all openness toward it.' He is a 'counter-violence' against the violence of the 'overwhelming sway' of being itself. *Dasein* triumphs over the violence of the overwhelming sway not by surviving, but by dying: 'Not-being-here is the ultimate victory over Being.' This is the danger not of *suicide* but of *ontocide*.[49]

In short, since there is no Being without Being-There, i.e., since the essence of man is to be the (only) "there" of the disclosure of being, suicide kills Being itself. Here one should not be afraid to pursue a naive line of questioning: are there other forms of ontocide, like the triumph of technology which threatens to reduce man to a natural organism, or psychotic illness? What lurks behind this question is the most fundamental philosophical issue: is the disclosure of Being the most elementary level of being-human? What if Heidegger's existential analytic of *Dasein* as being-towards-death fails to account for psychotics? A psychotic subject occupies an existential position for which there is no place in Heidegger's mapping—the position of someone who in a way "survives his own death." Psychotics no longer fit Heidegger's description of *Dasein*'s engaged existence, their life no longer moves within the coordinates of freely engaging in a futural project against the background of assuming one's past: their life is outside "care" (*Sorge*), their being is no longer directed "towards death."[50] In this sense, psychotics are the actual "living dead," alive but excluded from the big Other.

This, maybe, is why *Hamlet* is the first drama of modern subjectivity: the subject is in itself "thwarted," the paradoxical result of its own failure-to-be—or, in the simplified terms of the loop of symbolic representation: the subject endeavors to represent itself adequately, this representation fails, and the subject *is* the result of this failure. Recall the "Hugh Grant paradox" (referring to the famous scene from *Four Weddings and a Funeral*): the hero tries to express his love to his beloved only to get caught up in stumbling and confused repetitions; yet in his very failure to deliver his message in an articulate way he bears witness to its authenticity. We encounter a similar paradox in the history of Western music, which, "at least since 1500, has been organized in terms of a symmetrical correspondence and even a reciprocal influence between the largest aspects of form and the smallest detail.

49   Andrew Cutrofello, *All for Nothing: Hamlet's Negativity* (Cambridge, MA: MIT Press, forthcoming). The quotes within the quote are from Heidegger.

50   For a more detailed account of this limitation of Heidegger, see Chapter 13 of Žižek, *Less Than Nothing*.

A lack of correspondence is either a sign of the composer's incompetence, or else a source of expression."[51] Again, the very incompetence (inconsistency, clumsiness) can be the source of the expression of subjectivity.

If a "substance" is an X which expresses itself in its attributes or representations, even if this representation is failed and partial, then a "subject" is something much more radical: an X which emerges retroactively through the failure of its representation, with no substantial content preceding this loss or failure. It is from here that we can return to "the infamous hyphen in *Er-innerung*": "Even while graphically emphasizing the intensification of interiority, the mark registers a split within the self-remembering self. At this point of fracture thought is forced to pause at the memory of possibilities still unachieved."[52] Absolute Knowing (AK) is thus not just a moment of closure, but simultaneously the moment of closure *and* radical openness: "thought is forced to pause at the memory of possibilities still unachieved." How? Let us turn to another aspect of the Hegelian coincidence of opposites: symbol and object (pure signifier and its support, the material remainder), but also, in an organism, the highest and the lowest.[53] The classic case here is Hegel's analysis of the infinite judgment of phrenology ("The spirit is a bone"), which is illustrated by the example of the penis, at the same time the organ of the highest function of the organism (insemination) and the lowest (urination):

> The "depth" which mind brings out from within, but carries no further than to make it a presentation (*Vorstellung*), and lets it remain at this level—and the "ignorance" on the part of this consciousness as to what it really says, are the same kind of connexion of higher and lower which, in the case of the living being, nature naïvely expresses when it combines the organ of its highest

---

51   Charles Rosen, *Schoenberg*, London: Fontana Collins 1975, p. 44.
52   Comay, "Hegel's Last Words," p. 243.
53   Only from this perspective can one provide an adequate reading of Freud's infamous statement concerning the status of sexual difference: "Anatomy is destiny." This should be read as an Hegelian "speculative judgment" in which the predicate "passes over" into the subject. That is to say, its true meaning is not the obvious one, the standard target of the feminist critique (i.e., "the anatomical difference between the sexes directly founds, is directly responsible for, the different socio-symbolic roles of men and women"), but rather the opposite : the "truth" of anatomy is "destiny," i.e., a symbolic formation. In the case of sexual identity, an anatomic difference is "sublated," turned into the medium of appearance or expression—more precisely, into the material support—of a certain symbolic formation.

fulfillment, the organ of generation, with the organ of urination. The infinite judgment *qua* infinite would be the fulfillment of life that comprehends itself, while the consciousness of the infinite judgment that remains at the level of presentation corresponds to urination.[54]

In his *Naturphilosophie*, Hegel adds the case of the *mouth*, which "has the dual function of initiating the immediate conversion of food into organic structures in the animal organism and *also*, in contrast to this inwardizing of the outer, of completing the objectification of subjectivity occurring in the voice."[55] What if AK is also an *organ* (of Reason) in which the highest and the lowest overlap? The lowest: the false highest, the common idea of AK—"Hegel knew everything." The highest: what? Crucial here is the dialogic structure of this coincidence: the speculative truth of the proposition only emerges through a repeated reading. "Spirit is a bone"—this is nonsense, an utter contradiction—but spirit *is* this contradiction. The same holds for AK: "Hegel, this miserable, weak, mortal, and finite individual, deployed AK"—nonsense, a ridiculous impossibility, we cannot step out of the constraints of our historical epoch. But Hegel knew this—recall the famous lines from the Preface to the *Philosophy of Right*: "As for the individual, everyone is a son of his time; so philosophy also is its time apprehended in thoughts. It is just as foolish to fancy that any philosophy can transcend its present world, as that an individual could leap out of his time or jump over Rhodes."[56] But what about the teleological-historicist reading: Hegel was simply lucky to live in an epoch when access to AK became historically possible, in the same way that, as Marx noted, only in developed capitalist society does the abstract-universal notion of labor become social reality? We should be very precise here: it is not only that Hegel was also aware of the historical relativity of his thought; paradoxically, what AK means is that *only* Hegel was really ready to draw the consequences of his own historical relativization. In other words, AK is ultimately a name for historical *closure*. In a nice reversal of the "Spirit is a bone" type of proposition, in this case it is the "vulgar" reading which appears as "high" (access to the divine mind, etc.), and the speculative reading which introduces historical limitations.

Therein lies the ultimate "coincidence of the opposites" in the Hegelian system: *its closure is the very form (of appearance) of its openness.* That is to

---

54   Hegel, *Phenomenology of Spirit*, p. 210.
55   Hegel, *Encyclopaedia*, § 401, available at marxists.org.
56   Hegel, *Philosophy of Right*, Preface, available at marxists.org.

say, the idea that Hegel simply closes his system with the mirage of total knowledge about everything there is to know, somehow bringing the entire universe to its completion, is completely wrong: what Hegel calls AK is his name for a radical experience of self-limitation, of what Lacan referred to as *il n'y a pas de métalangage*. We reach AK not when we "know it all," but when we reach the point at which there is no longer any external point of reference by means of which we could relativize our own position—in AK, the very fact that no external limit is discernible, that we do not see the limits of our world, bears witness to our limitation, to our immersion in a world whose horizon we do not perceive. This is why the Hegelian totality is "non-All," incomplete, self-relativization brought to an extreme, and at the same time always already completed, totalized—these two aspects are the two sides of the same coin.

This, perhaps, brings us to the most concise definition of Hegelian Absolute Knowing: it means fully assuming the big Other's inexistence, that is to say, the inexistence of the big Other as the subject-supposed-to-know. There is a key difference between this knowing and what, in a certain Socratic or mystical tradition, is called *docta ignorantia*: the latter refers to the *subject*'s knowing its own ignorance, while the ignorance registered by the subject of Absolute Knowing is that of *the big Other itself*. The formula of true atheism is thus: divine knowing and existence are incompatible, God exists only insofar as He does not know (take note of, register) His own inexistence. The moment God knows, He collapses into the abyss of inexistence.

CHAPTER 6

God's Twisted Identity

GODS OF THE REAL

At the beginning of Ridley Scott's *Prometheus*, his sequel to the *Alien* trilogy, a spacecraft departs our Earth in prehistoric times, leaving behind a humanoid alien who drinks a dark bubbling liquid and then disintegrates. As his remains cascade into a waterfall, his DNA triggers a biogenetic reaction that leads to the genesis of human beings. The film then jumps to 2089 in Scotland, where two archeologists discover a star map that matches other maps from several disparate ancient cultures. They interpret it as representing an invitation from humanity's forerunners, the so-called "Engineers," and set out to follow the map to the distant moon LV-223 aboard the scientific vessel *Prometheus*. Once there, "they find a cryogenically preserved clone or sibling of the original alien 'creator' who seeded earth with DNA. The humans foolishly awaken him, perhaps expecting some sort of seminar on the purpose of life. Instead, the alien starts knocking heads off and strides away to resume his pre-nap project of traveling to and destroying the planet earth."[1] In the film's last scene, one of the archeologists (played by Noomi Rapace) desperately shouts at the homicidal alien: "I need to know why! What did we do wrong? Why do you hate us?" Is this not an exemplary case of the Lacanian "Che vuoi?"—of the impenetrability of the gods of the Real?

Where do we find these living gods? In the pagan Thing: God dies in Himself in Judaism and for Himself in Christianity. The destructive aspect of the divine that marks a living god—the brutal explosion of rage mixed with ecstatic bliss—is what Lacan is aiming at with his statement that the gods belong to the Real. An exemplary literary case of such an encounter with the divine Real can be found in Euripides' last play *The Bacchae*, which examines religious ecstasy and the resistance to it. Disguised as a young holy man traveling from Asia, the god Bacchus arrives in Thebes where he proclaims his godhood and preaches his orgiastic religion. Pentheus, the

---

1   Barbara Ehrenreich, "The Missionary Position," *The Baffler* 21 (2012), p. 132.

young Theban king, is horrified at the ensuing outbreak of sacred orgies and prohibits his people from worshiping Bacchus. Enraged by this, Bacchus leads Pentheus to a nearby mountain, a site of sacred orgies, where the women of Thebes—including Agave, Pentheus' own mother—tear him to pieces in a Bacchic destructive frenzy. The play outlines four existential positions towards the sacred orgiastic ritual. First, there is that of Pentheus himself, an enlightened rationalist and a skeptic in matters religious. He rejects the Bacchic orgies as mere cover for sensual indulgence, and is determined to suppress them by force:

> It so happens I've been away from Thebes,
> but I hear about disgusting things going on,
> here in the city—women leaving home
> to go to silly Bacchic rituals,
> cavorting there in mountain shadows,
> with dances honoring some upstart god,
> this Dionysus, whoever he may be. Mixing bowls
> in the middle of their meetings are filled with wine.
> They creep off one by one to lonely spots
> to have sex with men, claiming they're Maenads
> busy worshipping. But they rank Aphrodite,
> goddess of sexual desire, ahead of Bacchus.[2]

Then there are the two positions of wisdom. Teiresias, a blind man of pious and reverent soul, preaches fidelity to traditions as the sacred and imperishable heritage:

> To the gods we mortals are all ignorant.
> Those old traditions from our ancestors,
> the ones we've had as long as time itself,
> no argument will ever overthrow,
> in spite of subtleties sharp minds invent.

His advice is nonetheless sustained by a Marxist-like notion of religion as an opium of the people:

---

2   All quotations from *The Bacchae* are from the translation by Ian Johnston, available at https://records.viu.ca.

> [Bacchus] brought with him liquor from the grape,
> something to match the bread from Demeter.
> He introduced it among mortal men.
> When they can drink up what streams off the vine,
> unhappy mortals are released from pain.
> It grants them sleep, allows them to forget
> their daily troubles. Apart from wine,
> there is no cure for human hardship.

This line of thought is radicalized by Cadmus, the wise old counselor to the king who advises caution and submission:

> You should live among us,
> not outside traditions. At this point,
> you're flying around—thinking, but not clearly.
> For if, as you claim, this man is not a god,
> why not call him one? Why not tell a lie,
> a really good one?

In short, Cadmus' position is that of Plato in the *Republic*: ordinary people need beautiful lies, so we should pretend to believe in order to keep them in check.

Finally, beneath these three positions, there is that of the wild (feminine) mob itself: while the debate between the other positions goes on, from time to time we hear the passionate cries and wild ecstatic prayers of the Bacchantes, proclaiming their scorn for "the wisdom of deep thinkers," and their devotion to the "customs and beliefs of the multitude." The Bacchantes are anti-Platonic in the extreme: against abstract rationalism, they assert their fidelity to customs which form a particular life world; from their point of view, the true act of madness is the attempt to exclude madness, the madness of pure rationality. In other words, the true madman is Pentheus, not the orgiastic Bacchantes. Teiresias in fact draws the same conclusion:

> You've got a quick tongue and seem intelligent,
> but your words don't make any sense at all.
> … You unhappy man, you've no idea
> just what it is you're saying. You've gone mad!
> Even before now you weren't in your right mind.

In other words, as we saw earlier, the true "madness" is not the ecstatic excess of the Night of the World, but the madness of the passage to the symbolic itself. What is the madness caused merely by the loss of reason, like the crazy dancing of the Bacchantes, compared to the madness of reason itself?

The living god of *The Bacchae* continues his subterranean life and returns erratically in multiple forms, all of which are guises of the monstrous Thing. Recall J. Lee Thompson's film *The White Buffalo*, based on the novel by Richard Sale, definitely "one of the most bizarre curiosities ever released in cinemas."[3] In this strange Western variation on *Moby Dick*, Wild Bill Hickok (Charles Bronson) is an "Ahab of the West," haunted by dreams of a giant albino buffalo (also a sacred animal for native Americans). Hickok has just returned from play-acting on Eastern stages with Buffalo Bill; aged thirty-seven, he wears blue-tinted glasses to protect his fading eyes from the "Deep Serene"—the result of a gonorrheal infection—and his various bullet wounds have brought on premature rheumatism. On his travels he meets Chief Crazy Horse, who is roaming the plains in an obsessive search for a giant white buffalo that killed his young daughter. Hickok teams up with him to hunt down the beast.

Hickok's tinted glasses signify his blinded gaze, but his impotence is also explicitly ascertained in the film: when he meets his old love, Poker Jenny (Kim Novak, in her last role), he is unable to fulfill her expectations. However, paradoxically, the same (impotence) holds even more for the White Buffalo itself, so that it would be easy to propose an elementary Freudian reading: the White Buffalo is the primordial father who is not yet dead, and who thereby blocks the hero's sexual potency—his desperate sound is homologous to that of *shofar* in Jewish religion; the scene the hero endeavors to stage is thus that of parricide. The White Buffalo stands for the dying primordial father whose blind strength is the obverse of its impotence—in a way, the beast's impotence is the impotence of its raw strength itself. It is like the God encountered by Job: omnipotent, but morally insensitive and stupid.[4]

---

3   Jeff Bond, Review of *The White Buffalo*, available at creaturefeatures.com.

4   We encounter a similar impotence in Erich von Stroheim's two major sound roles, both with an ironic "great" in the title: *The Great Gabbo* (1929) and *The Great Flamarion* (1945). In both films, he plays a circus artist led to self-destruction by his jealousy and arrogance. Note the similar self-humiliation in Wilder's *Sunset Boulevard*, where Stroheim plays Max, Norma Desmond's servant and all-around attendant (butler, driver …), who is in reality Max von Mayerling, her director

The heroes track the sacred beast to a great cave where it lives with its cows. Hickok wants the pelt as a money-making display item, while Crazy Horse wants it for wrapping up his dead daughter, to ease her way across the great stars. The whole movie points towards their showdown with the demon, a delirium of action and horror. When it comes, the showdown is presented as a well-staged climactic *scene* in which, on a narrow mountain pass, the buffalo will attack the hero and he will kill him. It is crucial to bear in mind this aspect of the film: there is nothing spontaneous in the final showdown, it is presented as a carefully staged event—prior to the expected attack, Hickok and Crazy Horse carefully examine the mountain pass and arrange details here and there. The effect of artificiality is compounded by the mechanical nature of the beast (the film was shot before the invasion of digital creatures, and the Buffalo's movements are clearly those of a clumsy puppet) and by the obvious use of studio sets for the final confrontation (artificial snow, plastic rocks, etc.). Far from ruining the desired effect, however, all these features generate the somnambulistic and clumsy quality of a carefully prepared mechanical theatre scene.

Such an Event of encountering the Real Thing is taken to its extreme when the Thing is no longer an inner-worldly entity but the abyss itself, the void in which inner-worldly things disappear. This abyss exerts a strange mixture of horror and attraction, pulling us towards itself—but in what direction? The famous lines of the *chorus mysticus* that conclude *Faust* represent Goethe's "wisdom" at its worst: "Everything transient is just a simile; the deficient here really happens; the indescribable is here done; the eternal-feminine pulls us upwards." If nothing else, this pseudo-profound babbling gets the direction wrong: it pulls us *down*, not up—down like the Maelström from Edgar Allan Poe's "A Descent into the Maelström."[5] The story is told by a narrator who reports what an old Norwegian fisherman told him at the edge of a huge cliff overlooking the stormy sea. From time to time, a furious current shapes the smaller whirlpools into a huge

when she was still a star. *Sunset Boulevard* also contains one of the ultimate dialogue exchanges in the entire history of cinema: when the film's (un)dead hero Gillis (William Holden) notices a large portrait on the wall and realizes that Desmond was once a very famous silent movie star, he says: "You used to be big," and she retorts: "I am big. It's the pictures that got small." Is this not true today more than ever? Half-forgotten classics from Eisenstein to Lubitsch are still great, it's just that the movies have got small …

5   Incidentally, if ever there was a political regime in which the eternal feminine claims to draw its subjects upwards, it is today's North Korea.

mile-long funnel, the "great whirlpool of the Maelström." Whenever a ship comes within a mile of its full force, it is carried to the bottom and slammed against the rocks until the Maelström ceases. Since its sublime strength seems to defy rational explanation, the narrator is drawn to more fantastic explanations of the Maelström as an entrance to the abyss at the middle of the Earth. Years earlier, as the old fisherman relates, a terrible hurricane had torn off the masts of the ship on which he and his brother were returning home. When the two men discovered with horror that they were caught by the Maelström, they sensed their doom. But as the waves crashed around him, the old man becomes calm in his despair, thinking how magnificent it will be to die this way, exploring the Maelström's depths, even if it is at the cost of his life. As the force of the boat's whirling pins him to its sides, he sees a rainbow in the vortex, caused by the movement of the water spiraling downwards. He notices how in the wreckage that swirls around him the smaller cylinders seem to be descending more slowly into the abyss. He lashes himself to a water cask and cuts himself loose from the boat. His brother refuses to move and is lost. By the time the boat reaches the centre of the abyss, the funnel of the Maelström has become calm. The man finds himself on the surface where another ship soon picks him up—he has been saved, but, as he tells the narrator, his black hair has turned white and his face has rapidly aged.

In his ability to overcome his fear and reason his way to safety, the old man is similar to Auguste Dupin, Poe's arch-model of the private detective who is a master in the art of deduction. Although "A Descent into the Maelström" is an adventure horror story, it can also be read as a mystery story in which, at the end, the detective reveals how his powers of deduction brought him to the solution to the enigma. The old man here has already resolved the enigma, and is now recounting his thinking process to a rapt listener whose role is analogous to that of Dupin's commonsensical narrator friend, the forerunner of Holmes' Watson and Poirot's Captain Hastings: he is honest but lacks the spark that makes Dupin and the old fisherman the heroes of their respective stories. Indeed, the subtitle of the story might have been something like "The birth of rational thinking out of the spirit of the deadly vortex": in the story, cold rational thinking and the death drive overlap, since the latter (in its strict Freudian sense) refers not to the subject's willing surrender to the abyss, but to his repetitive circulation on the edge of the vortex. In other words, the death drive is on the side of reason rather than irrationality, which brings us back to Hegel's notion of the abyssal "Night of the World" as the very core of subjectivity: is not the abyss of subjectivity the ultimate Maelstrom? And is not rational thinking the art of circulating around the very edge of this abyss?

Another exemplary case can be found in the history of rock music. "In-A-Gadda-Da-Vida" is a song by Iron Butterfly from their 1968 album *In-A-Gadda-Da-Vida*; at a little over seventeen minutes, it occupies the entire second side of the album. (A slightly longer live version was released as part of their 1969 live album.) The simple lyrics are heard only at the beginning and at the end:

> In-a-gadda-da-vida, honey
> Don't you know that I love you?
> In-a-gadda-da-vida, baby
> Don't you know that I'll always be true?
> Oh, won't you come with me and take my hand?
> Or, won't you come with me and walk this land?
> Ah, please take my hand.

But the lyrics in themselves are insignificant—what matters is the hypnotic ostinato, a repetitive melodic phrase that casts a spell over the entire song (making it clear why this album marks the beginning of psychedelic hard rock), and which strangely echoes the song's weird title. According to rumor, the song's title was originally "In the Garden of Eden," but at one point in the course of rehearsals, singer Doug Ingle got drunk and slurred the words, creating the mondegreen that stuck as the title.[6] The title suggests at least three lines of semantic association: in the garden of Eden; in the garden of life (if one reads "vida" as a Spanish word); and in the garden of David (where the king had sex with Bathsheba). In all three cases, the garden in question is a prohibited Zone, a site of transgressive enjoyment. The song was used as background music during the final confrontation with the serial killer in Michael Mann's *Manhunter* (a version of *Red Dragon*, the first Hannibal Lecter novel, and much superior to the later version with Anthony Hopkins), and it strangely fits and reinforces the atmosphere of the killer preparing to ritually murder a helpless woman, rendering the uncanny coincidence of the sacred, the erotic,

---

6   A mondegreen is the result of a mishearing or misinterpretation of a phrase due to a near-homophony, in a way that gives it a new meaning. The term comes from a misheard version of Percy's *Reliques*—"They have slain the Earl o' Moray, / And Lady Mondegreen," where the actual second line is "And laid him on the green."

and cold murderous violence. No wonder the song causes such uneasiness, an uneasiness often covered up by a dismissive stance, as in the following comment from urbandictionary.com:

> In A Gadda Da Vida (drunk for "In the Garden of Eden") is an early heavy metal tune that became a classic solely through its sheer, mind-numbing length and incomprehensibility. At the time, this was confused for mysticism. The lyrics are but a few mere lines of sticky sweet romanticism, totally at odds with constipated metal vocals—the latter of which were appropriate for the time and genre, the former of which would not be appropriate under any circumstances.

The correct perception that the song's lyrics are "a few mere lines of sticky sweet romanticism, totally at odds with constipated metal vocals" totally misses the point—which is the very fact that they are at odds. Recall Heinrich von Kleist's short story "St. Cecilia or the Power of the Voice," which takes place in a German town torn between Protestants and Catholics during the Thirty Years War. The Protestants plan to trigger a slaughter in a large Catholic church during a midnight mass; four people are planted to start making trouble and thus give the signal to the others to wreak havoc. However, things take a strange turn when a beautiful nun, allegedly dead, miraculously awakens and leads the chorus in a beautiful song. When the song mesmerizes the four thugs, they fail to give the signal and the night passes peacefully. Even after the event, the four Protestants remain numbed: they are locked in an asylum where for years they just sit and pray all day long—at midnight each night, all four promptly stand up and sing the sublime song they heard that fateful night. Here, of course, the horror arises, since what was originally a divine chorus exerting a miraculous redemptive-pacifying effect is now a frightfully repulsive imitation. This grotesque singing inverts the standard version of the obscene turn—for example, the face of the innocent girl all of a sudden distorted by rage as she starts to spit out all sorts of profanities (the possessed girl in *The Exorcist*, etc.). The standard version renders visible the horror and corruption beneath the gentle surface—what could be worse than this? Precisely what takes place in Kleist's story: the ultimate horror occurs not when the mask of innocence disintegrates, but when the sublime text is (mis)appropriated by the wrong, the corrupted, speaker. In the standard version, we have the right object (the gentle innocent face) at the wrong place (issuing profanities), while in Kleist we have the wrong object (the brutal thugs) at the right place (trying to imitate the sublime religious ritual), which produces a much stronger profanation. And is it not the same discord at work in "In-A-Gadda-Da-Vida"? Sweet words of love sung by "constipated metal vocals" ... What the Urban Dictionary critic misses is precisely the effect of the song's "mind-numbing length and incomprehensibility," an effect of hypnotic repetitiveness whose stupid enjoyment obliterates all meaning. This is why the primary force of the song's title resides not in the multiplicity of its semantic associations, but in the way its weird sonority eclipses meaning and entangles us in the enjoyment of its meaningless obscenity—an exemplary case of the shift from meaning to enjoy-meant (*jouis-sense*).

The bond of the Word

So what happens when these living gods withdraw, when they no longer operate in a collective libidinal economy? Hegel had already noted that the word is the murder of the thing, which means that the death of the gods, far from liberating us from the symbolic link, enforces the power of the Word to the utmost. Let us take a perhaps surprising example, the 1947 film *Nightmare Alley* (dir. Edmund Goulding), which follows the rise and fall of a con man. The first thing to note about this outstanding *noir* is its circular narrative structure: it begins and ends at a seedy traveling carnival, with the figure of a circus freak or "geek." In the opening scene, Stanton Carlisle (Tyrone Power), who has just joined the carnival, expresses his weird fascination with the lowest attraction there, a half-crazy geek who lives totally isolated in his cage and amuses the public by eating live chickens. When Stanton asks how anyone can fall so low, other members of the carnival reproach him for raising a topic one should keep silent about. The figure of the geek, this "strange attractor" of the film's universe, stands for a *homo sacer*: the living dead, alive but excluded from the community, not to be talked about. "You never give up!" Stanton is told in the film—and, indeed, he goes to the end, fully realizing his fate and, like Oedipus, becoming fully human only when he ends up as no longer human. The geek-motif underlies the entire film: the geek's crazy laughter is regularly heard in the background at the key moments in the story.[7]

---

7   One should mention here Tyrone Power's personal commitment to the film: he bought the film rights to the novel and then blackmailed the studio into making it, allowing him to play a role which totally breaks with swashbuckling figures like

Stanton works with "Mademoiselle Zeena" and her alcoholic husband, Pete; they were once a top-billed act, using an ingenious code to make it appear that she had extraordinary mental powers, until her (unspecified) misdeeds drove Pete to drink and reduced them to working in a third-rate outfit. Stanton learns that many people want to buy the code from Zeena, but she will not sell. One night, he accidentally gives Pete the wrong bottle of alcohol and Pete dies. Zeena is now forced to tell Stanton the code and train him to be her assistant. Stanton, however, prefers the company of the younger Molly; when their affair is discovered, they are forced into a shotgun marriage. Stanton realizes this is a golden opportunity for him: now that he knows the code, he and his wife can leave the carnival. He becomes "The Great Stanton," performing with great success in expensive nightclubs. However, Stanton has even higher ambitions: with the help of crooked Chicago psychologist Lilith Ritter,[8] who provides him with information about her patients, he passes himself off as a medium able to communicate with the dead. At first it works brilliantly, but when he tries to swindle the skeptical Ezra Grindle, it all comes crashing down. Demanding proof from Stanton that he can really summon the ghosts of the dead, Grindle asks to see his long-lost love. Stanton convinces Molly to participate in the trick and play the role of the deceased, but when Grindle is totally taken in by the performance and kneels down in prayer, Molly breaks down and starts to shout she cannot go on. Stanton and Molly then have to leave town hurriedly. Stanton sends Molly back to the carnival world, while he gradually sinks into alcoholism. When he tries to find work at another carnival, he suffers the ultimate degradation: the only job he can get is playing the geek. Unable to stand his life any further, he goes berserk. Fortunately, as it turns out, Molly happens to work for the same carnival, and she brings him back from madness to normal life. The happy ending was, of course, imposed by the studio; there is nonetheless an unexpected echo between these final moments of the film and the scene in which Molly breaks down, unable to keep up the fake impersonation: it is as if here, at the end, *the (fake) recognition succeeds*—in contrast to Grindle, Stanton is fully duped and taken in by Molly's appearance.

Zorro. And his unique face seemed made for the part, with its strange sadness, colored with a touch of melancholic evil.

8   What makes the character of Lilith unique is the total absence of sexual tension between her and Stanton: although Lilith is the only figure in the film who comes close to a *femme fatale*, she is—in contrast to the *noir* formula—totally desexualized.

The loop of fate that closes upon itself in the film's circular structure is obvious to the point of ridicule: when Stanton encounters the geek at the start, he misses the dimension of *de te fabula narratur*, that is, he fails to recognize his own future, what awaits him at the end of the road. The (again, ridiculously naive) references to cards, which repeatedly point to a catastrophic future for Stanton, play the same role of emphasizing the closed loop. How does this loop stand with regard to the basic types of tragedy (classic, Christian, modern, *noir*)? It fits none of them. In classic tragedy, the doomed hero assumes the Fate that crushes him, but continues to protest against it, to curse it. In Christianity, the God of Fate is dead and the only bond remaining is that of the Word; tragedy ensues when, in the absence of the God of Fate, the subject overlooks this bond and wrongly thinks he can freely manipulate words without paying the price. Modern tragedy is best exemplified by the feminine *no* of the great literary heroines—from the Princesse de Clèves to Isabel Archer in *The Portrait of a Lady*—mysteriously rejecting happiness at the very point when it is within their reach. In the *noir*, the hero is a sucker betrayed by a *femme fatale*, and the tragic moment occurs at the end when, close to death, fully aware that he has been the victim of a brutal manipulation, the hero nonetheless has to admit that he regrets nothing—he would have made all the same choices even had he known his fate in advance.[9]

In what, then, does Stanton's "sin" consist? In playing tricks with others' beliefs, in ignoring the bond of the Word in a godless world—his tragedy is thus closest to the Christian type. When he tries to convince Molly to help him to perform the trick on Grindle, a strange debate ensues: when she accuses him of playing God in faking his contact with the spirit world, Stanton insists that he never mentions God, but merely performs harmless tricks which bring satisfaction to his customers—this strange respect for a God who remains off limits to his manipulations is curious, but crucial. Molly, dressed up as the ghost of Grindle's dead fiancée, cannot go on when the customer is fully duped and falls on his knees praying—but *why* could she not sustain the illusion, why did she find it unbearable and blasphemous to be identified as the object of the other's desire? To answer this question, we have to see how the bond of the Word which defines the religions of

---

9   Incidentally, if *Nightmare Alley* had been a traditional *noir*, the story would have been told in flashback, as in Tod Browning's *Freaks*: at the beginning, we would see a group of carnival-goers observing a geek who would remain off-screen; then, in flashback, somebody (a guide, usually) would tell the geek's story; and then, at the end, we would return to the carnival and get a full view of the geek.

the dead god necessarily culminates in the well-known words of *Kol Nidre*, sung on the evening before Yom Kippur:

> All [personal] vows we are likely to make, all [personal] oaths and pledges we are likely to take between this Yom Kippur and the next Yom Kippur, we publicly renounce. Let them all be relinquished and abandoned, null and void, neither firm nor established. Let our [personal] vows, pledges and oaths be considered neither vows nor pledges nor oaths.

For obvious reasons—not least to counter the charge that Jews are not to be trusted since their own sacred song enjoins them to break their vows—interpreters try to relativize these words, pointing out that they concern only personal vows, vows one makes to oneself, not vows made to others in public space. But such a reading obfuscates the much more radical dimension of *Kol Nidre*: the basic insight of Judeo-Christianity that dissolving the bond of the Word is immanent to *logos*, that it functions as its inner limit/excess, as the immanent negativity of the symbolic. This is why the "pragmatic paradox" of *Kol Nidre* has to be emphasized: it makes a *vow* to renounce vows, and the renunciation of vows has to be publicly proclaimed, performed as a symbolic act. Why? Because, as Lacan put it, there is no meta-language, there is no Other of the Other. Why do we make promises? Precisely because there is always the possibility that we will break them, and a pledge, an act of obligation, can only occur against the background of this possibility. The Other (the invisible core of another subject) is by definition an abyss lurking beneath all his or her pledges: "You say this, but how do I know that you really mean it?" The paradox resides in the fact that, if we are to dwell fully within the symbolic, this gap itself has to be reflexively inscribed into it, and this is what happens with *Kol Nidre*.

Historicizing God

How do we pass from the living gods of the Real to this dead god of the Word? The only consistent way is to move beyond merely describing historical changes in how we think about God and begin historicizing God Himself. This idea was too strong for Schelling, who introduced it: the key difference between the *Ages of the World* and the late Schelling's philosophy of mythology and revelation is that the earlier work thoroughly historicizes God (the becoming of the world is the becoming of God Himself,

His self-creation and self-revelation, so that the human awareness of God is the self-awareness of God Himself), while the late Schelling renounces this radical historicization (in a return to traditional theology, God is not affected by the process of creation, He remains in Himself what he is for all eternity, creation is a totally free and contingent divine decision/act). God as the Trinity exists in eternity, as the unity of the three potencies (contraction, expansion, and their reconciliation) in their atemporal or virtual state; with the process of creation which opens up temporality, the three potencies acquire autonomy and are actualized as Past, Present, and Future (the dark Ground of dense matter, the light of *logos*, and the reconciliation of the two in a living personality which is the Self as a point of contraction subordinated to the light of reason). The premise of the late Schelling's philosophy of mythology and revelation remains the self-division or self-alienation of divinity:

> It is absolutely necessary for the understanding of Christianity—the *conditio sine qua non* of perceiving its true meaning—that we comprehend this cutting-off [*Abgeschnittenheit*] of the Son from the Father, this being in his own form and hence in complete freedom and independence of the Father.[10]

However, God in Himself is not caught in this division—how can this be? Schelling sees creation as a process of the alienation of God from Himself which proceeds in three steps, with the separation of the Son from the Father being only the last in the series. First, God sets free His lowest potency, the egotistic principle of contraction, what in God is not God, thereby creating matter as something actually existing outside Himself. The goal of creation is for God to reveal Himself in it; however, creation takes a wrong turn, becoming the fallen world of decay and sorrow, nature impregnated by melancholy. God's first attempt to reconcile the created world to Himself by creating Adam also fails thanks to Adam's fall, his free choice of sin. At this moment, the second and higher potency of God, the principle of love, concretizes itself as the demiurge, the "lord of being." What Schelling saw clearly is that this demiurge of the fallen world is a Janus-like two-faced god: simultaneously the demiurge, the lord-creator, the transcendent Master elevated above the world, and a homeless god exiled from eternity and condemned to wander anonymously in his creation, like Wotan/Odin

---

10   F. W. J. Schelling, *Sämtliche Werke*, Stuttgart and Augsburg: J.G. Cotta 1856–61, Vol. 14, p. 39.

becoming the Wanderer in Wagner's *Ring*. In this ultimate theological coincidence of the opposites, the Master of the world has to appear within the world in its "oppositional determination" (*gegensaetzliche Bestimmung*), as its lowest element with no proper place in it, as an anonymous homeless wanderer excluded from all social groups.[11] We thus arrive at the first opposition in—or rather, splitting of—the divine: the "pure" God prior to the creation of the world, the anonymous "Godhead," set against the God-demiurge, the Master of creation, who is the God outside of God, the God of the fallen world. Schelling's achievement is to show how the Christian Incarnation can be understood only against the background of this split.

The God-demiurge who appears in different guises in pagan religion is the "pre-existing Christ," the mythological god, the god of pagan phantasmagorias, not the actually existing god but its shadowy double, "god outside himself": "Mythology is nothing less than the hidden history of the Christ before his historical birth, the peregrinations of the God outside God."[12] And it is crucial for Schelling that *the god who in the Incarnation becomes man is not God Himself or in Itself, but this "God outside God," the pagan demiurge*: "Christ must possess an independent ground of divinity, an extra-divine divinity, a claim to sovereignty which he renounces. ... as the God outside of God, Christ has his own proper claim to being the God of the fallen world, a claim which he renounces."[13] With the Christian Revelation, with the Incarnation proper in which Christ "enters into the being of the fallen world to the point of becoming himself a fallen being,"[14] myth becomes fact, an actually existing fully human individual, which is why, as Schelling says, pointing forward towards Kierkegaard, "Christ is not the teacher, as the saying goes, he is not the founder (of Christianity), he is the content of Christianity."[15] In the Incarnation, in becoming man, God does not empty Himself of his deity, but of the *morphe theou*, of the form of god as a sovereign demiurge: "he who was in the form of God willed to empty himself of this":[16] "'God becomes man' means: the divine became

---

11   Note how, in a strictly homologous way, a will that actively wills nothing is the oppositional determination of the will that wills nothing in particular, that is a mere possibility of willing.

12   S. J. McGrath, *The Dark Ground of Spirit*, London: Routledge 2012, p. 162.

13   Ibid., p. 166.

14   Ibid.

15   Schelling, *Sämtliche Werke*, p. 35.

16   F. W. J. Schelling, *Philosophy of Mythology and Revelation*, Armidale: Australian Association for the Study of Religion 1995, p. 273.

man, yet not the divine [in itself], but rather the extra-divine of the divine became man."[17]

We can see clearly here where Schelling deviates from Christian ortho-doxy—not so much in that, for him, the pagan religions are not simply wrong but are an organic part of the divine history, a process which culmi-nates in the Incarnation proper, but in how he complicates the process of Incarnation. For Schelling, the Incarnation is preceded by the self-splitting of God-in-itself (the Godhead), by God's contraction in a God outside the divine, the Lord of the fallen world, so that Christ as mediator does not mediate primarily between God and creation (the fallen world), but between the pure God and the God of the fallen world, the God outside the divine. What this means is that the God who incarnates Himself in Christ is not the pure Godhead but the God of the fallen world (the God-demiurge, the God outside the divine): it is *this* God who empties Himself of His divinity, renounces the "form of God," becomes purely human, and then dies on the cross. In short, what dies on the cross is the God-demiurge, the God who is outside the divine, and this is why the Crucifixion is simul-taneously the Reconciliation of the divine with itself.

We are thus in the midst of the topic of *kenosis* ("self-emptying"), which is operative at three distinct levels. First, we have *kenosis* as the self-emptying of one's own will, of its egotism and self-assertion, becoming entirely receptive to God and the divine will—this is the sense in which a true believer should be "poor in mind," an impassive medium of the divine message. Then, there is the *kenosis* at work in the Incarnation, in which the eternal God outside time and space renounces his divine attributes (or form), and enters into time and space to become human.[18] Finally, there is the most problematic *kenosis*, the self-emptying of the pure God(head) itself in the act of creation: does God empty Himself in the act of creation, does he contract to a vanishing punctuality and thus create the void to be filled by created things?

Furthermore, the link between *kenosis* and capitalism is absolutely crucial if we are to understand the dynamics of emancipation. As we all

---

17   Ibid., p. 275.

18   One can imagine the plethora of scholastic disputes about what divine attri-butes the incarnated Son chose to give up in order to assume his human nature: Did Christ really feel pain? Was he prone to human errors of judgment? Did he really think on the cross that his father had abandoned him? Were these changes only temporary, so that when Jesus ascended back to heaven, he reassumed fully all his original divine attributes?

know, capitalist progress entails the emptying (disintegration, desubstantialization) of traditional life forms, forms of communal life based on shared mores and skills—it is the passage from community to a society of atomized individuals. This emptying of life forms should be given all the weight of the Christian *kenosis* as a step towards redemption, as its necessary precondition, which is why one should absolutely avoid an anti-capitalism based on the defense of particular cultural life forms. (This is also how we should read Paul's famous claim that in Christianity there are neither Jews nor Greeks, the two great forms of life of his time.) In the choice between an irreducible plurality of life forms and universality, one should opt for universality—but not the abstract Habermasian universality shared by all particular life forms. Our only access to universality is through the gaps and inconsistencies of a particular life form: in order to arrive at universality, one should not move upwards, from particular life forms to what they all share, but downwards, from the totality of a particular life form to the elements which signal its instability and inconsistency. When critics of universality emphasize its violent character as a highly risky imposition (to proclaim something universal is always a risky hypothesis, since we can never be sure that the universality we propose is not colored by our particular position, so the building of universals is a patient infinite work which can only asymptotically approximate its goal), one is tempted to reply by paraphrasing the famous answer of the interrogator to Winston Smith who, in Orwell's *1984*, doubts the existence of Big Brother ("It is you who don't exist!"): does a universal dimension to which we refer really exist? But what if it is our particular identity which does not exist, i.e., which is always already traversed by universalities, caught up in them? What if, in today's global civilization, we are more universal than we think, and it is our particular identity that is a fragile ideological fantasy? When we take our particular life world identities as a starting point, we ignore how universality manifests itself in the gaps, failures, and antagonisms at the very heart of these very identities—as Susan Buck-Morss put it, "universal humanity is visible at the edges":

> rather than giving multiple, distinct cultures equal due, whereby people are recognized as part of humanity indirectly through the mediation of collective cultural identities, human universality emerges in the historical event at the point of rupture. It is in the discontinuities of history that people whose culture has been strained to the breaking point give expression to a humanity that goes beyond cultural limits. And it is in our emphatic identification with this raw,

free, and vulnerable state, that we have a chance of understanding what they say. Common humanity exists in spite of culture and its differences. A person's non-identity with the collective allows for subterranean solidarities that have a chance of appealing to universal, moral sentiment, the source today of enthusiasm and hope.[19]

The standard topic of how global capitalism corrodes and destroys particular life worlds should be countered by the topic of how these particular life worlds are always based on domination and oppression and conceal hidden (or not) antagonisms; the emerging emancipatory universality is then the universality of those who cannot find their "proper place" within their particular world, the lateral link of the excluded in each life world. For example, in the India of castes, political universality is embodied in the excluded caste of the untouchables.

Here, also, the logic of the retroactive positing of the immediate starting point has to be asserted: there is no God prior to His *kenosis*, God emerges through its loss, and in the Holy Spirit the loss is fully consummated. In a nice case of "absolute recoil," the (hi)story of God is the story of His loss and of the final full consummation of this loss. We *begin* with the self-splitting of God, with the loss of the mythic primordial unity of the Divine: *God emerges as split into the transcendent Lord of creation and the anonymous destitute wanderer roaming the world.* This self-divided and plural god is the god of pagan phantasmagorias, the god who spiritualizes external reality, leading us to perceive that reality as permeated by hidden magical forces, with ghosts in trees, rivers, and buildings. How do we pass from this spiritualized reality to hard, meaningless "external reality"? Not by directly erasing the spiritual dimension, but by giving it a body—not an ephemeral spiritualized body, but the ordinary body of an actually existing fully human individual—in this way, pagan myth becomes a fact, the fact of an actual individual living in Palestine 2,000 years ago. We reach actuality when God himself is reduced to an ordinary living individual, to a "ready-made God" (as Boris Groys has put it)—and to arrive at atheism, it is *this* God that has to be sacrificed and die.[20] Therein lies the genius of Christianity as the "religion of atheism": God cannot be negated directly,

---

19   Susan Buck-Morss, *Hegel, Haiti, and Universal History*, Pittsburgh: University of Pittsburgh Press 2009, p. 133.

20   We have to leave aside here the status of the two other "religions of the book"—Judaism, which already breaks with paganism and asserts a pure monotheism, as well as the repetition of Judaism in Islam.

it is the subsequent erasure of the individual that sets the Holy Spirit free from its embodiments, that sublates God into a virtual fiction sustained only by the collective of believers.

But should this Duchampian notion of Christ as a ready-made God be fully embraced? Does the reduction of God to an ordinary individual simply render visible the gap that separates a divine person from the place he occupies and that makes Him divine, in the same way as a *pissoir* becomes a work of art when exhibited in an art gallery (or a king is a king because people treat him as such)? If the result of this operation is the rise of a more authentic Sacred prior even to God, not yet "reified" in a God, then this, precisely, is a conclusion one should avoid at all costs. The Christian passage from myth to fact already kills every sacred aura, every misty spiritual envelope. The question thus arises again: why can't the transcendent substantial God be directly sublated into the Holy Spirit as the virtual big Other? Why does it first have to be "emptied" and externalized in a common individual? Did we not claim above that, in Christianity, the divine Substance is sublated: negated and simultaneously maintained in the elevated-transubstantiated form of the Holy Spirit which exists only as the virtual presupposition of the activity of finite individuals?

It is here that we approach the enigma of the Hegelian *Aufhebung*: does this term really designate a direct mediation of some immediate natural content, its elevation into a mediated ideal form? When he deals with sexuality, Hegel himself falls short of his own standards: he only describes how, in the process of culture, the natural substance of sexuality is sublated (cultivated, mediated)—how we humans no longer just copulate for procreation, but become involved in complex processes of seduction and marriage through which sexuality becomes an expression of the spiritual bond between a man and a woman, and so on. Here enters the standard criticism: what Hegel fails to see is that sublation never fully comes out, that there is always an indivisible remainder which resists being sublated. But does Hegel really not see this? Recall the process of the sublation of society in the rational totality of the state: for Hegel, this process realizes itself in the figure of the monarch, the conception of which is "of all conceptions the hardest for ratiocination, i.e., for the method of reflection employed by the Understanding"—why? While Understanding can well grasp the universal mediation of a living totality, what it cannot grasp is that this totality, in order to actualize itself, has to acquire actual existence in the guise of an immediate "natural" singularity:

This transition of the concept of pure self-determination into the immediacy of being and so into the realm of nature is of a purely speculative character, and the apprehension of it therefore belongs to logic. Moreover, this transition is on the whole the same as that familiar to us in the nature of willing, and there the process is to translate something from subjectivity (i.e. some purpose held before the mind) into existence.[21]

In other words, the process of sublation itself has to be sublated, sustained by an exception, by the unique point of a short-circuit between the highest (pure ideal self-determination) and the lowest (natural immediacy). It is significant that Hegel mentions here "the nature of willing." Schelling, Hegel's bitter critic, deploys this exception precisely apropos willing, apropos the passage from potential to actual willing. Schelling's problem is: how can the will which wills nothing, a mere possible will (or, rather, the possibility of willing), become an actual will? In the second version of *The Ages of the World*, he provides a precise answer:

> it can only become actual as what it is. Once and for all, it is impossible for anything to be sublated. The will can therefore only become actual as the will *that wills nothing*. But since it was previously a resting will that specifically did not will anything positive ... it becomes from itself the will that positively wills nothing ... That is, it becomes the will that opposes to itself the particularity, dispersion.[22]

The key to this passage lies in Schelling's anti-Hegelian stab: "it is impossible for anything to be sublated." An example from religion can help us clarify the point. In a complex system of beliefs and rules regulating what can be said or done, we often encounter a weird unstated prohibition: while something is not explicitly prohibited, one is nonetheless expected not to do or say it. If a naive observer explicitly raises the question of why not, the reply is that it is just an unimportant custom, a detail which means nothing, or something similar; however, the effect of raising the question or doing/ saying the implicitly prohibited thing is traumatic, and the offender is treated as if he has committed an unspeakable sacrilege. Do we not find something similar in the relationship between the dogmas of a religion and the rituals

---

21 G. W. F. Hegel, *Philosophy of Right*, Remark to § 280, available at marxists.org.

22 F. W. J. Schelling, *The Ages of the World* (2nd draft), Ann Arbor: Michigan University Press 1997, pp. 168–9.

prescribed by them? This relationship is as a rule much more ambiguous than it may appear: rituals do not merely or even primarily stage dogmas; rather, they often stage in a more or less coded form what is repressed or even outrightly prohibited by the teaching. For example, both Judaism and Islam repress their founding gestures—as the story of Abraham and his two sons with two different women shows, in both religions the father can become father, assume the paternal function, only through the mediation of *another* woman. Freud's hypothesis is that the repression in Judaism concerns the fact that Abraham was a foreigner (an Egyptian), not a Jew—the founding paternal figure, the one who brings revelation and establishes the covenant with God, had to come from the outside. With Islam, the repression concerns a woman—Hagar, the Egyptian slave who gave Abraham his first son. Although Abraham and Ishmail (the progenitor of all Arabs, according to the myth) are mentioned dozens of times in the Quran, Hagar is erased from the official history. As such, however, she continues to haunt Islam, traces of her surviving in rituals like the obligation of pilgrims to Mecca to run six times between the hills of Safa and Marwah, in a kind of neurotic repetition or reenactment of Hagar's desperate search for water for her son in the desert—the search which resists sublation.

How does it follow from this that the will can be actualized only as a will that actively wills nothing itself? What sustains Schelling's reasoning is a simplified notion of the dialectical movement as a progress in which the previous "lower" element or level is "sublated" in the next higher element or level: a crime is "sublated" and retroactively undone in its legal punishment, etc. For Schelling, the lower level cannot ever be sublated, it persists forever, and can only be brought into harmony with the higher level. With regard to willing, this means that the impassive potential willing cannot be "sublated" in an actual willing of something particular and determinate: it persists and inscribes itself into the very domain of actual willing in the guise of the will that actively wills nothing.

This brings us back to Christianity: in the same way that the willing which actively wills nothing is the impassive potential willing in its oppositional determination, Christ is God in His oppositional determination, God incarnated in/as an actual human person, and this is why, like the conception of monarch, the conception of the Incarnation is also "of all conceptions the hardest for ratiocination, i.e. for the method of reflection employed by the Understanding." The reference to Schelling here allows us to complicate further this figure of the Incarnation. As we have seen, two splits precede it: first the self-division of God into the pure Godhead

and the Lord of creation; then the splitting of the latter into the transcendent Demiurge and the anonymous Wanderer. The first figure of the God
in its oppositional determination, God outside Himself, is thus already
(the standard notion of) God as the transcendent creator and Master of
the universe; the fact that this God-Demiurge again redoubles himself
into himself and himself in its oppositional determination (the Wanderer)
signals his "abstract" character—signals that this God is already hampered
by an imperfection. How, then, can we get rid of (or rather, overcome) the
God-Demiurge? The Christian solution is: by way of making its double, the
Wanderer, a fully human god, a god incarnated, a fact.[23]

GOD IN STRUGGLE WITH HIMSELF

From this standpoint, we can return to the starting point of Badiou's ontology: his notion of multiplicities of multiplicities which are not multiplicities
of substantial ones, but infinitely divisible multiplicities whose only substance is the Void itself. Badiou is well aware that dialectical materialism
does not posit just the original multiplicity of being—such an assertion is
easily compatible with the One as the very space of these multiplicities (as
is the case with Spinoza and Deleuze). For dialectical materialism, one has
to think a Two prior to multiplicity—and the key question is: how are we to
think this Two with regard to the Void? Is One simply not yet there, in the
primordial Void? Or is this very lack of One a positive fact? Badiou goes
for the first option, Lacan for the second: from the Lacanian standpoint,
there are multiplicities because the One is "barred," divided, thwarted in
itself, unable to be(come) One. So, again, the key question of dialectical
materialism is: how are we to think the split or self-division of the One, its
non-coincidence with itself, without falling into Gnostic dualism or any
other form of the polarity of cosmic principles? The Christian-Hegelian
solution was outlined by G. K. Chesterton in his religious thriller *The*

---

23   In an homologous way, one can also claim that laziness is an immanent
negation of diligent work, of work-in-general, its essence itself appearing among its
species as one more paradoxical instance—in short, *laziness is work in its oppositional
determination*. A lazy subject refuses to engage in any particular work which would
satisfy some specific need, she persists in the universal stance of the possibility-of-
work, forever postponing its actualization in the guise of some particular work. In
other words, laziness is already "marked" by work, not just simple direct inactivity
but inactivity within the horizon of work. See Simon Hajdini, *Na kratko o dolgčasu,
lenobi in počitku*, Ljubljana: Analecta 2012, pp. 31–2.

Man Who Was Thursday.[24] The hero of the story, Gabriel Syme, is a young Englishman hired by the mysterious chief of a top-secret Scotland Yard department. Syme's first duty is to infiltrate the "Central Anarchist Council," the seven-member ruling body of a secret super-powerful organization bent on destroying our civilization. In order to preserve their anonymity, the members are known to each other only by days of the week. After some deft manipulation, Syme gets elected as "Thursday." At his first Council meeting, he is introduced to "Sunday," the larger-than-life president of the Council, a big man of great authority, mocking irony, and jovial ruthless- ness. In the ensuing series of adventures, Syme discovers that all the other members of the Council are also secret agents, indeed members of the same secret unit as himself, hired by the same chief whose voice they've heard but whose face they've never seen. They join forces and eventually, at a lavish masked ball, confront Sunday. Here, the novel passes from mystery to metaphysical comedy, and we discover two surprising things. First, that Sunday, the president of the Anarchist Council, is the same person as the mysterious chief who has hired them all to fight the anarchists; second, that he is none other than God Himself. These discoveries, of course, lead Syme and the other agents into a series of perplexed reflections. God's essential goodness is held against Him—when, after being asked who he really is, Sunday answers that he is the God of peace, one of the enraged detectives reproaches him, saying:

> it is exactly that that I cannot forgive you. I know you are contentment, opti- mism, what do they call the thing, an ultimate reconciliation. Well, I am not reconciled. If you were the man in the dark room, why were you also Sunday, an offense to the sunlight? If you were from the first our father and our friend, why were you also our greatest enemy? We wept, we fled in terror; the iron entered into our souls—and you are the peace of God! Oh, I can forgive God His anger, though it destroyed nations; but I cannot forgive Him His peace.[25]

As another detective notes in a terse English-style remark: "It seems so silly that you should have been on both sides and fought yourself."[26] If there

---

24   Here I resume (with a different accent) the reading of Chesterton's *Thursday* deployed in Chapter 1 of John Milbank and Slavoj Žižek, *The Monstrosity of Christ*, Cambridge, MA: MIT Press 2009.

25   G. K. Chesterton, *The Man Who Was Thursday*, Harmondsworth: Penguin 1986, p. 180.

26   Ibid.

ever was British Hegelianism, this is it—a literal transposition of Hegel's key thesis that, in fighting the alienated substance, the subject fights his own essence. Syme finally springs to his feet and, with mad excitement, spells out the mystery:

> I see everything, everything that there is. Why does each thing on the earth war against each other thing? Why does each small thing in the world have to fight against the world itself? Why does a fly have to fight the whole universe? Why does a dandelion have to fight the whole universe? For the same reason that I had to be alone in the dreadful Council of the Days. So that each thing that obeys law may have the glory and isolation of the anarchist. So that each man fighting for order may be as brave and good a man as the dynamiter. So that the real lie of Satan may be flung back in the face of this blasphemer, so that by tears and torture we may earn the right to say to this man, "You lie!" No agonies can be too great to buy the right to say to this accuser, "We also have suffered."[27]

This, then, is the formula provided: "So that each thing that obeys law may have the glory and isolation of the anarchist." So that Law is the greatest transgression, the defender of the Law the greatest rebel. But where is the limit of this dialectic? *Does it also hold for God Himself?* Is He, the embodiment of cosmic order and harmony, *also* the ultimate rebel, or is He a benign authority observing from a peaceful Above the follies of mortal men struggling with each other? Here is God's reply when Syme turns to him and asks "Have you ever suffered?"

> As [Syme] gazed, the great face grew to an awful size, grew larger than the colossal mask of Memnon, which had made him scream as a child. It grew larger and larger, filling the whole sky; then everything went black. Only in the blackness before it entirely destroyed his brain he seemed to hear a distant voice saying a commonplace text that he had heard somewhere, "Can ye drink of the cup that I drink of?"[28]

The final revelation is thus that God Himself suffers even more than us mortals: our struggles against our enemies are tearing apart God Himself, they are struggles God is fighting within Himself. However, this is not to be conceived as the struggle of an entity divided into multiple Selves unaware

---

27   Ibid., pp. 182–3.
28   Ibid., p. 183.

that, in fighting the other, they are striking at themselves: the self-division of God is not a substantial self-division, not that of two egos or powers fighting each other. The division is purely formal: there is substantially only one God, the two-ness is that of the Hegelian "coincidence of opposites" which has nothing to do with the "eternal harmony" of opposed forces characteristic of pagan cosmology. This, for Chesterton, is what makes Christianity "terribly revolutionary":

> That a good man may have his back to the wall is no more than we knew already; but that God could have His back to the wall is a boast for all insurgents for ever. Christianity is the only religion on earth that has felt that omnipotence made God incomplete. Christianity alone has felt that God, to be wholly God, must have been a rebel as well as a king.[29]

In *The Man Who Was Thursday* Chesterton twists around the standard topology of the struggle between Good and Evil: all the characters in the novel are good or on the side of Good; the entire anarchist committee is composed of secret agents fighting Evil—all of them with the exception of the top Scotland Yard figure (God) who is simultaneously the top criminal. Again, the standard topology is inverted: it is not that particular evil agents fight each other, and the result of their interaction is the common Good; on the contrary, each particular agent is good, but the entire space of their interaction is twisted so that Evil emerges out of the interaction of their particular good activities. The fish begins to smell from the head down, as the saying goes: a multiplicity of agents, each of them good, with the supreme Good overlapping with its opposite, radical Evil—the split here is thus not between particular agents fighting each other, but at the universal level of the supreme Good itself. The particular agents do not know—what, precisely? They do not know that the supreme Good is split within itself, that it coincides with the supreme Evil, or, in theological terms, they do not know that Devil is the obverse of God Himself.

So there are not two Gods, the benevolent King and the lone Rebel: in the twisted space of the barred One, God encounters Himself at the opposite end, as the Supreme criminal, in the same way that law is its own greatest transgression. This twisted space is the space of the Hegelian "negation of negation," which resides in the decisive shift from the *distortion of a notion* to a *distortion constitutive of this notion*, i.e., to this notion

---

29   Ibid.

as a distortion-in-itself. Recall Proudhon's old dialectical motto, "Property is theft": the negation of negation here lies in the shift from theft as a distortion (negation, violation) of property to the dimension of theft inscribed into the very notion of property (nobody has the right to fully own the means of production, their nature is inherently collective, so every claim "this is mine" is illegitimate). The same goes for crime and the law, for the passage from crime as the distortion (negation) of the law to crime as sustaining the law itself, that is, to the idea of the law itself as universalized crime. One should note that, in this notion of the negation of negation, the encompassing unity of the two opposed terms is the "lowest," "transgressive," one: it is not crime which is a moment of law's self-mediation (or theft which is a moment of property's self-mediation); the opposition of crime and law is inherent to crime, law is a subspecies of crime, crime's self-relating negation (in the same way that property is theft's self-relating negation).

A Habermasian "normative" approach imposes itself here immediately: how can we talk about crime if we do not have a prior notion of a legal order violated by the criminal transgression? In other words, is not the notion of law as universalized/self-negated crime ultimately self-destructive? But this is precisely what a properly dialectical approach rejects: what is before transgression is just a neutral state of things, neither good nor bad (neither property nor theft, neither law nor crime); the balance of this state is then violated, and the positive norm (law, property) arises as a secondary move, an attempt to counteract and contain the transgression.

In Martin Cruz Smith's novel *Havana Bay*, set in Cuba, a visiting American gets caught up in a high *nomenklatura* plot against Fidel Castro, but then discovers that the plot was organized by Castro himself.[30] Castro is well aware of the growing discontent with his rule even in the top circle of functionaries around him, so every couple of years his most trusted agent starts to organize a plot to overthrow him in order to entrap the discontented functionaries; just before the plot is supposed to be enacted, they are all arrested and liquidated. Why does Castro do this? He knows that the discontent will eventually culminate in a plot to depose him, so he organizes the plot himself to flush out potential plotters and eliminate them. What if we imagine God doing something similar? In order to prevent a rebellion against His rule by His creatures, He Himself—masked as the Devil—sets a rebellion in motion so that He can control it and crush it. But

---

30   Martin Cruz Smith, *Havana Bay*, New York: Random House 1999.

is this mode of the "coincidence of the opposites" radical enough? No, for a very precise reason: because Castro-God functions as the unity of himself (his regime) and his opposite (his political opponents), basically playing a game with himself. One has to imagine the same process under the domination of the opposite pole, as in the kind of paranoiac scenario often used in popular literature and films. For example: when the internet becomes infected by a series of dangerous viruses, a big digital company saves the day by creating the ultimate anti-virus program. The twist, however, is that this same company had manufactured the dangerous viruses in the first place—and the program designed to fight them is itself the virus that enables the company to control the entire network. Here we have a more accurate narrative version of the Hegelian identity of opposites.

V for Vendetta deploys a political version of this same identity. The film takes place in the near future when Britain is ruled by a totalitarian party called Norsefire; the film's main protagonists are a masked vigilante known as "V" and Adam Sutler, the country's leader. Although *V for Vendetta* was praised (by none other than Toni Negri, among others) and, even more so, criticized for its "radical"—pro-terrorist, even—stance, it does not have the courage of its convictions: in particular, it shrinks from drawing the consequences of the parallels between V and Sutler.[31] The Norsefire party, we learn, is the instigator of the terrorism it is fighting against—but what about the further identity of Sutler and V? We never see either of their faces in the flesh (except the scared Sutler at the very end, when he is about to die): we see Sutler only on TV screens, and V is a specialist in manipulating the screen. Furthermore, V's dead body is placed on a train with explosives, in a kind of Viking funeral strangely evoking the name of the ruling party: Norsefire. So when Evey—the young girl (played by Natalie Portman) who joins V—is imprisoned and tortured by V in order to learn to overcome her fear and be free, does this not parallel what Sutler does to the entire British population, terrorizing them so that they rebel? Since the model for V is Guy Fawkes (he wears a Guy mask), it is all the more strange that the film refuses to draw the obvious Chestertonian lesson of its own plot: that of the ultimate *identity* of V and Sutler. (There is a brief hint in this direction in the middle of the film, but it remains unexploited.) In other words, the missing scene in the film is the one in which, when Evey removes the mask from

---

31   There is another ironic coincidence of opposites in the casting of Sutler: the dictator is played by John Hurt who, in the film version of *1984*, played Winston Smith, the ultimate victim of a dictatorial regime.

the dying V, we see Sutler's face. How would we have to read this identity? Not in the sense of a totalitarian power manipulating its own opposition, playing a game with itself by creating its enemy and then destroying it, but in the opposite sense: in the unity of Sutler and V, V is the universal encompassing moment that contains both itself and Sutler as its two moments. Applying this logic to God himself, we are compelled to endorse the most radical reading of the Book of Job proposed in the 1930s by the Norwegian theologian Peter Wessel Zapffe, who accentuated Job's "boundless perplexity" when God himself finally appears to him. Expecting a sacred and pure God whose intellect is infinitely superior to ours, Job

> finds himself confronted with a world ruler of grotesque primitiveness, a cosmic cave-dweller, a braggart and blusterer, almost agreeable in his total ignorance of spiritual culture … What is new for Job is *not* God's greatness in quantifiable terms; that he knew fully in advance … what is new is the qualitative baseness.

In other words, God—the God of the Real—is like the Lady in courtly love, He is *das Ding*, a capricious cruel master who simply has no sense of universal justice. God-the-Father thus quite literally does not know what He is doing, and Christ is the one who does know, but is reduced to an impotent compassionate observer, addressing his father with "Father, can't you see I'm burning?"—burning together with all the victims of the father's rage. Only by falling into His own creation and wandering around in it as an impassive observer can God perceive the horror of His creation and the fact that He, the highest Law-giver, is Himself the supreme Criminal. Since God-the-Demiurge is not so much evil as a stupid brute lacking all moral sensitivity, we should forgive Him because He does not know what He is doing. In the standard onto-theological vision, only the demiurge elevated above reality sees the entire picture, while the particular agents caught up in their struggles have only partial misleading insights. At the core of Christianity, we find a different vision—the demiurge is a brute, unaware of the horror he has created, and only when he enters his own creation and experiences it from within, as its inhabitant, can he see the nightmare he has fathered. (It is easy to discern in this vision the old literary motif of the king who dresses up as a commoner in order to mingle with the poor and get the taste of how they live and feel.)

How are these two aspects of God related? Here we should introduce Kierkegaard's distinction between the genius and the apostle: the genius displays creativity, while the apostle is the bearer of a truth that transcends him (he just delivers it like a postman delivers a letter, without knowing what it means). This distinction is crucial for psychoanalysis: Lacan's ingenious notion is that the formations of the unconscious are not an expression of the subject's unconscious creativity, but articulations of a truth of which the subject is a bearer, an apostle. But the stakes can be raised much higher: the ultimate question here is the status of God Himself—is He the ultimate creative genius (author of the entire universe), or is He also an apostle, the bearer of a transcendent truth, and as such in Himself (with regard to his actual properties) no brighter than an ordinary human? Perhaps the Christian Kierkegaardian solution would be that, while God the Father is *the* creative genius, the Son is definitely an apostle—in the Incarnation, genius abdicates and appears as an apostle (the king appears as a beggar). Only an apostle (never a genius) can be a god of love—why?

As Lacan put it in his concise formula: love supplements the absence of sexual relationship. Love is not an illusory One of imaginary fusion covering up the underlying deadlock of the sexual relationship; authentic love is rather the ultimate case of a weird "one" in which this very non-relationship is embodied—therein resides the link between love and the *objet a*. How does love relate to the *objet a*? Let us approach this key point via the paradoxical status of the *objet a* as the product of the redoubled loss: the *objet a* can be best defined as a doubly reflected object, and precisely as such, it is real—the Lacanian Real is not the hard core underneath all the games of reflection and redoubling, but the elusive X that emerges through redoubled reflection (it was Freud who already noted that in this sense, in a dream, the Real as a rule appears in the guise of a dream within a dream). At the beginning of Fritz Lang's *Secret Beyond the Door*, the heroine (played by Joan Bennett) describes how she fell in love: "He looked at me and I felt as if he saw in me things I was not aware were in me!" Here, however, one should be very careful to avoid a pseudo-Lacanian cynical realism: what I see in the gaze of the other who looks at me is *not* a simple projection—or false appearance—of a treasure in me to be opposed to the miserable reality of what I really am. We should thus reject as false the pseudo-Kantian opposition of *agalma*, the treasure deep within me, as a phenomenal appearance, a fantasy-illusion, a projection of the other's desire, in contrast to the hard noumenal In-itself that I am in myself—an excremental nothing.

The first thing to add here is that it is precisely the experience of oneself as an excremental void that has to rely on the Other's gaze: one is never an excremental nothing in oneself, one appears as such only when measured against a symbolic ideal that one cannot live up to; one is never a void in oneself, one is a void with regard to an expected symbolic identity. Of course one is something outside of the relation to the Other, but only in a banal biological sense, as an impersonal piece of flesh. What *is* thoroughly sustained by the Other (not imaginary or symbolic, but the Real Other) for its very ex-sistence is the punctual abyss of subjectivity, in short, the Cartesian *cogito*. But Descartes was too quick here: there is no deduction needed to make the leap from the pure *cogito* to the divine big Other guaranteeing the consistency of the universe, as if I can first be sure of myself and only then, in a second step, am I compelled to introduce the big Other. Jean-Luc Marion has developed this point in detail: I only exist through being loved by the Other (God, ultimately). This, however, is not enough— God Himself only exists through ex-sistence, as the effect of our referring to Him (in *The Clash of the Titans*, Zeus is right to complain that if men stop praying to the gods and celebrating them in their rituals, the gods will cease to exist). This reversal—the insight of Christianity, the message of Christ's death—is *not* the standard humanist insight that the "gods are only projections of human desires, fears and ideals" (if this were the case, then humanity would be a full Subject positing its alienated divine Other). Such a properly comical notion of a God who depends on human approbation is, as one might expect, evoked by Kierkegaard who, in his *Concept of Anxiety*, describes in a mockingly anti-Hegelian way how Simon Tornacensis (the thirteenth-century scholastic theologian)

> thought that God must be obliged to him for having furnished a proof of the Trinity ... This story has numerous analogies, and in our time speculation has assumed such authority that it has practically tried to make God feel uncertain of himself, like a monarch who is anxiously waiting to learn whether the general assembly will make him an absolute or a limited monarch.[32]

What we are dealing with here is a properly dialectical mediation of knowing and being in which being itself hinges on (not-)knowing. As Lacan put it long ago, God does not know He is dead (that's why He is alive)—in this case, existence hinges on not-knowing, while in Christianity God learns that He is dead. The logical "god of philosophers," however, is already a dead god, although in a different way, so maybe Tornacensis was not wrong, or at least should be read in a more ambiguous way: if a

---

32   Søren Kierkegaard, *The Concept of Anxiety*, Princeton: Princeton University Press 1980, p. 151.

philosopher proves the existence of God, is the God who comes to exist in this way not a dead God? So, maybe, what God really dreads is the very success of the proof of His existence, and the situation is here the same as in the well-known anecdote about the Hearst editor: God fears that the proof of His existence will fail, but He fears even more that it will *not* fail. In short, God's impasse is that He is either alive, but caught in a state of terrifying suspense about His existence, or existing but dead.

Kierkegaard, of course, dismisses any attempt to logically demonstrate the existence of God as an absurd and pointless exercise (his model of such professorial blindness towards the authentic religious experience was Hegel's dialectical machinery); however, his sense of humor cannot withstand the wonderful image of an anxious God, dreading a decision on His own status as if it depends on the logical exercises of a philosopher, as if the philosopher's reasoning has consequences in the Real, so that, if the proof fails, God's existence itself is threatened. And one can go even further in this line of Kierkegaardian reasoning: what undoubtedly attracted him to Tornacensis' remark was the blasphemous idea of God Himself in a state of anxiety.

The divine impasse thus resides in the fact that the God whose existence is proven is like a monarch whom the assembly makes absolute: the very form by which his absolute power is confirmed (it depends on the whim of the assembly) undermines it. The political parallel is here crucial, since Kierkegaard himself resorts to the comparison of God and a king: God exposed to the philosopher's whimsy is like a king exposed to the caprice of a popular assembly. But what is his point here? Is it simply that, in both cases, we should reject liberal decadence and opt for absolute monarchy? What complicates this simple and apparently obvious solution is that, for Kierkegaard, the (properly comical) point of the Incarnation is that God becomes a beggar, a lowly, ordinary human. Would it thus not be more correct to conceive Christianity as the paradox of God's abdication—God steps down to be replaced by the assembly of believers called the Holy Spirit?

Our conclusion here should be that *every subject is ultimately in the position of Tornacensis' God*, forever in anxiety as to what will happen if others stop believing in them, presupposing them as a subject (for Lacan the subject as such is a presupposed subject)—we are dealing here with belief, not with knowledge. And here love enters: the most radical moment of love is not the belief of others which sustains the subject in its existence, but the subject's own counter-gesture, the terrifyingly daring act of fully accepting that its very existence depends on others, that—to put it in somewhat inappropriate poetic terms—I am nothing but a figure in the dreamspace of an inconsistent other.

This insight also compels us to renounce the cynical idea that the treasure the lover sees in the beloved is just an illusory projection: Lacan is not a cynic who thinks that there is really no treasure, that the subject is in itself only an excremental void. Recall the paradox of Kierkegaard's notion of "sickness unto death": the truly dreadful thing is not accepting that one is a mere mortal who will disappear into dust, leaving no trace behind, but accepting the hard fact that one is immortal and that, as such, one cannot escape one's conscience and the sins one has committed. In a homologous way, we should say that the truly dreadful thing is not accepting the fact that I am an excremental void, that the treasure others see in me is their projection and has nothing to do with the real core of my being—such a position ("What can I do? I'm in it for nothing, I am not responsible for what others project onto me") is all too facile, offering an all too easy escape. The truly dreadful thing is accepting the fact that there truly *is* a treasure in me and that I cannot escape from it—this is why the notion of a treasure in me triggers anxiety, since, as Lacan pointed out, anxiety is caused by the over-proximity of the object, not by its lack. This treasure is not a secret object that the beloved *has* deep in him/herself—the true treasure *is* the (beloved) subject him/herself. In other words, love does not occur when the loving subject desperately searches the beloved for some hidden treasure; love occurs when the loving subject discovers that the treasure in the beloved in just a deceiving fetish, that the true treasure is the fragile beloved himself, perplexed, at a loss, unable to relate his subjectivity to the treasure the beloved sees in him. It is this reflexive reversal from the object hidden in the subject to the subject itself which defines love, the move from blind fascination to love.

This is why the basic paradox of loving sex is that a tender consideration for the beloved other and the ruthless objectification of the other (reduction to a thing expected to provide intense enjoyment) are not mutually exclusive: the more the love that binds the sexual partners is truly profound, the more each of them is ready to offer themselves as the object of the other's enjoyment, and to use the other for their own enjoyment *as an act of love*. If, on the contrary, in the midst of an intense sexual encounter, one of the partners craves for "deeper", more tender acts, as if naked sexuality is somehow inadequate, as if it needs some kind of "spiritual" supplement, such a craving is an infallible sign of a spiritual love that is not authentic. Years ago, I read a Catholic sex manual recommending the missionary position on the basis that it is the best way to avoid reducing the act to crude sex, since, during the act, the two partners can exchange tender words—the brutal misreading of sexual activity, its implicit reduction to an animal coupling in need of a "spiritual" supplement, could not be more palpable.

It is this coincidence of apparent opposites—absolute subjectivity of love and radical self-objectification—that renders the Hegelian "infinite judgment" of sexual love. Without the step into complete self-objectification, into becoming an object or instrument of the Other's enjoyment, there can be no proper subjectivity in the act. A proof: in the most thorough self-objectification, the subject is still there, that is, the whole point of the self-objectification is that it is performed by two unique subjects. We are not dealing with the dissolution of subjectivity into an impersonal cosmic Enjoyment, but with something that takes place exclusively between two loving subjects. This is why, in a love relationship, intense sexual enjoyment is necessarily followed by an act (or rather process) of re-subjectification, arguably the most tender act in the world, through which the beloved Other re-emerges as a singular, vulnerable, and fragile human being.

THE PROSTHETIC GOD

This fragile coincidence of subjectivity and thorough self-objectification that characterizes authentic love gets lost in our postmodern universe, which imposes a different coincidence of opposites: that of the scientific self-objectification (naturalization) of man and his elevation into a prosthetic divinity. In his *Civilization and its Discontents*, Freud deployed his vision of the human being as a "prosthetic God," creating and using technological supplements to his finite body in order to approach the ideal of omnipotence and omniscience. As to be expected from Freud, his point is properly dialectical: it is not that man cannot approach these ideals, but that troubles emerge precisely when he seems to be nearing them, and things take an unexpected turn:

> Long ago [man] formed an ideal conception of omnipotence and omniscience which he embodied in his gods. To these gods he attributed everything that seemed unattainable to his wishes, or that was forbidden to him. One may say, therefore, that these gods were cultural ideals. Today he has come very close to

the attainment of this ideal, he has almost become a god himself. Only, it is true, in the fashion in which ideals are usually attained according to the general judgment of humanity: not completely, in some respects not at all, in others only half way. Man has, as it were, become a kind of prosthetic God. When he puts on all his auxiliary organs he is truly magnificent; but those organs have not grown on to him and they still give him much trouble at times ... Future ages will bring with them new and probably unimaginably great achievements in this field of civilization and will increase man's likeness to God still more. But in the interests of our investigations, we will not forget that present-day man does not feel happy in his Godlike character.[33]

Is not the cultural ideal of the "prosthetic God" embodied in superheroes like Batman, Spiderman, and Superman, who, to judge from the latest wave of movie remakes, are definitely not happy but haunted by anxieties and doubts (it is worth recalling that the title of the most recent Superman film, *Man of Steel*, is the English translation of "Stalin")? For us common mortals there is an unmistakable dimension of "beyond the pleasure principle" in our dealings with artificial organs and gadgets: instead of enhancing our pleasures and powers, they cause fear and anxiety. In recent decades, "troubles" have also exploded alongside the proliferation of prostheses and programs for the rewiring of our brains. Even Stephen Hawking's little finger—the proverbial minimal link between his mind and the outside world, the only part of his paralyzed body he can move—will no longer be necessary. With our minds alone, we will be able *directly* to cause objects to move, the brain itself serving as our remote control machine. In the terms of German Idealism, this means that what Kant called "intellectual intuition" (*intelektuelle Anschauung*)—in which the mind directly influences reality in a causal way, a capacity Kant attributed only to the infinite mind of God—is now potentially available to all of us, i.e., that we are potentially deprived of one of the basic features of our finitude. And since, as we learned from Kant as well as Freud, this gap of finitude is at the same time the resource of our creativity (the distance between "mere thought" and causal intervention in reality enables us to test our mental hypotheses, and, as Karl Popper put it, let them die instead of ourselves), a direct short-circuit between mind and reality implies the prospect of a radical closure. In his *Ethics* seminar, Lacan invokes the "point of the apocalypse,"[34] the impossible saturation of

---

33 Sigmund Freud, *Civilization and its Discontents*, New York: Norton 1961, p. 39.

34 Jacques Lacan, *The Ethics of Psychoanalysis*, New York: Routledge 1992, p. 207.

the symbolic by the Real of *jouissance*, the full immersion into massive *jouissance*. When, in a Heideggerian way, he asks "Have we crossed the line … in the world in which we live?,"[35] he refers to the fact that "the possibility of the death of the Symbolic has become a tangible reality."[36] Lacan himself invokes the threat of an atomic holocaust; today, however, we are in a position to offer other versions of this death of the symbolic, principal among them the full scientific naturalization of the human mind. The apocalyptic process will reach its zero point when prostheses no longer merely supplement the human body but in a way supplant it, leaving behind the notion of the human being as a worker whose know-how enables him to use prosthetic instruments. We should note that Lacan engaged in these reflections as part of a critical confrontation with the Maoist notion of the knowledge inherent in manual work (hence the intellectuals must learn from the manual workers, etc.), a notion which was not foreign even to Heidegger, who in 1933 answered Jaspers' question as to how a man as coarse as Hitler could govern Germany with: "Culture is of no importance, just look at his marvelous hands!"[37] Lacan, for his part, asks how,

> in a world in which there has emerged, in a way that indeed exists and is a presence in the world, not the thinking of science, but science in some way objectified, I mean these things entirely forged by science, Hertzian waves, simply these little things, gadgets and things, which for the moment occupy the same space as us, in a world in which this emergence has taken place, can know-how at the level of manual work carry enough weight to be a subversive factor? This is how, for me, the question arises.[38]

In mentioning Hertzian waves, Lacan draws attention to another uncanny aspect of prosthetic gadgets: they are increasingly becoming invisible to us, doing their job at a level well below the threshold of our perception. What makes nanotechnology so thrilling is the prospect of constructing objects and processes in such a small dimension that all correlation with

---

35   Ibid., p. 231.

36   Lorenzo Chiesa, *Imaginary, Symbolic and Real Otherness: The Lacanian Subject and His Vicissitudes*, Doctoral Thesis, University of Warwick, Department of Philosophy, 2004, p. 233.

37   Quoted from Daniel Maier-Katkin, *Stranger from Abroad*, New York: Norton 2010, p. 99.

38   Jacques Lacan, *The Other Side of Psychoanalysis*, New York: Norton 2007, p. 149.

our ordinary life world is lost, so in effect we are dealing with an alternative reality: there is no shared scale between nano-reality and our ordinary reality, and yet we can nonetheless influence our reality through nano-processes. As Ray Kurzweil remarked apropos *Blade Runner*:

> The scenario of humans hunting cyborgs doesn't wash because those entities won't be separate. Today, we treat Parkinson's with a pea-sized brain implant. Increase that device's capability by a billion and decrease its size by a hundred thousand, and you get some idea of what will be feasible in 25 years. It won't be, "OK, cyborgs on the left, humans on the right." The two will be all mixed up.[39]

While in principle this may be true, the problem is that when the prosthesis is no longer experienced as such, but becomes invisible, part of our immediate-organic experience, those who technologically control the prosthesis effectively control us at the very heart of our self-experience.

Lacan elaborates further on the changed status of science implied by the profusion of objects "entirely forged by science": "the characteristic of our science is not that it introduced a better and more extensive knowledge of the world, but that it made emerge into the world things that did not exist in it in any way at the level of our perception."[40] Science and technology today no longer aim only at understanding and reproducing natural processes, but also at generating new forms of life that will surprise us. The goal is not just to dominate nature (the way it is), but to generate something new, greater, stronger than ordinary nature, including ourselves—exemplary is here the obsession with artificial intelligence, which aims at producing a brain stronger than the human brain. The dream that sustains the scientific-technological endeavor is to trigger a process with no return, a process that will exponentially reproduce itself all on its own. The notion of "second nature" is therefore today more pertinent than ever, in both its main meanings. First, in the literal sense of an artificially generated nature: deformed animals and plants, or—in a more positive spin—genetically manipulated organisms "enhanced" in directions that suit us. Second, in the more standard sense of the autonomization of the results of our own activity: the way our acts elude us in their consequences, the way they can generate a monster with a life of its own. It is *this* horror at the unforeseen

---

39   Quoted from Ian Sample, "Frankenstein's Mycoplasma," *Guardian*, June 8, 2007.

40   Lacan, *The Other Side of Psychoanalysis*, p. 158.

effects of our own acts that causes shock and awe, not the power of nature over which we have no control; and it is *this* horror that religion tries to domesticate. What is new today is the short-circuit between these two senses of "second nature": second nature in the sense of objective Fate, the autonomized social process, is generating second nature in the sense of an artificially created nature, of natural monsters. The kind of processes which now threaten to run out of control are no longer just the social processes of economic and political development, but new forms of natural processes themselves, from nuclear catastrophe to global warming to the unforeseen consequences of biogenetic manipulation. Can we even imagine what the consequences of nanotechnological experiments might be: new life forms reproducing themselves in an out-of-control cancer-like way? Here is a standard description of this fear:

> Within fifty to a hundred years, a new class of organisms is likely to emerge. These organisms will be artificial in the sense that they will originally be designed by humans. However, they will reproduce, and will "evolve" into something other than their original form; they will be "alive" under any reasonable definition of the word … the pace of evolutionary change will be extremely rapid … The impact on humanity and the biosphere could be enormous, larger than the industrial revolution, nuclear weapons, or environmental pollution.[41]

This fear also has a clear libidinal dimension: it is the fear of the asexual reproduction of Life, the fear of a life that is indestructible, constantly expanding, reproducing itself through self-division—in short, the fear of that mythic creature Lacan called *lamella* (which can be loosely translated as "manlet," a condensation of "man" and "omelet"), the libido as an organ, an inhuman-human organ without a body, the mythical pre-subjective "undead" life-substance. The line that leads from simple techno-gadgets to the undead *lamella* is not difficult to reconstruct: what makes such gadgets so uncanny is that, far from simply supplementing human organs, they introduce a logic that fundamentally differs from, and so unsettles, the "normal" libidinal economy of sexed human beings *qua* beings of language. Techno-gadgets are potentially "undead," they function as parasitic "organs without bodies" which impose their repetitive rhythms onto the

---

41   Doyne Farmer and Aletta Belin, "Artificial Life: The Coming Evolution," in C. G. Langton, C. Taylor, J. D. Farmer, and S. Rasmussen, eds., *Artificial Life*, Redwood City: Addison-Wesley 1992, p. 815.

beings they are supposed to serve and supplement. Recall the Jim Carrey film *The Mask*, in which the plastic mask changes the ordinary guy into a superhero. The Mask is the asexual "partial object" that allows the subject to remain in (or regress to) the pre-Oedipal anal-oral universe in which there is no death and guilt, just endless fun and fighting—no wonder the character played by Carrey is obsessed with cartoons: the world of cartoons is just such an undead universe without sex or guilt, a universe of infinite plasticity in which every time a character is destroyed it magically recomposes itself and the struggle goes on.

Lacan proposed the neologism *lathouses* as a name for these "things that did not exist" prior to the scientific intervention into the Real, from mobile phones to remote-controlled toys, from air conditioners to artificial hearts:

> The world is increasingly populated by *lathouses*. Since you seem to find that amusing, I am going to show you how it is written. Notice that I could have called it *lathousies*. That would have gone better with *ousia*, it is open to all sorts of ambiguity ... And for the tiny little *a*-objects that you are going to encounter when you leave, on the pavement at every street corner, behind every shop window, in the superabundance of these objects designed to cause your desire in so far as it is now science that governs it, think of them as *lathouses*. I notice a bit late since I invented it not too long ago that it rhymes with *ventouse* [windy].[42]

(And, we might add, it also echoes *vente*, sale, to bring out the capitalist link.) As such, *lathouse* is to be opposed to *symptom* (in the precise Freudian sense of the term): *lathouse* is knowledge embodied (in a new "unnatural" object). We can see why, apropos *lathouses*, we have to include capitalism— we are dealing here with a whole chain of surpluses: scientific technology with its surplus-knowledge (a knowledge beyond mere *connaissance* of already existing reality, a knowledge which gets embodied in new objects); capitalist surplus-value (the commodification of this surplus-knowledge in the proliferation of gadgets); and, last but not least, surplus-enjoyment (gadgets as forms of the *objet a*), which accounts for the libidinal economy of the hold of *lathouses* over us.

---

42   Lacan, *The Other Side of Psychoanalysis*, p. 162.

Lubitsch, the Poet of Cynical Wisdom?

THE THREE WHITES AND THE TWO BLACKS

The subject's symbolic identification always has an *anticipatory*, hastening character (similar to, yet not to be confused with, the anticipatory recognition of "myself" in the mirror image). As pointed out by Lacan already in the 1940s, in his famous paper on logical time, the fundamental form of symbolic identification—i.e., of assuming a symbolic mandate—is for me to "recognize myself as X," to proclaim, to promulgate myself as X, *in order to overtake others who might expel me from the community of those who "belong to X."* Here is a somewhat simplified version of the logical puzzle of the three prisoners apropos of which Lacan develops the three modalities of the logical time:[1] the prison governor is allowed, on the basis of an amnesty, to release one of the three prisoners. In order to decide which one, he sets them a logical test. The prisoners know that there are five hats, three white and two black. Each prisoner has a hat placed on his head, and they all then sit down in a triangle, so that each of them can see the color of the others' hats, but not the color of his own. The winner is the first one to guess the color of his own hat, which he signifies by standing up and leaving the room.[2] We thus have three possible situations:

If one prisoner has a white hat and the other two have black hats, the one with the white hat can immediately "see" that his is white by way of a simple deduction: "There are only two black hats; I can see them on the others' heads, so mine must be white." Here there is no time lapse involved, only an "instant of the gaze."

In the second case there are two white hats and one black. If mine is white, I will reason this way: "I can see one black hat and one white, so mine may be either white or black. However, if mine were black, then the prisoner with the

---

1   See Jacques Lacan, "Logical Time and the Assertion of Anticipated Certainty," in *Écrits*, New York: Norton 2006, pp. 161–75.

2   Here I develop further the analysis from Chapter 3 of Slavoj Žižek, *Tarrying With the Negative*, Durham, NC: Duke University Press 1993.

white hat would see two black hats and immediately conclude that his is white; since he hasn't done that, mine must also be white." In this case, some time had to elapse, that is, a certain "time for understanding" is needed: I must as it were "transpose" myself into the reasoning of the other, arriving at my conclusion on the basis of the fact that the other does not act.

The third situation, in which there are three white hats, is the most complex. Here, the reasoning goes like this: "I can see two white hats, so mine may be either white or black. If mine were black, then either of the two other prisoners would reason the following way: 'I see a black hat and a white hat. So if mine were black, the prisoner with the white hat would see two black hats and would stand up and leave immediately. However, he hasn't done that. So, mine must be white. I shall stand up and leave.' But since neither of the other two prisoners has stood up, mine must be white." Here, however, Lacan points out how this solution requires a double delay and a hindered or interrupted gesture. That is to say, assuming all three prisoners are of equal intelligence, then, after the first delay, i.e., upon each noticing that neither of the others is making a move, they will all rise at the same moment—and then stiffen, exchanging perplexed glances. The problem is that they will not know the meaning of the other's gesture—each will ask himself: "Did the others rise for the same reason as me, or because they can see a *black* hat on my head?" Only now, upon seeing that they all share the same hesitation, will they be able to jump to the final conclusion: the very fact of their shared hesitation is proof that they are all in the same situation, i.e., that they all have white hats. At this precise moment, delay turns into haste, as each prisoner realizes "I must rush to the door before the others overtake me!"

It is easy to see how a specific mode of subjectivity corresponds to each of the three moments of logical time: the "instant of the gaze" implies the impersonal "one" ("one sees"), the neutral subject of logical reasoning without any intersubjective dialectic; the "time for understanding" already involves intersubjectivity, i.e., in order for me to arrive at the conclusion that my hat is white, I have to "transpose" myself into the other's reasoning. However, this instance of intersubjectivity remains that of the "indefinite reciprocal subject," as Lacan puts it: a simple reciprocal capability of taking the other's reasoning into account. Only with the third moment, the "moment of conclusion," do we reach the true "genesis of the I": what takes place in it is the shift from $ to S_1, from the void of the subject epitomized by a radical uncertainty as to what I am, i.e., by the utter undecidability of my status, to the conclusion that "I am white," to the assumption of the symbolic identity—"That's me!"

We must bear in mind the anti-Lévi-Straussian thrust of Lacan's rumi-nations here. Lévi-Strauss conceived the symbolic order as an asubjective structure, an objective field within which every individual occupies, fills in, his or her preordained place. What Lacan invokes is the "genesis" of this objective socio-symbolic identity: if we simply wait for a symbolic place to be allotted to us, we will never live to see it. That is, in the case of a symbolic mandate, we never simply ascertain what we are; we "become what we are" by means of a precipitous subjective gesture. This precipitous identifica-tion involves the shift from object to signifier: the (white or black) hat is the object I am, and its invisibility to me renders the fact that I can never get an insight into "what I am as an object" (i.e., $ and a are topologically incompatible). When I say "I am white," I assume a symbolic identity that fills out the void of the uncertainty as to my being. What accounts for this anticipatory overtaking is the *inconclusive* character of the causal chain: the symbolic order is ruled by the "principle of insufficient reason": within the space of symbolic intersubjectivity, I can never simply ascertain what I am, which is why my "objective" social identity is established by means of "sub-jective" anticipation. A significant detail in Lacan's text on logical time—a detail usually passed over in silence—is that he quotes as the exemplary political case of such collective identification the Stalinist communist's affirmation of orthodoxy: I hasten to proclaim my true communist creden-tials out of fear that others will expel me as a revisionist traitor.

Anticipatory identification is therefore a kind of preemptive strike, an attempt to answer in advance the question "what am I for the Other?" and thus assuage the anxiety that pertains to the desire of the Other: the *signi-fier* which represents me in the Other resolves the impasse of *what object I am for the Other*. What I actually overtake by way of symbolic identifica-tion is therefore the *objet a* in myself; as to its formal structure, symbolic identification is always a "flight forward" from the object that I am. By way of saying "You are my wife," for example, I elude and obliterate my radical uncertainty as to what you are in the very kernel of your being, qua Thing. This is what is missing from Althusser's account of interpellation: it does justice to the moment of retroactivity, to the illusion of the "always already," yet it leaves out of consideration the anticipatory overtaking qua inherent reverse of this retroactivity.

This point can be nicely illustrated by an incident that occurred recently in Iceland: on August 25, 2012, a foreign tourist was reported missing in the volcanic canyon Eldgjá after she failed to return to her tour bus, and search and rescue teams were immediately dispatched to the area. However, the search was called off after a couple of hours when it turned out that the missing woman had been on the bus all along and even participated in the search for herself. The explanation for the confusion is rather simple: during the stop at Eldgjá, the woman had changed her clothes and freshened up, so the other passengers had not recognized her when she returned to the bus. The tour guide then made a mistake in counting the passengers, so it appeared that one was missing, and thanks to a sloppy description of the missing person, the woman didn't recognize herself in it. The result—in the wonderful formulation from the police report on the incident—was that she "had no idea that she was missing."[3] The source of the weird fascination of this story is that it echoes and simultaneously mocks the New Age spiritualist topic of self-loss, of someone losing contact with the intimate core of their being and then desperately trying to discover "who they really are"—this is precisely the temptation to which one should not succumb. It is much more productive to formulate the problem in terms of the tension between signifying representation and identity: insofar as signifying representations designate our properties, what a subject "is like," the question is that of the old Marx brothers' paradox: do I look like myself? In other words, not "who" but "what" (for an object) am I?

What is not so well known is that the original form of the three prisoners puzzle comes from the era of eighteenth-century French libertinage, with its mixture of sex and cold logic (which culminates in Sade).[4] In this sexualized version, the governor of a woman's prison has decided that he will give an amnesty to one of the three prisoners, and the winner will be decided by a test of her intelligence. The three women—note how the story replaces men with women—will be placed in a triangle around a large circular table, each naked from the waist down and leaning forward on the table to enable penetration *a tergo*. Each woman will then be penetrated from behind by either a black man or a white man, so she will only be able to see the color of the men who are penetrating the other two women. All

---

3 "Lost Woman Looks for Herself in Iceland's Highlands," available at icelandreview.com. As the article also reports: "a similar incident occurred in 1954 when an extensive search was carried out for a young girl in a red coat who had been berry picking with a group of people but didn't return with them. Or so they thought. People searched for the girl for hours until it turned out that she wasn't missing at all but had participated in the search herself. The misunderstanding was based on a false description of the girl's clothing."

4 Since we live in times increasingly bereft of even an elementary sense of irony, I feel obliged to add that this sexualized version is in fact my own invention.

that she will know is that there are only five men available to the governor for this experiment, three white and two black. Given these constraints, the winner will be the woman to establish the skin color of the man fucking her, pushing him away and leaving the room. As before, there are three possible situations here, of increasing complexity:

In the first case, there are two black men and one white man fucking the women. Since the woman being fucked by a white man knows that there are only two black men in the pool, she can immediately rise and leave the room.

In the second case, one black man and two white men are doing the fucking. The two women fucked by the white men can thus see one white man and one black man. The woman fucked by a black man can see two white men, but—since there are three white men in the pool—she cannot immediately rise. The only way for a winner to emerge in this second case is if one of the two women being fucked by a white man reasons as follows: "I can see one white man and one black man, so the guy fucking me might be white or black. However, if my fucker was black, the woman in front of me being fucked by a white man would see two black men and immediately conclude that her fucker was white—she would have stood up and moved immediately. But she hasn't done this, so my fucker must be white."

In the third case, all three women are being fucked by white men, so each of them sees two other white men. Each can accordingly reason in the same mode as the winner in case two does, in the following way: "I can see two white men, so the man fucking me may be white or black. But if mine was black, either of the two others could reason (as the winner in 2 does): 'I can see a black man and a white man. So if my fucker is black, the woman fucked by a white man would see two black man and immediately conclude that her fucker was white and leave. But she hasn't done this. So my fucker must be white.' But since neither of the other two has stood up, my fucker must not be black, but white too."

Here enters, as before, the logical time proper: assuming all three women are of equal intelligence and arise at the same time, this would cast each of them into a radical uncertainty about who is fucking them—why? Because each woman could not know whether the other two women have stood up as a result of the same reasoning process she has undertaken, since she was being fucked by a white man; or whether each had reasoned as the winner in the second case had, because she was being fucked by a black man. The winner will be the first woman to interpret this indecision correctly and jump to the conclusion that it indicates that all three are fucked by white men.

The consolation prize for the other two is that at least they will be fucked to the end, a fact that becomes significant the moment one takes note of the political overdetermination surrounding the choice of this particular group of men: among upper-class ladies in mid-eighteenth-century France, black men were, of course, socially unacceptable as sexual partners, but were nonetheless coveted as secret lovers because of their alleged higher potency and extra-large penises. Consequently, being fucked by a white man involves socially acceptable but ultimately unsatisfying sex, while being fucked by a black man involves socially inadmissible but much more satisfying sex. This choice is, however, more complex than it may appear, since, in sexual activity, the fantasy gaze observing us is always there: the most elementary fantasmatic scene is not that of a fascinating scene to be looked at, but the notion that "there is someone out there looking at us"; not a dream but the notion that "we are objects in someone else's dream" … (In his novel *La Lenteur*, Milan Kundera offers as representative of today's aseptic pseudo-voluptuous sex a scene in which a couple feign anal sex close to a hotel pool, in full view of the guests in the rooms above, faking pleasurable cries but not even accomplishing penetration—to this Kundera opposes the slow, gallant, and intimate erotic games of eighteenth-century France, the era of our original puzzle.) The message of the puzzle thus becomes more ambiguous: what the three women observing each other while having sex have to establish is not simply "Who is fucking me, a black guy or a white guy?" but, rather, "What am I for the Other's gaze while I am being fucked?", as if their very identity is established through this gaze.

Does not this triad yet again follow the logic of the Imaginary-Symbolic-Real? If one of the prisoners sees two black men, she "sees" directly, in the imaginary, that hers is white. If she sees one white and one black, she reasons that, as there is no reaction from the woman being fucked by a white man, hers also has to be white—the order of reasoning is here purely symbolic. If she sees two whites, her reasoning is temporally more complex: it cannot just rely on a clear logical structure, since what enters in here is the contingent Real of a precipitous decision that follows postponement (one waits too long, then one acts too early).

But the key element in this ridiculous retelling of the story is the intervention of knowledge: *there is no human sexuality without knowledge*. One is reminded here of the vulgar Serb formula *"Koji kurac te jebe?"* ("What prick is fucking you?"), which in a more interpretative translation means something like: "What's bothering you so much that you have to act like a complete asshole?" In our puzzle, this question is raised directly: each of the women has to guess what prick is fucking her. The choice may appear to be simple—white or black, i.e., respectability (status) versus the raw real of *jouissance* ("blacks fuck better")—but the underlying issue is more complex: the need for a decentered gaze to sustain our sexual activity.

THE LESSON OF PLAYING GOLF ON THE SHORES OF GALILEE

Needing a short break from his dull Messianic work of preaching and performing miracles, Jesus decided to go for a round of golf with one of his disciples on the shores of the Galilean sea. Faced with a particularly difficult shot, Jesus botched it and the ball ended up in the sea. Undeterred, he walked across the water (his standard trick) to where the ball had dropped, reached down and picked it up. As he teed up to try again, the disciple warned him that it was a very tricky shot that only someone like Tiger Woods could hope to pull off. Jesus replied, "What the hell, I'm the son of God, I can do anything a miserable mortal like Woods can do!" and took another strike. Again, the ball ended up in the sea, and again Jesus took to walking on the water to retrieve it. At this point, a group of American tourists passing by turned to the disciple and said, "My God, who does that guy think he is? Jesus Christ?" To which the disciple replied, "No, he thinks he's Tiger Woods." This, then, is how fantasmatic identification works: no one, not even God himself, is directly what he is—even God needs an external decentered point of identification in some minimal fantasy scenario.

The filmmaker whose opus consists of multiple variations on this kind of decentering is Ernst Lubitsch. The theme of a decentered fantasy sustaining a sexual relationship takes a weird turn in his *Broken Lullaby* (1932—the film's original title, *The Man I Killed*, was initially changed to *The Fifth Commandment* to avoid creating "wrong impressions in the minds of the public about the character of the story," before ultimately being released as *Broken Lullaby*). Here is an outline of the story: haunted by the memory of Walter Holderlin, a soldier he killed during World War I, the French musician Paul Renard travels to Germany to find Holderlin's family, using the address on a letter he found on the dead man's body. Mindful of the anti-French sentiment that continues to permeate Germany, Dr. Holderlin initially refuses to welcome Paul into his home, but changes his mind when his son's fiancée Elsa identifies him as the man who has been leaving flowers on Walter's grave. Rather than reveal the real connection between them, Paul tells the Holderlins that he was a friend of Walter's from their days studying at the same musical conservatory. Although the hostile townspeople and local gossips disapprove, the Holderlins befriend Paul, who duly falls in love with Elsa. However, when she shows Paul her former fiancé's bedroom, he becomes distraught and tells her the truth. She convinces him not to confess to Walter's parents, who have embraced him as their second son, and Paul agrees to forgo easing his conscience and stay with his adopted family. Dr. Holderlin presents him with Walter's violin which, in the film's final scene, Paul plays while Elsa accompanies him on the piano, both observed by the loving gazes of the parental couple ... No wonder that Pauline Kael dismissed the film, claiming that Lubitsch "mistook drab, sentimental hokum for ironic, poetic tragedy."[5]

There is something disturbing in the film, a weird oscillation between poetic melodrama and obscene humor. The couple (the girl and the killer of her fiancé) are happily united under the protective gaze of the fiancé's parents—it is this gaze that provides the fantasy frame for their relationship, and the obvious question is: are they really doing it just for the sake of the parents, or is this gaze an excuse for them to engage in sex? This obvious question is, of course, a false one, because it doesn't matter which of the alternatives is true: even if the parents' gaze is just an excuse for sex, it is still a necessary excuse. We find a further variation of this same motif in Lubitsch's *One Hour With You*:

> A woman and a man, Mitzi and Andre, both married but not to each other, accidentally find themselves in the same taxi. Their affair is set in motion by the fact that, to an imagined external observer, it seems *as if* they are lovers, although they are just sitting in the privacy of a cab ... Andre cannot resist the power of appearance. Although he clearly loves his wife, the appearance of his sharing the cab with another woman is incriminating and its effects, which are quite real, cannot be erased. Mitzi does not refer here primarily to an instance which is physically present, in the sense of "if someone actually sees us now, he will automatically conclude we are having an affair." What she has in mind is much more complex and calls for a notion deployed by, among others, Robert Pfaller—that of a naive observer who judges a situation not with regard to a subject's true intentions but exclusively in terms of how things appear.[6]

5   Pauline Kael, *5001 Nights at the Movies*, New York: Macmillan 1991, p. 107.
6   Ivana Novak and Jela Krečič, "Introduction," in Ivana Novak, Jela Krečič, and Mladen Dolar, eds., *Lubitsch Can't Wait*, Ljubljana: Kineteka 2014, p. 4. See also

What we are dealing with here is the so-called "drama of false appearances":[7] the hero and/or heroine find themselves in a potentially compromising situation, and their actions are observed by a character who sees things mistakenly, reading illicit implications into their innocent behavior. In the standard version of this drama, the misunderstanding is eventually cleared up and the heroes are absolved of any wrongdoing. The point is, however, that through this game of false appearances a censored thought is allowed to be articulated: the spectator can imagine the hero or heroine acting on forbidden wishes but escaping any penalty, since he knows that despite appearances to the contrary, nothing bad has happened, i.e. they are innocent. The dirty mind of the onlooker who misreads innocent signs or coincidences is here a stand-in for the spectator's "pleasurably aberrant viewing": this is what Lacan had in mind when he claimed that truth has the structure of a fiction—the very suspension of literal truth opens the way for the articulation of the libidinal truth.

In Lubitsch, his direct staging of the gaze as the fantasy frame undermines its hold by way of openly displaying its decentered character. This same decentering or distance towards the fantasy frame sustains one of the most efficient jokes in Lubitsch's absolute masterpiece, *To Be or Not to Be*: the Polish actor Joseph Tura impersonates Colonel Ehrhardt of the Gestapo in conversation with a high-level Polish collaborator. In (what we take as) a ridiculously exaggerated way, he comments on rumors about himself— "So, they call me Concentration-Camp-Ehrhardt?"—accompanying his words with vulgar laughter. A little later, Tura has to escape and the real Ehrhardt arrives; when the conversation again touches on the rumors about him, the real Ehrhardt reacts in exactly the same ridiculously exaggerated way as did his impersonator. The message is clear: even Ehrhardt himself is not immediately himself, he also imitates his own copy or, more precisely, the ridiculous idea of himself. While Tura acts him, Ehrhardt acts himself.

The Shop Around the Corner (1940) deals with this decentering in the guise of overlapping fantasies. Set in a Budapest store, it tells the story of co-workers Klara Novak and Alfred Kralik who, though they dislike each other intensely, are maintaining an anonymous letter-writing relationship with each other, neither of them realizing who their pen-pal is. They duly fall

---

Robert Pfaller, *Das schmutzige Heilige und die reine Vernunft*, Frankfurt: Fischer Verlag 2012.

    7 On this notion, see Martha Wolfenstein and Nathan Leites, *Movies: A Psychological Study*, Glencoe, Ill.: The Free Press 1950.

in love via their correspondence, while being hostile and peevish towards one another in real life. (The more recent Hollywood hit *You've Got Mail* was a remake of *The Shop Around the Corner* for the email era. One might also mention here a curious incident which took place a couple of years ago in—of all places—Sarajevo: a husband and wife were both involved in an intense email love affair with an anonymous partner; only when they decided to meet in the flesh did they discover that they had been flirting with each other all along ... Was the final outcome then a happy rejuvenated marriage, now they had discovered that they were each other's dream partner? Probably not—such a realization of one's dreams as a rule turns into a nightmare.)

The lesson of such decentering is simply that, in a love relationship, we are never alone with our partner: we are always playing a role for a foreign gaze, imagined or real. Which brings us back to *Broken Lullaby*, where the implicit question raised by the couple at the film's end is precisely: "What are we for the parents' gaze while we are fucking?"

THE FALL, AGAIN

Another key feature of Lubitsch's universe, and the counterpart to the subject's decentering or alienation in the signifier, is the topic of the subject's fall. Exemplary here is *Ninotchka*, a film which was publicized as a departure for its star Greta Garbo—after a series of pathos-heavy melodramas (*Grand Hotel, Queen Christina, Anna Karenina* ...), finally here was a film in which Garbo laughs. The scene in which Garbo (as Ninotchka) first bursts into laughter thus deserves a closer look. Leon and Ninotchka are sitting in a simple working-class restaurant in Paris, and Leon has been trying without success to make her laugh by telling her a series of jokes. Here is his last desperate attempt: "A man comes into a restaurant. He sits down at the table and says, 'Waiter! Bring me a cup of coffee without cream.' Five minutes later the waiter comes back and says, 'I'm sorry, sir, we have no cream, can it be without milk?'" A group of workmen sitting at the next table all burst into laughter, but Ninotchka continues to eat her soup without so much as a smile. Leon reacts furiously: "Not funny huh? ... Well it is funny! Everybody else thought it was funny! Maybe you didn't get the point. I'll tell it to you again. A man comes into a restaurant. Did you get that?" "Yes." "He sits down at the table and says to the waiter ... Did you get that too?" "Yes." "All right, it isn't funny so far, but wait a minute. He says to the waiter, 'Waiter! Bring me a cup of coffee.' So the waiter comes back five minutes later and says, 'I'm sorry, sir, we're all out of coffee.'" (He realizes he has made a mistake.) "Oh no, you've got me all mixed up now ..." (He starts over again.) "... That's it ... he says, 'Waiter! Bring me a cup of coffee without cream,' and five minutes later the waiter comes back and says, 'I'm sorry, sir, we have no cream, can it be a glass of milk!'" Ninotchka still doesn't react, and Leon berates her angrily: "Oh! You have no sense of humor! None whatsoever!" In his excitement he leans back too far on his chair and topples over, crashing into the table behind him. At this, the whole restaurant erupts into laughter and the camera cuts back to Garbo now in uncontrollable spasms. Leon snaps back indignantly: "What's so funny about this?"

What is striking here is the contrast between the subtlety of the joke and the vulgarity of Leon's fall. The joke is a supreme one, an exemplary case of sophisticated Hegelian humor, exploiting the basic dialectical fact that the absence of a feature also defines the identity of an object—even if a coffee without milk is materially exactly the same as a coffee without cream, its symbolic identity is not the same. We thus find ourselves in the field of symbolic alienation, of the differential game of signifiers—no wonder the joke has been subjected to detailed Lacanian readings, most recently by Ivana Novak and Jela Krečič:

What, then, can follow such an excellent joke? Only a *fall*, a collapse into mere vulgarity—which, of course, is not merely that, since it complicates the signifying dialectic even further, adding another turn of the screw: the fall out of the signifying chain. Indeed, what follows is a whole series of falls: First, there is a fall in the immediate physical sense: Leon falls on his ass in the most embarrassing and clumsy way. But this also signals a fall from his symbolic status as a sophisticated charmer, a fact directly registered by his expression of anger ("What's so funny about this?")—he no longer controls the game of seduction and is momentarily lost. And, as befits true love, Ninotchka does not react to this fall with condescending grace ("don't worry, when you stumble, I love you even more"), but with *her own fall*—the two falls overlap. At the immediate level, she *falls into incontrollable laughter*—loses control of herself in exactly the same way one loses control when one falls into tears. Her fall, however, goes much deeper, providing an exemplary instance of what Lacan calls "subjective destitution."[8]

---

8 Novak and Krečič, "Introduction," in *Lubitsch Can't Wait*, pp. 14–15.

The scene is also profoundly political—with her laughter, Ninotchka expresses her solidarity with the workers in the restaurant against the aristocratic and sophisticated Leon, the target of their shared laughter. Ninotchka's famous outburst should therefore be precisely located: it is not the cynical laughter of the powerful who mock the clumsiness of their uneducated and perplexed subjects; neither is it the conformist laughter permitted to those subjects as a consolation prize, allowing them to ease their tensions and thus endure their miserable lives more easily (as was the function of political jokes in communist regimes). But nor is it the laughter of wisdom (in the sense of: "Isn't our dignity an imposture not to be taken too seriously? Are we not all ultimately helpless dolls thrown around by unknown forces?"). This last is not a laughter into which we fall, but the laughter of those who take a knowing distance towards the game of life, towards those who take life too seriously. Ninotchka's laughter is, on the contrary, the laughter of a complete and utter fall, of the collapse of any such distance, the laughter of solidarity. Ninotchka doesn't simply laugh at Leon's fall, she herself falls into laughter.

Alain Badiou wrote about this in his wonderful short book *In Praise of Love*, in which he opposes the authentic experience of "falling in love" to the "search for an adequate partner" through dating agencies: what gets lost in such a search is simply love itself as a Fall—as a crazy event, a contingent traumatic encounter that derails my life and through which I am reborn as a new subject.[9] Is this not what happens with the double fall in *Ninotchka*? When Ninotchka starts to laugh wildly, she doesn't only fall into laughter, she also falls in love. With Leon, the same process takes place in two steps: at first he falls only physically, not yet subjectively, as signaled by his bitter complaint: "What's so funny about this?" But when he joins in the laughter with Ninotchka and the restaurant crowd, his old subjectivity also falls and he changes from a decadent sophisticated seducer into a true proletarian in love. Here, then, we must supplement Badiou's theory of love with Lubitsch: *Badiou avec Lubitsch*. In his elaboration of love as a fall, Badiou neglects its comical (pre)condition: prior to falling in love, both subjects have to "fall" in the sense of falling out of their (socially, hierarchically) established form of subjectivity—there is no love, no authentic love encounter, without this moment of comedy.

The fall also means that love is singular—we never fall in love with a collective like a nation (whether our own or some other—when it seems

---

9   See Alain Badiou, *In Praise of Love*, London: Serpent's Tail 2012.

that we do, the mechanism is totally different). During a debate on sexual harassment in which I participated several years ago, a woman claimed that, whenever she reads a report of a rape, she feels as if the perpetrator is not just a single man, but the whole of man-kind. Somewhat in poor taste, I was tempted to ask her if, when she hears of a woman enjoying a nice bout of love-making, she also feels as if not only a single lover, but the whole of man-kind, were responsible ... I didn't say it, not just because it would have been tasteless, but because it immediately struck me that it would also have been theoretically wrong. There is no symmetry between the two experiences: an act of violence can be experienced as universalized, as performed by the entire group to which the perpetrator belongs, while an act of love is always singular. This is also why humanitarian universal love is lifeless compared to racist passion: one can hate all Jews (Arabs, Blacks ...), but one can never love all of them with the same intensity.

The topic of the fall takes us to the most elementary ethical level, confronting us with the two basic approaches: on the one hand, there is the tradition of spiritual meditation, which locates the ethical attitude in the subject's resistance to the fall, or ability to maintain some degree of distance towards the objects of libidinal investment—from a melancholic admission of their vanity through benevolent irony up to a contemptuous rejection of all worldly goods (the common thread is here the old Buddhist motto, "Don't become too attached to worldly things"). On the other hand, there is the tradition from Christianity to Lacan which locates the ethical attitude in the subject's unrestrained fall into the world, in the unconditional surrender and fidelity to the contingent object of love. And it is here that appearances deceive: Lubitsch is not a wise man preaching benevolent irony ("don't take human follies and attachments too seriously"); on the contrary, he insists on the unconditional Fall and fidelity to this Fall.

This elementary contrast needs to be elaborated further: Buddhist practice begins with conduct—with analyzing (and changing) the way we act. There are no higher powers dictating or judging our actions from outside; our acts as it were create their own immanent criteria in the way they fit into their overall context, either increasing or diminishing suffering (our own and that of all sentient beings). This is what is meant by the notion of karma: we never act in isolation, and our actions always leave traces— traces which, whether good, bad, or indifferent, continue to haunt the agent long after the act is done. Here enters common morality: the first step of Buddhist practice is to train us to identify and gradually reduce unwholesome actions that occur at three levels: body, speech, and mind. There are

296 THE HEGELIAN EVENT

three unwholesome actions of the body that are to be avoided (killing, stealing, sexual misconduct), four actions of speech (lying, slander, harsh speech, malicious gossip), and the three actions of mind (greed, anger, delusion). As we gradually diminish these unwholesome acts following the "middle way" of avoiding extremes, we approach—although are not yet ready to enter—the state of Enlightenment in which we will acquire dispassion for all objects of desire, and thus be liberated from suffering (*dukkha*) and from the cycle of incessant rebirths (*samsara*). An individual who reaches this stage is called a bodhisattva. However, ambiguities emerge here concerning the ethical dimension and the determination to free *all* sentient beings (not just myself and other humans) from *samsara* and its cycle of death, rebirth, and suffering. There are a variety of different conceptions of the nature of a bodhisattva in Buddhism; according to the Tibetan text *Kun-bzang bla-ma'i zhal-lung*, a bodhisattva can choose from three paths in helping sentient beings in the process of achieving buddhahood:

—a *king-like bodhisattva* aspires to achieve buddhahood as soon as possible and then help sentient beings to do the same;

—a *boatman-like bodhisattva* aspires to achieve buddhahood along with other sentient beings;

—a *shepherd-like bodhisattva* aspires to delay buddhahood until all other sentient beings achieve buddhahood.

This last level can be taken to a sublime extreme: there was a shepherd-like bodhisattva who included among "all sentient beings" not just the living but also the souls of those suffering eternal torment in Hell because of their sinful lives—they too should be redeemed before he would enter nirvana. According to some schools, the lowest level is the way of the king who primarily seeks his own benefit but recognizes that this depends crucially on the benefit of his kingdom and his subjects. The middle level is the path of the boatman who ferries his passengers across the river and simultaneously, of course, ferries himself as well. The highest level is that of the shepherd who makes sure that all his sheep arrive safely ahead of him and places their welfare above his own. Other schools claim that only the first level is the real one: buddhas remain in the world, able to help others, so there is no point in delaying one's entry into nirvana—it is only possible to lead others to Enlightenment once we have attained Enlightenment ourselves.

So what happens to our karma when we find ourselves in nirvana (the Buddhist "subjective destitution")? It is not that our acts leave only good traces—if this were the case, then we would simply have to oppose good and bad karma, in the sense that the traces of our good acts compose our good karma which provides a kind of safety shelter for our life, a positive Wheel of Desire. The point is that, when we find ourselves in nirvana, our acts leave *no* traces, we are at a distance—*subtracted*—from the Wheel of Desire. But here the problem emerges: if performing moderately good acts (the elementary morality with which Buddhist practice begins) helps us to get rid of our excessive attachments, is it then not the case that, when we reach nirvana, we should be able to perform even brutal acts in such a way that they leave no traces, because we perform them at a distance? Would not precisely this ability be the mark of a true bodhisattva? The answers given in the classic Buddhist texts are inconsistent here. The *Milindapanha*, an authoritative Theravadin text, argues that punitive violence should be understood as the fruition of the victim's own karma: "If a robber deserves death, he should be put to death ... it is the robber's *own* karma that causes the execution ... The king merely facilitates this fruition ... Even the death penalty can be seen as a benefit from this perspective. The victim is benefited through relief of a karmic burden." The king who orders the execution is thus just a neutral "dispenser of karmic outcomes." And the same goes for torture: "compassionate torture that does not result in permanent physical damage may have a beneficial influence on the character of the victim."[10] Like the dedicated Stalinist communist acting as a mere "instrument of historical necessity," the bodhisattva is here just a kind of vanishing mediator, a "dispenser of karmic outcomes" who merely effectuates the karmic necessity of punishment following our sinful acts. And, as in the case of Stalinism, the bodhisattva adopts the perverse position of being the instrument of the big Other, shifting the burden of responsibility and decision onto his victim: "I'm not in it for anything, I am just a conveyor of the objective necessity of your karma, so it's up to you to avoid sinful deeds." This reasoning may be sustained by one of three underlying logics. According to the first, a bodhisattva sees the void of all existence and is thus aware that his acts are not crimes because there is nothing to be killed: "If every living being is just a phantasm or a dream, is it a sin to kill them?— If one 'sees' them as living beings, it is a sin to kill them. If one does not

---

10   Michael Jerryson and Mark Juergensmeyer, *Buddhist Warfare*, Oxford: Oxford University Press 2010, p. 65.

'see' them as living beings, then there are not any living beings that can be killed; as when one kills another man in a dream: upon awakening, there is absolutely no one there."[11] According to the second logic, since a bodhisattva has succeeded in stepping out of the karmic cycle, his deeds have no karmic consequences and he can do whatever he wants. According to the third logic, a bodhisattva's deeds have karmic consequences like all human deeds, but since he does what he does out of compassion, he "may do what is ordinarily forbidden or inauspicious, including killing, and make merit as long as they remain compassionate."[12] So if killing or torture is done with compassion, committing such acts not only doesn't hurt my karma, it may even strengthen my good karma. That is to say, in a more radical version of this line of reasoning, a bodhisattva's killing and torturing is presented as an act of supreme self-sacrifice which

> allows the bodhisattva to engage in the slaughter of thieves or brigands ... so that the bodhisattva could go to hell instead of the criminals ... the bodhisattva replaces himself for the other and suffers in his stead ... the bodhisattva killer is compassionately freeing his victim from the karmic outcome of great crimes and has the wish that he, rather than the criminal, should be born in hell. However ... the result of killing with this intention, far from going to hell, is that the bodhisattva actually becomes blameless and produces great merit ... the more willing bodhisattvas are to go to hell, the more certain it is that they will not.[13]

The obscenity of the final reversal is difficult to miss: when I kill to prevent a murder, I prevent the (potential) murderer from becoming one, i.e., I sin instead of him and increase my bad karma; however, since this sinful act is done to save the (potential) murderer from hell, I will not be punished by bad karma for my act, in fact my good karma will even profit.

Here we have another instance of the paradox of the borrowed kettle: I can kill without bad karma because 1) there is nothing to kill, reality is a void; 2) there is reality, and living beings, but if I kill as bodhisattva, I am not caught in the karmic cycle; 3) there is reality and I have karma, but if I kill out of compassion, the killing enhances my good karma. Another aspect of this ambiguity is the question confronting contemporary Buddhists: how

---

11   Ibid., pp. 56–7.

12   Ibid., p. 68.

13   Ibid., p. 69.

are we to distinguish between the Buddhist Enlightenment achieved by the hard work of discipline and meditation, and Enlightenment generated through chemical means ("Enlightenment pills")? Owen Flanagan here introduces a "normative exclusion clause": "cases where happiness is gained by magic pills or is due to false belief do not count because the allegedly happy person must be involved in cultivating her own virtue and happiness; happy states born of delusion are undeserved."[14] However, this clause is clearly an external normative device, where what is needed is an immanent criterion. In other words, the "undeserved" Enlightenment is still Enlightenment. Plus, once we know that Enlightenment can be achieved through chemical means, do we not have to accept that *all* Enlightenment is based on chemical processes (going on in our brain when we meditate)? So there is really no difference between deserved and non-deserved Enlightenment: in both cases, the immanent process is chemical … It is like two people competing in exams: one works hard, the other enhances his abilities with a pill—but if one can win with a pill, does this not mean that the same chemical process is going on also in the hard worker?

But what if we were to apply the Hegelian lesson that the identity of a thing is mediated/constituted by the negations implied in this identity, i.e., by what this thing is not? Couldn't we then say that there is nonetheless a difference between the two Enlightenments? One Enlightenment (say, the "chemical" one) is like a coffee without milk, while the other Enlightenment (say, the "meditative" one) is like a coffee without cream, so that, although with regard to their positive features they are exactly the same, they differ with regard to what they are *not* (i.e., in terms of how the non-enlightened existence was negated or overcome on the way to Enlightenment).[15] This counter-argument misses the critical point, however: the moment there is no phenomenal difference between "chemical" Enlightenment and "meditative" Enlightenment, the two Enlightenments themselves *become the same also with regard to their causality*; that is to say, even when we meditate, we just trigger in our brain the same chemical processes that can also be triggered by direct chemical intervention.

---

14 Owen Flanagan, *The Boddhisattva's Brain: Buddhism Naturalized*, Cambridge, MA: MIT Press 2011, p. 186.

15 This idea was suggested to me by Benjamin Inouye (personal communication).

WHY WE SHOULD MARRY A DOLL

To return to Lubitsch: even this endorsement of the Fall is not enough to circumscribe the so-called "Lubitsch touch"—what one must add is a feature most clearly discernible in his *Design for Living* (1933), based on a play by Noël Coward. "Trouble in Paradise," the title of a film made by Lubitsch a year earlier, is actually a much better fit for the story of *Design for Living*: commercial artist Gilda Farrell works for advertising executive Max Plunkett, who tries in vain to seduce her. On a train to Paris, she meets artist George Curtis and playwright Thomas Chambers, fellow Americans who share an apartment there; they both fall in love with her. Unable to choose between the two, Gilda proposes to live with them as a friend, muse, and critic—on the understanding they will not have sex. However, when Tom goes to London to oversee the staging of his play, Gilda and George become involved romantically. After his return to Paris, Tom discovers that George is in Nice painting a portrait, and uses the opportunity to seduce Gilda himself. When the three meet again, Gilda orders both men out and decides to end their rivalry by marrying Max in New York; but when she receives potted plants as a wedding gift from Tom and George she is so upset that she fails to consummate the marriage. When Max hosts a party for his advertising clients in New York, Tom and George crash the event and hide in Gilda's bedroom. Max finds the three of them laughing on the bed and orders the men out. In the ensuing brawl, Gilda announces that she is leaving her husband, and she, Tom, and George decide to return to Paris and their previous *ménage à trois*.

What then is the trouble that occurs in the paradise of the happy *ménage à trois*? Is it the monogamous marriage, which introduces the dimension of the Fall, of Law and its transgression, into the happy prelapsarian promiscuity, or is it the competitive jealousy of the two men, which disturbs the peace and forces Gilda to escape into marriage? Is the film's conclusion then "better a little trouble in paradise than happiness in the hell of marriage"? Whichever is the answer, the ending stages a return to paradise, so that the overall result can be paraphrased in G. K. Chesterton's terms: marriage itself is the most sensational of departures and the most romantic of rebellions. When the couple proclaim their marriage vows, alone and somewhat fatuously fearless amid the multiple temptations to promiscuous pleasure, it certainly does serve to remind us that marriage is the original and poetic figure, while cheaters and participants in orgies are merely placid old cosmic conservatives, happy in the immemorial respectability of promiscuous apes and wolves. The marriage vow is based on the fact that marriage is the most dark and daring of conspiracies.[16]

In 1916, when Lenin's (at that point ex-)mistress Inessa Armand wrote him that even a fleeting passion was more poetic and cleaner than kisses without love between a man and a woman, he replied: "Kisses without love between vulgar spouses are filthy. I agree. These need to be contrasted ... with what? ... It would seem: kisses with love. But you contrast 'a fleeting (why a fleeting) passion (why not love?)'—and it comes out logically as if kisses without love (fleeting) are contrasted to marital kisses without love ... This is odd."[17] Lenin's reply is usually dismissed as proof of his personal petit-bourgeois sexual constraints, sustained by his bitter memory of the past affair; but there is more to it than this: namely, the insight that the marital "kisses without love" and the extramarital "fleeting affair" are two sides of the same coin—both shirk from *combining* the Real of an unconditional passionate attachment with the form of symbolic proclamation. The implicit presupposition (or, rather, injunction) of the standard ideology of marriage is that, precisely, there should be no love in it: one gets married in order to cure oneself of the excessive passionate attachment, to replace it with boring daily custom (and if one cannot resist passion's temptation, there are always extra-marital affairs ...).

From the very beginning of his career, Lubitsch was well aware of these complications pertaining to the formula "trouble in paradise." In his first masterpiece, *The Doll* (1919), the Baron of Chanterelle demands that his nephew Lancelot get married to preserve the family line. A skittish and effeminate fellow, Lancelot does not wish to marry, so when his uncle presents him with forty enthusiastic brides, he hides out with a group of monks. The gluttonous monks learn about Lancelot's potential cash reward for his nuptials, so they cook up a plan: since Lancelot doesn't want to marry a real "dirty" woman, he can marry a doll. However, after the toymaker Hilarius finishes making the doll, her arms are accidentally broken; in order not to lose the reward, the monks convince Ossi, Hilarius' daughter, to take the place of the doll and pretend to be artificial. The wedding ceremony is a success, Ossi plays her role well, Lancelot gets the promised money from the Baron and returns with his bride to the monastery where he falls asleep in his cell and dreams that Ossi is alive, not a doll. When he awakens, Ossi

---

16   Cf. G. K. Chesterton, "A Defense of Detective Stories," in H. Haycraft, ed., *The Art of the Mystery Story*, New York: The Universal Library 1946, p. 6.

17   Quoted from Robert Service, *Lenin*, London: Macmillan 2000, p. 232.

tells him that she really is alive, but Lancelot only believes her when she cries out in fear upon seeing a mouse. They both promptly escape from the monastery to a river bank, where they embrace and kiss passionately. In the meantime, his hair having gone grey from worry, Hilarius is desperately looking for his daughter; when he finally locates the couple, they show him their marriage certificate—they have married again properly, this time as real persons. When Hilarius sees this his worries are over and his hair goes dark again ... Surprisingly, we can discern here the motif of remarriage which characterizes later Hollywood screwball comedies: the first marriage is without true love, an opportunistic marriage with a doll; only the second marriage is the true one.

At the film's beginning, we see Lubitsch himself behind a miniature of the film's set: he begins by unpacking a toy box, first placing its wedge-shaped landscape atop a table, then attaching a cabin, trees, a white background and a small bench to the base. After placing a pair of wooden dolls in the house, Lubitsch cuts for the first time to a full-size facsimile of the toy set with the two human figures stepping out of the cabin. This artificiality characterizes the film's entire set design and costuming: paper trees, a cut-out moon, a horse replaced with two people under a black sheet, etc. Lubitsch thus directly presents the film as a product of his manipulation, reducing the film's human subjects to inanimate objects (dolls) and positing himself as the puppet master of his actors-marionettes. Here, however, one has to avoid the trap of a simple humanist reading that would oppose woman as a mere doll (mechanically obeying male whims) to a "real" living woman. What does a puppet (more precisely: a marionette) stand for as a subjective stance? We can turn here to Heinrich von Kleist's essay *Über das Marionettentheater* from 1810,[18] which is crucial with regard to his relationship to Kant's philosophy (we know that reading Kant threw Kleist into a shattering spiritual crisis—this reading was *the* traumatic encounter of his life). Where, in Kant, do we find the term "Marionette"? In a mysterious subchapter of his *Critique of Practical Reason* entitled "Of the Wise Adaptation of Man's Cognitive Faculties to His Practical Vocation," in which he endeavors to answer the question of what would happen to us were we to gain access to the noumenal domain, to the *Ding an sich*:

---

18   Reprinted in Vol. 5 of *Heinrich von Kleist. dtv Gesamtausgabe*, Munich: dtv 1969.

instead of the conflict which now the moral disposition has to wage with inclinations and in which, after some defeats, moral strength of mind may be gradually
won, God and eternity in their awful majesty would stand unceasingly before
our eyes ... Thus most actions conforming to the law would be done from fear,
few would be done from hope, none from duty. The moral worth of actions, on
which alone the worth of the person and even of the world depends in the eyes
of supreme wisdom, would not exist at all. The conduct of man, so long as his
nature remained as it is now, would be changed into mere mechanism, where, as
in a puppet show, everything would gesticulate well but no life would be found
in the figures.[19]

So, for Kant, direct access to the noumenal domain would deprive us of
the very "spontaneity" which forms the kernel of transcendental freedom:
it would turn us into lifeless automata, or, in contemporary terms, into
"thinking machines." What Kleist does is present the *obverse* of this horror:
the bliss and grace of marionettes, of those creatures who have direct access
to the noumenal divine dimension, who are *directly* guided by it. For Kleist,
marionettes display the perfection of spontaneous, unconscious movements: they have only one center of gravity, their movements are controlled
from only one point. The puppeteer has control only of this point, and as
he moves it in a simple straight line, the limbs of the marionette follow
inevitably and naturally because the figure of the marionette is completely
coordinated. Marionettes thus symbolize beings of an innocent, pristine
nature: they respond naturally and gracefully to divine guidance, in contrast
to ordinary humans who have to struggle constantly with their ineradicable
propensity to Evil, which is the price they have to pay for their freedom.
This grace of the marionettes is underscored by their apparent weight-
lessness: they hardly touch the floor—they are not bound to the earth, for
they are held up from above. They represent a state of grace, a paradise lost
to man whose willful "free" self-assertions make him self-conscious. The
dancer exemplifies this fallen state of man: he is not upheld from above,
but feels himself bound to the earth, and yet must appear weightless in
order to perform his feats with apparent ease. He must try consciously to
attain grace, which is why the effect of his dance is affectation rather than
grace. Therein resides the paradox of man: he is neither an animal wholly
immersed in his earthly surroundings, nor an angelic marionette floating

---

19   Immanuel Kant, *Critique of Practical Reason*, New York: Macmillan 1956,
pp. 152–3.

gracefully in the air, but a free being who, thanks to his very freedom, feels the unbearable pressure that attracts and ties him to the earth where, ultimately, he does *not* belong. It is in terms of this tragic split that we should read figures like Käthchen von Heilbronn from Kleist's play of the same name, this fairy-tale figure of a woman who wanders through life with angelic equanimity: like a marionette, she is guided from above and fulfill her glorious destiny merely by following the spontaneous assertions of her heart. Against this background then, new light can be thrown upon the Lubitsch motif of "trouble in paradise":

> What is the nature of the Lubitschean comic object? One hint may be discerned from an aphorism by Emil Cioran: "I ponder C., for whom drinking in a café was the sole reason to exist. One day when I was eloquently vaunting Buddhism to him, he replied, 'Well, yes, nirvana, all right, but not without a café.'" For Cioran's colleague, the café is the "troublesome object" which both disturbs the peacefulness of paradise and, through this very disturbance, renders it bearable. One could reiterate, "Well, yes, paradise is wonderful, but only on one condition: the odd detail that messes it up." This would also seem to be Lubitsch's underlying message, that the trouble *in* paradise is also the trouble *with* paradise: imbalance and disharmony are the very soul of desire, so that the object of desire is what embodies this turbulence rather than putting a "happy end" to it.[20]

One should nonetheless add to this general point (about the odd detail that disturbs the harmonious order as the cause of desire) a more specific turn of the screw: the true trouble in paradise is the very fall from the state of grace (that characterizes the doll) to the ordinary human life of mortal passions. In other words, the move from doll to real woman is a fall, not a growth towards maturity. The point is thus not that women should stop playing stupid sexy dolls for the sake of men and act like real women—the detour through the doll figure is a necessary one, as it is only against the background of such a figure, i.e., as a fall from it, that the "real" woman can emerge.

No wonder *Die Puppe* echoes "the Sandman," one of the best known of Hoffmann's tales about a poet falling in love with a beauty who turns out to be a doll: the three most famous tales (brought together in Offenbach's opera) render precisely the three principal modes of the failure of a

---

20   Aaron Schuster, "Comedy in Times of Austerity," in Novak et al., eds., *Lubitsch Can't Wait*, pp. 27–8.

sexual relationship—the woman either turns out to be a mechanical doll (Olympia), or she prefers her vocation to love and dies singing (Antonia), or she is simply a promiscuous cheat (Giulietta). (And, as Offenbach's opera makes clear, all three adventures are fantasies of Hoffmann's, ways to postpone or avoid the encounter with his actual love.)

Where, exactly, is the trouble in paradise?

This brings us back to *Trouble in Paradise*, Lubitsch's first absolute masterpiece and, one should never forget, the first part of his *political* trilogy:

> If *Ninotchka* is a film about communism and *To Be or Not to Be* about fascism, *Trouble in Paradise* is a comic treatment of the worst economic crisis the world has seen, the Great Depression. These three films, the most socially conscious in Lubitsch's *oeuvre*, form a kind of trilogy which deals with the crisis of capitalism and its two historic solutions: fascism and communism.[21]

Shall we reproach Lubitsch for keeping this social-political topic at a distance, as the mere background for a comedy? This would be to miss a dimension also present in the work of Preston Sturges. Sturges' *Sullivan's Travels* tells the story of John Sullivan, a popular young Hollywood director who has made a series of profitable but shallow comedies. Dissatisfied with his output so far, he decides that his next project will be a serious exploration of the plight of the downtrodden, so he dresses as a penniless hobo and takes to the road. Due to a confusion, he is mistaken for a criminal and sentenced to six years in a labor camp, where he learns the importance of laughter in the otherwise dreary lives of his fellow prisoners when they are allowed to attend a showing of Walt Disney's *Playful Pluto* cartoon. Sullivan comes to realize that comedy can do more good for the poor than respectful social dramas, so when the confusion is cleared up and he is released, he decides to continue making his shallow comedies, and the film ends with a montage of laughing faces watching his new offering ... *Sullivan's Travels* can of course be read as advocating blind escapism, and as a condemnation of the futile pretensions of socially engaged art—however, what escapes this framing is *the film itself as a narrative act*. That is to say, it *directly shows* the misery and despair of the homeless tramps and of the

---

21 Ibid., p. 29.

low-class prisoners—had the film taken its own message seriously, it could not have been shot. And the same goes for dismissing Lubitsch's trilogy as mere escapist comedies.

In *Trouble in Paradise*, the lyrics of the song heard during the opening credits provide a definition of the "trouble" in store (as does the image that accompanies the song: first we see the words "Trouble in," then beneath them a large double bed appears, and then, over the bed in large letters, "Paradise"). So "paradise" is the paradise of a full sexual relationship: "That's paradise / while arms entwine and lips are kissing / but if there's something missing / that signifies / trouble in paradise." To put it in a brutally direct way, "trouble in paradise" is thus Lubitsch's name for the fact that *il n'y a pas de rapport sexuel*. Perhaps this brings us to what the "Lubitsch touch" represents at its most elementary—an ingenious way of making this failure work. That is to say, instead of reading the fact that there is no sexual relationship as a traumatic obstacle on account of which every love affair has to end in some kind of tragic failure, this very obstacle can be turned into a comic resource, can function as something to be circumvented, alluded to, played with, exploited, manipulated, made fun of ... in short, sexualized. Sexuality is here an exploit which thrives on its own ultimate failure.

So where is the trouble in paradise in *Trouble in Paradise*? As has been noted by perspicuous critics, there is a fundamental (and irreducible) ambiguity surrounding this key point, an ambiguity which echoes that in *Design for Living*. The first answer to suggest itself is that although Gaston loves Lily as well as Mariette, the true "paradisiacal" sexual relationship would have been the one with Mariette, which is why it is this relationship that has to remain impossible/unfulfilled. This unfulfillment confers a touch of melancholy on the film's ending: all the laughter and boisterousness, all the merry display of partnership between Gaston and Lily as they exchange their stolen goods, only fill in the void of this melancholy. Does Lubitsch not point in this direction with the repeated shot of the big empty double bed in Mariette's house, a shot which recalls the empty bed of the film's opening credits? What about the poignant romantic exchange between Gaston and Mariette when he leaves her—"It could have been glorious." "Lovely." "Divine ..."? It is all too easy to read the excessive romantic sentimentality of this parting scene as a parody, as a case of the characters directly acting as actors, reciting the lines they have learned. Undoubtedly there is an ironic distance in this scene, but it is a properly Mozartean irony: it is not the excessive romantic passion which conceals the ironic distance, it is the appearance of ironic distance itself, the ridicule of the sentimental scene, which conceals the utter seriousness of the situation. In short, the two (prospective) lovers are play acting in order to obfuscate the Real of their passion.

There is, however, also the possibility of the exact opposite reading:

> Could it be that paradise is actually the scandalous love affair of Gaston and Lily, two chic thieves fending for themselves, and trouble is the sublimely statuesque Mariette? That, in a tantalizing irony, Mariette is the snake luring Gaston from his blissfully sinful Garden of Eden? ... Paradise, the good life, is the life of crime full of glamour and risks, and evil temptation comes in the form of Madame Colet, whose wealth holds the promise of an easy-going *dolce vita* without real criminal daring or subterfuge, only the humdrum hypocrisy of the respectable classes.[22]

The beauty of this reading is that paradisiacal innocence is located in the glamorous and dynamic life of crime, so that the Garden of Eden is equated with that life while the call of high society respectability is equated with the snake's temptation. However, this paradoxical reversal is easily explained by Gaston's sincere and raw outburst, enacted with no elegance or ironic distance, the first and only one in the film, after Mariette refuses to call the police when he tells her that the chairman of the board of her company has for years been systematically stealing millions from her. Gaston's reproach is that, while Mariette was immediately ready to call the police when an ordinary burglar like him steals from her a comparatively small amount of wealth, she is ready to turn a blind eye when a member of her own respectable class steals millions. Is Gaston here not paraphrasing Brecht's famous question, "What is the robbing of a bank compared to the founding of a bank?" What are direct robberies like those of Gaston and Lily compared to the theft of millions through obscure financial operations?

There is, however, another aspect which has to be noted here: is Gaston's and Lily's life of crime really so "full of glamour and risks"? Beneath all the surface glamour and risk, they are perhaps

> a quintessential bourgeois couple, conscientious professional types with expensive tastes—yuppies before their time. Gaston and Mariette, on the other hand, are the really romantic pair, the adventurous and risk-taking lovers. In returning to Lily and lawlessness, Gaston is doing the sensible thing—returning to his

---

22   Ibid., p. 28.

"station," as it were, opting for the mundane life he knows. And he does so full of regret, apparent in his lingering final exchange with Mariette, full of rue and stylish ardor on both sides.[23]

This brings us back to Chesterton, and the already mentioned passage from his famous "Defense of Detective Stories" in which he notes how the detective story in some sense keeps before the mind the fact that civilization itself is the most sensational of departures and the most romantic of rebellions:

> When the detective in a police romance stands alone, and somewhat fatuously fearless amid the knives and fists of a thief's kitchen, it does certainly serve to make us remember that it is the agent of social justice who is the original and poetic figure, while the burglars and footpads are merely placid old cosmic conservatives, happy in the immemorial respectability of apes and wolves... [The police romance is thus] based on the fact that morality is the most dark and daring of conspiracies.[24]

Does this not also offer the best description of Gaston and Lily? Are these two burglars not "placid old cosmic conservatives, happy in the immemorial respectability of apes and wolves," i.e., living in their paradise before the fall into ethical passion? What is crucial here is the parallel between crime (theft) and sexual promiscuity: what if, in our postmodern world of ordained transgression, in which marital commitment is perceived as ridiculously anachronistic, those who cling to it are the true subversives? What if, today, straight marriage is "the most dark and daring of all transgressions"? As we have already seen, this is exactly the underlying premise of Lubitsch's *Design for Living*: a woman leads a calm and satisfied life with two men; as a dangerous experiment she tries single marriage; the attempt fails miserably and she returns to the safety of living with the two men— the participants in this *ménage à trois* are "placid old cosmic conservatives, happy in the immemorial respectability of apes and wolves." Exactly the same thing happens in *Trouble in Paradise*, wherein the true temptation is the respectful marriage of Gaston and Mariette.[25]

---

23   James Harvey, *Romantic Comedy in Hollywood: From Lubitsch to Sturges,* New York: Da Capo 1987, p. 56.

24   Chesterton, "A Defense of Detective Stories," p. 6.

25   Aaron Schuster has pointed out the Hitchcockian object in *Trouble in Paradise*: Mariette's expensive purse which circulates between the principal figures (Mariette, Gaston, Lily), embodying their intersubjective tension and imbalance,

Lubitsch's sensitivity to the paradoxes of marriage is also clearly discernible in his *To Be or Not to Be*, where there is something quite unique
about the marriage of Maria and Joseph Tura: it is firm as a rock not in spite
of her serial cheating but because of it—it is this very infidelity that ensures
the marriage persists through all its vicissitudes. There is also a nice opposition between the couple at work here: while Maria is cheating her husband
in reality, Joseph's case is more subtle—while not really sleeping with other
women, the complex game of masking locates him in the symbolic position
of the extramarital lover of his own wife. In the middle of the film, Professor
Siletsky (the Polish traitor who is a German agent) tries to seduce Maria,
but following a series of displacements, his place is taken by Joseph himself,
now playing his wife's potential lover. This comic version of the speculative
"identity of opposites" is profoundly Christian: in the same way that, in the
figure of Christ, God rebels against himself, a true husband has to act as his
wife's illegitimate lover. Did not Lubitsch himself indicate this parallel in an
obscene detail: the names of the couple—Maria and Joseph—are the same
as those of Christ's parents, where one can also surmise a certain cheating? (That is to say, assuming one discards the hypothesis of immaculate
conception, is it not clear that Mary had to have had an illegitimate lover
who made her pregnant—a kind of biblical version of the Polish pilot who
is Maria's lover in *To Be or Not to Be*?)

But, again, there is a further complication in *Trouble in Paradise*. We
should always bear in mind that first impressions do not deceive, in spite of
the numerous proverbs and wisdoms that try to convince us otherwise (in
the style of "I fell in love at first sight—what should I do?" "Take another
look!"). It is the first impression which, as a rule, provides the encounter
with the object in the freshness of the Real, and it is the function of second
impressions to obfuscate and domesticate this encounter. What cannot
but strike us on a first encounter with the finale of *Trouble in Paradise* is

---

similarly to Poe's purloined letter ("Comedy in Times of Austerity," p. 37). However,
in contrast to Poe and Hitchcock in whose work the letter does reach its destination
(returns to its proper place)—say, at the very end of *Strangers on a Train*, Guy gets
back his cigarette lighter—in *Trouble in Paradise* the object does not get back to its
rightful owner (it is again stolen by Lily). It would be all too easy to take this as
proof of Lubitsch's subversive dimension, as an indication that he rejects narrative
closure (established when the object returns to its proper place); we should rather
risk a move which may appear naive and instead read the fact that the purse does not
return to its proper place as a melancholic reminder and remainder of a loss which
persists in the merry atmosphere of the film's ending.

the sudden, "psychologically unconvincing and unfounded" reversal of the subjective position of Gaston and Lily: after the ultra-romantic sad farewell between Gaston and Mariette, we are all of a sudden thrown into the screwball universe of Gaston and Lily, a couple of thieves exchanging witty repartees, lovingly making fun of each other, mischievously penetrating each other's clothes, and clearly fully enjoying each other's presence. How to account for the thorough emotional dissonance between these two closing scenes? How come the preceding sad farewell leaves no bitter aftertaste? The easy explanation would be that the sad farewell scene is a fake, a cynical performance which should not be taken seriously. Such a reading, however, would flatten the emotional dissonance, leaving no space for obviously sincere moments like Lily's earlier expression of cynical despair or Gaston's outburst about the hypocrisy of the rich. We must therefore fully embrace the "psychologically unfounded" reversal of tone from pathos to comedy—what does it indicate?

Let us make a (perhaps unexpected) detour. At the end of Howard Hawks' classic Western *Red River*, another "psychologically unfounded" twist occurs which is usually dismissed as a simple weakness in the scenario. The entire film moves towards the climactic confrontation between Dunson and Matt—a duel of almost mythic proportions, predestined by fate, as an inexorable conflict between two incompatible subjective stances. In the final scene, Dunson approaches Matt with the determinacy of a tragic hero blinded by hatred and marching towards his ruin. The brutal fist fight which ensues ends unexpectedly when Tess, who is in love with Matt, fires a gun into the air and shouts at the two men that "any fool with half a mind can see that you two love each other"—a quick reconciliation follows, with Dunson and Matt talking like buddies. This "transition of Dunson from anger incarnate, all Achilles all the time, to sweetness and light, happily yielding to Matt ... is breathtaking in its rapidity."[26] Robert Pippin is fully justified in detecting beneath this technical weakness in the scenario a deeper message, the same message uncovered by Alenka Zupančič in her reading of the final moments of Lubitsch's *Cluny Brown*. After the lively dialogue between the Professor and Cluny at the train station, the Professor simply orders her to get into the carriage with him (implying that they will get married and live together), and she obeys without a moment's hesitation. The Professor's order can be read as a case of successful psychoanalytic

---

26   Robert Pippin, *Hollywood Western and American Myth*, New Haven: Yale University Press 2010, p. 52.

intervention: it brings about in the analysand (Cluny) a radical sub-jective transformation that cannot be accounted for in psychological terms.

Similarly, as was noted by Russell Grigg, Lily's unexpected and appar-ently nonsensical moves towards the end of *Trouble in Paradise* display the same quality of an analytic intervention. How does Lily get Gaston back? It is again all too easy merely to oppose the romantic couple (Gaston-Mariette) to the vivacity of the risky pragmatic partnership (Gaston-Lily). To paraphrase Marx, the secret lies in the form itself, in the apparently nonsensical and repetitive circulation of money between Mariette and Lily. Lily proceeds in three moves, which effectively form a nice Hegelian triad. First, in a moment of cynical realism, she steals the 100,000 francs from Mariette's hidden safe in front of Gaston, declaring hysterically that money is the only thing that matters, that everything else is just empty sentimen-tality. Then—her second move—she throws the cash back on Mariette's bed in a gesture of pride, renouncing the money out of fidelity to ethical princi-ples: "I don't want your money, you can have my man for free, you already bought him cheaply and he deserves you!" But what makes Gaston return to her is not this "ethical turn," i.e., her renunciation of her initial cynical realism, since she then makes a third move: taking the money back and running away with it. The key here lies in the repetition of the same gesture (stealing the money), which acquires the second time a totally different, even opposite, meaning: Lily gets Gaston back by again *taking* the money, not, as one might have expected, just by throwing it back at Mariette and in this way proving her sincerity. Lily's second move resembles the so-called empty gesture, the gesture meant to be rejected: she returns the money only to take it away again. Why does the money have to be taken (stolen) twice? The first theft is a simple act of cynical despair: "OK, I've got it, you love Mariette, so let's forget the sentimentality, I will act as a cold realist." The second theft, however, changes the entire terrain: it repeats the "egotist" act within the field of ethics, i.e., it suspends the ethical (sacrifice of material goods), but does not return to an immediate cynical realism/egotism—in short, it does something similar to Kierkegaard's religious suspension of the ethical. With the second theft, Lily sets Gaston free: her taking the money plays the same role as does the payment of the psychoanalyst; its message is "by accepting money I am out of the game, there are no symbolic debts between us, I renounce all moral blackmail, it's up to you now whether to choose Mariette or not." Only at this point does Gaston break down and return to Lily.

CYNICAL WISDOM

Unfortunately, Lubitsch seems not to embrace fully the consequences of this "suspension of the ethical." He sees marriage as the supreme transgression, as a daring conspiracy, but ultimately he opts for the placid old conservative *ménage à trois*. Lubitsch thus remains within the cynical position of respecting appearances while secretly transgressing them. So if Lubitsch does act as an analyst-director, the subjective position implied by his movies is close to that advocated by Jacques-Alain Miller, for whom a psychoanalyst

> occupies the position of the ironist who takes care not to intervene in the political field. He acts so that semblances remain at their places while making sure that subjects under his care do not take them for *real* … one should somehow bring oneself to remain *taken in by them* (fooled by them). Lacan could say that "those who are not taken in err": if one doesn't act as if semblances are real, if one doesn't leave their efficiency undisturbed, things take a turn for the worse. Those who think that all the signs of power are mere semblances and rely on the arbitrariness of the discourse of the master are bad boys: they are even more alienated.[27]

In the matter of politics, a psychoanalyst thus "doesn't propose projects, he cannot propose them, he can only mock the projects of others, which limits the scope of his statements. The ironist has no great design, he waits for the other to speak first and then brings about his fall as fast as possible … Let us say this is a political wisdom, nothing more."[28] The axiom of this "wisdom" is that

> one should protect the semblances of power for the good reason that one should be able to continue to *enjoy*. The point is not to attach oneself to the semblances of the existing power, but to consider them necessary. "This defines a cynicism in the mode of Voltaire who let it be understood that god is our invention which is necessary to maintain people in a proper decorum." Society is held together only by semblances, "which means: there is no society without repression, without identification, and above all without routine. Routine is essential."[29]

---

27   Nicolas Fleury, *Le réel insensé. Introduction à la pensée de Jacques-Alain Miller*, Paris: Germina 2010, pp. 93–4.

28   Jacques-Alain Miller, "La psychanalyse, la cité, les communautés," *Revue de la Cause freudienne* 68 (2008), pp. 109–10.

29   Fleury, *Le réel insensé*, p. 95, quotations are from Miller.

How can one miss here the echo of Kafka's *Trial* affirming the public Law and Order as a semblance which is not true but is nonetheless necessary? Having listened to the priest's explanation of the story about the Door of the Law, Joseph K. shakes his head and says:

> "I can't say I'm in complete agreement with this view, as if you accept it you'll have to accept that everything said by the doorkeeper is true. But you've already explained very fully that that's not possible." "No," said the priest, "you don't need to accept everything as true, you only have to accept it as necessary." "Depressing view," said K. "The lie made into the rule of the world."

Is this not also Lubitsch's basic position? Law and Order are a semblance, but we should pretend to respect them and meanwhile enjoy our small pleasures and other transgressions ... Nowhere is this position of wisdom revealed more clearly than in *Heaven Can Wait* (1943). At the film's beginning, the old Henry van Cleve enters the opulent reception area of Hell and is personally greeted by "His Excellency" (the Devil) to whom he relates the story of his dissolute life so that his place in Hell can be determined. After hearing Henry's story, His Excellency, a charming old man, denies him entry and suggests he try "the other place," where his dead wife Martha and his good grandfather are waiting for him—there might be "a small room vacant in the annex" up there. So the Devil is nothing but God himself with a touch of wisdom, not taking prohibitions too seriously, well aware that small transgressions make us human ... But if the Devil is a good and wise being, is it then God himself who is the true Evil, insofar as he lacks ironic wisdom and blindly insists on obedience to his Law?[30]

This last step into what Hegel would have called speculative identity is the one that Lubitsch was unable to take; it is what is absent from his universe. It is a limitation that can be felt in the pathetic moment in *To Be or Not to Be* when the old Jewish actor recites the famous lines from Shylock's speech in front of Hitler—the truly subversive thing would have been to imagine something like Hitler making the same speech if, by some miracle, he were to have been brought to trial at Nuremberg and accused of inhuman monstrosities: "I am a Nazi German. Hath not a Nazi eyes? hath not a Nazi hands, organs, dimensions, senses, affections, passions? fed with

---

30   There is a weird inconsistency in the figure of the Devil: he is evil embodied, he pushes us towards sin, but he is simultaneously the executioner of the punishment for our evil deeds, i.e., he runs Hell where we will be punished—how can the supreme criminal be the very agent of justice?

the same food, hurt with the same weapons, subject to the same diseases, healed by the same means, warmed and cooled by the same winter and summer, as a Jew is? If you prick us, do we not bleed? if you tickle us, do we not laugh? if you poison us, do we not die? and if you wrong us with your Jewish plot, shall we not revenge?" In short, the murdered Jews are just the "pound of flesh" extracted for all the injustices Germany has suffered in its recent history ... Such a paraphrase is, of course, a disgusting obscenity—but it makes one thing clear: a general appeal to a shared humanity can cover up any particular horror; it holds as well for the victim as for his or her executioner. The truth of such an appeal would have been in its extreme form—imagine Shylock saying something like: "If we are constipated, don't we need a laxative? If we hear a dirty rumor, don't we like to spread it further just like you do? If we get a chance to steal or cheat, don't we take it just like you do?" The true defense of a Jew should not have been the appeal to a common humanity that we all share, but precisely an appeal to the specific and unique character of the Jews (it was, surprisingly, none other than Hegel who claimed that the problem with Napoleon's emancipation of Jews was not that it granted them full citizenship in spite— or irrespective of—their religion, but that it did not emancipate them on account of the special features that make them unique). It should not have been "You should accept us because, in spite of our differences, we are all human!" but "You should accept us because of what we are in our uniqueness!"

Not all of Lubitsch's work can be reduced to this position of a humanist cynical wisdom—in many of his films (*Broken Lullaby*, *To Be or Not to Be* ...) there are elements which point to an uncanny dimension beyond wisdom, and his last (completed) film, *Cluny Brown* (1946), definitely leaves wisdom behind, effecting a kind of "epistemological break" in Lubitsch's *oeuvre*—but this is already a topic for another analysis.[31]

31   For a close reading of *Cluny Brown* see Alenka Zupančič, "Squirrels to the Nuts, or, How Many Does it Take to Not Give up on Your Desire," in Novak et al., eds., *Lubitsch Can't Wait*, pp. 165–80.

Part III

HEGEL BEYOND HEGEL

CHAPTER 7

Varieties of the "Negation of Negation"

SUICIDE AS THE ACT OF ASSUMING THE IMPOSSIBLE/
REAL OF FREEDOM

From the 1950s to the early 1980s, the Egyptian-French singer Dalida was a mega-star in Europe and the Middle East, and even today has a cult following in France. In January 1967, Dalida competed at the San Remo Festival with her Italian lover, the singer, songwriter, and actor Luigi Tenco. After learning that their song had been eliminated from the final competition, Tenco committed suicide in their hotel room. In September 1970, her Pygmalion and former husband Lucien Morisse, with whom she was still on good terms, committed suicide by shooting himself in the head. In April 1975, her close friend the singer Mike Brant leapt to his death from an apartment in Paris. In July 1983 Richard Chanfray, her lover from 1972 to 1981, committed suicide by inhaling the exhaust gases of his car. In early 1987, coming home one night, Dalida found her beloved bulldog dead. And finally, on Saturday, May 2, 1987, she committed suicide herself by overdosing on barbiturates, leaving behind a note: "*La vie m'est insupportable ... Pardonnez-moi*" ("Life has become unbearable for me... Forgive me.")

Was not Dalida's life exemplary of a type of subject—not a loser but as a rule a successful and charismatic personality—who seems to draw people around them towards death, and who finally succumbs to its temptation themselves? Should we dismiss such cases as simply pathological, or is there a way to conceive them as signs of an authentic life lived in all its intensity?

We can approach this question by way of *film noir*, in which Robert Pippin has discerned a double inversion: the "reflexive" flashback narrative forms part of the events portrayed, but the hero appears to be more a spectator of his own acts than their agent. On the one hand, "often the flashback telling of the story is not so much a perspective *on* what is shown (although it is partly that), but yet another element *of* what is being shown. The narration is another event, and so it and the events narrated then *both* require interpreting."[1] On the other hand, "one can sometimes get the sense that ... the narrator feels he was in much the same position as the events actually unfolded, more a spectator than a participant."[2] Pippin develops this point in his perspicuous reading of the deaths of Jeff and Kathie in Jacques Tourneur's *Out of the Past*. Kathie proposes that they should stop pretending, accept they are both corrupt, and escape together. This represents the comfortable position of accepting one's character and fate as inevitable—it is what it is, we can't do anything about it, it is our nature ... Jeff counteracts this position with a suicidal act, anonymously phoning the police to inform them of his and Kathie's escape route, giving them time to set up a roadblock. It is not a direct act, but a case of "passive agency" or "weak intentionality"[3]—Jeff lets himself and Kathie be shot to death. In a weird reversal of an active engagement that reveals itself as manipulated, here it is the passive intervention that generates an authentic act.

The falsity of accepting fate is perfectly exemplified by Ted Hughes in his relationship with Sylvia Plath—if ever, in the history of modern literature, there was a person who stands for ethical defeat, it is Hughes. The true Other Woman, the focus of the Hughes–Plath saga ignored by both camps, was Assia Wevill, the dark-haired Jewish beauty and Holocaust survivor who became Ted's mistress. When he left Sylvia for Assia, this was like leaving a wife to marry the mad woman in the attic. But how did she become mad in the first place? In 1969 she killed herself the same way Sylvia had (by gassing herself), but she also killed Shura, her daughter with Ted. Why? What drove *her* into this uncanny repetition? This was Ted's true ethical betrayal—here his *Birthday Letters* with their fake mythologizing turn into an ethically repulsive text, putting the blame on the dark forces of Fate that run our lives, casting Assia as the dark seductress: "You are the dark force. You are the dark destructive force that destroyed Sylvia."[4] No wonder Hughes invites the Wildean reproach that while losing one wife to suicide may be regarded as a misfortune, losing two looks like carelessness ... Hughes' betrayal is one long variation on Valmont's "*ce n'est pas ma faute*" from *Liaisons dangereuses*: it wasn't me, it was Fate—as one critic

---

1   Robert Pippin, *Fatalism in American Film Noir*, Charlottesville: University of Virginia Press 2012, p. 38.

2   Ibid., p. 39.

3   Ibid., p. 47.

4   Quoted from Elaine Feinstein, *Ted Hughes*, London: Weidenfeld & Nicolson 2001, p. 166. The psychoanalytic notion of the Unconscious is the very opposite of this instinctual, irrational Fate onto which we can transpose our responsibility.

put it, capturing Hughes' point of view, responsibility is "a figment valid only in a world of lawyers as moralists."⁵ All his babble about the Feminine Goddess, Fate, astrology, etc., is ethically worthless; this is how sexual difference played out here: *she* was hysterical, probing, authentic, self-destructive, while *he* mythologized and shifted the blame onto the Other.

Did not Heidegger do something quite similar in 1934? A month after he had resigned as Dean of Freiburg University, he was invited to teach in Berlin; unsure whether to accept, he "went to see an old friend … a seventy-five-year-old farmer. He had read about the call to Berlin in the newspapers. What would he say? Slowly he fixed the sure gaze of his clear eyes on mine, and keeping his mouth tightly shut, he thoughtfully put his faithful hand on my shoulder. Ever so slightly he shook his head. That meant: absolutely no!"⁶ There are good reasons to surmise that Heidegger's decision to "remain in the provinces" was a belated reaction to his failure to realize his ambitions in Berlin. In the summer of 1933, Heidegger had been under consideration for the prestigious chair in philosophy at the University of Berlin and for the leadership of the Prussian Academy of University Lecturers; however, his enemies within the Nazi party strongly opposed the move. Heidegger travelled to Berlin hoping to meet Hitler and establish a personal relationship with him, but failed to gain access even to the appropriate ministers. It was after his return to Freiburg, when it had become clear that he had no chance of getting the desired post in Berlin, that he wrote his provinces text (first read out as a radio speech)—a nice case of retroactively presenting a defeat as a matter of high-principled personal choice.⁷

Therein resides, as Pippin notes, the finesse of the hero's predicament in *film noir*: yes, we are doomed, Fate pulls the strings, every manipulator is in his turn manipulated, every semblance of a free agent deciding his own fate

---

5   Quoted in ibid., p. 234.

6   Martin Heidegger, "Why Do I Stay in the Provinces? (1934)," in *Philosophical and Political Writings*, London and New York: Continuum 2003, p. 18. One can only imagine what the old farmer was really thinking—in all probability, he knew the answer Heidegger wanted from him and politely provided it. But more importantly, is it not possible to imagine Heidegger going to see his old farmer friend when he was deciding whether to get involved in Nazi university politics? The farmer's reaction, hopefully, would have been exactly the same—a silent no—but this time implying a different meaning: not some primordial wisdom, but a simple fear of the consequences of speaking out publicly against Nazi commitment.

7   See Daniel Maier-Katkin, *Stranger from Abroad*, New York: Norton 2010, pp. 101–2.

is illusory—but simply to endorse and assume this predicament is also an illusion, an escapist avoidance of the burden of responsibility:

> If traditional assumptions about self-knowing, deliberation-guided, causally effective agents are becoming less credible and are under increasing pressure, *what difference should it make in how we comport ourselves?* What would it actually be to *acknowledge* "the truth" or take into practical account the uncertainty? It is difficult to imagine what *simply* acknowledging the facts would be, to *give up* all pretensions to agency ... when Jeff refuses to accept Kathie's fatalistic characterization that both of them simply *are* "no good," implying that it is useless to fight, and he calls the police, he ... assumes a stance, a practical point of view, that in effect concedes how limited is the room for action allowed him by this point, but which does not assume that he is simply "carried along" by the consequences of his history (his past) or his nature ("no good"). He ends up an agent, however restricted and compromised, in the only way one can be. He acts like one.[8]

We may not be able to escape the clutches of Fate, but neither can we escape the burden of responsibility by appealing to Fate. "Many of the best *noirs* are quite good at conveying to us the sense that this, this complicated and paradoxical situation, is what could more properly be said to be our modern fate."[9] Is this not why psychoanalysis is exemplary of our predicament? Yes, we are decentered, caught in a web, overdetermined by unconscious mechanisms; yes, I am "spoken" more than speaking, the Other speaks through me—but simply assuming this fact (in the sense of rejecting any responsibility) is also false, a case of self-deception. Psychoanalysis thus makes us even more responsible than traditional morality, makes us responsible even for what is beyond our (conscious) control. Here we have a nice case of "negation of negation": first subjective autonomy is negated, but then this negation itself is "negated," denounced as a subjective stratagem.

This redoubled impossibility is what defines the status of the Lacanian Real. *Jouissance* is not only inaccessible, forever lost in its incestuous intensity; it is simultaneously that which we cannot get rid of—no matter how we censor or repress it, the very gestures destined to erase it become infected by what they try to obliterate (recall the obsessional neurotic who practices rituals to keep his illicit desires at bay, but the performance of these very

---

8   Pippin, *Fatalism in American Film Noir*, pp. 48–9.
9   Ibid., p. 97.

rituals only reproduces the illicit desires). The same goes for "free associations" in psychoanalytic treatment: while the patient's associations are, of course, never fully "free," in the sense of completely exempt from conscious manipulation, whatever the patient says during the treatment formally acquires the status of a free association. In a strictly homologous way, freedom itself also has this status of an impossible-real: while we are never fully free, at the same time we cannot ever escape being free. Likewise for ethics as the highest expression of our freedom—as they say in *Cloud Atlas*: "You have to do whatever you can't not do." The reason this statement is not a tautology in the traditional style of "Duty is duty!" lies in the gap between direct affirmation and double negation: in ethics, direct affirmation is the result (consequence) of a double negation, i.e., it is not that you cannot not do something (some difficult deed) because you have to do it, it is rather that you have to do it *because you cannot not do it*. In the domain of ethics, necessity is grounded in a deadlock of unavoidability.

Note how the relationship between these two impossibilities is asymmetrical: first, we are forced to accept the impossibility of reaching a certain goal (radical incestuous *jouissance*; the total spontaneity of free associations); then, we are unable to get rid of what we were in vain trying to reach (everything we do is stained by *jouissance*; every association is treated as "free"). In other words, the Real is simultaneously impossible and necessary (unavoidable). Therein resides the properly dialectical status of universality: first, in the classic Marxist move, we have to accept that pure abstract universality is impossible to reach—every universality is already overdetermined by some particular content which is privileged with regard to all other particular content, a privileged content which—as Marx would have put it—provides the specific color of the universality in question. (Marx's example: in capitalism, industrial production is not just one species of production, it colors the entire scope of production, so that all other kinds of production—agricultural, artisanal—get "mediated" by it, get "industrialized.") Then, in the second step, we have to ascertain that this universality which is impossible to reach is also inescapable: no matter how we try to contextualize a universality, to reduce it to its particular components, the empty form of universality continues to haunt us. Recall the ambiguous status of universal human rights: although we can always discern a particular content privileged by the universal form ("human rights are really the rights of white property-owning males"), the universal form nonetheless keeps a gap open, a gap in which others (women, workers, other racial groups …) can inscribe their demands in the course a struggle for hegemony.

It is in this sense that, for Lacan, desire is indestructible (eternal, absolute) insofar as it is impossible—it is indestructible not because it is a permanent unchangeable substance impervious to all pressures, but precisely because it is thoroughly non-substantial: a barely perceptible scintillation of an X that erases itself before it even fully comes to be. In other words, desire is Real—an inconsistent fragile X which, although we can never get hold of it, is forever doomed to return, to continue to haunt us:

> although desire merely conveys what it maintains of an image of the past towards an ever short and limited future, Freud declares that it is nevertheless indestructible. Notice that in the term indestructible, it is precisely the most inconsistent reality of all that is affirmed. If indestructible desire escapes from time, to what register does it belong in the order of things? For what is a thing, if not that which endures, in an identical state, for a certain time? Is not this the place to distinguish in addition to duration, the substance of things, another mode of time—a logical time?[10]

Here we encounter Lacan's version of Hegel's basic axiom: the subject (of desire) is not substance—not a thing which persists in time, but an entirely non-substantial evental entity which disappears even before it appears, which appears in/through its very disappearance, as the result of its very failure to be. This is why its structure involves a specific temporality—the temporality of something that never is but always only *will have been.*

This brings us back to freedom which, in Kant's practical philosophy, has the same status of an impossible-real. A truly free act is, first, impossible in the simple (common) sense that we can never be sure that what we did was really a free act—it always might be the case that, even if it appeared to us that we acted solely for the sake of duty, we were, unbeknownst to us, effectively motivated by some pathological desire (say, for the esteem of others). This, however, is only one side of the story—what causes true anxiety is the prospect that our act really *was* free, and this trauma is domesticated by reducing it to some pathological motivation.

For Kant, freedom is real in the most radical (Lacanian even) sense: freedom is an inexplicable, "irrational," unaccountable "fact of reason," a *Real* which disturbs our notion of (phenomenal) spatio-temporal *reality* as governed by natural laws. It is for this reason that our experience

---

10 Jacques Lacan, *The Four Fundamental Concepts of Psychoanalysis*, New York: Norton 1998, pp. 31–2.

of freedom is properly *traumatic*. In other words, in Kantian ethics, the true tension is not between the subject's idea that he is acting only for the sake of duty, and the hidden fact that there was indeed some pathological motivation at work (vulgar psychoanalysis); the true tension is exactly the opposite one: the free act in its abyss is unbearable, traumatic, so that when we accomplish an act out of freedom, and in order to be able to sustain it, we experience it as being conditioned by some pathological motivation. This is also why, as Kierkegaard put it, the true trauma is not our mortality, but our immortality: it is easy to accept that we are just a speck of dust in the infinite universe; what is much more difficult to accept is that we really *are* immortal free beings who, as such, cannot escape the terrible responsibility of their freedom.

Kierkegaard's notion of "sickness unto death" also relies on this difference between two deaths. That is to say, the "sickness unto death" proper is to be opposed to the standard despair of the individual torn between the certainty that death is the end, that there is no Beyond of eternal life, and his unquenchable desire to believe that death is not final, that there is another life with its promise of eternal bliss. The true "sickness unto death" rather involves the opposite paradox of the subject who knows that death is not the end, that he has an immortal soul, etc., but who cannot face the exorbitant demands that follow from this fact (the necessity of abandoning vain aesthetic pleasures and working for his salvation) and so desperately wants to believe that death *is* the end, that there is no divine unconditional demand exerting its pressure upon him. The standard religious *je sais bien, mais quand même* is inverted here: not "I know very well that I am a mere mortal, but I nonetheless desperately want to believe that there is redemption in eternal life," but rather "I know very well that I have an eternal soul responsible to God's unconditional commandments, but I desperately want to believe that there is nothing beyond death, to be relieved of the unbearable pressure of the divine injunction." In other words, in contrast to the individual caught in the standard skeptical despair, who knows he will die but cannot accept it and hopes for eternal life, we have here, in the case of "sickness unto death," the individual who desperately wants to die, to disappear forever, but knows that he cannot, i.e., that he is condemned to eternal life.

Is not the privileged case of the impossible-real that of subjectivity itself? The reason is obvious: subjectivity is in its very notion a universal singularity, the singularity of an "I" that is not only simultaneously universal (I am an abstract I, all my particular content is contingent, I "have" all my properties, but I "am" not them), but in which only universality becomes "for itself" (only a singular self-consciousness is aware of the universality as such, in contrast to its particular cases). The subject is thus the exception, a crack in the "great chain of being," and simultaneously the disharmonious excess which grounds harmony. Recall the fate of Stella Dallas in the final scene of the Hollywood melodrama of the same name: through a window of the mansion where the ceremony is in progress, Stella watches the marriage of her daughter to her rich suitor, observing the harmonious paradise of a wealthy happy family from which she is excluded. This, precisely, is the illusion of fantasy: that by erasing oneself (the disturbing excess) from the picture, the picture will be that of a harmonious Whole. At its most radical, this erasure takes the form of suicide—as in *Out of the Past*, where the final act asserting the hero's freedom is suicidal. Rian Johnson's science-fiction thriller *Looper* (2012) stages the same suicidal act as the resolution of a symbolic deadlock: at the climax of the film's twisted time-travel plot, the hero must kill himself in order to erase his future self, thereby cutting the closed loop of Fate and restoring harmony in the present.

The two butterflies

There is a famous ancient anecdote about Chuang-Tse, the great Daoist thinker: waking from a sleep in which he dreamt he was a butterfly, he asks himself if he is Chuang-Tse who has dreamt he was a butterfly, or if he is now a butterfly dreaming that he is Chuang-Tse. The correct reading of this story should avoid at all costs the postmodern topic of multiple realities and insist that in reality there is only Chuang-Tse who dreams he is a butterfly—nonetheless, the lesson is that in order to be Chuang-Tse in reality, Chuang-Tse has to dream he is a butterfly. Even if reality is "more real" than fantasy, it needs fantasy in order to retain its consistency: if we subtract fantasy, the fantasmatic frame, from reality, reality itself loses its consistency and disintegrates.

How is this butterfly—the butterfly that stands for my fantasmatic identity—related to the butterfly of the so-called "butterfly effect"? The latter refers to some tiny feature (object, occurrence) that tips a fragile balance and sets in motion a process that ends in catastrophe—a butterfly flaps its wings off the coast of Scotland and there is a devastating tornado on the US east coast ... On a first approach, it may appear that the two butterflies play exactly opposite roles: the first stands for the ideal image I have of myself while the second is the proverbial stain that ruins the harmony of the ideal image. But what if this contrast conceals a deeper paradoxical identity of the opposites? Let us take an exemplary case of this object-stain, the alternate reality drama *The Butterfly Effect* (Eric Bress and J. Mackye Gruber, 2004). It begins when Evan Treborn, a medical patient, breaks into a doctor's office at night, finds some old home movies and starts to watch them, while security guards try to break into the room. What follows is a series of flashbacks in which we discover that as a young child and adolescent, Evan suffered many sexual and psychological traumas—he was forced to take part in child pornography by a neighbor (the father of Kayleigh, Evan's great love, and her brother Tommy); he was nearly strangled to death by his institutionalized mentally ill father, who is then killed in front of him by guards; he accidentally murders a mother and her infant daughter while playing with dynamite with his friends; he sees his dog being burned alive by Tommy. A couple of years later Evan realizes that when he reads from his adolescent journals, he can travel back in time and is able to alter parts of his past—these time traveling episodes account for the frequent blackouts he experienced as a child. Evan's editing of his personal timeline creates alternative futures in which he finds himself, variously, a college student in a fraternity, an inmate imprisoned for murdering Tommy, and an amputee. Evan intervenes in his past in order to undo the most unpleasant events of his childhood that coincide with his mysterious blackouts, like saving Kayleigh from being molested by her father and from being tormented by her brother Tommy.

However, Evan soon realizes that even though his intentions are good, his actions have unforeseen consequences: his attempts to alter the past only end up harming those he cares about, and he comes to see that the main cause of everyone's suffering in all the different timelines is himself. So he decides to travel back one final time, to the backyard party where he first met Kayleigh as a child. This time, as they meet, he whispers into Kayleigh's ear: "I hate you and if you ever talk to me, I'll kill you and your family." She runs away crying, and later, when her parents divorce, she will choose to live with her mother, in a different neighborhood, instead of with her father. She is thus never subjected to an abusive upbringing and goes on to be successful in life, at the cost of Evan's acquaintance with her. In the very last scene of the film, set eight years later in New York, an adult Evan passes Kayleigh on the street. Though a brief look of recognition passes over Kayleigh's face, it quickly fades as she walks away without talking to Evan, confirming that she doesn't know him.

There are three alternate endings to the film, two of which are "happy" and open-ended. In the first, after passing her on the sidewalk, Evan turns and follows Kayleigh. In the second, they introduce themselves and Evan asks her out for coffee. The third ending, however, is much more radical (the rumor is that the directors preferred it from the very beginning, but the studio vetoed it for commercial reasons): after breaking into the doctor's office, Evan begins watching the films, only this time, instead of watching a home movie of a neighborhood gathering, he's watching the video of his own birth shot by his father. We see Evan's mother in the delivery room, and in a voiceover hear her telling Evan about her losing previous babies, and he being her miracle child. Aware of the catastrophes his birth will entail, the unborn Evan strangles himself in the womb with his umbilical cord; after he dies we see his mother crying in her hospital room. Since he was never born, he was never there to change the timeline in the first place; his suicide also explains why his mother had two stillborn children before him—they also killed themselves in the same way. One is tempted to call this ending the Sophocles version, after the famous line sung by the Chorus in *Oedipus* about how the best thing is not to be born at all.

There is a kind of negation of negation at work here, a reversal from the ideal fantasy image of the subject to the fantasy of the self-erasure of the subject from the ideal picture. The lesson of *The Butterfly Effect* is thus that it is not enough for the subject to search for the butterfly among the objects in reality: in this vast domain, anything can ultimately play the role of the butterfly. The subject has to realize that he is himself the butterfly he is searching for, so that the only way to prevent things from taking the wrong turn is to eliminate himself. The result is a again a pure fantasy scene: after the (imagined) suicide, I survive as a pure disembodied gaze observing the utopia of the world from which I am absent. As an external observer of a paradise barred to him, Evan assumes the same position as Stella Dallas who commits social suicide, reducing her to a pure gaze observing the happy family that emerges through her erasure from the picture. (Capra's classic *It's a Wonderful Life* seems to present the opposite case: when the hero is on the verge of suicide, his guardian angel shows him how life in his little town would have turned out in his absence—and we get a realist portrait of a vulgar, commercialized main street, etc. The irony of the film is that here the alternate reality is not a utopia, but simply the reality of life in the US.)

Herein lies the limit of abstract ethical atheism: its ultimate conse-quence is not unbridled hedonism but an ethically motivated suicide as the only way out of the burden of total responsibility. Or, in terms of time-travel narratives: the more I try to correct the past by intervening in it, the more things take a wrong turn. In Stephen Fry's alternate reality novel *Making History* (1997), for example, a scientist discovers a way to intervene minimally in the past—having been traumatized by the Nazi holocaust, he changes the chemical composure of the stream that provides water for the village in which Hitler was born, making the local women infertile at around the time when Frau Schickelgruber was pregnant with Adolf. When the scientist returns to the present, he sees that his intervention has succeeded: Hitler was not born ... However, another ambitious politician, a Prussian nobleman much more able and well versed in modern science, took over the Nazi party and, by pushing for the faster development of the atomic bomb, ensured a German victory in World War II. The desperate scientist now dedicates his life to undoing the effects of his first intervention and bringing Hitler back ...

We might mention here the often noted parallel between Dostoyevsky and Sartre. In his "Existentialism Is a Humanism," Sartre formulated the premise of his radical atheism: as free beings, we are responsible for all elements of ourselves, for our consciousness, our actions, and even the conditions under which we act (by accepting them we made them the conditions of our acts). This is why with total freedom comes total responsibility: even those who wish not to be responsible, who declare themselves not responsible for themselves or their actions, are still making a conscious choice and are thus responsible for anything that happens as a consequence of their action *or* inaction. In a similar vein, Father Zosima in Dostoyevsky's *Brothers Karamazov* claims that there is only one way to salvation: each of us must make ourselves responsible for all men's sins, i.e., we are all responsible for everyone else—but I am more responsible than all the others: "As soon as you make yourself responsible in all sincerity for everything and for everyone, you will see at once that this is really so, and that you are in fact to blame for everyone and for all things."

We can see now why Lacan's reversal of Dostoyevsky's well-known motto "If God doesn't exist, then everything is permitted" into "If God doesn't exist, then everything is prohibited" is fully justified: from a radical atheist perspective, I am responsible for everyone and everything, which means that whatever I do (or don't do) may have catastrophic consequences, so that not only is everything prohibited in full atheism, but ultimately *I myself* should be prohibited, liquidated, erased from the picture ... The extreme form of this responsibility would be the ecological one:

since humanity itself is the ultimate big fat butterfly responsible for the destruction of the environment, it should repay its debt by erasing itself from the picture altogether and committing collective suicide. Even this solution might not work, however, as humanity's collective suicide could itself trigger an unheard-of catastrophe insofar as life on earth is already adapted to human pollution, so the sudden discontinuity would disturb the established balance. What should be problematized here is the very notion of balance. According to one legend about Darwin, he lost his faith in God when on the coast of a Pacific island he witnessed hundreds of turtles dying slowly and in great pain: having turned on their backs, they were unable to reach the sea and were now condemned to wait for their death, exposed to the weather and predators. What depressed Darwin was that this terrifying scene was obviously part of the normal life span of a turtle—the turtles were already "adapted" to it, this form of death was not an accident. So when, much later, some ecologists tried to organize a group to spend days turning the turtles back on their bellies, other more radical ecologists protested, claiming that such an intervention into the natural balance would disturb the entire biosphere of the island.

This ethics of one's asymmetric responsibility towards the Other was taken a step further by Levinas, who radicalized it into a questioning of one's own right to exist: am I not, merely on account of my very existence, occupying a place potentially available to others and thus constraining their existence? Arguably, however, there is something inherently false in this link between my responsibility for/to the other and my right to exist. Although Levinas asserts its universality (*every one* of us is in the position of primordial responsibility towards all others), this asymmetry effectively ends up privileging *one* particular group which assumes the responsibility for all others, which embodies it in a privileged way or directly stands for it—in this case, of course, the Jews, so that, once again, one is ironically tempted to speak of the "Jewish man's (ethical) burden":

> The idea of a chosen people must not be taken as a sign of pride. It does not involve being aware of exceptional rights, but of exceptional duties. It is the prerogative of a moral consciousness itself. It knows itself at the centre of the world and for it the world is not homogeneous: for I am always alone in being able to answer the call, I am irreplaceable in my assumption of responsibility.[11]

---

11   Emmanuel Levinas, *Difficult Freedom*, Baltimore: Johns Hopkins University Press 1997, pp. 176–7.

In other words, do we not get here—by analogy with Marx's forms of the expression of value—a necessary passage from simple and developed form (I am responsible for you, for all of you) to the general equivalent, and then its reversal (I am the privileged site of responsibility for all of you, which is why you are all effectively responsible for me …)? And is this not the "truth" of such an ethical stance, thereby confirming the old Hegelian suspicion that every expression of self-denigration secretly asserts its contrary? Self-questioning is always by definition the obverse of self-privileging; there is always something false about a respect for others that is based on a questioning of one's own right to exist.

A Spinozan answer to Levinas would be that our existence is not at the expense of others, but forms part of the network of reality: for Spinoza there is no Hobbesian "Self," as extracted from and opposed to reality—Spinoza's ontology is one of full immanence to the world, I "am" just the network of my relations with the world, totally "externalized" in it. My *conatus*, my tendency to assert myself, is thus not an assertion at the expense of the world, but a full acceptance of being part of it, my assertion of the wider reality within which alone I can thrive. The opposition of egotism and altruism is thus overcome: I fully am not as an isolated Self, but in the thriving reality of which I am a part. When Levinas writes that "enjoyment is the singularization of an ego … it is the very work of egoism,"[12] and concludes from this that "giving has meaning only as a tearing from oneself despite oneself … Only a subject that eats can be for-the-Other,"[13] he thereby secretly imputes to Spinoza an egotistic "subjectivist" notion of (my) existence—his anti-Spinozan questioning of my right to exist is effectively an inverted arrogance: as if I am the center whose existence threatens all others.

The response should not be to assert my right to exist in harmony with and tolerance of others, but to raise an even more radical question: do I exist in the first place? Am I not, rather, a *hole in the order of being*? This brings us to the ultimate paradox on account of which Levinas' answer is not sufficient: I am a threat to the entire order of being not insofar as I positively exist as part of it, but precisely insofar as I am a hole in this order—as such, as nothing, I "am" a striving to reach out and appropriate all (only a Nothing can desire to become Everything—it was Schelling who already defined the subject as the endless striving of the Nothing to become

---

12   Emmanuel Levinas, *Otherwise than Being*, The Hague: Martinus Nijhoff 1981, p. 73.
13   Ibid., p. 74.

Everything). By contrast, a positive living being occupying a determinate space in reality, rooted in it, is by definition a moment of its circulation and reproduction.

BETWEEN THE TWO IMPOSSIBILITIES

Recall Voltaire's old quip about God: even if He didn't exist, it would be necessary to invent Him (to keep the rabble under control). Here the notion, or essence, precedes existence (a symbolic place precedes the entity that fits into it). Is the father not also such an entity? He doesn't exist (there is no father who matches up to his notion), but we have to imagine him ... The Real is the opposite: it exists even if we cannot imagine/invent it, i.e., only its being-there convinces us of its possibility—here (and only here) existence precedes essence, the fact that X is there occurs in spite of its notional impossibility. But is this all? Is the Real qua construct not also something that doesn't exist, that insists only as a point in a formal structure (like the second proposition of Freud's "A child is being beaten"). It is crucial to distinguish between the two cases, between the priority of the symbolic place over the existing bit of reality that fills it in, and the X that can only be logically inferred (or rather, that emerges through the very impossibility of symbolizing it fully). This reversal from the Real as the hard core that resists symbolization to the purely virtual Real which is only an empty point of reference is crucial if we are to avoid a naive misreading of Lacan.

The tension that characterizes the notion of the Real can also be formulated as a weird kind of *negation of negation*: the impossibility of asserting or achieving X reverts into the even more radical impossibility of asserting the opposite—in the first move, our freedom is negated; but in the second move, our direct recourse into non-freedom is also negated. At its most radical, the negation of negation should thus be conceived as a failed negation: first, a negation is enforced, but it fails, and the negation of negation draws the consequences of that failure, giving it, as it were, a positive spin. It is here that one should invoke Lacan's couple of alienation and separation, where separation is ultimately nothing but the failed alienation. If the alienation of the subject in the symbolic order were to succeed, we would be totally integrated into that order and thereby reduced to being puppets of the big Other; what gives us space to breathe is thus the very failure of our efforts—through this failure, the subject separates itself from its symbolic representations. Since the subject does not exist outside of these representations, is itself an effect of them, it can only gain a space of freedom through the failure of its representations.[14] And does not the same hold for the Freudian "return of the repressed," which can also be conceived as a kind of negation of negation? Repression is a form of psychic negation: something is pushed out of the system Cs/Pcs (Consciousness/Preconscious), and when the repressed returns (in symptoms etc.), this means that the repression failed.

Can Hegel think *this* kind of negation of negation, the negation of negation at work in Lacan's couple of alienation and separation? Or, to make the same point in a slightly different way, can the Hegelian move of the "negation of negation" account for the rise of an object which is "less than nothing"? Philosophical common sense tells us that the Hegelian triad culminates in a higher synthesis (a return to unity), while Lacanian separation is more like the emergence of an excremental excess or leftover. Furthermore, for Lacan, alienation is constitutive of the subject: there is *stricto sensu* no subject that alienates itself into its otherness, a subject is rather the result of the process of (its) alienation, emerging through the loss of its substantial content. And this is why the counter-move, dis-alienation, can and should involve not the direct reappropriation by the subject of its alienated substantial content, but rather the reflexive redoubling or reiteration of the alienation/loss constitutive of the subject itself—the subject's alienation from the other gets redoubled by the alienation of the Other from itself, by the subtraction of the small a from the big A, or, to quote Hegel, by the subject's realization that the secrets of the Egyptians were secrets also for the Egyptians themselves. The *objet a*, Lacan's name for "less than nothing," is the inscription of this redoubling of the lack, not simply the lacking object—a nothing where there should have been something—but the object that redoubles the lack and is thus a paradoxical something subtracted from nothing.

We can now formulate the link between the "negation of negation" and the enigmatic element that is "less than nothing": while the negation of Something gives Nothing, the negated Nothing does not bring us back to Something but rather engenders a "less than nothing." While negated life is death, negated death is not life but "undeadness," the life of the living dead who are "less than nothing," i.e., not even dead. In her outstanding *Hegel and Shakespeare on Moral Imagination*, Jennifer Bates distinguishes "upward-*Aufhebung*" from its uncanny double, "downward-*Aufhebung*."[15]

---

14 I owe this idea to a conversation with Aaron Schuster.
15 See Jennifer Ann Bates, *Hegel and Shakespeare on Moral Imagination*,

This distinction can be explained by way of drawing attention to the basic ambiguity in the term "spirit" (*Geist*), referring either to pure thought (spirituality as opposed to material and sensual inertia) or to ghosts (obscene undead apparitions possessing a spectral materiality). Spirituality is self-present in the mode of conceptual clarity, while spirits haunt us. The standard Hegelian "upward-*Aufhebung*" spiritualizes the immediacy of reality, reconciling its struggles and/or contradictions in an ideal/notional form, while in the case of the "downward-*Aufhebung*," the contradiction remains unresolved and is merely patched up in an obscene spectral appearance. In the case of life and death, for example, the "normal" *Aufhebung* that follows the death of a person is its idealization in the notion that will remain of him in the collective memory (i.e., the "negation of the negation" of his life is his posthumous life preserved in the collective memory, in which, stripped of its accidental properties, his life is reduced to its notional essence). When this symbolic reconciliation fails, however, the life of the deceased is not properly *aufgehoben* (sublated) but returns in the guise of the obscene pseudo-materiality of a ghost who haunts the living. The "downward-*Aufhebung*" thus involves a different negation of the negation (alive-dead-undead) whose outcome is a spectral apparition that haunts the living as something that resists sublation in its inertia, something that, precisely insofar as it is nothing in itself, having no substance, cannot be negated and/or sublated. To quote Shakespeare's *Troilus and Cressida*, insofar as there is an obvious element of madness involved in seeing ghosts, can the absolute spirit, while engaged in the work of the negative (and this work *is* the absolute spirit), ever truly say "my negation has no taste of madness"?

It would be (all too) easy to read this distinction in the standard deconstructionist way—seeing the ghost as the spectral remainder of the rational dialectical progress of gradual spiritualization/idealization, as something that resists this progress, continuing to haunt it. This, however, is not the end-point, the final deadlock, of the Hegelian *Aufhebung*: as Bates herself perspicuously indicates, Hegel does offer a way to de-ghostify a situation in which we are haunted by ghosts, to exorcize the ghosts, as it were, not by somehow finally succeeding in sublating their inertia but, paradoxically, by bringing inertia to an extreme in the infinite judgment of identifying spirit with the most non-spectral, inert, and vulgar materiality of a bone—the

---

Albany: State University of New York Press 2010, esp. Chapter 3, "Aufhebung and Anti-Aufhebung: Geist and Ghosts in Hamlet."

reference is to the famous infinite judgment that summarizes the subchapter on phrenology in Hegel's *Phenomenology of Spirit*: "*der Geist ist ein Knochen*" ("Spirit is a bone"). In *Hamlet*, a play in which the hero is haunted by the ghost of his dead father, Hamlet rids himself of the ghost towards the end of the play when, over a fresh grave, he contemplates the skull (i.e., dead bone) of his beloved clown Yorick—only such a confrontation with materiality at its most inert can purify it of the obscene spirituality of the ghost and thereby set free the space of pure spirituality.

So what if one could construct an Hegelian theory of ghosts, comparable to Hegel's theory of historical repetition? While repetition may also appear as *something* that, in its blind persistence, resists dialectical *Aufhebung*, Hegel triumphantly finds a way to include it in his account of historical movement: a historical event is, in its first appearance, a contingent occurrence; only in its repetition is its inner notional necessity asserted, as Hegel illustrates with reference to the fate of Julius Caesar:

> we see the noblest men of Rome supposing Caesar's rule to be a merely adventitious thing, and the entire position of affairs to be dependent on his individuality. So thought Cicero, so Brutus and Cassius. They believed that if this one individual were out of the way, the Republic would be *ipso facto* restored. Possessed by this remarkable hallucination, Brutus, a man of highly noble character, and Cassius, endowed with greater practical energy than Cicero, assassinated the man whose virtues they appreciated. But it became immediately manifest that only a *single* will could guide the Roman State, and now the Romans were compelled to adopt that opinion; since in all periods of the world a political revolution is sanctioned in men's opinions, when it repeats itself. Thus Napoleon was twice defeated, and the Bourbons twice expelled. By repetition that which at first appeared merely a matter of chance and contingency becomes a real and ratified existence.[16]

The example of Caesar is especially pertinent because it concerns the fate of a name: what in its first occurrence was the contingent name of a *particular individual* becomes through its repetition a *universal title* (Augustus as the first Caesar). What if we proceed in the same way with ghosts? In this case, the failed sublation of the dead (after which they continue to haunt us as ghosts) is not simply a non-dialectical complication that perturbs the "normal" dialectical progress, but a *necessary* complication that creates the

---

16   G. W. F. Hegel, *Philosophy of History*, Part III: The Roman World, available at marxists.org.

conditions for the second step, the successful sublation. Recall that, according to legend, Caesar appeared to Brutus as a ghost in the night before the battle which the conspirators lost—if we read Caesar's story through *Hamlet*, it is only after Caesar is reduced to his skull, when he no longer haunts the living as a ghost, that he can transform himself into a universal title "Caesar."

Is Hegel then unable to do the downward-*Aufhebung*? Or does his notion of comedy as the reconciliation of tragic conflict not point precisely in the direction of a downward-*Aufhebung* in which the tragic failure itself fails? The field of comedy is defined by two strangely opposed features: on the one hand, comedy is seen as the intrusion of the vulgar materiality of ordinary life into a pretentious world of high seriousness—as when the Leader, entering a majestic hall to preside at a formal meeting, slips on the proverbial banana peel. On the other hand, there is a strange immortality that pertains to comic figures, homologous to the ability of de Sade's victims to survive all their misfortunes—for example, when the Leader slips on the banana peel, the truly comic thing is that he pretends to retain his dignity and carries on as if nothing has happened ... (where this is not the case, we have the sad, if not outright tragic, spectacle of a Leader deprived of his dignity). How are we to think these two features together? Alenka Zupančič provides a properly Hegelian answer:[17] it is true that the space of the comic is the space between the dignified symbolic mask and the ridiculous vulgarity of common life with its petty passions and weaknesses, but the properly comic procedure is not simply that of undermining the mask (the serious task or sublime passion) with an injection of everyday reality, but that of effecting a kind of structural short-circuit or, rather, an exchange of places between the two in which the very mask (or task or passion) itself appears as a pathetic idiosyncrasy, as a properly human weakness. Recall the standard generic comic characters (the Miser, the Drunkard, the Seducer): it is their very attachment to some excessive task or passion that *makes them human*. This is why Chaplin was right in his *Great Dictator*: Hitler's *hubris* was not "inhuman," beyond the range of sympathy for common human pleasures and weaknesses—Hitler was rather "human, all too human," his political *hubris* was an "all too human" idiosyncrasy which made him ridiculous. In short, Hitler was a burlesque figure of the Evil Dictator who belongs in the same series as the Seducer, the Miser, and the Deceiving Servant.

---

17   See Alenka Zupančič, *The Shortest Shadow*, Cambridge, MA: MIT Press 2004.

How, then, does utter tragedy turn into comedy? Hegel noticed something weird happening to Antigone after she pathetically assumes her fate—to put it bluntly, she starts to *act*; her statements begin to display a level of self-awareness about her "role" which undermines her immediate ethical spontaneity from within:

> I've heard about a guest of ours,
> daughter of Tantalus, from Phrygia—
> she went to an excruciating death
> in Sipylus, right on the mountain peak.
> The stone there, just like clinging ivy,
> wore her down, and now, so people say,
> the snow and rain never leave her there,
> as she laments. Below her weeping eyes
> her neck is wet with tears. God brings me
> to a final rest which most resembles hers.

Antigone is acting here, modeling her predicament on mythical examples—in short, she is aware of the immanent theatricality of her tragic predicament, a theatricality which by definition confers on it a minimal touch of comedy—one can (and should) imagine her interrupting her pathetic complaint, worrying briefly whether her outburst of spontaneous passion is being acted well enough.

The passage from tragedy to comedy thus concerns overcoming the limits of representation: while in a tragedy the individual actor represents the universal character he plays, in a comedy he immediately *is* this character. The gap of representation is thus closed, which, however, does not mean that the comic actor coincides with the person he plays in the way that he plays himself on the stage, that there he just "is what he really is." It is rather that, in a properly Hegelian way, the gap that separates the actor from his stage persona in a tragedy is transposed into the stage persona itself: a comic character is never fully identified with his role, he always retains the ability to observe himself from outside, making fun of himself.[18]

What kind of immortality does comedy then give birth to? As we have just seen, comedy is not about de-sublimation, the reduction of our dignity and high aspirations to the vulgar finitude of our earthly existence—the

---

18   For a more detailed analysis of the comical turn in Antigone, see Chapter 5 of Slavoj Žižek, *Less Than Nothing*, London: Verso Books 2013.

comic effect occurs when spirituality survives and persists through its failure. However, the immortality in a comedy is not the noble immortality of a spirit triumphing over biological death, but the weird immortality of, for example, those who survive a suicide attempt, who bungle even their effort to die, or, in a more uncanny mode, the obscene immortality of the undead in gothic and horror fiction. The fact that films featuring the undead are always on the verge of turning into comedy is a clear sign of how undeadness oscillates between comedy and horror, between laughter and nightmare.

Comedy as reconciliation, as the overcoming of tragic conflict, is usually seen as expressing a wise insight into how "tragedy is an illusion", how all our conflicts are mere shadow games, it is all a play, etc.—that is, it adopts a position of universality elevated above tragic conflicts. The approach outlined above opens up a totally different perspective: comedy at its most radical points towards a dimension beyond tragedy, a dimension too terrifying to appear as tragic—a strange negation of the tragic negation itself, the failure of its failure.

THE "DOWNWARD-SYNTHESIS"

So, again, can this Hegelian mechanism account for the weird negation of negation with no positive synthetic result? There is a specific version of the Hegelian triad which finishes with what one can only call a "downward-synthesis"—a move similar to what Bates calls "downward-*Aufhebung*," although the concluding moment here is not a ghost but rather a bone or some other form of immediacy. Exemplary here is the case of Christianity. Although Christianity remains within the confines of the sublime, it brings about the sublime effect in a way exactly opposite to Kant: not through the extreme exertions of our capacity to represent (which nonetheless fails to render the suprasensible Idea and thus paradoxically succeeds in delineating its space), but as it were *a contrario*, through the reduction of the representative content to the lowest imaginable level. At the level of representation, Christ was the "son of a man," a ragged, miserable creature crucified between two common brigands; and it is against the background of this wretched character of his earthly appearance that his divine essence shines through all the more powerfully. In the late Victorian age, the same mechanism was responsible for the ideological impact of the tragic figure of the "elephant-man," as the subtitle of one of the books about him suggests (*A Study in Human Dignity*): it was the monstrous and nauseating distortion of his body which itself made visible the simple dignity of his inner spiritual life. And was not the same logic an essential ingredient in the tremendous success of Stephen Hawking's *A Brief History of Time*? Would his ruminations on the fate of the universe have been so attractive to the public were it not for the fact that they belonged to a crippled, paralyzed body communicating only through the feeble movement of one finger and speaking with an impersonal machine-generated voice? Therein consists the "Christian Sublime": in this wretched "little piece of the real" lies the necessary counterpart (the form of appearance) of pure spirituality.

Here we must be very careful not to miss the Hegelian point: what Hegel aims at is not the simple fact that, since the suprasensible is indifferent to the domain of sensible representations, it can appear even in the guise of the lowest representation. Hegel insists again and again that there is no special "suprasensible realm" beyond or apart from our universe of sensible experience; the reduction to the nauseating "little piece of the real" is thus *stricto sensu* performative, productive of the spiritual dimension: the spiritual "depth" is *generated* by the monstrous distortion of the surface. In other words, the point is not only that God's embodiment in a wretched creature renders visible His true nature by way of the contrast—the ridiculous, extreme discord—between Him and the lowest form of human existence; the point is rather that this extreme discord, this absolute gap, is the divine power of "absolute negativity." Both Judaism and Christianity insist on the absolute discord between God (Spirit) and the domain of (sensible) representations; their difference is of a purely formal nature: in the Jewish religion God dwells in an unrepresentable Beyond, separated from us by an unbridgeable gap, whereas the Christian God *is this gap itself*. It is this shift that causes the change in the logic of the Sublime: from a prohibition on representation to an acceptance of the most null representation.

This "Christian Sublime" involves that specific mode of dialectical movement which we are here calling the "downward-synthesis": the concluding moment is not a triumphant "synthesis," but the lowest point at which the common ground of position and negation is worn away. What we are then stuck with is a remainder that falls out from the symbolic order: the order of universal symbolic mediation as it were collapses into an inert left-over. Apart from the Christian Sublime, other examples of this movement are the triad of positive-negative-infinite judgment, the dialectic of phrenology ("Spirit is a bone"), and, of course, the triad of Law that concludes the chapter on Reason and sets up the passage into Spirit, into History, in the *Phenomenology of Spirit*: reason as lawgiver; reason as testing laws; the acceptance of law simply because it is the law. Reason first directly *posits* laws qua universal ethical precepts ("Everyone ought to speak the truth," etc.); once it gains an insight into the contingent content and possible conflictual nature of these laws (different ethical norms may impose on us mutually exclusive forms of behavior), it assumes a kind of *reflective* distance and limits itself to testing laws, assessing how far they meet formal standards of universality and consistency; finally, Reason becomes aware of the empty, purely formal character of this procedure, of its incapacity to procure actual spiritual substance filled out with concrete, positive content. Reason is thus compelled to reconcile itself to the fact that it can neither posit nor reflect upon laws without presupposing our inveterate involvement in some concrete, *determinate* ethical substance, in a law which is in force simply *because it is law*, i.e., because it is accepted as a constitutive part of our community's historical tradition. We pass to History *stricto sensu*, to the succession of actual historical figures of Spirit, only on the basis of having accepted that we are embedded in some historically specified "spiritual substance." The logic of these three stages follows the triad of 1) positing, 2) external and determinate reflection, and 3) the concluding moment consisting in an immediate acceptance of the given ethical substance—which someone not well versed in Hegel might rather expect to constitute the "lowest" moment, the immediate starting point from which we then "progress" by way of reflective mediation. The triad of Law in its entirety thus exemplifies the breakdown of reflection: it ends with the reflecting subject getting accustomed to the ethical substance qua universal, presupposed medium that mediates his very attempt at reflective mediation. This resigned acceptance of the immediate character of the totality-of-mediation itself is what Hegel has in mind with "determinate reflection": the reflective totality is "held together" by a contingent, non-reflected remainder which is "simply there."[19]

Another exemplary case of "downward-synthesis" is provided by the existential position of self-negated pessimism: by the breakdown of the principled form of pessimism when, in a weird *eppur si muove*, life goes on, too weak even to follow its self-renunciation. So it is not the usual "Hegelian" negation of negation that would bring us to optimism (even if

---

19   I first elaborated this notion of "downward-synthesis" in Chapter 2 of Slavoj Žižek, *Tarrying With the Negative*, Durham, NC: Duke University Press 1993.

a deeper non-naive one), but a step even lower: first, optimism is negated, the subject assumes the insight that life is shit, etc., but then the very *form* of the principled pessimist position is negated, so that the subject remains stuck in what is "in pessimism more than pessimism":

> Optimism is not the opposite of pessimism, it has no positive substance or consistency, no resilient spirit that could stand on its own, but is a further elaboration of pessimism's relentless negativity: it is what is subtracted from the nothingness of pessimism, the thorn that doesn't allow pessimism to comfortably settle into itself, to vanish into its own nihilism, yet without converting it into its opposite … Against this common sense, one should rather defend the mad "idealist" claim that the concept is correct and life itself is wrong: if there were any ontological justice, the human species would disappear in a puff of logical smoke, like the computer in *Star Trek* that explodes when ordered to solve a logical paradox. The fact that life doesn't do so does not refute pessimism but requires us to admit a certain ironic twist: rather than the proof of an indomitable vitality and richness this clinging to life is the supreme ontological injustice, a violent perturbation of the self-canceling nothing.[20]

This passage clearly alludes to Hegel's (in)famous claim that, if the concept does not fit reality, so much the worse for reality. Perhaps melancholy is a desperate attempt to live the truth of the concept existentially. But is this really beyond Hegel? Is this not, on the contrary, an exemplary case of self-relating negation of negation relying on the gap between form and content: first, the optimist content is negated, but the "optimist" universal-principled form remains; then this form itself disintegrates. Principled pessimism is inconsistent, since the principled approach as such implies a minimum of formal optimism. And, again, should we not read this move as an example of the "downward-synthesis" in which the dialectical movement culminates in the most miserable moment, like phrenology?

And exactly the same goes for the tension between immortality and mortality.[21] Mortality is the first negation of immortality: we have to accept our finitude, we will return to dust, ultimately nothing will remain of us. However, the "negation of negation" that follows is not some kind of magical or symbolic return of immortality, or some kind of "synthesis" of

---

20 Aaron Schuster, *The Third Kind of Complaint* (unpublished manuscript).

21 I rely here on Alenka Zupančič, "Die Sexualität innerhalb der Grenzen der bloßen Vernunft" (manuscript).

mortality and immortality (say, in the standard humanist sense of "even if we die, we live on in our works and the memories of those who loved us"). The immortality that remains after we assume our mortality is a "low" immortality, "lower" than mortality, no longer the sublime immortality of a spiritual eternity. In popular culture, as noted above, we get a glimpse of this low immortality in the obscene figure of the "undead," those who cannot even die properly but continue to haunt the living. In psychoanalytic theory, the name for this immortality is the "death drive," the obscene persistence of life just going on, not even ready to follow its natural path and dissolve itself in death. The undead are in a way less than dead.

And is not comedy the supreme case of such a downward negation of negation?[22] As we have seen, it is wrong to locate the properly comical effect simply in the unexpected reduction of the sublime to the ridiculous, the infinite to the finite, the spiritual to the vulgar material (the Leader slips on the banana peel). Something more has to happen: the sublime dimension has to persist against all the odds (the Leader gets up and carries on in the same pompous way as before, pretending not to notice the massive tear in his trousers exposing his multicolored polka-dot shorts). The properly comical effect resides in this ridiculous sublime surviving its own demise. And since the ultimate mark of our finitude is death, the most extreme comical moment is that of a subject's failed attempt(s) to kill himself, as if the subject is too weak even to fully assume his finitude—the effect is then one of an obscene immortality lower even than mortality, a life that persists only insofar as it is too bungled even to finish itself off. At the end of Milan Kundera's first novel *The Joke* (much superior to his later bestsellers), the hero's abandoned mistress tries to kill herself with an overdose, but mistakes laxatives for sleeping pills and ends up shitting on the toilet for hours—obscene immortality at its purest. Again, is there a place for this weird kind of immortality in Hegel?

Here is another example of such a failed negation: in what is arguably her single greatest achievement, *Those Who Walk Away*, Patricia Highsmith took crime fiction, the most "narrative" genre of them all, and imbued it with the inertia of the Real, the lack of resolution, the dragging-on of "empty time," which characterize the stupid factuality of life. In Rome, Ed Coleman tries to murder his son-in-law, Ray Garrett, a failed painter

---

22   I rely here extensively on Alenka Zupančič, *The Odd Man In*, Cambridge, MA: MIT Press 2008.

and gallery-owner in his late twenties. Ed blames for Ray for the recent suicide of his only child, Peggy, Ray's wife. Rather than flee, Ray follows Ed to Venice, where Ed is wintering with Inez, his girlfriend. What follows is Highsmith's paradigmatic portrayal of the agonizing symbiotic relationship of two men inextricably linked to each other in their very hatred. Ray himself is haunted by a sense of guilt for his wife's death, so he exposes himself to Ed's violent intentions. Driven by his death wish, he accepts a lift from Ed in a motor-boat, and in the middle of the lagoon Ed pushes Ray overboard. Ray escapes by pretending to be dead, and goes on to assume a false name and a different identity, experiencing both exhilarating freedom and overwhelming emptiness. He roams like one of the living dead through the cold streets of wintry Venice. We have here a crime novel with no actual murder, only failed attempts; and there is no clear resolution at the novel's end—except, perhaps, the resigned acceptance on the part of both Ray and Ed that they are condemned to haunt each other to the end, in a case of what we might call an endlessly suspended murder.

In the ethical domain proper, utter self-humiliation can generate a similar paradox. In this regard, Laurent de Sutter has offered a perspicuous reading of Jean Eustache's *Une sale histoire* (*A Dirty Story*, 1977), a fifty-minute film in two parts—each part tells the same story, first as fiction (with Michael Londsale as narrator), then as a (pseudo)documentary. A group of friends listen as one man relates a story about a time when, years ago, while regularly visiting a small café, he noticed a group of men at the bar who from time to time would disappear into the basement. When he had to make a phone call—the phone was also in the basement—he saw one of them crouched in a strange position outside the ladies' toilet and discovered what the weird ritual was all about. There was a peephole into the toilet, but at floor level, so that the voyeur had to lean down and put his head on the floor, "as in the Muslim prayer," to get a full and unobstructed view. The position was extremely humiliating, but the narrator himself nonetheless became addicted to the ritual, the maxim of which was "No pleasure without pain." However, as de Sutter notes, "because this maxim is ironic, its meaning takes the form of an inversion: 'No pleasure without pain' means 'No pain without pleasure.'"[23] "No pleasure without pain" thus means: "the default of pleasure is the pleasure of default."[24] What is interesting here is that, in a properly perverse way, the ritual was experienced as

23   Laurent de Sutter, *Théorie du trou*, Paris: Leo Scheer 2012, p. 21.
24   Ibid., p. 23.

being profoundly ethical, or, as the narrator himself puts it: "In doing all this, I have my dignity." A dignity in the extreme self-humiliation which reaches beyond ascesis:

> From the moment every ascesis has to be considered worthless [null and void, *nulle*], and the moment pleasure has to be conceived as at fault [*en défaut*] with regard to ascesis, one has to conclude that the pleasure is not null and void. But this non-nullity is a negative one; pleasure is *less than null*—it displays itself in zones which are inferior to nothing. To the terminal "I want to be nothing" of the client of Bernard-Marie Koltes, Eustache's narrator opposes an infinite "I want to be less than zero."[25]

The obvious reproach would be that here we are dealing with an extreme existential position which is more the fantasized option of a real-impossible than a real possibility. However, it is here that we should return to the basic ambiguity of the Real—as impossible and unavoidable. Yes, the position of "less than zero" may be an impossible extreme, but is it not simultaneously always already there? Are we not, insofar as we are simply alive, always already in this zone of less than nothing, of a remainder that survives its own radical self-annihilation? In other words, the movement of double negation whose outcome is the existential position of "less than nothing" amounts to a kind of transcendental pre-history of subjectivity—something which never "really happened" in empirical time but has to be presupposed as a timeless, always already past process (*zeitlos vergangenes*, as Hegel would have put it).

It is difficult to overlook the Christian overtone of such excremental identification. In his reading of Christianity, Hegel emphasizes the inconsistency of the Evil position: the Devil is presented as courageous, following a principle, etc., which undermines his Evil—following Milton, one can say that Evil is his Good. So we can imagine here the same "downward-synthesis": Good negated by (principled) Evil is in its turn negated—but not in some kind of "synthesis" in which Evil is sublated as a subordinate moment of the self-deployment of the Good. Rather, what we get is a kind of "stupid" goodness, the purely opportunistic inertia of not doing anything radically evil out of a lack of a sense of purpose, out of a lack of principle, which is required if one is to be truly evil. In short, the end result is that Evil is deprived of its principled form. (But how does this relate to the

---

25   Ibid., pp. 25–6.

fact that the Good *is* self-negated Evil, i.e., Evil elevated into a universal principle?)

At the ontological level, we can discern the same logic: first, something is negated, we get nothing; then, in a second negation, we get less than nothing, not even nothing—not a Something mediated by nothing, but a kind of pre-ontological inconsistency which lacks the principled purity of the Void. (It is out of this pre-ontological inconsistency that, in the Kabbala, God first has to create nothingness.) Here, one should move beyond the "Oriental" approach (taken over by quantum physics) for which everything emerges out of the primordial Void (and returns into it): it is not only that no One can be fully One, that every One is always thwarted by an immanent impossibility; *even the Nothing cannot be fully Nothing.* The point is not only that the Void is always already disturbed, but that the Void is secondary, a retroactive effect of its own disturbance.[26]

Again, there is a similar logic at work in the ethical triad of utilitarianism, Kantian ethics, and their "synthesis." For a utilitarian, ethical rules are justified by their efficacy; for a Kantian, duty should be done for its own sake, not because of its consequences. But, paradoxically, one can also justify Kantianism on pragmatic-utilitarian grounds: if people believe they have to act ethically for the sake of duty, irrespective of consequences, such an attitude will in the long term have the best pragmatic consequences. Is this not again a case of "downward-synthesis," i.e., the assertion of a necessary or benevolent lie?

But is there not also a further type of downward-synthesis, one that we have already encountered: that of the redoubled impossibility which defines the status of the Lacanian Real? *Jouissance* is simultaneously both inaccessible and something we can never get rid of (everything we do is stained by it); likewise, while we are never fully free, we cannot ever escape being free. There is again a structure of negation of negation here: 1) the first negation posits the impossibility of the asserted element (*jouissance*, freedom); 2)

---

26   It is here that Peter Osborne, in his critical review of my *Less Than Nothing*, totally misses the point when he claims that in my "materialism, as the affirmation of an irreducible multiplicity, in opposition to the idealistic 'One'," this multiplicity is derived "not from nothing (Deleuze's alleged error) but from the void, which is 'less than nothing'. Reality, in its irreducible multiplicity comes from, or fundamentally is, the void" (Peter Osborne, "More Than Everything," *Radical Philosophy* 177 [January/February 2013], p. 23). What I refer to as "less than nothing" is precisely not the void but the minimum of content that functions as the "bone in the throat" destabilizing the void.

the second negation negates this negation itself, i.e., posits the inevitability of what the first negation posited as impossible: freedom is impossible, but it is also impossible to escape it and put all the blame on Fate. What we encounter here is a not-not which does not bring us back to positivity—precisely the paradox that defines the non-All of Lacan: a no-man is a woman, but a no-woman is not a man. Or: there are the living and there are the dead, but there are also the undead—the dead are not-living, but the undead are not-not-living. *Jouissance* does not not exist—which does not mean that it simply exists—it merely insists in a pre-ontological state. The *objet a* is not not-something—which does not mean that it is something; it is, rather, less than nothing, it negates not nothing but the entire field of nothing-and-something—nothing is less-than-nothing viewed from the formal field of something. Is not the Real of the redoubled impossibility thus a case of downward-synthesis, of the negation of content-form?

Against the "Hölderlin-paradigm"

These persisting deadlocks and oscillations bear witness to the fact that Hegel does not fit the key metaphysical narrative shared by thinkers as different as Nietzsche, Heidegger, and Derrida, who all conceive their own age as that of the critical turning point of metaphysics: in their (our) time, metaphysics has exhausted its potential, and the thinker's duty is to prepare the ground for a new, post-metaphysical thinking. More generally, the entire Judeo-Christian history, up to postmodernity, is determined by what one is tempted to call the "Hölderlin paradigm": "Where the danger is, grows also what can save us" ("*Wo aber Gefahr ist weachst das Rettende auch*"). The present moment appears as the lowest point in a long process of historical decadence (the flight of Gods, alienation …), but the danger of the catastrophic loss of the essential dimension of being-human also opens up the possibility of a reversal (*Kehre*)—proletarian revolution, the arrival of new gods (which, according to the late Heidegger, alone can save us), etc. Are we able to imagine a "pagan" *non-historical* universe, a universe thoroughly outside this paradigm, a universe in which (historical) time just flows, with no teleological curvature, in which the idea of a dangerous moment of decision (Benjamin's *Jetzt-Zeit*) out of which a "bright future" will emerge, a future that will redeem the past itself, is simply meaningless?

Although this paradigm is usually identified with Christianity, the latter, at its most radical, nonetheless seems to give it a unique twist: everything that has to happen has *already happened*, there is nothing to wait for, we do not have to wait for the Event, the arrival of Messiah, the Messiah has already arrived, the Event has already taken place, and we live in its aftermath. And Hegel? This basic attitude of historical *closure* is also the message of Hegel, of his dictum that the owl of Minerva takes off in the twilight—but the crucial point, however difficult to grasp, is that this stance, far from condemning us to passive reflection, opens up the space for active intervention.

What this means is that Hegel is *not* part of the "Hölderlin-paradigm," even if he is usually considered its main representative. A certain historical teleology is wrongly associated with Hegel: there is a naive beginning, an immediacy that lacks inner wealth and articulation; development then means dispersion, a fall, right up to the total alienation that opens up the possibility of reversal. Marx deployed this type of teleological scheme of history in his famous manuscript on "Pre-capitalist modes of economic production" according to which the uniqueness of the capitalist mode of production lies in the fact that, in it, "labor is torn out from its primordial immersion in its objective conditions, and, because of this, it appears on the one side itself as labor, and, on the other side, as the labor's own product, as objectified labor, obtains against labor a completely autonomous existence as value."[27] The worker thus appears as the "objectless, purely subjective capacity of labor, confronted with the objective conditions of production as its non-property, as a foreign property, as value which exists for itself, as capital." However, this

> extreme form of alienation, in which, in the guise of the relationship of the capital towards wage labor, labor, productive activity, appears as opposed to its own conditions and to its own product, is a necessary point of transition—and, for that reason, in itself, in an inverted form, posited on its head, it already contains the disintegration of all limited presuppositions of production, and even creates and produces the unconditional presuppositions of production, and thereby all material conditions for the total, universal development of the productive forces of the individuals.[28]

---

27   Karl Marx and Friedrich Engels, *Gesamtausgabe*, Abteilung II, Band 1, Berlin: Dietz Verlag 1976, p. 431.

28   Ibid., p. 432.

History is thus the gradual process of the separation of subjective activity from its objective conditions, that is, from its immersion in the substantial totality. This process reaches its culmination in modern capitalism with the emergence of the proletariat, the substance-less subjectivity of workers totally separated from their objective conditions. This separation, however, is in itself already their liberation, since it creates pure subjectivity, exempted from all substantial ties, which has only to appropriate its objective conditions. In this sense, Marx remains within the "Hölderlin-paradigm": where there is danger (utter alienation), the redemptive force also grows. Marx's notion of historical process therefore remains fundamentally a teleological one: all history hitherto points towards the present moment, we live in *kairos*, the time of shift, and are able to discern in the miserable present the possibility of an act to come.

But, again, is this process (that unfolds from substantial unity through subjective alienation to the reunification of subject with substance, in which substance is thoroughly subjectivized, reappropriated by the subject) really a Hegelian one? The first thing to note is that the *kairos* position of finding oneself on the brink of the reversal of Danger into Redemption, of attending (or acting as an agent of) the *telos* of history, is not a position ever adopted by Hegel. The conclusive moment of the dialectical process is not a synthetic unity, a dis-alienation conceived as a return to the (subjective or substantial) One. For Hegel, alienation is constitutive of the subject, in the radical sense that the subject does not pre-exist its alienation, but emerges through it: the subject emerges through its own loss. Consequently, the Hegelian "reconciliation" is not an overcoming of alienation, but a reconciliation with alienation itself. So when Hegel says that, in dis-alienation, the subject "recognizes itself in its Other," the radical ambiguity of this statement should be kept in mind: it is not only that the subject recognizes in its Other the alienated result of its own activity, it is also (and primarily) that the subject recognizes the decentered Other as its own site, i.e., that it recognizes its own decentered character.

More precisely, alienation can be "overcome"—if, by alienation, we mean the subject's self-experience as a subordinated moment of some substantial big Other that runs the show (History, Destiny, God, Nature …). Alienation is "overcome" when the subject experiences that "there is no big Other" (Lacan), that its status is that of a semblance, its character inconsistent and antagonistic. This, however, does not mean that the subject reappropriates the big Other: rather, the subject's lack with regard to the Other is transposed into the big Other itself. Such a redoubling of the lack, this overlapping of my lack with the lack in the Other itself, does not cancel the lack—on the contrary, what the subject experiences is that the lack/gap in the (substantial) Other is the condition of possibility, the site, of the subject itself.

What this implies is that there is a gap prior to alienation: alienation does not introduce a gap or loss into a pre-existing organic unity, on the contrary, *it covers up the gap in the Other*. In alienation, the subject experiences the Other as the full agent running the show, as the one who "has it" (what the subject is lacking), i.e., the illusion of alienation is the same as the illusion of transference—that the Other knows. (Dis-alienation is thus basically the same move as the fall of the subject-supposed-to-know at the end of the analytic process.) What we then have is a dialectical process with a structure wholly different from the triad of substantial immediacy/alienation/reconciliation in a new higher unity: there is no original unity preceding loss, what is lost is retroactively constituted through its loss, and the properly dialectical reconciliation resides in fully assuming the consequences of this retroactivity. Let us go back to the previously cited example of India, and the complaint of the cultural theorists that being compelled to use the English language is a form of cultural colonialism, censoring their true identity. In this case, "reconciliation" means a reconciliation with the English language, which is to be accepted not as an obstacle to a new India which should be discarded in favor of some local language, but as an enabling medium, indeed, as a positive condition of liberation. The true victory over colonization lies not in the return to some authentic pre-colonial substance, even less in a "synthesis" of modern civilization and pre-modern origins, but, paradoxically, in the *fully accomplished loss of these pre-modern origins*. In other words, colonialism is not overcome when the intrusion of English as a medium is abolished, but when the colonizers are as it were beaten at their own game—when the new Indian identity is effortlessly formulated in English, when the English language is "denaturalized," losing its privileged link to its "native" Anglo-Saxon speakers.

If we discard the obscene notion that it is better to be "authentically" tortured by one's "own" language than by an imposed foreign one, then we should first emphasize the liberating aspect of being compelled to use a foreign "universal" language. There was a certain historical wisdom contained in the fact that, from medieval times until fairly recently, the *lingua franca* of the West was Latin, a "secondary" inauthentic language, a "fall" from Greek with all its authentic burden. It was this very emptiness and "inauthenticity" of Latin that allowed Europeans to fill it in with their own particular contents, in contrast to the stuffy overbearing nature of Greek. Beckett learned this same lesson when he started to write in French, a foreign language, leaving behind the "authenticity" of his roots. In short, the function of treating a foreign language as an oppressive imposition is to obfuscate the oppressive dimensions of our own language, to retroactively elevate our own maternal tongue into a lost paradise of full authentic expression. The move to be accomplished when we experience an imposed foreign language as oppressive, as out of sync with our innermost life, is thus to transpose this discord into our own maternal tongue.[29]

Exactly the same holds for the Fall in Christianity: the way out of the Fall into sin lies not in a return to God, but in the *full consummation of the Fall*, the death of God. This is how we should read Christ's last words: "It is accomplished"—with the death of God (of Beyond), the reconciliation is accomplished ... This is why Lacan rejects the standard Christian idea that Jesus saved us by taking our sins upon himself and paying the price for them with his sacrifice: "It is true that the historical tale of Christ does not present itself as the project to save mankind, but to save God. One has to acknowledge that he who took on this project, Christ, that he has paid the price for it, that is the least one can say."[30] To save God in what sense? By way of assuming guilt for the Fall, the lack in the Other is obfuscated: God is pure; had we not Fallen, we would be able to dwell in the Paradise of full, non-castrated *jouissance*.[31] This, however, is precisely *not* what happens in Christ's death: his sacrifice does not obfuscate the Other's (God-the-Father's) lack—on the contrary, *it displays this lack*, the inexistence of the big Other. It was already Hegel who noted that what dies on the cross is the God of Beyond himself: instead of us sacrificing ourselves to (or for) Him,

---

29   But there is also the opposite experience of our own language as provincial, primitive, marked by private passions and obscenities which only obscure clear reasoning and expression, an experience which pushes us towards using a universal second language in order to think clearly and freely. Is this not how a national language emerges and comes to replace the multiplicity of dialects?

30   Jacques Lacan, *Le séminaire, livre XX*: Encore, Paris: Seuil 1975, p. 98.

31   This same logic was at work in Stalinist show trials: by confessing their guilt, by assuming responsibility for the problems and failures of the Soviet system, the accused did a great service to the Party, maintaining its purity—the troubles of daily life were not the Party's responsibility ... Likewise, the same effort to rescue the Other sustains the neurotic's feelings of guilt: the neurotic blames himself, he takes the failure upon himself in order to maintain the fantasy of an ideal father.

God sacrifices Himself and dies—the message of this paradox can only be that *there is no one to sacrifice to (or for)*. In other words, as René Girard once said, the sacrifice of Christ is the act destined to end the very logic of sacrifice. Christ takes the sins of the world upon himself—literally: they are not ours, the lack is in God Himself.

CHAPTER 8

"There Is a Non-Relationship"

Two films on subjectivity

Let us begin with Hegel's good old distinction between an external limit (*Grenze*) and an immanent limitation (*Schranke*): a *Grenze* is a simple external limit which is not reflected back into the entity that encounters it. As such, when I encounter a *Grenze*, I don't even perceive it as a limitation since I have no access to any external point with which to compare it. I see things within a certain horizon which allows me to see only certain things and only in a certain way, but I do not perceive the horizon as such—from within, it appears to me endless, infinite, or, to put it in Rumsfeldian terms, when I am limited by a *Grenze*, I don't know what I don't know. When *Grenze* changes into *Schranke*, it becomes a limitation proper, an obstacle I am aware of and try to overcome—now I know what I don't know. For example, the ecological threat of extinction forces humankind to perceive itself as a *species*, as one among the many on Earth, and with this idea of humans as a species, the universality of humankind falls back into the particularity of an animal species: phenomena like global warming make us aware that, for all the universality of our theoretical and practical activity, we are at a certain basic level just another living species on planet Earth. However, in order to see ourselves as one among many species, we have to extract ourselves from our particular position and somehow adopt a universal standpoint: in order to claim that we humans are just a speck of dust in the endless universe, we have to be able to look at ourselves from a quasi-divine global point of view. (Here again we encounter the Lacanian distinction between the subject of the enunciated and the subject of enunciation.) This is what Hegel meant by the passage from limit to limitation: a species which becomes aware of its limitation as a species (i.e., which becomes a species "for itself") has to overcome its limit and adopt a position of universality.

Another example: the Kantian Thing-in-itself is unknown and unknowable, but I am aware that the reality I have access to is only a transcendentally constituted phenomenal reality, so I know there is an unknowable X beyond it. Hegel's point here, predictably, is that such a limitation leads to what he calls the "bad" (or "spurious") infinity: I know there is something beyond, but all I can do is replace one phenomenal determination with another in a process that goes on endlessly. In short, I merely replace one finite entity with another without ever reaching Infinity itself, so that Infinity is present only as a void that pushes me from one to another finite determination. In effect, I find myself in a world divided into Something(s) and Nothing, and all that is left to me is to produce more and more new Somethings to fill in the void of Nothing. The Hegelian solution here is to shift the entire perspective from the objective to the subjective standpoint: we move beyond the "bad infinity" by abandoning the search for some infinite Absolute in the transcendent objectivity beyond the series of finite entities. Instead, we make a reflexive move towards the subject engaged in the endless activity of "overpassing" each finite entity—the true infinity is precisely this subjective dynamic stance of the incessant overpassing of finitude. The objective and the subjective aspect of infinity are here opposed as Being versus Becoming: the infinite Absolute in its Being is a transcendent entity outside our reach, while in its Becoming it is the incessant process of overcoming all finite determinations—and Hegel's point, of course, is that Becoming is the Truth of Being, i.e., that the infinite Absolute as Being is a reified result of the productive process of Becoming. In other words, *true Infinity is nothing but finitude as such*, its immanent limitation which pushes it into a constant self-overcoming.

A further feature to be noted apropos the distinction between *Grenze* and *Schranke* is that a proper limit never emerges as such: in the case of *Grenze*, we are *not yet* there, we are effectively limited but without even being aware of it; in the case of *Schranke*, we are *already over it*, aware of it and in this sense overpassing it, knowing both sides. The resolution of this tension is provided by the limit's radical internalization: the limit is finally posited as such when it is no longer conceived as an external limitation, but as an immanent self-limitation constitutive of the identity of the limited entity. One more step is needed to reach true infinity: the organism's self-relating has to sublate (encompass and overcome) its relation to the Other, as, for example, in the case of human freedom. To account for how freedom is possible in a determinist universe, Kant proposed the so-called "incorporation thesis": I am determined by causes, but I retroactively determine which causes will determine me. As subjects, we are passively affected by pathological objects and motivations; nevertheless, we have a minimal reflexive power to accept (or reject) being affected in this way. Or, to risk a Deleuzian-Hegelian formulation: the subject is a reflexive fold by means of which I retroactively determine the causes that will determine me, or, at least, the *mode* of this linear determination. "Freedom" is thus inherently retroactive: at its most elementary, it is not simply a free act which, out of nowhere, starts a new causal link, but a retroactive act of endorsing which link or sequence of necessities will determine me. Here, one should add a Hegelian twist on Spinoza: freedom is not simply "recognized/known necessity," but recognized/assumed necessity, a necessity constituted/actualized through this recognition.

In the passage from Life to the Subject, however, a further step has to be made: the immanent limitation constitutive of a living organism, the limit that separates an organism from its outside, has to be reflected back into the organism itself as the limit that prevents the organism from fully becoming itself. It is in this sense that Lacan defines a human subject as $, as a barred subject: a subject is literally the outcome of a failure to be—in order to clarify this paradox, let us make a detour through two films.

Alfonso Cuarón's *Gravity* (2013) tells the story of a US space team (consisting among others of Dr. Ryan Stone, played by Sandra Bullock, and Matthew Kowalski, played by George Clooney) preparing the Hubble Telescope for re-entry to Earth along with the shuttle Atlantis. When the Russians launch a missile to destroy one of their own defunct satellites, and the resulting cloud of debris flies around at high speed destroying everything in its path, Ryan finds herself trapped in space. After a series of setbacks, including losing her whole crew, she makes her way to the damaged Chinese space station Tiangong 8 to use one of their escape pods to return to Earth and claim back her life and freedom. There are three stupid criticisms of the film: 1) although it portrays superbly the experience of floating freely in empty space, it lacks the metaphysical depth of *2001* and other similar works; 2) the dialogue in the film is ridiculously clichéd; 3) while it follows the proto-feminist model of the "last surviving girl" (as well as, more ambiguously, giving the girl a masculine-sounding name—Ryan, similar to Ripley from *Alien*), the girl survives only with male help (from Kowalski, who guides her up until his own death, and even afterwards appears in an hallucination at the crucial moment of despair).

As to the first criticism, it is plainly wrong: if anything, *Gravity* captures an experience of reality that is much more authentic than the New Age platitudes of *2001*. Its authenticity lies in the way that, rather than representing, it directly *renders* the experience of floating in space in all its dreadful helplessness.¹ Just as, to return to Fredric Jameson's point, Hemingway did not adopt a terse style in order to represent a certain type of (narrative) subjectivity but rather invented a narrative content so as to be able to write in a certain style, so too in *Gravity* the minimal narrative elements are there to enable Cuarón to stage the formal experience of floating in space. The film inverts the classic *topos* of a human being bound to Earth by gravity and longing to free themselves from its hold. Jameson had already noted how weird it is that an extremely unpleasant and claustrophobic experience can be celebrated as a model of freedom, and here Cuarón, as if following this insight, presents gravity itself, the enduring of its impact, as the object of desire of a subject freely floating in space, as, precisely, her point of gravity. (However, Cuarón is at the same time refined enough not to depict empty space as itself a source of danger: all the trouble in the film comes from the Earth, or from the debris orbiting it.)

Consequently, what we should avoid at all costs is any precipitous "psychoanalytic" reading that would reduce this adventure in external space to some kind of projection of the protagonist's inner turmoil. True, we learn that some years earlier, as a single mother, Ryan lost her four-year-old child in a school playground accident. Perhaps it would not be an over-interpretation to read this inconsistency as an indication that the story of Ryan's traumatic loss is a fantasmatic false memory, but in any case, what *Gravity* is decidedly *not* is a film in which the external adventure serves as a screen for the presentation of the heroine's "true" inner journey. The film's title could have been *The Young Woman and Space*—a much better story than Hemingway's *The Old Man and the Sea*, which itself could also have worked as the title for Robert Redford's *All Is Lost*. There is a clear parallel between *Gravity* and *All Is Lost*: both films reduce the hero to a minimal point of absolute loss, both are loners trying to survive. This is not to suggest that the social background of the loner's confrontation with absolute loss is unimportant; the point is rather that, instead of reading it as an expression of some social turmoil, we should read *the hero's absolute isolation itself as a social fact*, as a metaphor for the predicament of every one of us in contemporary global capitalism, as we come to function more and more like monads struggling for survival.

---

1   The same holds for *Pacific Rim*, directed by Cuarón's colleague Guillermo del Toro: what should be celebrated is the film's material texture, the way the machinery is presented in all its materiality, as rusting, clumsy, and heavy.

This is why the second criticism—concerning the film's clichéd dialogue—also misses its mark: abstractly the observation is true, but one should rather read it as an elegant reminder of the fact that the basic raw experience of the film lies elsewhere, and that the words are there only to circumscribe the real of this experience. More generally, in the complex relationship between enjoyment and interpretation, it is not simply that the direct enjoyment of a text, its fascination, is there to obfuscate the "deeper meaning" to be unearthed by interpretation—more often than not, the compulsion to interpret imposes itself in order to obfuscate the stupid immediacy of enjoyment. When Boris Pahor, a Slovene writer who recently celebrated his centenary, was asked to comment on a passage from his work on good men, he tartly quoted a Serb proverb: "Even a rabbit is ready to lick the prick of a good man" ("*Dobrom čoveku i zec kurac liže*"). One can imagine the hermeneutic endeavour this statement triggered among journalists and commentators unable to accept the fact that the old man might simply enjoy a casual obscenity. And is this not one of the secret motivations for the hermeneutic endeavour? The point of discovering an author's "deeper meaning" is (more often than we think) to interpret away the unpleasant fact of direct enjoyment, to transubstantiate enjoyment into an expression of some "more profound" intellectual attitude. Exactly the same holds for *Gravity*: all the narrative content about Ryan's traumatic past is a symbolic semblance obfuscating the trauma of her present.

And what about the final criticism: that Ryan is presented as a help-less hysterical woman in need of male intervention to save her at crucial moments? While, again, this is a more or less accurate observation, it should be read in the exactly opposite way: at the crucial turning point of the film, Kowalski appears to Ryan as an hallucination—so the act (the decision) remains *hers*, and the man is reduced to an imagined prop to enable the feminine act. The key moment occurs when Ryan is caught in suicidal despair: she aligns her Soyuz vessel with the Tiangong space station only to discover her craft's thrusters have no fuel. After a brief com-munication with a Greenland Inuit fisherman, listening to him cooing to a baby, she resigns herself to her fate and shuts down the oxygen supply in the cabin in order to commit suicide. As she begins to lose consciousness, Kowalski appears outside and enters the capsule; berating her for giving up, he tells her to use the Soyuz's landing rockets to propel the capsule towards Tiangong. Realizing that Kowalski's return was an hallucination, Ryan nonetheless gains new strength and the will to live; she restores the flow of oxygen and uses the landing rockets to navigate towards Tiangong.

Kowalski's hallucinated advice is very precisely worded. Describing the choice Ryan faces, he does not paint suicide as a terrible defeat, but as the easy way out: she will float freely in empty space, free of pain and bad memories, full of lifeless joy and peace. The hard choice, on the contrary, is the choice of life (of returning to gravity): the choice of painful commitment and worry. Therein resides Ryan's ultimate metaphysical decision, the pure zero-point choice of all of us: engagement or withdrawal, a Yes or a No to external reality. Consequently, gravity-less empty space is here not just another part of reality, but stands for absolute death, for the real of the primordial void. There is only life if a kind of swerve or *clinamen*, as the ancient materialists put it, disturbs the symmetry of the neutral balance by introducing an asymmetrical point of gravity.

So why can Ryan not make this choice alone, why does she need the support of a (hallucinated) Other? Because, strictly viewed, the choice involved here is not the choice of an (already constituted) subject, but the choice constitutive of the very dimension of subjectivity. For common sense, the subject precedes free choice: in order for a free choice to take place, there has to be a subject who enacts it. For Badiou, on the contrary, the free choice precedes the subject: the subject is not the agent of a free choice (the one who chooses freely), but the result of a positive free choice— a subject emerges after the choice of fidelity to an Event, as the agent that engages itself in the work of enforcing its consequences. This choice is itself a forced one, however, since the whole weight of ethics pressurizes me into making the positive choice and not missing the evental encounter. It is a choice in which the choosing subject has to choose himself. And this is why the detour through the figure of an Other is necessary here—for the same reason that, in psychoanalysis, a subject cannot simply analyze itself in an act of self-reflection, but needs the external figure of the psychoanalyst as its object of transference. If Ryan had chosen all by herself, this would have elevated her into the god-like position of an absolute subject able to choose or create itself in a perfect closed circle of a retroactive *causa sui*.

This requisite virtual Other need not necessarily be another human being, it can also be an animal, as is the case in Ang Lee's *Life of Pi*, based on Yann Martel's bestselling novel. What makes this blockbuster unique is that 80 percent of its takings of $600 million was earned outside the United States, mostly in the Far East. The film tells the story of the maturation of Pi Patel, an Indian whose father named him Piscine (meaning a swimming pool in French); as a child, he changed his name to "Pi" (the Greek letter π) because he was tired of being called "Pissing Patel" (due to the pronunciation of his name). Pi's family owned a zoo, and Pi took great interest in the animals, especially a Bengal tiger named Richard Parker. When Pi is 16, his father decides to move the family to Canada where he intends to sell the zoo animals and settle down. On board the Japanese freighter taking them to Canada, Pi's father gets into an argument with the ship's cook when he speaks to Pi's mother rudely. After a storm in which the ship founders while Pi is on deck, Pi finds himself in the lifeboat with an injured zebra and an orangutan who has lost her offspring in the shipwreck. A spotted hyena emerges from the tarp covering half of the boat, and kills the zebra. To Pi's distress, the hyena also mortally wounds the orangutan in a fight. Suddenly, Richard Parker also emerges from under the tarp, and kills and eats the hyena.

When the lifeboat eventually reaches the coast of Mexico, Richard Parker stumbles away from Pi and disappears into the jungle. Pi, too weak to follow, lies in the sand until he is rescued by a group who carry him to hospital. While there, insurance agents for the Japanese freighter come to hear his account of the incident. They find his story unbelievable, and ask him to tell them what "really" happened, if only for the credibility of their report. He then gives them a less fantastic but detailed account of sharing the lifeboat with his mother, a sailor with a broken leg, and the cook: the cook kills the sailor to use him as bait and food; in a later struggle, Pi's mother pushes him to safety on a smaller raft, and the cook stabs her as she falls overboard to the sharks; later, Pi returns to grab the knife and kills the cook. In the present, the writer-narrator notes parallels between the two stories: the orangutan was Pi's mother, the zebra was the sailor, the hyena was the cook, and Richard Parker, the tiger, was Pi himself. Pi asks the writer which story he prefers, and he chooses the one with the tiger because it is "the better story," to which Pi responds, "And so it is with God."

Glancing at a copy of the insurance report, the writer notices that the insurance agents chose that story as well, following John Ford's well-known motto "Print the legend, not the facts." One cannot but recall here the rabbi's famous reply to a kid who, after hearing a beautiful myth from him, asked: "But is it true? Did it really happen?" The rabbi replied: "It did not really happen, but it is true." Does this mean that, in a postmodern-Nietzschean way, the film ultimately asserts the primacy of fiction over reality? Here we should be attentive to the difference between the novel and the film: the book does indeed radiate a New Age postmodern spirituality, but the film totally changes the entire terrain (similar in a way to what Cuarón, in his *Children of Men*, did with the P. D. James novel on which his film is based).

The two series in the stories—the human (Pi, his mother, the cook, the sailor) and the animal (tiger, orangutan, hyena, zebra)—can (should, even) be conceived along the lines of Kierkegaard's famous division of humans into officers, maids, and chimney sweepers: all humans can be divided into mothers, cooks, and sailors—or, all animals can be divided into orangutans, hyenas, and zebras. Pi is the exception here, a fourth element sticking out: he appears in both series, but with a twist. In the human series, he is simply himself, while in the animal series, he is doubly present, as himself and as the tiger, his animal counterpart, his more-than-human dimension. This reflexive moment is crucial: in order to have the two series (human and animal), there has to be an excessive element which is the stand-in for the subject; as such, it has to be divided, doubly inscribed, and interact directly with its double. In other words, the boy cannot just tell the story with the four animals, he has to be part of the story himself and encounter himself in it in the guise of the tiger as his "oppositional determination" (Hegel). What this entails is that *the tiger does not exist*, that effectively he is there in neither of the stories. What, then, is his status? In some of Francis Bacon's drawings, we find a (naked, usually) body accompanied by a weird dark stain-like formless form that seems to grow out of it, barely attached to it, as a kind of uncanny protuberance that the body can never fully recuperate or reintegrate, and which thereby destabilizes beyond repair the organic Whole of the body—this is what Lacan was aiming at with his notion of the *lamella*. This forever lost excess of pure indestructible life is—in its guise as the *objet a*, the object-cause of desire—also what "eternalizes" human desire, making it infinitely plastic and unsatisfiable (in contrast to instinctual needs). In relation to the film then, we can now see why the tiger has to disappear into the jungle at the end of Pi's adventure: the film is a story of the hero's maturation, and the moment of maturity occurs when the subject renounces its uncanny protuberance, finally accepting that it must stand alone.

This brings us to the difference between Badiou and Lacan: to put it in the terms of *Life of Pi*, in Badiou's universe there is no place for the non-existing tiger. For Badiou, the subject is object-less, while for Lacan, the subject is strictly correlative to a paradoxical object, the *objet a*. Badiou's point is, of course, that the subject should not be constrained to the transcendental correlation between subject and object, where "object" stands for the order of objective reality; not without irony, the best term with which to designate the Lacanian operation left out by Badiou is the Badiouian one: *subtraction*. And, again, not without irony, it is Lacan who is the materialist here, i.e., who adds a pathological "stain," a contingent remainder and/or excess, as the (im)material support of the subject correlative to transcendentally constituted objective reality. The *objet a* is what has to be subtracted from reality so that reality can emerge as a transcendentally constituted field of phenomena. Lacan's thesis is that *there are (transcendentally constituted) objects (of the "external reality") because there is a split subject*. This constitutive split of the subject (which precedes the split between subject and object) is the split between the void that "is" the subject ($) and the impossible-real objectal counterpart of the subject, the purely virtual *objet a*. What we call "external reality" (as a consistent field of positively existing objects) arises through subtraction, when something is subtracted from it, and this something is the *objet a*. The correlation between subject and object (objective reality) is thus sustained by the correlation between this same subject and its objectal correlate, the impossible-real *objet a*, and this second correlation is of a totally different kind: it is a kind of negative correlation, an impossible link, a non-relationship, between the two moments which cannot ever meet within the same space (like subject and object), not because they are too far away, but because they are one and the same entity on the two sides of the Möbius band. And we should not be surprised to find a strictly homologous paradox in a totally different context, that of the Cold War strategy of Mutually Assured Destruction (MAD):

> It is a strange paradox of our time that one of the crucial factors which make the [nuclear] dissuasion effectively function, and function so well, is the underlying fear that, in a really serious crisis, it can fail. In such circumstances, *one does not play with fate*. If we were absolutely certain that the nuclear dissuasion is one hundred per cent efficient in its role of protecting us against a nuclear assault, then its dissuasive value against a conventional war would have dropped to close to zero.[2]

The paradox is here a very precise one: the MAD strategy works not because it is perfect, but *on account of its very imperfection*. That is to say, a perfect strategy (if one side nukes the other, the other will automatically respond, and both sides will thus be destroyed) has a fatal flaw: what if the attacking side counts on the fact that, even after its first strike, the opponent will continue to act as a rational agent? His choice will be this: with his country mostly destroyed, he can either strike back, thereby causing total

---

2   Bernard Brodie, *War and Politics*, New York: Macmillan 1973, pp. 430–1.

catastrophe and the end of humanity, or not strike back, thus enabling the survival of humanity and thereby at least the possibility of a later revival of his own country. A rational agent would choose the second option. What makes the strategy effective is the very fact that we can never be sure it will work perfectly: what if a situation spirals out of control for any of a variety of easily imaginable reasons (from the "irrational" aggression of one party to simple technological failures or miscommunications)? It is because of this permanent threat that neither side wants to come even close to the prospect of MAD, *so they avoid even conventional war*: if the strategy were perfect, it would, on the contrary, encourage the attitude: "Let's fight a full conventional war, since we both know that neither of us will risk the fateful nuclear strike!" The actual constellation of deterrence is thus not "If we follow the MAD strategy, the nuclear catastrophe will not take place," but "If we follow the MAD strategy, the nuclear catastrophe will not take place, *except for some unpredictable incident*." And the same goes today for the prospect of the ecological catastrophe: if we do nothing, it will occur, and if we do all we can do, it will not occur, *except for some unpredictable accident*. This unpredictable factor "e" is precisely the remainder of the Real which disturbs the perfect self-closure of the projected perfect strategy—it is a cut which prevents the full closure of the circle (exactly the way Lacan writes *l'objet petit a*). What confirms the paradoxical status of e is that, in it, possibility and impossibility, positive and negative, coincide: *it renders the strategy of prevention effective precisely insofar as it hinders its full efficacy*. In short, is not this factor quite literally (a something that is) *less than nothing*? It is negative, an obstacle, an index that something has been taken away from the thing (in this case, the perfectly functioning dissuasion strategy), but if we abolish the obstacle and fill in the lack, we lose what it is an obstacle to, i.e., we get less than we had before.

This twisted space of the *objet a* brings us to the erotic dimension. A voluptuous lady from Portugal once told me a wonderful anecdote: when her most recent lover had first seen her fully naked, he told her that, if she lost just one or two kilos, her body would be perfect. The truth was, of course, that had she lost the kilos, she would probably have looked more ordinary—the very element that seems to disturb perfection itself creates the illusion of the perfection it disturbs: if we take away the excessive element, we lose the perfection itself.

THE NECESSITY OF A CHIMNEY SWEEP

As we might expect, this excessive element, the *objet a*, disturbs every system of classification, of division of a genus into species. Let us return to Kierkegaard's "immortal division"³ of mankind:

> A wit has said that one might divide mankind into officers, serving maids, and chimney sweeps. To my mind this remark is not only witty but profound, and it would require a great speculative talent to devise a better classification. When a classification does not ideally exhaust its object, a haphazard classification is altogether preferable, because it sets imagination in motion.⁴

In Marx, Kierkegaard's contemporary, we find two different versions of the same paradoxical classification. First, in *Capital*, there is Marx's characterization of the market exchange between worker and capitalist as

> a very Eden of the innate rights of man. There alone rule Freedom, Equality, Property and Bentham. Freedom, because both buyer and seller of a commodity, say of labor-power, are constrained only by their own free will. They contract as free agents, and the agreement they come to is but the form in which they give legal expression to their common will. Equality, because each enters into relations with the other, as with a simple owner of commodities, and they exchange equivalent for equivalent. Property, because each disposes only of what is his own. And Bentham, because each looks only to himself. The only force that brings them together and puts them in relation with each other is the selfishness, the gain and the private interests of each.⁵

One is tempted to submit this passage from Marx to a double Kierkegaardian correction: first, the terms should be just three, not four—freedom, equality, *and Bentham*—then, one should bring to light the underlying triad of the French Revolution to which Marx obviously refers: freedom, equality, *fraternity*. We are thus dealing with a metaphoric substitution (fraternity is pushed below the bar, out of sight, substituted by Bentham) which makes

3   Jacques Lacan, *Écrits*, New York: Norton 2006, p. 600.

4   Søren Kierkegaard, *Fear and Trembling/Repetition*, Princeton: Princeton University Press 1983, p. 162. I am indebted to Mladen Dolar for the reference to Kierkegaard, Heine and Marx.

5   Karl Marx, *Capital*, Vol. 1, Chapter 6, "The Buying and Selling of Labour Power," available at marxists.org.

a clear point: the actual result of the bourgeois revolution is that, instead of the fraternity of free individuals, we get narrow egotism.

Marx's second version of the paradoxical classification, also in *Capital*, concerns the status of the "general equivalent" among other commodities:

> It is as if, alongside and external to lions, tigers, rabbits, and all other actual animals, which form when grouped together the various kinds, species, subspecies, families, etc., of the animal kingdom, there existed in addition *the animal*, the individual incarnation of the entire animal kingdom.[6]

The two types of paradoxical classification are clearly opposed: in the second case, the supplementary element (money, *the* animal) directly gives body to the universal dimension as such, i.e., in it, the universal (of commodities or of animals) encounters itself among its species; in the first case, the supplementary element (Bentham) stands for ridiculous particularity (which is also universal in the precise sense that it gives a specific color to the universality—in Marx's case, the key to what freedom and equality effectively mean in capitalist society). The difference relies on the structure of the preceding set: if it is a couple (man and woman, rich class and poor class), the third element is the "lowest" one (the chimney sweep who disturbs a harmonious sex relationship, or, in anti-Semitism, the Jew who disturbs the harmonious class relationship); if it is an (open, in principle) series (of commodities, of people, etc.), the supplementary term is the highest one (money, the king, gold, etc.). In the first case, the excessive element disunites, introduces antagonism and struggle; in the second case, it introduces unity, it totalizes. Or, in the terms of Lacan's formulae of sexuation: the stand-in for universality (money among commodities) follows the "masculine" logic of the exception which grounds universality, while the supplement to the Two (chimney sweep, rabble) follows the "feminine" logic, for it makes the couple non-All, inconsistent.

In the case of Bentham, we can also introduce the same triadic logic of the antagonistic couple plus its supplement—there is an antagonism between freedom and equality (which Étienne Balibar tries to overcome with his formula *égaliberté*), and "Bentham" names the cause of this antagonism: it is because freedom means freedom of market exchange that, when we are dealing with the "free" exchange between capital and labor, formal equality turns into factual inequality; and vice versa, it is

---

6   Ibid., Chapter 1, "The Commodity."

because equality is formal equality in the eyes of the law that free exchange on the market turns into unfreedom for the one selling his or her labor power. In short, the condition of *égaliberté* is to obliterate "Bentham" from the picture.

True, the chimneysweep element is a particular supplement that gives a specific coloring to all the preceding terms (what they "really mean" in the concrete historical totality); however, this is not to be read as if the chimneysweep element represents common sense, as in Heinrich Heine's (yet another contemporary of Marx and Kierkegaard) well-known saying that one should value above all else "truth, freedom, and crab soup." "Crab soup" here stands for all those small pleasures in the absence of which we become (mental, if not real) terrorists following an abstract idea and forcing it onto reality without any consideration for the concrete circumstances. One should emphasize here that such "wisdom" is precisely what Kierkegaard and Marx did *not* have in mind—their message is rather the opposite one: the principle itself, in its purity, is already stained by the particularity of "crab soup," i.e., the particularity sustains the very purity of the principle. The difference that separates Heine from Marx is thus clear, and it concerns the status of universality: while Heine advocates the commonsensical wisdom that warns us against a direct literal devotion to and application of universal norms, Marx's point is the opposite one—the addition of "Bentham" implies that, in capitalist society, freedom/equality is not authentic, so we should get rid of "Bentham" and strive to actualize freedom/equality in its true universality.

We should also note here the difference between this supplementary element and the Derridean supplement: the latter is a supplement to One (to Presence, to Origin), while for Kierkegaard, Marx, *and Lacan* (whose name should be added here as the chimney sweep to both of them), the excessive element is a supplement to the Two, to the harmonious couple (*yin* and *yang*, the two classes, etc.)—capitalist, worker, *and the Jew*; or, maybe, upper class, lower class, *plus the rabble.*[7] In the triad of officer, maid, and chimney sweep, the latter can effectively be seen as the *Liebes-Stoerer*, the obscene intruder who cuts short their love-making.[8]

---

7 Stalin's position seems ambiguous here: one can imagine a Stalinist purge as the effort to liquidate all chimney sweeps who disturb the socialist harmony—but was not Stalin himself also the supreme sweep?

8 Let us go to the end and imagine the ultimate obscenity: after the officer and the maid have finished having sex, the chimney sweep quickly intervenes with an act of belated contraception, cleaning out her "channel" with his brush ... We should

Insofar as this supplementary element embodies trash with no proper place in the hierarchy of things, no wonder that the same paradox reproduces itself within the world of trash itself. Public trash bins are today more and more differentiated: there are special bins for paper, glass, cans, cardboard packaging, plastics, etc. Here already, things sometimes get complicated: if I have to dispose of a paper bag or notebook with a tiny plastic band, where does it belong, in paper or plastics? No wonder we often find on the bins detailed instructions beneath the general designation: *paper*—books, newspapers, etc., but *not* hardcover books or books with plastic covers, etc. In such cases, properly disposing of one's waste could take up to half an hour or more of detailed reading and tough decision making. To make things easier, we then get a supplementary bin for *general waste* where we throw everything that does not meet the criteria specified on the other bins—again, as if, apart from paper trash, plastic trash, etc., there is also trash as such, universal trash.

The chimney sweep is the element embodying the non-relationship, sustaining it as a non-relationship: if we take it away, we get a simple duality of polar opposites, like the eternal struggle of masculine and feminine cosmic principles, instead of a true antagonism. In other words, it is not enough to oppose the level of evental flow or of antagonism to the material elements: the evental flow or antagonism has to be inscribed in, reflected into, the field of material elements as one of its elements, as a pseudo-element that gives body to what cannot be reduced to material elements.

The place of this excessive element can also be discerned in the imbalance between the universal and the particular—the excess of the universal over its actual particularities points towards a weird excessive particular element, as in Chesterton's well-known remark addressed to "my readers most of whom are human"—or, as a well-known Slovene soccer player once put it after an important victory: "My gratitude goes to my parents, especially my mum and my dad." Who then is the remaining parent, the third one, neither mother nor father? A remark by the French Communist Party leader Georges Marchais, during an electoral meeting in the early 1980s, created a similar comic effect when he emphatically claimed: "Not only are we Communists not wrong in our analysis of the situation, we are also right!" Again, what would be the third position, neither right nor wrong?

---

also not forget that the maid and the chimney sweep themselves form a couple—recall the old myth of the chimney sweep as a seducer of innocent maids.

Everyone knows Winston Churchill's quip about democracy, usually quoted as: "Democracy is the worst possible system, except for all the others." What Churchill actually said (in the House of Commons on November 11, 1947) was slightly less paradoxical and scintillating: "Many forms of Government have been tried, and will be tried in this world of sin and woe. No one pretends that democracy is perfect or all-wise. Indeed it has been said that democracy is the worst form of Government except for all those other forms that have been tried from time to time."[9] The underlying logic is best rendered by applying Lacan's "formulae of sexuation" to Churchill's dictum and rephrasing it as follows: "Democracy is the worst of all systems; however, compared to democracy, any other system is worse." If we take all possible systems together and grade them with regard to their worth, democracy is the worst and finishes at the bottom; if, however, we compare democracy one to one with all other systems, it is better than any of them.[10] Does not something similar hold (or seem to hold) for capitalism? If one analyses it in an abstract way, trying to locate it in the hierarchy of all possible systems, it appears as the worst—chaotic, unjust, destructive, etc.; however, if we compare it in a concrete pragmatic way to each alternative, it is still better than any of them.

This "illogical" imbalance between the universal and the particular is a direct indication of the efficacy of ideology. An opinion poll in the US at the end of June 2012, just before the Supreme Court decision on Obama's healthcare reform, showed that "strong majorities favor most of what is in the law":

> Most Americans oppose President Barack Obama's healthcare reform even though they strongly support most of its provisions, a Reuters/Ipsos poll showed

---

9   Incidentally, it is not known to whom "it has been said" refers—to a particular individual or just to the common wisdom?

10   In logic and theory of judgment, we sometimes encounter a similar paradox of intransitivity: if A is better than B and B is better than C, it does not always follow that A is better than C—when one compares A and C directly, C can appear better. It would be all too easy to explain away this paradox as relying on a change in criteria (comparing all three, one applies the same criteria, but when comparing them one to one, the criteria imperceptibly shift). In some way, of course, this has to be true, but the point is that the shift is immanent, not arbitrary. That is to say, the shift can occur because of the differentiality of features: say we compare the beauty of three people— A appears more beautiful than B and B more beautiful than C. However, when we compare A and C, it may happen that a strong contrast in some minor feature will ruin the beauty of A, so that A will appear inferior to C.

... The survey results suggest that Republicans are convincing voters to reject Obama's reform even when they like much of what is in it, such as allowing children to stay on their parents' insurance until age 26.[11]

Here we encounter ideology at its purest: the majority wants to have its (ideological) cake and eat it (the real cake), i.e., they want the real benefits of the healthcare reform, while rejecting its ideological form (which they perceive as a threat to "freedom of choice")—they reject water, but accept H_2O, or, rather, they reject (the concept of) fruit, but they want apples, plums, strawberries, etc. Early on in Jo Nesbø's thriller *Headhunters*, there is a joke involving a similar paradoxical series: "The tangy saline taste of exhaust fumes in the autumn air evoked associations of sea, oil extraction and gross national product."[12] The eccentric moment added to the series of natural and physical elements here is GNP, shorthand for the brutal exploitation of nature. Another version, from Bob Dylan in a recent *Rolling Stone* interview (September 2012):

> This country is too fucked up about color. It's a distraction. People at each other's throats just because they are of a different color. It's the height of insanity and it will hold any nation back—or any neighborhood back. Or anything back. Blacks know that some whites didn't want to give up slavery—that if they had their way, they would still be under the yoke, and they can't pretend they don't know that. If you've got a slave master or Klan in your blood, blacks can sense that. That stuff lingers to this day. Just like Jews can sense Nazi blood and the Serbs can sense Croatian blood. It's doubtful that America's ever going to get rid of that stigmatization. It's a country formed on the backs of slaves ... If slavery had been given up in a more peaceful way, America would be far ahead today.

A weird series of blood-smelling people: a black man versus a slave-owner, a Jew versus a Nazi, a Serb versus a Croat. The first two couples oppose a general ethnic category (black, Jew) to a specific economic/social/political subcategory (slave-owner, Nazi), not to an entire group (whites, Germans), while in the case of the Serbs, it is not the Ustashi subset of Croats but Croats as such.[13] This is a clear step towards racism: a couple, plus the third

11   "Most Americans Oppose Health Law Provisions," reuters.com, June 24, 2012.

12   Jo Nesbo, *Headhunters*, New York: Vintage Books 2011, p. 18.

13   It is true that there is a massive historic memory of World War II crimes against the Serbs—but the same holds even more for Germans, so why not a Jew who can smell a German? Plus what about Serb ethnic cleansing in the early 1990s?

term that displays the true underlying racist stance. More precisely: what makes it racist is not the special status of Croats, but the fact that it is *only* Croats who have this status. That is to say, the correct formulation would not be to replace Croats with Ustashi (the Croat Nazi collaborators), but in the first two cases to replace slave-owners with whites and Nazis with Germans. The terrible acts of the slave-owners and of the Nazis are a stain on white Americans as such and on Germans as such—it is too easy to say that the Nazis were guilty, while all other Germans were innocent (and the same goes for what the Ustashi did during World War II). So when a black man looks at a white man, he can (and has the right to) "smell slave-owner blood" in him, even if this individual white man has nothing to do with slavery.

There is a similar categorization in which a set is divided into ridiculously unbalanced subsets, as in the Eugene Wigner quip: "There are two kinds of people in the world: Johnny von Neumann and the rest of us." Recall also the cynical wisdom formula: "There are two kinds of people, those who ... and those who ...," where the point is the arbitrary nature of the distinction: those who get hanged and those who hold the rope; those who enjoy Armagnac and those who hate it ... And would not the ultimate categorization be the very division into something and nothing: "There are two kinds of people in the world: those who will die and no one else." Or: "There are two kinds of people in the world: those who will die and the immortals"—the point being that the second set is empty. In terms of Marx's notion of a commodity in general, his version would be: "There are two kinds of commodities on the market, particular commodities with specific use values and the commodity in general." Along the same lines, recall again Walter Benjamin's essay "On Language in General and Human Language in Particular," in which the point is not that human language is a species of some universal language "as such" which also comprises other species: there is no actually existing language other than human language— but, in order to comprehend this "particular" language, one *has* to introduce a minimal difference, conceiving it with regard to the gap which separates it from language "as such." The particular language is thus the "really existing language," language as the series of actually uttered statements, in contrast to the formal linguistic structure. This Benjaminian lesson is missed by Habermas, who does precisely what one should *not* do—he posits the ideal "language in general" (pragmatic universals) *directly* as the norm of the actually existing language. Along the lines of Benjamin's title, we should describe the basic constellation of the social law as that of the "Law in general and its obscene superego underside in particular." The "Part" as such is thus the "sinful" unredeemed and unredeemable aspect of the Universal—in concrete political terms, every politics that grounds itself in a reference to some substantial (ethnic, religious, sexual, lifestyle …) particularity is by definition reactionary. Consequently, the division introduced and sustained by the emancipatory ("class") struggle is *not* that between the two particular classes of the Whole, but that between the Whole-in-its-parts and its Remainder which, within the Particulars, stands for the Universal, for the Whole "as such," opposed to its parts. One should bear in mind here the two aspects of the notion of the remnant: the rest as what remains after the subtraction of all particular content (elements, specific parts of the Whole), and the rest as the ultimate result of the subdivision of the Whole into its parts, when, in the final act of subdivision, we no longer get two particular parts or elements, two Somethings, but a Something (the Rest) and a Nothing.

Is the triad of the two opposites plus the chimney sweep Hegelian? Perhaps the fact that we have referred to Kierkegaard, Heine, and Marx, each of whom tried to break out of the constraints of Hegel's idealist logic, indicates that the aim of such paradoxical classifications or divisions is precisely to unsettle the consistent logical frame of the Hegelian scheme? Upon a closer look, however, things become more complicated: as we have already seen, the monarch in Hegel's *Philosophy of Right* displays the coincidence of the highest (pure signifier) and lowest (biology, contingency) which characterizes the excessive element. And was not the young Marx, on account of this overlapping of the pure symbolic element (the royal title) and a contingent bodily element (the penis), more right than he was aware of when, in his early critique of Hegel's philosophy of right, he remarked acerbically that the Hegelian Monarch is just an appendix to his phallus?[14]

In Lacan's precise sense of the term, the chimney sweep effectively stands for the phallic element. How? Insofar as he stands for pure difference: officer, maid, and chimney sweep are the masculine, the feminine, *plus their difference as such*, as a particular contingent object—again, why? Because not only is difference differential, in an antagonistic (non)

---

14   We encounter a similar figure of a person reduced to the stupidity of his body in Alexander Sokurov's *Telec* (*Body*), a film depicting a day in the life of Lenin when he was already approaching death, living isolated in a forest mansion. It renders the painfully desublimated body of a Leader, shown as a helplessly fragile individual unable to stand or walk unaided, prattling nonsense and making obscene gestures, oscillating between senile smiles and outbursts of suppressed rage.

relationship, it precedes the terms it differentiates: not only is woman not-man and vice versa, woman is also what prevents man from being fully man and vice versa. It is like the difference between the Left and the Right in political space: their difference is a difference in the very way difference is perceived—the whole political space appears differently structured if we look at it from the Left or from the Right; there is no third "objective" way (for a leftist, the political divide cuts across the entire social body, while for a rightist, society is a hierarchical Whole disturbed by marginal intruders). Difference "in itself" is thus not symbolic/differential, but real-impossible—something that eludes and resists the symbolic grasp. This difference is the universal as such—universal not as a neutral frame elevated above its two species, but as their constitutive antagonism, and the third element (chimney sweep, Jew, *objet a*) stands for the difference as such, for the "pure" difference/antagonism that precedes the differentiated terms. If the division of the social body into two classes had been complete, without the excessive element (Jew, rabble ...), there would have been no class struggle, just two clearly divided classes—this third element is not the mark of an empirical remainder that escapes the class classification (the pure division of society into two classes), but *the materialization of their antagonistic difference itself*, insofar as this difference precedes the differentiated terms. In the space of anti-Semitism, the "Jew" stands for the social antagonism as such: without the Jewish intruder, the two classes would live in harmony. We can see now how the third intruding element is evental: it is not just another positive entity, it stands for what is forever unsettling the harmony of the Two, opening it up to an incessant process of re-accommodation.

A supreme example of this third element, the *objet a* which supplements the couple, is provided by a weird incident that occurred in Kemalist Turkey in 1926. Part of the Kemalist modernization program was to enforce new "European" models for women, how they should dress, talk, and act, in order to get rid of the oppressive Oriental traditions—as is well known, there was indeed a Hat Law prescribing how men and women, at least in big cities, should cover their heads. Then,

> in Erzurum in 1926 there was a woman among the people who were executed under the pretext of "opposing the Hat Law." She was a very tall (almost 2 m.) and very masculine-looking woman who peddled shawls for a living (hence her name "Şalcı Bacı" [Shawl Sister]). Reporter Nimet Arzık described her as "two meters tall, with a sooty face and snakelike thin dreadlocks ... and with manlike steps." Of course as a woman she was not supposed to wear the fedora, so she

could not have been "guilty" of anything, but probably in their haste the gen-
darmes mistook her for a man and hurried her to the scaffold. Şalcı Bacı was
the first woman to be executed by hanging in Turkish history. She was definitely
not "normal" since the description by Arzık does not fit in any framework of
feminine normalcy at that particular time, and she probably belonged to the old
tradition of tolerated and culturally included "special people" with some kind of
genetic "disorder." The coerced and hasty transition to "modernity," however, did
not allow for such an inclusion to exist, and therefore she had to be eliminated,
crossed out of the equation. "Would a woman wear a hat that she be hanged?"
were the last words she was reported to have muttered on the way to the scaffold. Apart from making no sense at all, these words represented a semantic void
and only indicated that this was definitely a scene from the Real, subverting the
rules of semiotics: she was first emasculated (in its primary etymological sense
of "making masculine"), so that she could be "emasculated."[15]

How are we to interpret this weird and ridiculously excessive act of killing?
The obvious reading would be a Butlerian one: through her provocative
trans-sexual appearance and acting, Şalcı Bacı rendered visible the contingent character of sexual difference, of how it is symbolically constructed—as
such, she was a threat to normatively established sexual identities. My
reading is slightly (or not so slightly) different: rather than undermining
sexual difference, Şalcı Bacı stood for this difference as such, in its traumatic Real, irreducible to any clear symbolic opposition; her disturbing
appearance transformed clear symbolic difference into the impossible-real
of an antagonism.

Yet another supreme example of this excessive element is the most
brilliant hallucinatory legend of the Great War: the persistent rumor that,
somewhere in no-man's-land—in this desolate wasteland of scorched earth
full of rotting corpses, water-logged shell craters, abandoned trenches and
tunnels—gangs of half-crazy deserters lived.[16] They were composed of men
from all the combatant nations—Germans, French, British, Australians,
Poles, Croats, Belgians, Italians—and they lived their hidden lives in friendship and peace, avoiding detection and helping each other out. Dressed in
rags, with long beards, they never allowed themselves to be seen, although
from time to time one might hear their crazy shouts and songs. They left

15   Bulent Somay, L'Orient n'existe pas, Doctoral Thesis defended at Birkbeck
College, University of London, November 29, 2013.
16   I rely here on Paul Fussell, The Great War and Modern Memory, Oxford:
Oxford University Press 2000.

their subterranean netherworld only at night, after a battle, in order to scavenge the corpses and collect water and food. The beauty of this legend is that it clearly describes a kind of alternative community, a great *no* to the madness unfolding on the battlefield: a group in which members of the warring nations lived in peace with each other, their only enemy being War itself. While they may appear as an image of War at its most crazy—outcasts living a wild life—they are simultaneously its self-negation, literally an island of peace in between the front lines, a universal fraternity that ignores these lines. Precisely by ignoring the official lines of division between Us and Them, they stand for the real division, the only one that matters, the negation of the entire space of imperialist warfare. They are the third element that belies the false duality of the War—in short, they are the true Leninists of the situation, repeating Lenin's gesture of refusing to be drawn into the patriotic fervor. So it is not that they just stand for indifference: they stand for the real difference (the class antagonism), in the same way that the chimney sweep stands for sexual difference as such.[17]

Insofar as the antagonism is another name for non-relationship (*il n'y a pas de rapport sexuel*, there is no class relationship), this third excessive element which always haunts the Two (sexes, classes) as their obscene shadow can also be said to stand for Lacan's "there is (something of the) One (*Y a d'l'Un*)" which is the obverse of *il n'y a pas de l'Autre*. Or, to put it with a slightly different accent, insofar as the One of *Y a d'l'Un* is an "indivisible remainder" which makes sexual relationship inexistent, *Y a d'l'Un* is also strictly correlative to *il n'y a pas de rapport sexuel*: it is the very object-obstacle to this *rapport*. The One of *Y a d'l'Un* is not primarily the mystical all-encompassing One of the infamous "oceanic feeling" derided by Freud, but a "little piece of the real," the excremental remainder that disturbs the harmony of the Two. Clarifying this crucial distinction, Guy le Gaufey drew attention to a subtle passage in late Lacan from "*il n'y a pas de rapport sexuel*" to "*il y a du non-rapport (sexuel)*," a shift which precisely fits

---

17   The link between antagonism, the *objet a*, and failed interpellation resides in the fact that interpellation as such always displaces-betrays-obfuscates the antagonism. The antagonistic character of "class struggle" means precisely that members of the two classes are never directly interpellated as pure class subjects (capitalists and proletarians), but always in a mystified-displaced way (e.g. in the case of fashion: rich people are interpellated as populists, wearing jeans, etc.). In this precise way, the *objet a* is the remainder that emerges as the index of the failed interpellation, i.e., as the index of how the interpellation of individuals into their symbolic identity always displaces the antagonism.

Kant's distinction between a negative judgment (the negation of a predicate) and an infinite judgment (the affirmation of a non-predicate), as in "he isn't dead" versus the much more uncanny "he is undead." "There is no sexual relationship" can still be read as a variation on the old motif of the eternal conflict between the sexes: there is no harmony between men and women because men are from Mars and women from Venus, they move in different universes, so their encounter is always missed. "There is a non-relationship" implies something much more radical: the positivization of this impossibility of the sexual relationship in a paradoxical "trans-finite" object that overlaps with its own lack or which is in excess with regard to itself. What this means is that masculine and feminine are not simply two entities out of sync, but that sexual difference in a way precedes the two sexes (the difference of which it is), so that the two sexes somehow come (logically) later, reacting to, and endeavoring to resolve or symbolize, the deadlock of the Difference, a deadlock materialized in the pseudo-object called the *objet a*. This is why we should not say of the *objet a* simply that it is not sexual: it is un-sexual in exactly the same sense in which vampires are undead: the "undead" are neither alive nor dead but the monstrous living dead; likewise, the *objet a* is neither sexual nor non-sexual but "sexually asexual," a monstrosity which does not fit the coordinates of either of the two sexes, but is still sexual. As Lacan pointed out, what is at stake here is nothing less than a change of the "principle of all principles," from the ontological principle of non-contradiction to the principle that there is no sexual relationship.[18]

Desire, Drive, Deleuze, Lacan

How does this passage from "there is no ..." to "there is a no-" affect Lacan's elementary couple of desire and drive? Is it not that in desire "there is no relationship" while for the drive "there is a non-relationship"? Desire is Kantian (which is why we can think of Lacan's classic teaching from the 1950s as a kind of "critique of pure desire"), drive is Hegelian. There is no relationship between desire and its object, desire concerns the gap that forever separates it from its object, it is about the lacking object; drive, by contrast, takes the lack itself as object, finding a satisfaction in

---

18   I resume here the line of thought from Chapter 11 of Slavoj Žižek, *Less Than Nothing*, London: Verso Books 2012.

the circular movement of missing satisfaction itself. Desire versus drive, masculine and feminine, and other similar couples (up to the duality of waves and particles in physics) form an unsurpassable parallax— the alternative is absolute and unmediated, there is no higher unity or shared ground between the two poles. What one should thus especially avoid is asserting, openly or implicitly, the primacy of one of the sides—to claim, say, that particles ultimately condense or materialize the intersections of waves, or, with regard to Lacan's opposition of the "masculine" All grounded in an exception and the "feminine" non-All, that the dispersed multiplicity of non-All gets totalized into a universal Whole through the exclusion of an exception.[19] Does this not amount, however, to the ultimate form of transcendentalism, positing a limit beyond which we cannot reach? Is there a way to move beyond or, rather, beneath the parallactic couple? The Hegelian wager is that such a move is possible: it is possible to formulate not some shared ground between the two poles but the gap itself, the deadlock that can be formalized in two ways, "masculine" and "feminine," particle and wave, etc.[20]

For Lacan, desire and drive are opposed with regard to their formal structure: desire drifts in an endless metonymy of lack, while drive is a closed circular movement; desire is always unsatisfied, but drive generates its own satisfaction; desire is sustained by the symbolic Law/Prohibition,

---

19   With regard to the parallax of drive and desire, the obvious candidate is the drive, so that desire would emerge as the drive submitted to castration, to the regime of Law and its prohibition, circulating around a lack.

20   The standard model of physics postulates space and time as the two "primitive" features of reality that cannot be reduced to or deduced from some more "primitive" state of things: there is nothing in reality which is not in space and time. However, some ongoing attempts to bring together (and thereby overcome the split between) general relativity theory and quantum physics postulate a state in which there is no time: time emerged out of a kind of "infra-world," so has to be conceptually deduced from a substrate in which there is no time. According to this hypothesis, it should be possible to construct a kind of "thermodynamics of time" in which time appears as the outcome of micro-processes outside temporal coordinates. See Chapter 8 of Etienne Klein, *Le facteur temps ne sonne jamais deux fois*, Paris: Flammarion 2009. (The title—"the time-postman never rings twice"—is of course a play on the title of James Cain's hard-boiled classic *The Postman Always Rings Twice*.) At a pre-scientific level, something similar was proposed already by Schelling who, in his *Weltalter* drafts, imagines a proto-real atemporal dynamics of divine drives— time then emerges when this vortex of drives is "repressed." In short, time emerges to resolve a debilitating deadlock of drives, it is equal to the "repression" of some traumatic X into the primordial past.

while drive remains outside the dialectic of the Law. Desire and drive thus form a parallax unity of mutual exclusion: each is irreducible to the other, there is no shared space within which we can bring them together. In contrast to Lacan, Deleuze asserts the flux of desire, this endless productive movement (logically) prior to the totalizing intervention of the paternal Law, a positive assertion of life prior to all negativity.

Aaron Schuster has proposed a simple and direct solution to this tension between Lacan and Deleuze: what Deleuze calls desire is equivalent to what Lacan calls drive: a machinic productive movement prior to all dialectics of lack and negativity. There is nonetheless a feature which disturbs this equation: Deleuzian desire is open, drifting, expanding, productive, while the Lacanian drive is self-enclosed, repetitive. The point of the Lacanian opposition between desire and drive is that there is an alienating *vel* at work here, a choice to be made: you cannot have it both ways, have both the expanding openness *and* the positive affirmation without any lack or negativity. Paradoxically, it is the prohibitory Law itself which opens up the field, "deterritorializing" the agent, cutting off the roots which constrain it to a particular identity—what the Law prohibits is our incestuous immersion in a particular narrow territory.

The difference between Deleuze and Lacan here is radical, concerning the basic coordinates of the ontological space. Deleuze remains within the paradigmatic modern opposition between production and (the scene of) representation: the basic ontological fact is the productive affirmative process, always in excess with regard to the scene of representation; negativity, lack, etc., enter only afterwards, through the immanent split, self-sabotage, of this process. Lacan's coordinates are wholly different, and the first indication of his difference is his surprising rehabilitation of the notion of representation ("a signifier represents the subject for another signifier"): for Lacan, representation is never a mere screen or scene that mirrors the productive process in a limited and distorted way, it is rather the void or gap that splits the process of life from within, introducing subjectivity and death.

It is, however, at this point that things start to get really interesting, since the parallax split returns in Deleuze's work with a vengeance. Deleuze's conceptual edifice relies on *two* logics which coexist within it, although they are mutually exclusive:

—On the one hand, the logic of sense, of the immaterial becoming as the sense-event, as the *effect* of bodily-material processes-causes, the logic of the radical gap between generative process and its immaterial sense-effect: "multiplicities, being incorporeal effects of material causes, are impassible or causally sterile entities. The time of a pure becoming, always already passed and eternally yet to come, forms the temporal dimension of this impassibility or sterility of multiplicities."[21] And is not cinema the ultimate case of the sterile flow of surface becoming? The cinema image is inherently sterile and impassive, the pure effect of corporeal causes, although nonetheless acquiring its pseudo-autonomy.

—On the other hand, the logic of becoming as the *production* of Beings: "the emergence of metric or extensive properties should be treated as a single process in which a continuous *virtual spacetime* progressively differentiates itself into actual discontinuous spatio-temporal structures."[22]

In his analyses of films and literature, Deleuze emphasizes the desubstantialization of affects: in a work of art, an affect (boredom, for instance) is no longer attributable to actual persons, but becomes a free-floating event. How, then, does this impersonal intensity of an affect-event relate to bodies or persons? Here we encounter the same ambiguity: either this immaterial affect is generated by interacting bodies as a sterile surface of pure Becoming, or it is among those virtual intensities out of which bodies emerge through actualization (the passage from Becoming to Being).[23]

And is not this opposition, yet again, that of materialism versus idealism? In Deleuze, this means: *The Logic of Sense* versus *Anti-Oedipus. Either* the Sense-Event, the flow of pure Becoming, is the immaterial (neutral, neither active nor passive) effect of the intrication of bodily-material causes, *or* the positive bodily entities are themselves the product of the pure flow of Becoming. Either the infinite field of virtuality is an immaterial effect of the interacting bodies, or bodies themselves emerge, actualize themselves, from this field of virtuality. So, on the one hand, Manuel DeLanda, in his excellent *compte-rendu* of Deleuze's ontology, affirms the logic of the "disappearance of process under product," the logic which relies on a long (also Hegelian-Marxist!) tradition of "reification": "This theme of the disguising of process under product is key to Deleuze's philosophy since his

21 Manuel DeLanda, *Intensive Science and Virtual Philosophy*, New York: Continuum 2002, pp. 107–8.

22 Ibid., p. 102.

23 For a more detailed elaboration of this line of thought, see Slavoj Žižek, *Organs Without Bodies*, New York: Routledge 2003.

philosophical method is, at least in part, designed to overcome the objective illusion fostered by this concealment."[24] On the other hand, the proper level of production is also *unambiguously* designated as that of the virtual: in and beneath the constituted reality, "the extensive and qualitative properties of the final product,"[25] one should discover the traces of the intensive process of virtualities—Being and Becoming relate as Actual and Virtual. How, then, are we to combine this unambiguous affirmation of the Virtual as the site of production that generates constituted reality, with the no less unambiguous statement that *"the virtual is produced* out of the actual"?—

> Multiplicities should not be conceived as possessing the capacity to actively interact with one another through these series. Deleuze thinks about them as endowed with only a mere capacity to be affected, since they are, in his words, "impassive entities—impassive results." The neutrality or sterility of multiplicities may be explained in the following way. Although their divergent universality makes them independent of any particular mechanism (the same multiplicity may be actualized by several causal mechanisms) *they do depend on the empirical fact that some causal mechanism or another actually exists* ... Deleuze views multiplicities as *incorporeal effects of corporeal causes*, that is, as historical results of actual causes possessing no causal powers of their own.[26]

And does not this ambiguity of Deleuzian Becoming (as both productive process and sterile effect) bring us back to the Lacanian couple of desire and drive? Is the opposition between the productive flux of desire and the sterility of the event not the Deleuzian parallax, his version of the opposition between desire and drive? It is crucial to note that Hegel lies at the core of this dispute, in particular the two opposite readings of his thought. Along Deleuzian lines (paradoxically, since Deleuze is the ultimate anti-Hegelian) we have the predominant historicist "dynamic" reading of Hegel: reality is a dynamic process of continuous change in the course of which everything solid sooner or later melts away, all static shapes (or "essences") are just frozen moments of this process, which disintegrate after their brief time is over, all negativity and lack are just perspectival illusions generated by the all-encompassing affirmative process of generating differences. The properly Hegelian reply to this vision of the dialectical process begins by rejecting its underlying evolutionary premise: if there is anything absolutely

---

24   DeLanda, *Intensive Science*, p. 73.
25   Ibid., p. 74.
26   Ibid., p. 75.

alien to Hegel, it is the idea that, in the course of historical change, a certain form of life gradually emerges, first in the guise of confused indications, then it reaches maturity, has its moment of glory, and finally follows the way of all living things and passes away. The very core of what we may call the basic Hegelian intuition is that *there never is a "proper" moment*: a form of life is thwarted from the very beginning, it deploys its potentials as a desperate strategy to cope with its immanent deadlock. This is why Hegel emphasized that "*one should not begin with oneness and then pass to duality*"²⁷—why not? Because the One is only constituted through the passage to duality, through its division. This same point was made by Jameson when, apropos *Antigone*, he insisted that the opposition between human law and divine law has to be read

> not as a struggle between the state and the family or clan that tears society apart; but first and foremost as the division which brings society itself into being in the first place by articulating its first great differentiations, that of warrior versus priest, or of city versus clan, or even outside versus inside ... Each of these larval powers brings the other into being and reinforces the distinctiveness of its opposite number ... the contradiction which ultimately tears the polis apart and destroys it ... is the same opposition that brings it into being as a viable structure in the first place.²⁸

Here we can see again the gap that separates Hegel from historicist evolutionism: from the historicist standpoint, every historical figure has its moment of maturity which is then followed by the period of decay. Capitalism, say, was progressive up until the middle of the nineteenth century, when it had to be supported in its struggle against pre-modern forms of life; but with the aggravation of class struggle, capitalism became an obstacle to the further progress of humanity and will have to be overcome in its turn. For a proper dialectician, there is no moment of maturity when a system functions in a non-antagonistic way: paradoxical as it may sound, capitalism was at the same time "progressive" and antagonistic, in decay, and the threat of its decay is the very motor of its "progress" (capitalism has to revolutionize itself constantly to cope with its constitutive "obstacle"). The family and the state are thus not simply the two poles of the social Whole; it is rather that society has to split itself from itself in order to become One—it is this

---

27 G. W. F. Hegel, *Werke*, Frankfurt: Suhrkamp 1986, Band. 19, p. 450; emphasis added.

28 Fredric Jameson, *The Hegel Variations*, London: Verso Books 2010, pp. 82–3.

tearing apart of the social Whole, this division itself, which "brings society itself into being in the first place by articulating its first great differentiations, that of warrior versus priest." It is in this precise sense that one should read Badiou's claim: "The real is not what brings together, but what separates." Even more pointedly, we should add that the real is the separation (antagonistic split) which, as such, brings together a socio-symbolic field. In short, *Antigone* is not a play about the disintegration of the harmonious Greek polis, it is a story about the *constitution* of this polis. The Hegelian reading of *Antigone* as a play dealing with "the emergence of an articulated society as such"[29] thus demonstrates the radically anti-corporatist nature of Hegel's social thought: the underlying premise of this thought is that every social articulation is by definition always "inorganic," antagonistic. The lesson of this insight is that, whenever we read a description of how an original unity gets corrupted and splits, we should remember that we are dealing with a retroactive ideological fantasy that obfuscates the fact that this original unity never existed, that it is a retroactive projection generated by the process of splitting—there never was a harmonious state whose unity was split into warriors and priests.

The Absolute

Those critics of Marxism who point out that there are never just two classes opposed in social life miss the point: as we have seen, it is precisely because there are never just two opposed classes that there is class struggle. There are always third elements (the Jew, the rabble …) that displace the struggle, and these third elements are not just a "complication" of the class struggle, *they are the class struggle*. In short, class struggle is precisely the struggle for hegemony, i.e., for the appropriation of these third elements.

In this precise sense, class struggle should be "absolutized": what makes it absolute is that it is never the direct conflict of the two classes but the very excess which displaces such pure confrontation. What is absolute is this coincidence of the pure antagonistic difference with the excess that blurs the difference—it is as if the pure difference exists as a particular element aside from the differentiated terms. In this element, pure relationality (the form of difference) again coincides with its opposite, a positive element assuming immediate existence. This is why the Hegelian Absolute

---

29   Ibid., p. 80.

should be understood against the background of the key Hegelian notion of *Entschluss*, decision, as the act of ab-solution, of *ent-schliessen*: a totality becomes absolute when a final reversal ab-solves it from its own processuality. This is why, at the end of the *Logic*, the absolute Idea "decides" to externalize itself in Nature, to release Nature from itself, to dis-close itself in Nature. This is also why the term "absolute recoil" (*absoluter Gegenstoss*) has to be read with the accent on "absolute": we reach the absolute standpoint when a process of sublation/mediation of the contingent material stuff in its notional form is supplemented by the fall into its immediate opposite. To return to the case of the State as a totality sublating its own particular elements into moments of a rational Whole: the process can be brought to a conclusion, i.e., the State can establish itself as an actually existing rational totality, only when the process reaches its peak in an additional element in which the sublated natural immediacy returns at its most brutal—in the person of the king whose right to rule is determined by the most stupid natural contingency, the fact of biological descendancy. And the same goes for the absolute recoil: we reach the standpoint of the Absolute when a thing (or process) under consideration immediately coincides with (falls back into) its starting point, when it fully overlaps with its own loss.

This is why the medium of the absolute recoil is the symbolic order: while it holds for every entity that it becomes what it is only through the "recoil" from itself, the symbolic order *is directly this structure of recoiling as such*—in it, a thing becomes what it is by way of disappearing in its sign. If we define literature in the broadest possible sense, as the entire field of explicit or implicit references to any kind of narrative, we can say that there is nothing which is not literature—literature serves as a kind of universal medium, even the most intense and violent political or military struggle is traversed and sustained by references to ideological myths. However, precisely insofar as everything is literature, literature is simultaneously nothing in itself: it is never present "as such," but always already withdrawn, deprived of its purity, traversed and distorted by social and political struggles, economic interests, eroticism, and so on and so forth. It may appear that we can make a similar claim about every domain of social life (is not the economy also universal and simultaneously pervaded by all other spheres—law, ideology, private traumas and interests—so that while there is nothing which is not economic, the "pure" economy does not exist?); however, "literature" (the symbolic sphere of narratives) is unique here since it is not a special sphere like economy or law but a medium structuring the entire field of social life.

It is crucial to take the adjective "absolute" in "absolute recoil" in the strict Hegelian sense, in contrast to the standard view according to which there is no direct access to the Absolute, it can be approached only in recoil, over a distance, as the transcendent X that always eludes our grasp. From the Hegelian standpoint, one need only add that the Absolute *is* nothing but this recoil, the counter-movement that creates that from which it withdraws—*what is "absolute" is this very coincidence between withdrawing-from and creating.* This is also how we should understand the Hegelian notion of the identity of the One, i.e., this is why, for Hegel, identity is a "reflexive determination." Apropos the One, a deconstructionist would deploy endless variations on how it can never fully actualize itself as one, how it is always already traversed by traces of irreducible multiplicity, how the One is always "more than One" (without already becoming Two), supplemented by an additional feature or trace which undermines its Oneness, and so on. The speculative Hegelian reply to such a deconstructive procedure is not that the One is nonetheless the encompassing unity which "mediates" and "sublates" all multiplicity, but a much more radical move: the One is *in itself* a "plus-One" (or, rather, a "One-in-surplus," *le-plus-Un*), a supplementary feature, something that adds itself to what it unifies.

This brings us back to the notion of *den*, Democritus' term for the particles the primordial Void is composed of and whose ontological status is that of "less than nothing." It may seem that *den* signals a key limitation of Hegel's thought, his inability to think the Real. One has to be very precise here since Hegel obviously *can* think the Real in the sense of "lack in the Other" or structural impossibility. This Real is most clearly discernible if we oppose it to the standard notion of the Real as the substantial Thing—recall how Lacan accomplishes a reversal which can be illuminated by the passage from the special to the general theory of relativity in Einstein. While the special theory already introduces the notion of curved space, it conceives of this curvature as the effect of matter: it is the presence of matter which curves space, i.e., only an empty space would be non-curved. With the passage to the general theory, the causality is reversed: far from *causing* the curvature of space, matter is its *effect*, and the presence of matter signals that space is curved. What does this have to do with psychoanalysis? Much more than it may appear: in a way exactly homologous to Einstein, for Lacan, the Real—the Thing—is not so much the inert presence that curves the symbolic space, introducing gaps and inconsistencies into it, but rather an effect of these gaps and inconsistencies. Already, in the development of his theory of trauma, Freud had changed his position in a way strangely homologous to Einstein's above-described shift. He started with the notion of trauma as something that intrudes from outside into our psychic life, disturbing its balance, throwing out of joint the symbolic coordinates that organize our experience (a rape or torture for example). From this perspective, the problem is how to symbolize the trauma, how to integrate it into our universe of meaning and cancel its disorienting impact. Later, Freud opted for the opposite approach. His analysis of the "Wolf Man," his famous Russian patient, isolated as the early traumatic event that marked his life the fact that, aged 18 months, he had witnessed his parents engaged in *coitus a tergo* (in which the man penetrates the woman from behind). At the time the scene took place, however, there was nothing originally traumatic in it: far from shattering the child, he just inscribed it into his memory as an event the sense of which was not at all clear to him. Only years later, when the child became obsessed with the question "where do children come from?" and started to develop infantile sexual theories, did he draw out this memory in order to use it as a traumatic scene embodying the mystery of sexuality. The scene was traumatized, elevated into a traumatic Real, only retroactively, in order to help the child cope with the impasse of his symbolic universe (his inability to find answers to the enigma of sexuality). In an exact homology with Einstein's shift, the original fact here is the symbolic deadlock, and the traumatic event is resuscitated to fill in the gaps in the universe of meaning.

Does not exactly the same hold for the Real of a social antagonism? Anti-Semitism "reifies" (embodies in a particular group) the inherent social antagonism: it treats Jewishness as the Thing which, from outside, intrudes into the social body and disturbs its balance. What happens in the passage from the position of strict class struggle to fascist anti-Semitism is not just a simple replacement of one figure of the enemy (the bourgeoisie, the ruling class) with another (the Jews); the logic of the struggle is totally different. In the class struggle, the classes themselves are caught up in the antagonism which is inherent to the social structure, while in anti-Semitism the Jew is conceived as a foreign intruder that causes the social antagonism, so that all we need to do in order to restore social harmony is annihilate the Jews. That is to say, in exactly the same way that the Wolf Man as a child resuscitated the scene of parental coitus in order to organize his infantile sexual theories, a fascist anti-Semite elevates the Jew into the monstrous Thing that causes social decadence.

So far so good, we may say: Hegel not only carries out this Einsteinian "curved space reversal," he practices it again and again. The problem is:

is the Real *only* (or, rather, *nothing but*) the inconsistency and/or uncon-
sciousness (*ics*) of appearances, the gap of appearances, their immanent
impossibility, or is it something more? To put it in an even more direct way:
can the Real qua Thing be fully dissolved into the ics of symbolic semblances?
What we stumble upon here is the limit of the standard critique of fetish-
ism, of the approach that reduces the Thing to the fetishized effect of an
inner deadlock. Lacan struggled for years with the passage from "there is
no (sexual) relationship" to "there is a non-relationship": he was repeatedly
trying "to *give body* to the difference, to isolate the non-relationship as an
indispensable ingredient of the constitution of the subject."[30] When Lacan
opposes the One, he targets two of its modalities, the imaginary One (of the
specular fusion into One-ness) and the symbolic One (which is reductive,
concerning the unary feature—*le trait unaire*—to which an object is reduced
in its symbolic registration; this one is the One of differential articulation,
not of fusion). The question is: is there also a One which would be that of
the Real? Is this not the role played by *Y a d'l'Un* in Lacan's *Encore*, which is
a One prior to the differential articulation of the big Other, a non-delimited
but nonetheless particular One, a One which is neither qualitatively nor
quantitatively determined, a "there is something of the One" designating a
minimal contraction, a condensation, of the libidinal flow?

---

30   Guy le Gaufey, *Le Pastout de Lacan*, Paris: EPEL 2006, p. 151.

CHAPTER 9

From Here to *Den*

Eric Frank Russell's short science-fiction story "The Sole Solution" begins with the confused ramblings of a solitary old man:

> *He brooded in darkness and there was no one else. Not a voice, not a whisper. Not the touch of a hand. Not the warmth of another heart. Darkness. Solitude. Eternal confinement where all was black and silent and nothing stirred. Imprisonment without prior condemnation. Punishment without sin. The unbearable that had to be borne unless some mode of escape could be devised. No hope of rescue from elsewhere. No sorrow or sympathy or pity in another soul, another mind.*

The old man then starts to dream about a solution:

> *The easiest escape is via the imagination. One hangs in a strait-jacket and flees the corporeal trap by adventuring in a dreamland of one's own. But dreams are not enough. They are unreal and all too brief. The freedom to be gained must be genuine and of long duration. That meant he must make a stern reality of dreams, a reality so contrived that it would persist for all time.*

After the long hard work of planning all the details, the time then comes to act:

> *The time was now. The experiment must begin.*
> *Leaning forward, he gazed into the dark and said, "Let there be light."*
> *And there was light.*

Here we get the ultimate *point de capiton* ("quilting-point"): the last lines retroactively make it clear that the ramblings of the old man are the thoughts of God Himself just prior to the act of Creation. The beauty of this final reversal is that it inverts the more obvious version, which would be to present the divine thought processes as nothing more than the delusional ramblings of a madman who thinks he is God. For a philosopher, the denouement of the story comes as no surprise: that the beginning is not at the beginning is the first lesson of the fragment from Schelling's *Ages of the World* in which he focuses precisely on what goes on *before* the beginning. The beginning of all beginnings is, of course, "In the beginning was the Word" from the Gospel of John; prior to it, there was nothing, that is, the void of divine eternity. According to Schelling, however, eternity is not a nondescript mass—much takes place in it. Prior to the Word, there is the chaotic-psychotic universe of blind drives, in their rotary motion, with their undifferentiated pulsating; and the Beginning occurs when the Word is pronounced which represses, rejects into the eternal Past, this self-enclosed circuit of drives. In short, at the Beginning proper stands a Resolution, an act of Decision which, by differentiating between past and present, resolves the preceding unbearable tension of the rotary motion of drives. The true Beginning is the passage from the "closed" rotary motion to "open" progress, from drive to desire—or, in Lacanian terms, from the Real to the symbolic.[1]

As all the really perspicuous Gnostics and mystics knew very well, there is something missing in this narrative: one cannot pass directly from the confused and blind rotary motion to the act of creation—something has to occur in between, the formless primordial abyss has to be reduced to pure Nothingness. One has thus to distinguish between the Nothingness of the primordial abyss (the impersonal "Godhead," not yet God proper but what is in God more than God Himself) and the Nothingness of the primordial gesture of contraction (what Schelling called *Zusammenziehung*), the gesture of supreme egoism, of withdrawing from reality and reducing oneself to the punctuality of Self. (In the mystical tradition, it was Jacob Böhme who took this crucial step forward.) This withdrawal-into-the-self is the primordial form of Evil, and there is a necessity in this shift from Nothingness as the abyss of the Godhead to Nothingness as the void of the Self, the necessity of the passage from potentiality to actuality: *the divine void is a pure potentiality which can actualize itself only in the guise of the punctuality of Evil*—and giving birth to the Son-Word is the way to move beyond this Evil.[2]

---

1   For a more detailed account of this topic, see the first part of Slavoj Žižek, *The Indivisible Remainder*, London: Verso Books 2007.

2   The Kabbala was also aware of this with its claim that, prior to creating the world, God has to create nothingness itself, the void to be filled in by creation; what comes before creation is thus the divine self-contraction.

This line of reasoning may appear to be totally foreign to Hegel: there seems to be no place for the pre-conceptual chaos in Hegel—his system begins with Being as the first and emptiest pure concept. But is this really the case? Hegel's first words at the beginning proper of his *Science of Logic* (First Chapter, A., Being) are: "Being, pure being—without any further determination" (*"Sein, reines Sein,—ohne alle weitere Bestimmung"*). The paradox is, of course, that this negative qualification, "without any further determination," adds the key feature, the minimal idealization. One should therefore read this repetition in a Wittgensteinian way, like a phrase which echoes everyday statements of the type "What made you do it?" "Duty, pure duty." Is this not the first Hegelian repetition, a repetition which introduces a minimal idealization? It is not the repetition of the same, since, through it, the pre-ontological X achieves its ideal purity. In short, what happens in this minimal repetition is that we pass from something that one can only designate as "less than nothing" to Nothing. The first being is not yet pure being which coincides with its opposite, but a pre-ontological "less than nothing" whose name in Democritus is *den*; through the primordial repetition, this (proto-)being is placed into the purity (the empty space) of Nothing and thus becomes something.[3]

BETWEEN *DEN* AND *CLINAMEN*

It is not only with Plato that metaphysics and idealism emerge: the battle between idealism and materialism was already being fought out in pre-Socratic thought, as best exemplified by the opposition between Parmenides and Democritus. Parmenides stands for what Meillassoux would call *ur*-correlationism: being and thinking (*logos*) are correlated as the same; furthermore, only being exists, while non-being does not exist. For Democritus, on the contrary, non-being exists no less than being, it is inherent to being as its original split. Heidegger was thus right, although in the wrong sense: yes, pre-Socratic thought was pre-metaphysical, but not that of Parmenides, only the line that begins with Democritus. The history of philosophy is this struggle of the two lines, the Parmenidean versus the Democritean.

To express this "less than nothing," Democritus had recourse to the wonderful neologism *den* (first coined by the sixth-century BC poet Alcaeus), so

---

3   See Frank Ruda's outstanding "Dialectics, Contradiction, Iteration. Thinking by Dividing" (manuscript, 2012).

the basic axiom of his ontology became: "Nothing is no less than Othing," or, as the German translation goes, *"Das Nichts existiert ebenso sehr wie das Ichts."* This translation probably relies on Meister Eckhart, who already coined *"Ichts"* as a positive version of *"Nichts,"* i.e., the void in its positive/ generating dimension—the *nihil* out of which every creation proceeds. What Eckhart saw was the link between the subject (I, *Ich*) and negativity. It is crucial to note how, *contra* the late Wittgensteinian move towards ordinary language as part of a life world, materialism begins with a violation of the rules of ordinary language, by thinking against language.[4]

According to philosophical common sense, with his notion of the *clinamen*, Epicurus radicalized Democritus: in Democritus, atoms are Ones floating in empty space, while the Epicurean notion of the *clinamen* is the first philosophical model of the idea that an entity only is insofar as it "comes too late" with regard to itself, to its own identity: it is not that there are first atoms, which then deviate from their straight path (or not)—atoms are nothing but their *clinamen*. There is no substantial "something" prior to the *clinamen* that gets caught up in it; this "something" which deviates is created, emerges, through the *clinamen itself*. The *clinamen* is thus like the photon with no mass: we imagine an ordinary particle (if there is such a thing) as an object with mass, such that when its movement is accelerated its mass grows; a photon, however, has no mass in itself, its entire mass is the result of its acceleration. The paradox here is the paradox of a thing which is always (and nothing but) an excess with regard to itself: in its "normal" state, it is nothing. This brings us back to Lacan's notion of the *objet a* as surplus-enjoyment: there is no "basic enjoyment" to which one adds surplus-enjoyment; enjoyment is always a surplus, in excess. The object-in-itself (photon, atom) is here not negated/mediated, it *emerges as the (retroactive) result of its mediation.*

This retroactivity, the idea that a thing is nothing but its own deviation or excess, can be read in two ways, Deleuzian and Lacanian. In the Deleuzian reading of Spinoza, Substance is nothing but the constant process of "falling" (into its determinate, particular modes); everything there is is a fall (if we are permitted to read the famous proposition from Wittgenstein's *Tractatus—Die Welt ist alles, was der Fall ist*—more literally than he meant it, discerning in *der Fall* also the meaning "fall"). There is no Substance which falls, curves, interrupts the flow, etc.; Substance simply *is*

---

4   For a more detailed account of *den*, see Chapter 1 of Slavoj Žižek, *Less Than Nothimg*, London: Verso Books 2012.

the infinitely productive capacity of such falls, they are its only reality. On such a reading of Spinoza, Substance and the *clinamen* (the curvature of the Substance which generates determinate entities) directly coincide; in this ultimate speculative identity, Substance is nothing but the process of its own "fall," the negativity that pushes it towards productive determination. The difference between Spinoza and Hegel is crucial here: while for Spinoza Substance remains a stable and peaceful immanent frame of the incessant movement of its modes, a frame that can be envisaged in a blissful intuition, for Hegel, the Substance that engenders its modes is in itself antagonistic, "barred," marked by an irreducible inner tension—it is this immanent "contradiction" that pushes the Substance towards the continuous generation of its particular modes. In short, the move from Spinoza to Hegel is the move from S to $, from Substance to Subject.

Is such a clinamenesque move not signaled by the *ver* that occurs in a whole series of Freud's concepts: *Verdrängung* (repression), *Verdichtung* (condensation), *Verschiebung* (displacement), *Verneinung* (negation), *Verwerfung* (foreclosure) …, all of which are to be opposed to direct negation (*nein*)? In contrast to the basic Hegelian move of radicalized (self-relating) negation, Freud's *ver* indicates a different move: a conflict is not resolved when the self-contradiction is brought to an extreme and thus, with its self-cancellation, a new dimension emerges; on the contrary, the conflict is not resolved at all, the "contradiction" is not brought to a climax, but is rather stalled, brought to a temporary stasis in the guise of a compromise formation. This compromise is not the "unity of the opposites" in the Hegelian sense of the "negation of negation," but a ridiculously *failed* negation, a negation that is hindered, derailed, distorted, twisted, sidetracked.[5] The Freudian event (*Ereignis*) could thus be named *Vereignis*, an event of derailment/detraction—or, maybe, the zero level of *ver* is *verfangen*: to become caught up or entangled in something. In this sense, perhaps *ver* renders the minimal form of the drive: getting entangled/caught.[6] The (death) drive is thus not a destructive force of negativity that needs to be bound or constrained, because in its unbounded state it threatens to swallow all positive shapes into its abyss; the (death) drive is rather *this bounding itself in its minimal form*, this minimal "clinamenization." The

---

5   I owe this point to Mladen Dolar.

6   *Verfangen*: entanglement. *Sich verfangen*: to get entangled, to entangle, to be caught, to catch something, like a disease, to get/become entangled. *Sich in etwas verfangen*: to get caught up in something. *Sich in der eigenen Schlinge verfangen*: to be/get caught in one's own trap.

drive is on the side of *ver*, not on the side of *nein* (no). And is not the disturbed equilibrium, the broken symmetry, of which quantum physics speaks, and through which particular reality emerges out of a vacuum, also a version of the *ver*?[7]

There is a long tradition of dismissive argumentation against Lucretius' *clinamen*, from Cicero's claim that chance without cause is sheer nonsense, up to Einstein's famous quip about quantum physics, "God doesn't play dice." Why such resistance to this notion? The *clinamen* designates a deviation *from* (a straight path), a partial aspect *of* (or less than a full) X, etc., and things get interesting when we ask: what if this X is nothing? Can we think of the *clinamen* as primordial, so that there is nothing that precedes it, and the mirage of a fully existing thing is a retroactive effect of the thing's deviation from its identity? There are, along these lines, two possible readings of the *clinamen* which follow Lacan's formulae of sexuation:

—The masculine version: the *clinamen* as exception—there is a pre-existing substantial reality of Ones, and the *clinamen* designates secondary deviations from it, exceptions from the norm.[8]

—The feminine version: the universalized *clinamen*—there is an irreducible plurality of twists, turns, folds, nonlinearities, inconsistencies, deviations, exceptions, etc., but since there is nothing else, no exception to exception, no positive reality from which the exceptions deviate, this crazy multiple reality gets normalized, losing its tension, so that we end up in a Deleuzian ontology of the One out of which, without any mediation of negativity, the multiplicity of deviations continuously flows.

This couple, however, does not exhaust all the possibilities: there is another, more properly Lacanian, feminine version in which the *clinamen* is not

---

7   Another *ver* should be added to the Freudian series, the *ver* of what, following Freud, Lacan calls *Versagung*: the radical (self-relating) loss/renunciation of the fantasmatic core of the subject's being: first, I sacrifice all I have for the Cause-Thing which is for me more than my life; what I then get in exchange for this sacrifice is *the loss of this Cause-Thing itself*. Lacan provided a detailed interpretation of Claudel's *L'otage* in his Seminar VIII on transference (*Le séminaire, livre VIII: Le transfert*, Paris: Seuil 1982); see also my reading of *Versagung* in Chapter 2 of *The Indivisible Remainder*.

8   One should add here Badiou's version which inverts Deleuze's postmodern universalization of the *clinamen*: for Badiou, the Event-*clinamen* is singular, a singular excess which interrupts the series of positive causal links in the order of Being.

opposed to radical self-relating negativity, but designates its very existence. In this way, we can avoid the Deleuzian One of generative substance: *clinamens* multiply against the background of the blocked/impossible One. This is also how we should read "in defence of lost causes," inclusive of the political sense of the term: it is not "*Ablata causa tollitur effectus*," but the other way round—like the mice who play freely when the cat's away, effects proliferate when their cause is lost. This is why, for Lacan, the Real Cause is the absent/lost Cause: when the One is barred, *dens* multiply.

Far from belonging to the curiosities of the history of philosophy, the topic of the *clinamen* thus brings us to *the* question that quantum cosmology is tackling today: why is there something and not nothing? Science offers here two models: the Big Bang and symmetry breaking, both of which refer to a kind of clinamenesque disturbance or Fall. It is not that, prior to our fully constituted reality, there is a pre-Fall non-All proto-reality wherein multiple virtualities happily coexist in their superpositions, and this plural paradise is then ruined by the Fall into a single reality—the proto-reality is in itself barred, thwarted, so that the Fall has always already taken place.

Big Bang theory, currently the predominant theory of the origin of the universe, claims that (our) universe began from an initial point or singularity which has expanded over billions of years to form the universe as we now know it. Singularity refers to a point or region in space-time in which gravitational forces cause matter to have an infinite density, so that the laws of physics are suspended. This suspension of the laws as the key feature of a singularity allows us to use the term in other contexts—Ray Kurzweil, for example, defined the Technological Singularity as

> a future period during which the pace of technological change will be so rapid, its impact so deep, that human life will be irreversibly transformed. Although neither utopian nor dystopian, this epoch will transform the concepts that we rely on to give meaning to our lives, from our business models to the cycle of human life, including death itself.[9]

For understandable reasons, Catholics see the Big Bang as providing an opening for God: the suspension of the laws of nature at the point of singularity means that this event is not natural, indicating a direct supernatural intervention—singularity is thus the scientific name for the moment of

---

9   Ray Kurzweil, *The Singularity Is Near*, New York: Penguin Books 2006, p. 9.

creation (Catholics like to point out that the "father of Big Bang Theory" was Father Georges Lemaître, a Catholic priest from Belgium, who proposed its first formulation in 1933). What complicates this picture, however, is the collapse of a field into the singularity of a Black Hole, which is a kind of counter-movement to the Big Bang, so that we can imagine a plurality of Big Bangs and Black Holes, with a Big Bang as the obverse of a Black Hole (what disappears in a Black Hole reappears in a different universe through a Big Bang). Such a repetitive rhythm suggests a materialist perspective for the Big Bang.

Philosophically much more interesting is the notion of broken symmetry, since it explains how something can emerge out of nothing by way of redefining nothingness itself.[10] The vacuum state or the quantum vacuum is not some absolutely empty void—it contains fleeting electromagnetic waves and particles that pop into and out of existence. When these (infinitesimally) small fluctuations act on a system that is crossing a critical point, they decide the system's fate by determining which branch of a bifurcation it will take; to an outside observer unaware of the fluctuations (or "noise"), the choice will appear arbitrary. The process is called symmetry breaking because such a transition takes the system from a homogenous disorderly state into one of two definite states. The best-known physical example is a ball balanced on a (symmetrical) hill: an imperceptibly small disturbance of the ball's position will cause it to quickly roll down the hill into its lowest energy state, so that a perfectly symmetrical situation will collapse into an asymmetrical state. The key point is that this collapse is genuinely contingent: it is not that the causes are so tiny that we cannot perceive them; much more radically, the fluctuations take place at the level of not-fully-existing (pre-ontological) virtual entities which are in a way "less than nothing," like Democritus' *den*.[11]

---

10   It is interesting to note the gap that separates the event as Fall (broken symmetry, disturbed balance) and the Badiouian event as a break in the normal flow of things (a love encounter, a scientific discovery, etc.). The key asymmetry between the two is that the Fall breaks with (disturbs) the Void and thereby creates the "normal run of life," while the Badiouian Event breaks with this normal flow of things itself. One should nonetheless note that a love event is also a kind of Fall—falling in love—something that traumatically disturbs the emptiness of our previous existence.

11   Furthermore, we should note the fundamental asymmetry between the two events, the Big Bang and the breaking of symmetry: the Big Bang is the explosion of an infinitely compressed singularity, while broken symmetry involves the collapse of an infinite field of potentialities into a determined finite reality. The two events can be opposed in many ways: relativity theory (within which the notion of the Big

The step from Democritus to Epicurus, from *den* to *clinamen*, thus involves a minimal of "Aristotelianization": in its notional structure, the *clinamen* already functions as a deviation from the presupposed atom as the One (a substance with weight, etc.), i.e., *den* becomes *clinamen* when the atom is "Aristotelianized" into the substantial One, in clear contrast to the Democritean atom which is not yet One but *den*, "less than nothing." Is the solution then to imagine a *clinamen without* the presupposed substantial One, an excess/deviation which is excessive with regard to *nothing*? Then the primordial move is not the subtraction from Nothing through which less than nothing (*den*) emerges, but the minimal repetition through which Nothingness itself emerges out of *den*. Or: the primordial triad of negation is not Something-Nothing-*den*—which already presupposes Something as given—but *den*-Nothing-Something. At the beginning, *y a de den*. (The "One" in Lacan's *Y a d'l'Un* is not the pure signifier, the signifying One, but the "less than nothing," the minimal stain of *den*.) If we read in this way Hegel's *Sein, reines Sein*, we can formulate a reply to the standard reproach to Hegel (first formulated by Schelling) that the Hegelian passage from Being-Nothing to (Becoming and) Something is a fake, a sophism, since we pass from the mere logical coincidence of pure Being and Nothing to actual Becoming and Something—where does the surplus of actual contingent existence come from? The Hegelian answer: it comes from the pre-ontological density of *den*, of what is less than nothing—all that was erased in the passage from first to second (pure) Being as it were provides the stuff. On the other side, there is no *den* without Nothing (Void), Nothing is the "barred" One of "absolute contradiction" which is the background of the proliferation of *den(s)*.

What this means is that we should move beyond the topic of the Fall, of how Something emerges out of Nothing (through disturbed symmetry, etc.). It is not enough to claim that the Fall always already took place, that Nothing is just a retroactive presupposition of clinamenesque deviations; one has to move back from the *clinamen* to *den*, from a Something which emerges as the deviation from Nothing to less than Nothing. This move can also be formulated as a weird version of the "negation of the negation." We begin with a Something and its effects/shadows/distortions, and this topic can be deployed in its full range of dialectical mediations (a Something

---

Bang emerged) versus quantum cosmology, idealism versus materialism, even—why not?—masculine (the logic of universality grounded in an exception) versus feminine (a non-All field of potentialities).

deploys its potential through its deviations, these deviations comprise its entire wealth, so that a Something is the unity of itself and its deviations). The first negation of this starting point is the radicalized version of the *clinamen*: there are no atoms/Ones which then deviate, something only is in its distortions. This same paradox is exemplified by the Lacanian *objet a* whose status is that of an anamorphosis: a part of a picture which, when the picture is viewed in a direct frontal way, appears as a meaningless stain, but which acquires the contours of a known object when we change our position and look at the picture from the side. Lacan's point is even more radical: the object-cause of desire is something that, when viewed frontally, is nothing at all, just a void—it acquires the contours of something only when viewed sideways. One of the most beautiful cases in literature occurs when, in Shakespeare's *Richard II* (Act 2, Scene 2), Bushy tries to comfort the Queen, worried about the unfortunate King on a military campaign:

> Each substance of a grief hath twenty shadows,
> Which shows like grief itself, but is not so;
> For sorrow's eye, glazed with blinding tears,
> Divides one thing entire to many objects;
> Like perspectives, which rightly gazed upon
> Show nothing but confusion, eyed awry
> Distinguish form: so your sweet majesty,
> Looking awry upon your lord's departure,
> Find shapes of grief, more than himself, to wail;
> Which, look'd on as it is, is nought but shadows
> Of what it is not.

This is the *objet a*: an entity that has no substantial consistency, which is in itself "nothing but confusion," and which acquires a definite shape only when looked upon from a standpoint distorted by the subject's desires and fears—as such, as a mere "shadow of what it is not." As such, the *objet a* is the strange object which is nothing but the inscription of the subject itself into the field of objects, in the guise of a stain which acquires form only when part of this field is anamorphically distorted by the subject's desire.

Here, however, one should imagine a further step, the "negation of the negation": not only an object which is a shadow of nothing, a spectral appearance with no substance beneath or behind it, but an object which is less than nothing, an object which has to be *added* to a state of things so that we get nothing. Theosophical speculations focus on the idea that, at the very beginning (or, more precisely, *before* the beginning), there is nothing, the void of pure potentiality, the will which wants nothing, the divine abyss prior to God, and this void is then inexplicably disturbed, lost. The materialist solution to this enigma is very precise, and concerns the key paradox of the Higgs field in quantum physics: like every field, the Higgs field is characterized by its energy density and by its strength—however, "it is energetically favorable for the Higgs field to be switched on and for the symmetries between particles and forces to be broken."[12] In short, when we have the pure vacuum (with the Higgs field switched off, inoperative), the Higgs field has to spend some energy—nothing does not come for free, it is not the zero-point at which the universe is just "resting in itself" in a state of total release—nothing has to be sustained by an investment of energy, i.e., energetically, it costs something to maintain the nothing (the void of the pure vacuum).

This paradox compels us to introduce the distinction between two vacuums: first, there is the "false" vacuum in which the Higgs field is switched off, in which there is pure symmetry with no differentiated particles or forces—this vacuum is "false" because it can only be sustained by a certain amount of energy expenditure. Then, there is the "true" vacuum in which, although the Higgs field is switched on and the symmetry is broken, there is a certain differentiation of particles and forces, the amount of energy spent is zero, i.e., energetically, the Higgs field is in the state of inactivity, of absolute repose.[13] At the beginning, there is the false vacuum; this vacuum is disturbed and the symmetry is broken because, like every energetic system, the Higgs field tends towards the minimization of its energy expenditure. This is why "there is something and not nothing": because, energetically, *something is cheaper than nothing*. We are here back at the notion of *den* in Democritus: a "something cheaper than nothing," a weird pre-ontological "something" which is less than nothing.

As we have already seen, it is thus crucial to distinguish between the two Nothings: the Nothing of the pre-ontological *den*, of "less than nothings," and the Nothing posited as such, as direct negation—in order for Something to emerge, the pre-ontological Nothing has to be negated, i.e., it has to be posited as a direct/explicit emptiness, and it is only within

---

12   Paul J. Steinhardt and Neil Turok, *Endless Universe: Beyond the Big Bang*, London: Phoenix 2008, p. 82.

13   Ibid., p. 92.

this emptiness that Something can emerge, that there can be "Something instead of Nothing." The first act of creation is thus the emptying of the space, the creation of Nothing (or, in Freudian terms, the death drive and creative sublimation are intricately linked).

Perhaps this gives us a minimal definition of materialism: the irreducible distance between the two vacuums. And this is why even Buddhism remains "idealist": the two vacuums are there confused in the notion of nirvana. This is also what Freud did not grasp quite clearly, sometimes confounding the death drive with the "nirvana-principle," i.e., missing the core of his notion of the death drive as the "undead" obscene immortality of a repetition which insists beyond life and death: nirvana as the return to a pre-organic peace is a "false" vacuum, since it costs more than the circular movement of the drive. Within the domain of the drive, the same gap appears in the guise of the difference between the *goal* and the *aim* of a drive, as elaborated by Lacan: the drive's goal—to reach its object—is "false," it masks its "true" aim, which is to reproduce its own circular movement by way of repeatedly missing its object. If the fantasized unity with the object brings about full/impossible incestuous *jouissance*, the drive's repeated missing of its object does not simply compel us to be satisfied with a lesser enjoyment, but generates a surplus-enjoyment of its own, the *plus-de-jouir*. The paradox of the death drive is thus strictly homologous to that of the Higgs field: from the standpoint of libidinal economy, it is "cheaper" for the system to repeatedly traverse the circle of the drive than to stay at absolute rest.[14]

DEN AND THE ONE

How, exactly, is *den* related to One? The question is: are the One (the signifying feature/trace) and *den*, S and *a*, the original *unhintergehbares* couple? Or is this only the masculine version, so that we should also posit a feminine version in which there is a "primordial" *den* not yet accompanied by the One? In other words, can we think beyond the signifying cut (One) plus its remainder/excess? If we do not think this, do we not remain within the transcendental horizon of the symbolic order as the ultimate horizon of our thinking? Insofar as *den* is subtracted from Nothing, is this Nothing

---

14   I resume here the line of thought fully deployed in Chapter 14 of Žižek, *Less Than Nothing.*

already the result of the negation of the One, so that *den* emerges out of a weird non-Hegelian "negation of the negation," or does it precede the One?

It is crucial to note that this nothing is not external to something (like the empty space between Ones-Atoms in the primitive notion of atomism) but immanent to it: it is a nothing which makes the One in itself incomplete, partial, non-All—and this void is filled by the fantasy object, the *objet a*, or, in Stoicism, by the immaterial *lekta*, "sayables," or by other fillers of the void, forms of non-being—the *objet a* is a "positivized negativity." This holds even for the Cartesian *cogito*, which relates to *res cogitans* in the same way, as a purely evental non-being relates to substantial being; the move from *cogito* to *res cogitans* thus turns around the Hegelian move from substance to subject—with *res cogitans*, subject becomes substance. Is the *clinamen* then the fall/deviation from the One in the same way that the Subject is the fall/deviation from Substance, its self-division? It is crucial to clarify the difference between these multiple levels: the pure self-relating negativity of the Void (the thwarted/barred One); the multiplicity of *den*, of "less than nothings" which dwell in (and, in a way, *are*) this Void; the *objet a* as the excess/remainder over the signifying One. Is it then that *den* becomes the *objet a* when the One emerges, so that *a* is *den* under the condition of the One, what remains of *den* within the regime of the One, the excess that cannot be reduced to the One? Or can we think an *a* prior to the One?

As Heinz Wismann put it concisely: "being is a privative state of non-being," i.e., being emerges as *othing*, by way of subtracting something from nothing. We are here back at the key critical question about subtraction: is the subtractive movement beyond the reach of an Hegelian approach, or can it still be conceived as a form of the Hegelian negation of the negation? Even those who (beginning with Lacan) emphasize Hegel's limitation at this point, continue to use the term "negation of the negation," usually qualifying it with predicates like "weird." Their main argument is that subtraction clearly does not fit the Hegelian logic of negating the positive starting point and then returning to it at a higher level: there is no higher synthesis in subtraction, just a weird negation which does not go all the way—when we negate nothing, we get the Democritean "othing." But does the Hegelian process really stand for the higher "mediated" return to the starting position? Does not Hegel *begin* with Nothing, so that the process unfolds "from nothing through nothing to nothing," as Hegel put it in his *Logic*? Consequently, Democritus' atom *qua den* and Epicurus' *clinamen* do not form a couple, they do not dwell within the same conceptual space: for the Epicurean *clinamen* to emerge, the atom must already be the Aristotelian

One. Could we then risk the hypothesis that *den* is a *clinamen* of *nothing*, i.e., that we arrive at *den* when we try to think the *clinamen* as a deviation without any positive entity from which it deviates? We are here back at the topic of the "undead," the outcome of the Kantian "infinite judgment": are the undead not like *den*, a spectral entity which is neither not something nor nothing, but also not between something and nothing—it is rather *less* than nothing, like an image in the mirror with no original in reality.

Do we encounter here a kind of primordial parallax, in other words, is the duality of atom/void and the *clinamen* irreducible, so that there is no way to reach behind or beneath it? And does not the same hold for the duality of the One and *den*? We should nonetheless add that if the split between the One and *den* is, as one says in German, *das Unhintergehbare*, the ultimate unsurpassable horizon of our thinking, then the One (the signifying trace) nonetheless enjoys priority, i.e., we are always already within the symbolic: *den* is the result, not the beginning; it is, in exact homology to the *objet a* as the result of the double operation of alienation-separation, the result of a weird negation of the negation (the negation of being which gives nothing, and then the subtraction from nothing itself). However, is it enough to conceive *den* as an outcome of a previous double operation, and in this sense dependent on the signifying One? Does not Democritus already begin with a multiplicity of *den*? So how are we to think a *den* which is prior to the signifying One? The key is provided by the weird status of the *objet a*.

As we have just stated, the *objet a*—the embodiment of Nothing—is the result of double negation, its outcome/remainder: first the subject's alienation (in the Other), then the subject's separation—not dis-alienation, not the subject's reappropriation of the Other, but the separation of/in the Other itself from its Other, so that the subject's alienation from the Other is transposed into the Other itself, as its self-alienation. The *objet a* is as such primarily not the lost object of the subject, what the subject lacks, but that which the Other itself lacks, that which *subtracts itself from the Other*. In an homologous way, *den* is the result of a double negation, the negation of 1 which results in zero plus the subtraction from zero which results in *den*. It is, however, crucial not to stop here: we should also invert this operation, otherwise we get stuck in a kind of theology of the symbolic which appears from nowhere: the symbolic alienation is not the beginning, something has to be there before, the remainder—*den*—must be already a starting point, as it is for Democritus for whom *den* is the name of the indivisible atom.

In what precise sense is the atom indivisible? Gilbert Ryle once played with the idea that the only way to bring to an end the Zeno-like interminable division of an entity into smaller and smaller parts would be to reach the point of the "last division," the point at which One no longer divides into two positive parts, but into *a part and nothingness*. Therein resides the paradox of the atom: it cannot be divided (into two somethings) because it is the something of the last division between something and nothing. Hegel saw this clearly: atoms are not Ones floating in the empty space-void, negativity is immanent to them, in their very core—is this nonsense? It is if we conceive the atom as more than nothing and less than One; it is not if we make the atom *less* than nothing, not something between 0 and 1—*something has to be added to the atom not to make it One but to make it Nothing*.

This zero-level of *den* is, however, not simply previous to the One—Lacan differs here from Deleuze as well as from Badiou, all three deploying different versions of the relationship between multiplicity and the One. For Badiou, the primary fact is the multiplicity of multiplicities and the One comes after, through counting-as-One; for Deleuze, the productive-immanent One of the Life flux immanently generates multiplicity; for Lacan, multiplicity emerges against the background of minus One—in short, the absence/failure of One is immanent to multiplicity, it is its determining absence, i.e., there is multiplicity *because* the One is barred by its immanent impossibility. Or, to put it in more speculative Hegelian terms: the One arises as the effect of its own impossibility (like the subject which is the result of its own failure to become a subject). In Berlin, you can order beer "*mit ohne*," "with without" (or just with-out!), to distinguish it from beers flavored with different fruit extracts ("*Berliner Weiss*," white, which can be green or red ...). So, insofar as "white" is the neutral color, it is this non-existing "white" that has three species: *rot*, *grün*, and *ohne*—red, green, and without (in the same way that the empty set is an element of every set, or the proletarians are "*mit ohne*" in society, since their proper place is no place). The primordial state is thus not a simple innumerable and inconsistent multiplicity, but a multiplicity with/out One, marked by an immanent obstacle which prevents it becoming One.[15] One lacks, it is "one less," and this lack is in itself a positive fact, it triggers repetition/drive. It is precisely because the One is lacking that the ics multiplicity appears to itself, re-presents itself.

---

15   For this line of thought, I am deeply indebted to Alenka Zupančič.

The unrepresentable, un-countable "floating excess" (the rabble etc.) is not directly the Real, but a symptom of the Real—a symptom of something that does not exist but can only be constructed as a virtual point of reference, as the pure antagonism. The floating excess is the symptom of the antagonism/the Real. One has thus to drop the whole metaphor of marginal excesses resisting and fighting the Center embodied in the Master-Signifier: the true struggle is the antagonism that cuts from within the field. The original excess is therefore the Master-Signifier itself which emerges to contain the antagonism. (In the case of social life, it is not the marginal against the state: the state itself emerges to contain the antagonism—"class struggle"— in the heart of the social body.)

The first move of a radical emancipatory act is thus not one of identification with the marginal excess—pathetic solidary identification with the symptom, its elevation into a new universality ("we are all rabble," "we are all Jews," "we are all in Gaza," etc.)—but the formalization of the underlying antagonism in a new signifier (S of $\cancel{A}$). In Lacan's terms, to see an element "in its becoming" would be to see S_1, the Master-Signifier, in its dimension of $S(\cancel{A})$, as the signifier of the Other's inconsistency. As Spinoza would have put it, it is to see the notion of "God" as the positive form of our very ignorance. Or, in social life, it is to see how class struggle/ antagonism, the condition of (im)possibility, the obstacle to unity, the not-One, makes the One possible. But how are we to think together the two elementary structures, that of *den* ("less than nothing") and that of an antagonism beyond the transcendental, i.e., of the twisted space of the subjectivization of substance in which it is our very distance from the Thing that includes us in it? Is the solution to conceive the *objet a* as the subject's fossil, as an entity which is simultaneously *den* and the mode of the inscription of the subject into the Real?

FROM ISR TO A, S($\cancel{A}$), $

To clarify this crucial point, let us begin with the Lacanian triangle of Imaginary-Symbolic-Real (ISR), a triad which is far from exclusively Lacanian. Another version of it was proposed by none other than Karl Popper in his theory of the Third World.[16] Popper came to see that the usual classification of phenomena into external material reality (from

---

16 See Karl Popper, *Objective Knowledge*, Oxford: Oxford University Press 1972.

atoms to arms) and inner psychic reality (emotions, wishes, experiences) is insufficient: the ideas we talk about are not just passing thoughts in our minds, since these thoughts refer to something which remains the same while our thoughts pass away or change (when I think about 2 + 2 = 4 and my colleague also thinks about it, we are thinking about the same thing, although our thoughts are materially different; when, in a dialogue, a group of people talk about a triangle, they are somehow talking about the same thing; etc.). Popper is, of course, not an idealist: ideas do not exist independently of our minds, they are the result of our mental operations, but they are nonetheless not directly reducible to them—they possess a minimum of ideal objectivity. It was in order to capture this realm of ideal objects that Popper coined the term "Third World," which is more or less equivalent to what Lacan calls the symbolic order or the "big Other." However, the word "order" should not lead us astray here: Lacan's symbolic order is not a fixed network of ideal categories or norms. The standard deconstructionist and feminist reproach to Lacanian theory targets its alleged implicit normative content: Lacan's notion of the Name-of-the-Father, the agent of the symbolic Law which regulates sexual difference, allegedly introduces a norm which, even if it is never fully actualized, nonetheless imposes a standard on sexuality, somehow excluding those who occupy a marginal position (gays, transvestites, etc.); furthermore, this norm is clearly historically conditioned, not a universal feature of being human, as Lacan allegedly claims. This reproach, however, relies on a confusion over the word "order" in the phrase "symbolic order":

> "Order," in the legitimate sense of the term, designates nothing more than a specific domain: it does not indicate an order to be respected or obeyed, and even less an ideal to be conformed to or a harmony. The symbolic in Lacan's sense says nothing but the essential disorder which emerges at the juncture of language and the sexual.[17]

The Lacanian symbolic order is thus inherently inconsistent, antagonistic, flawed, "barred," an order of fictions whose authority is that of an imposture. One author who does effectively conceive of Popper's Third World as an eternal ideal order is Roger Penrose, who gives the notion a distinctly Platonic-idealist twist: (mathematical) Ideas not only exist independently of our minds, they even engender material reality. Penrose proposed a

---

17   François Balmès, *Structure, logique, aliénation*, Toulouse: eres 2011, p. 16.

version of the three worlds in which they are intertwined, as in Escher's famous "Waterfall" drawing of a perpetually descending circuit of water. As Jim Holt summarizes:

> There are three worlds: the Platonic world, the physical world, and the mental world. And each of the worlds somehow engenders one of the others. The Platonic world, through the magic of mathematics, engenders the physical world. The physical world, through the magic of brain chemistry, engenders the mental world. And the mental world, through the magic of conscious intuition, engenders the Platonic world—which, in turn, engenders the physical world, which engenders the mental world, and so on, around and around. Through this self-contained causal loop—Math creates Matter, Matter creates Mind, and Mind creates Math—the three worlds mutually support one another, hovering in midair over the abyss of Nothingness.[18]

This Escher-style interdependence of the three worlds nonetheless differs from Lacan's knot of ISR: the three Lacanian dimensions are intertwined (knotted) in such a way that no two dimensions are directly connected but are held together only through the third, so that if we cut out the third dimension, the other two are also disconnected—the point being that there is no (direct) relationship between any two dimensions, since each of them relates to another only through the third. It is only through the imaginary—the *objet a*—that the Real is linked to the symbolic; it is only through the symbolic—$S(\cancel{A})$—that the imaginary is linked to the Real; it is only through the Real—$, the barred subject—that the symbolic is linked to the Imaginary. If we apply this triad to the notion of the Event, we thus get three evental dimensions:

The *imaginary event*: the incorporeal flux of sense, the pure de-substantialized sense-event, what the ancient Stoics called *lekta* (the "sayables"), or, at its poetic purest, a haiku poem whose final line names a pure impassive evental flash, a fleeting appearance that disappears as soon as it arises—a splash of water, a blurred shadow ...

The *symbolic event*: the quasi-magical effect of "finding the right word," the intervention of a Master-Signifier (S_1), a *point de capiton*, the "quilting point" at which signifier falls into signified and which thus introduces a

---

18   Jim Holt, *Why Does the World Exist?*, New York: Norton 2012, p. 180.

new Order ("harmony"), providing a new structuring principle of a field in question.

And, finally, what is usually considered the specifically Freudian notion of the Event, the *real event* (or, rather, the event as/in the Real): a *trauma*, something "impossible" (or unthinkable) that nonetheless happens, a shattering encounter or intrusion impossible to symbolize, to integrate into our horizon of meaning, from rape to cosmic catastrophe.[19]

This simple triangle of Imaginary-Symbolic-Real is, however, inadequate— we need to add another three excessive entities, each of them registering the constitutive failure/deadlock of one of the three basic dimensions:

Imaginary: the flux of sense is always sustained by a singular point of non-sense—in order to flow, it has to get stuck on a glitch whose Lacanian name is the *objet a*, the object-cause of desire.

Symbolic: the "harmony" imposed by a Master-Signifier always covers up a constitutive disharmony, and the signifier of this disharmony is what Lacan calls the signifier of the barred Other—the move to be made is thus from S_1 to $S(\cancel{A})$ (say, from Nation to Class Struggle, to the name of the antagonism/impossibility that cuts across the social edifice).

And, finally, *Real*: the traumatic external Thing reaches its limit in the void of the subject itself ($, the barred subject): Gandhi's well-known dictum "Be the change you want to see in the world!" should be rephrased as "You are already the horror you are looking for and fear in the world!"—the true trauma is the subject itself, its abyssal focal point what Hegel called the Night of the World. Perhaps this is how we should read the famous chorus lines from *Antigone*: "There are many uncanny/terrifying things in the world, but nothing more uncanny/terrifying than man himself."

In this way, we get to Lacan's scheme from his seminar *Encore* (slightly modified here):[20]

19   For a more detailed account of this triad, see Slavoj Žižek, *Event*, London: Penguin Books 2014.

20   Jacques Lacan, *Encore*, Paris: Seuil 1975, p. 99.

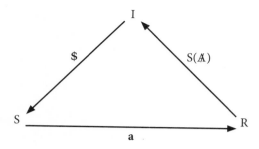

What we find in the middle of the triangle is the central Void of the impossible Thing which threatens to swallow us up if we get too close to it.[21] Where Lacan agrees with Penrose is in the idea that the three worlds "hover in midair over the abyss of Nothingness"; in terms of general relativity and quantum cosmology, we can designate this central Void as that of an Event-Horizon. In general relativity theory, an event horizon is a boundary in space-time beyond which events cannot affect an outside observer; it is "the point of no return," the point at which the gravitational pull becomes so great as to make escape impossible. Its best-known case is a black hole: it is "black" because light emitted from beyond the horizon can never reach the observer. As is always the case in relativity theory, it is crucial to specify from which standpoint we observe an object approaching the horizon: for an external observer, the object appears to slow down and never quite pass through the horizon; however, if an observer were to be placed on the traveling object itself, she would experience no strange effects, for the object would pass through the horizon in a finite amount of time.

Although the three additional elements—S($\bar{\text{A}}$), $, a—are to be strictly distinguished, they nonetheless display the same reflexive structure of an element filling in its own lack: the signifier of the lack of a signifier; the object which stands in for the very lack of an object; the subject which arises out of its own impossibility, the failure of its own symbolic representation. So let us begin with a: Lacan defines *objets a* as objects which "cannot be grasped in the mirror" since—like vampires—they "have no specular image."[22] But what if they are the exact opposite, the virtual organ visible *only* in the mirror, as in the horror movies where I see something in the mirror that is not there in reality? Such a paradoxical object

---

21   For Lacan, the central void is designated as J, the void of the *Jouissance-Thing*.

22   Jacques Lacan, *Écrits*, New York: Norton 2006, p. 819.

standing for the very absence of an object cannot be deployed only at
the level of content (a system of signs or objects)—one has to include the
subject. Let us imagine a mythical original situation in which signs refer
to objects in reality; in such a situation, a strange sign then emerges, like
a zero among numbers which is one in the series of signs/numbers, but at
the same time

> a sign intended to counter the absence of sign in a situation of absence of object.
> It is thus not a sign which is primarily turned towards the world in order to indi-
> cate there a *hic et nunc* quality, but a sign intended to show that, in this domain
> where a sign is required (but by whom, for whom?), we *fabricate* one to signal
> and *designate* the absence of object.
>
> With this zero, we are thus dealing with a peculiar sign: since it does not
> point towards anything, *the fact that it points* indirectly designates "the-one-
> for-whom-there-is-nothing" as an essential part of the process of counting ...
> With zero, the-one-who-counts is included in the account, not as an object to be
> counted (if this happens, it is a banality), but as the one who sustains the activity
> of counting *independently of the very counted objects* which are there only as a
> background.[23]

The *objet a* is the point at which the subject encounters itself, its own impossible objectal counterpoint, among objects—"impossible" means here that *a*
is the obverse of the subject, they can never encounter each other in a direct
opposition or mirroring, i.e., there is no relationship between $ and *a*, they
are like the two sides of the same spot on a Möbius band. What this means
is that the *objet a* stands for the "object as such," the frame of a variable; it
is in this sense (Lacan's version of) the transcendental object, a mark of the
"pure" faculty of desire: it has no substantial consistency of its own, it is just
a spectral materialization of a certain cut or inadequacy—or, as Lacan put
it concisely: "The object *a* is a cut" ("*l'objet a est une coupure*").[24] To render
the hysterical frustration with every attained object of desire, Lacan often
repeated the formula: "*I demand that you refuse what I offer you because this
is not that.*" The point of this formula is not simply that a positive object we
can get hold of in reality never fits the ideal object—this ideal itself is just
an imaginary representation, and if we were to get exactly such an object
(with regard to its properties), the same gap would be repeated. In other

---

23   Guy le Gaufey, *L'objet a*, Paris: EPEL 2012, pp. 141–2.
24   Jacques Lacan, in his unpublished seminar *Le désir et son interprétation*
(May 1959).

words, the *objet a* is not the inaccessible ideal object to which no empirical object is adequate—"*the* object a *is this inadequacy itself.*"[25] In this sense, the *objet a* is "the presupposed void in a demand,"[26] the void that sustains the experience of "this is never *that*": the universal ("object as such") comes to exists as a pure gap.

Recall the joke from Lubitsch's *Ninotchka*: "'Waiter! Get me a cup of coffee without cream!' 'I'm sorry, sir, we have no cream, but I can get you a coffee without milk!'" This is a joke about the *objet a*—but where is the *objet a* here? We have to ask a simple question: why do we add milk or cream to coffee? Because there is something missing in straight coffee, and it is this void in coffee—the non-identity of coffee with itself—that we try to fill with a series of supplements. What this means (among other things) is that there is no full self-identical "plain coffee," that every "plain coffee" is already a "coffee without." And it is here that the *objet a* is located: coffee is in itself not One but a One plus something. This reflexive logic of filling in the void is at work even (and especially) when we are offered a product in its pure, authentic state, with nothing added, like "plain coffee," any addition to which would just ruin the taste. In this case, the object (coffee) is not just directly itself, but is redoubled, functioning as its own supplement—it itself fills the void its mere existence creates: "this coffee is … just simple coffee."

So, first there is the coffee's non-identity with itself, its immanent impossibility, and then the excessive element fills in this lack. Or, in the social field, first there is the class antagonism, and then there is the "part of no-part" as the excessive element. Again, here we must avoid the poetry of marginal symptoms, of excessive unaccountable elements ranged against a System whose disturbance they materialize.[27] In a moment of social crisis, "plain coffee" becomes "coffee without X"—i.e., a situation previously perceived as normal or "fair" is suddenly experienced as unjust, as lacking something—but the ensuing revolt against the situation itself enters a crisis when people become aware that no determinate X can fill in the tautological lack inherent in "coffee without … coffee."

---

25 Le Gaufey, *L'objet a*, p. 211.

26 Ibid.

27 However, the fact that antagonism comes first does not entail the simple primacy of non-relationship: it is crucial to make the step from "there is no relationship" to "there is a non-relationship"—the chimney sweep *is* a non-relationship between man and woman, between the officer and the maid, the (anti-Semitic figure of the) Jew *is* the non-relationship between the antagonistic classes.

We can thus distinguish: (1) plain coffee; (2) coffee with … (milk, cream, vanilla, chocolate …); (3) coffee with no … (milk, cream …); (4) coffee with no-milk (but with another supplementary ingredient—cream, vanilla …); (5) coffee without no-milk (but without another no- …); (6) coffee without "coffee" (deprived of its crucial ingredient—caffeine); (7) coffee without coffee as the lack constitutive of it; (8) coffee which claims to already have the X, i.e., to be functioning as its own supplement. The basic form is here 7—coffee is already in itself without … (X, *objet a*). 1, 3, 5, 7, and 8 are "empirically" the same, while 2, 4, and 6 add to or subtract something from the plain coffee; 2 and 4 are also "empirically" the same, coffee with something, but with or without the mediation through absence (coffee just with milk or with cream instead of milk). This is symmetrical to 3 and 5: both are coffee without something, but with or without the additional mediation through absence (coffee just with no milk or with no milk instead of no cream). The other two couples are 1 and 8 (plain coffee and coffee which is reflexively plain, i.e., which supplements itself) and 6 and 7 (coffee without coffee/caffeine and coffee without …). Other pairings are possible, and one can also construct a mythical Hegelian narrative: one begins with (1) plain coffee, and experiences that (7) it comes with a lack, *ce n'est pas ça*; then (2) one fills in this lack with something (milk, cream …); after establishing that this supplement cannot fill in the lack, (4) one replaces it with another supplement (milk instead of cream); when all these fail, (5) one posits coffee as its own supplement; what logically follows is to reject, out of purity, all supplements, which just ruin the true taste—we want (3) coffee without any supplement, and also (5) if we are especially bothered by one supplement, we pointedly want coffee without *that* one, not without another one. Finally, this obsession with "no" ends up with our really taking something from coffee: (6) we turn lack into excess and establish that what is wrong with coffee is not that it lacks something but that it has too much of something (like caffeine), so we take this poisonous excess away from it. So to get a truly "pure" coffee, it must be deprived of its excess. But, of course, in this way, once again we get caught in a trap: what we take away is the very gist of coffee, caffeine; for this reason, the coffee has to be supplemented with something else to make sure it still tastes like coffee (like saccharine instead of sugar). We thus get a potentially dangerous fake coffee which carries its own risks (cancer etc.), and the reaction can only be a return to (1) plain coffee.

Here we must return to another incident involving coffee from popular cinema, this time from the English working-class drama *Brassed*

Off.[28] The hero walks home a pretty young woman who, when they reach the entrance to her flat, asks him if he would like to come in for a coffee. To his answer—"There's a problem—I don't drink coffee"—she replies with a smile: "No problem—I don't have any …" The erotic power of her reply lies in how—again through a double negation—she makes an embarrassingly direct sexual invitation without ever mentioning sex: when she first invites the guy in for a coffee and then admits she has no coffee, she does not cancel her invitation, she just makes it clear that the coffee invitation was a stand-in or pretext, indifferent in itself, for the sexual invitation. We can imagine multiple levels here, beginning with the direct communication: "I would like you to come up to my flat and fuck me." "I would also like to fuck you, so let's just go up and do it!" Then, the direct mention of the detour as a detour: "I would like you to come up to my flat and fuck me, but I'm embarrassed to ask directly, so I will be polite and ask if you want to come up for a coffee." "I don't drink coffee, but I would also like to fuck you, so let's just go up and do it!" Then, the idiot's answer: "Would you like to come up to my flat for a cup of coffee?" "Sorry, I don't drink coffee." "You idiot, it's not about coffee, it's about sex, the coffee was just a pretext!" "Oh, I get it! Yes, let's go up and do it!" Then a version with immediate jumps between levels: "Would you like to come up to my flat for a cup of coffee?" "Yes, I would love to fuck you!" (Or: "Sorry, I'm too tired for sex"). And the inverted version: "Would you like to come up to my flat and fuck me?" "Sorry, I'm not in the mood for a coffee right now." (This retreat into politeness is, of course, an act of extreme aggression and humiliation.) We can also imagine a version along the lines of "coffee without …": "I'm tired tonight, so I would love to come up to your place just for a cup of coffee—without sex." "I have my period right now, so I cannot give you coffee without sex—but I have a good DVD to watch, so what about coffee without a DVD?" Up to the ultimate self-reflexive version: "Would you like to come up to my place?" "I'm not sure if I want to have sex or watch a movie, so what if we just go up and have a cup of coffee?"

Why does the direct invitation for sex not work? Because the true problem is not that coffee is never fully coffee, but that sex is never fully sex, that there is no sexual relationship, which is why the sexual act needs a fantasmatic supplement. So it is not just polite censorship that prevents the direct invitation, "Let's go up and have sex!"—coffee or something like it has to be mentioned to provide the fantasmatic frame for sex. In other

---

28   I resume here the analysis from Chapter 8 of *Less Than Nothing*.

words, what is primordially repressed in the scene from *Brassed Off* is not sex (which, for this reason, has to be replaced in the explicit text by coffee); what is repressed is what is missing in sex itself, the inherent impossibility/ failure of sex—the replacement of sex by coffee is a secondary repression whose function is to obfuscate the primordial repression.[29]

What is missing in sex itself is simply its cause. When Lacan approaches the topic of cause and causality, the reference to Kant is crucial.[30] For Kant, the texture of phenomenal reality is that of a complete causal link with no gaps or discontinuities: a thing exists only if there are sufficient reasons for it to exist. But the Freudian unconscious emerges precisely in the discontinuities and gaps of phenomenal causality: an eccentric absent X intervenes and disturbs the flow of causality, introducing discontinuity:

> Cause is to be distinguished from that which is determinate in a chain, in other words the law. By way of example, think of what is pictured in the law of action and reaction. There is here, one might say, a single principle. One does not go without the other. The mass of a body that is crushed on the ground is not the cause of that which it receives in return for its vital force—its mass is integrated in this force that comes back to it in order to dissolve its coherence by a return effect. There is no gap here, except perhaps at the end. Whenever we speak of cause, on the other hand, there is always something anti-conceptual, something indefinite. The phases of the moon are the cause of tides—we know this from experience, we know that the word cause is correctly used here. Or again, miasmas are the cause of fever—that doesn't mean anything either, there is a hole, and something that oscillates in the interval. In short, there is cause only in something that doesn't work. Well! It is at this point that I am trying to make you see by approximation that the Freudian unconscious is situated at that point,

---

29   Darian Leader mentions a similar anecdote from his analytic work, when a patient reported a slip of tongue that had embarrassed him: he was taking a lady to a restaurant in a luxury hotel, secretly planning to take her to a room after lunch; as a waiter approached, the patient said: "A bed for two, please!" instead of "A table for two, please!" Leader rejects the obvious "Freudian" reading (his real wish for sex erupted directly) and proposes the opposite one: the slip of the tongue should be read as a warning not to enjoy the food too much, as a reminder that the shared lunch is just a pretext, a *Vorlust*, and that the true goal is sex. The slip of the tongue was thus a desperate attempt to repress the gnawing suspicion that even sex is not "the real thing," that something is missing in it also.

30   I rely here on Simon Hajdini, "Why the Unconscious Doesn't Know Time," *Problemi* 5–6 (2012) (in Slovene).

where, between cause and that which it effects, there is always something wrong. The important thing is not that the unconscious determines neurosis—of that one Freud can quite happily, like Pontius Pilate, wash his hands. Sooner or later, something would have been found, humoral determinates, for example—for Freud, it would be quite immaterial ... Discontinuity, then, is the essential form in which the unconscious first appears to us as a phenomenon—discontinuity, in which something is manifested as a vacillation.[31]

Freud's name for this gap between cause and effect is *Nachträglichkeit*: a cause is not in direct continuous contact with the effect, it generates effects at a distance, after a temporal gap. One should go even further here: in a way, the cause is also a retroactive effect of its effects. (In the case of the Wolf Man, the scene of the parental *coitus a tergo* became the traumatic scene long after the fact.) But, it will be objected, is not the whole point of Freud's discovery of the unconscious precisely that this discontinuity is only a first appearance, which can then be abolished and the gap filled in? Is not "the unconscious" the name of another causal chain which enables us to reassert the complete chain of determinism? Lacan's wager is a decisive *no*: "the unconscious" does not designate the complete substantial causal chain which fills in the gaps, but the radical discontinuity that threatens the consistency of every symbolic formation. It is not the unconscious but the fantasy that stands for the attempt to fill in the gap and reimpose a narrative that establishes a full causal link. (The model here is Marx's fantasy of primitive accumulation, which tells the story of the origins of capitalism.) One should bear in mind that Kant's notion of freedom also implies this discontinuity, the entry of another dimension into the order of phenomenal causality—what if, then, the discontinuity of the unconscious is another name for freedom?

This brings us back to the joke about coffee without milk, which works against the background of the standard conversation: "Coffee with cream, please!" "Sorry, we're out of cream, but I can give you coffee with milk." The joke can also be retold as a slip of the tongue: the man wants to say "cream," but says "milk" instead, not because cream would have been the true incestuous object that has to remain repressed, but *in order to repress the primordial lack in coffee which neither milk nor cream can fill in*, by way of creating the illusion that cream (the elided supplement) would have filled

---

31   Jacques Lacan, *The Four Fundamental Concepts of Psycho-Analysis*, New York: Norton 1979, pp. 21–2.

in this lack. In other words, what is repressed is not cream but the *without* in cream—the ontological lack (the fact that coffee is in itself not fully coffee, and that no supplement can fill this gap) is replaced by an ontic-empirical one. We should distinguish here between the absent Cause (the Real of an antagonism) and the *objet a* as the object-cause (of desire). They are not the same: the true "absent cause" is the Real as impossible, the impossibility of the One, the antagonism constitutive of the field (like the antagonism or impossibility inscribed into the very heart of capitalism as its "concrete universality"); then comes the object-cause of desire, the excessive element which has no proper place within the structured symbolic space.[32]

To recapitulate, a coffee "not without cream" is not a coffee *without* milk, but a coffee without *milk*, i.e., the negation of another supplement. There is a difference between "plain coffee" and "coffee not without cream" (i.e., "coffee without milk"): the second is still marked by a lack, but the place of the lack has shifted. Towards the end of Neil Gordon's *The Company You Keep*, Mimi Lourie, an ex-Weather Underground member hiding from US authorities, faces a tough decision: should she escape into Canada and remain free, or surrender to the authorities and face prison in order to exculpate Jason Sinai, her Weatherman ex-lover, from the charges against him? When Jason presents Mimi's choice to a sympathetic journalist, Benny Schulberg, Benny expresses his doubt that Mimi is ready to surrender, and Jason concedes that he is probably right. The surprised Benny then asks why he is helping Mimi to escape; Jason explains that, in order to make her testimony acceptable and thus exculpate him, Mimi should freely surrender to the authorities, not just be captured by them. He then adds: "Before she can *not* surrender, she has *not* to be caught."[33]

The underlying logic is clear: in order to choose between surrendering and not surrendering, Mimi has to be in a position to make this choice, and she will be in this position only if she is free, which means in Canada, not threatened by imminent arrest. This, however, is not all—if it were, if Jason's point were simply the obvious fact that Mimi can only surrender if she is not already caught, then he would have said: "Before she *can* surrender, she has *not* to be caught." But Jason does not say this because he shares Benny's opinion that Mimi will (probably) not surrender, which means that, in respect of Jason's exculpation, it does not matter if Mimi is

32   See Alenka Zupančič, "Where Does the Dirt Come From?" (*Od kod prihaja umazanija?*), *Problemi* 5–6 (2012), p. 16.

33   Neil Gordon, *The Company You Keep*, London: Penguin Books 2013, p. 364.

caught or not. So why help her to escape? What Jason wants to do is just to give Mimi a chance to surrender and thereby exculpate him; what he also wants is to give Mimi a chance *not* to surrender and thus put her in a situation of authentic ethical choice. A parallel would be for me to leave a heap of money on the table before I leave the room, knowing that the person who remains in the room will be tempted to steal it even though he is my friend—I do it not in order to give him a chance to steal the money and run away, but in order to give him a chance *not* to steal it. Again, the point is not that I simply want to keep the money: if that were the case, I would not put the money on the table at all. Here the parallel with the *Ninotchka* joke enters: the causal connection Jason establishes is not between two positive facts (Mimi remaining free and Mimi surrendering), but between two negative facts—i.e., something not happening is a condition of something else not happening, as in the joke, where the waiter offers coffee without milk instead of coffee without cream.

And the status of the subject is determined by the same uncanny logic: the subject is like a pronoun, a name of a name where no name is pointing to a determinate object/person: a subject *is* "subject as such," and this is why it is "barred," with all its positive content obliterated. In insisting on the abstract singularity of the *cogito* (I = I), Descartes and his transcendental followers were right, as against the post-Hegelian assertion of the positive concrete human being: the subject is "abstract," voided, the paradox of an actually existing abstraction, and all the wealth of "concrete personality" comes secondarily, to fill in this void. To reach the dimension of the subject, we thus have to accomplish the purifying move from the imaginary person to $ (empty-barred subject), from fellow-man to neighbor, from the wealth of inner life to the abyss of subjectivity.

But the key point here is that this subject cannot come to be without the *objet a* as its objectal support: the modern tradition from Sartre (with his notion of the subject as a negativity transcending every object) up to Badiou (whose formula is *sujet sans objet*) ignores this negativity which has to be sustained by its impossible objectal counterpart—there is no subject without the object "as such," or, as Lacan put it in *Encore*: "the reciprocity between the subject and the *objet a* is total."[34] The *objet a* is usually perceived as a singular remainder which eludes signifying capture; however, we should bear in mind that in the *objet a* the extremes coincide, as in the Hegelian infinite judgment: the object as such and the indivisible remainder

---

34   Lacan, *Encore*, p. 114.

(itself split between the sublime *je ne sais quoi*, the cause of my desire, and the excremental).

As Lacan put it in his seminar on the ethics of psychoanalysis, the subject is "that [part-aspect] of the real which suffers from the signifier [*ce que du réel pâtit du significant*]":[35] a subject is the answer of the (living) Real to the invasion of the signifier, to its "colonization" by the symbolic order, the loss imposed by this "colonization." As such, the subject does not pre-exist its loss, it emerges from its loss as a return to itself: a subject aims at representing itself, this representation fails, and the subject *is* the void left behind by this failure of its own representation. This brings us to Lacan's definition of the signifier as that which "represents the subject for another signifier": in a symbolic structure, there is always a lack, and this lack is filled in, sustained even, re-marked, by a "reflexive" signifier which is the signifier of the lack of the signifier; identifying the subject with the lack, we can thus say that the reflexive signifier of the lack represents the subject for the other signifiers. This is why there is always an element of imposture in a Master-Signifier (the signifier which represents the subject): its power of fascination conceals a lack, a failure.[36] This is why we should accomplish the third move here: a Master-Signifier is an imposture destined to cover up a lack (failure, inconsistency) of the symbolic order; it is effectively the signifier of the lack/inconsistency of the Other, the signifier of the "barred" Other. What this means is that the rise of a new Master-Signifier is *not* the ultimate definition of the symbolic event: there is a further turn of the screw, the move from S_1 to $S(\cancel{A})$, from new harmony to new disharmony, which is an exemplary case of *subtraction*. That is to say, is not subtraction by definition a subtraction from the hold of a Master-Signifier? Is not the politics of radical emancipation a politics which practices subtraction from the reign of a Master-Signifier, its suspension through the production of the signifier of the Other's inconsistency/antagonism?

The signifier of the barred Other is produced in the passage from the distortion of a notion to a distortion constitutive of this notion: it names the constitutive inconsistency (antagonism, impossibility) of the big Other—it names the dimension of crime inherent in the very notion of Law; it names the "theft" inherent in the very notion of (private) property. It names the

---

35   Jacques Lacan, *The Ethics of Psychoanalysis*, New York: Norton 1997, p. 142.

36   Recall Spinoza's insight that the traditional notion of "God" as a person dwelling above in heaven obfuscates a lack of our knowledge: the glory of "God" should not blind us to the fact that God is indeed a negative designation, a name for what we do not know.

antagonism which is not an effect of "things going wrong," but constitutive of the "normal" order of things itself. "Class struggle," say, becomes S($\cancel{A}$) when it no longer only designates the conflicts between labor and capital (strikes, protests, etc.), but becomes the name for the structuring principle of the relation between labor and capital as such, so that even when there are periods of "class peace," this "peace" has to be interpreted as the (temporary) victory of one side in the struggle. So what if this—the production of the signifier of the barred Other, and not just the production of a new Master-Signifier—is the symbolic Event at its most radical?

SINTHOME, OBJET A, $

From this standpoint, we can also clearly perceive the difference between *den* and *objet a*: while *den* is "less than nothing," the *objet a* is "more than one, but less than two," a spectral supplement that haunts the One, preventing its ontological closure. The crucial implication of this opposition is that *there is nothing between Nothing and One*, no "just barely something, almost nothing, more than nothing and less than One." This is the key axiom of materialism: there is nothing between zero and one—in contrast to idealism which likes so much to discern traces ("almost nothings") of some higher spiritual order. At the same time, one should bear in mind that Lacan is not a poet of the Two, of the respect for Otherness: his lesson is that of Gorgias' paradox on Achilles and the turtle—one cannot ever get from One to Two (this is why the binary signifier is primordially repressed, this is why there is no sexual relationship). In short, the *objet a* is *den* processed through the One. And if we take into account the third excessive element, the chimney sweep in Kierkegaard's example, we can articulate three levels of the functioning of the excessive element:

(3) *Between Two and Three*. As Lacan put it, 3 is not the set of three 1s, but, at its most elementary, 2 + *a*, the two plus an excess which disturbs their harmony—Masculine and Feminine plus the *objet a* (the *a*-sexual object, as Lacan calls it), the two principal classes plus the rabble (the excess of no-class).[37] It is this excess that makes out of a difference more than a mere

---

37   There is a limit to the parallel between sexual difference and class difference, but not where we would expect it: it is not that one is eternal and the other historically limited. They are both "eternal" in the sense that the antagonism cannot be resolved within its own field—there is no reconciliation, since the antagonism is a

symbolic difference, the Real of an antagonism. To designate this excess, we can also use Lacan's neologism *sinthome* (symptom at its most elementary): the Two, a couple (*yin-yang*, masculine-feminine, the two classes in society), plus the One of *Y a d'l'Un* which makes the sexual (or class) relationship impossible and possible at the same time as its constitutive obstacle (chimney sweep, Jew, rabble).

(2) *Between One and Two.* Then, there is 1 + *a*: the One is never a pure One, it is always supplemented by its shadowy double, a "more than one but less than two." To put it slightly differently: for Lacan, sexual difference is not a difference between two sexes, but a difference separating One (Sex) *from itself*—the One cannot ever reach the Two, its complementary counterpart, i.e., as Lacan put it, there is no Other Sex. This excessive element is the *objet a*: more than One and less than 2, the shadow that accompanies every One, making it incomplete.

(1) *Less Than Zero.* Finally, there is a paradoxical element which can only be counted as *less* than zero, and whose figures reach from Democritus' *den* to Higgs' boson in quantum physics, an element which "makes nothing cost more than something," i.e., which should be added to the pre-ontological chaos so that we get the pure vacuum—although here we must introduce an additional distinction ...

The zero-level, the starting point, is not zero but less than zero, a pure minus without a positive term with regard to which it would function as a lack/excess. Nothing (void) is the mirror (screen) through which less than nothing appears as something, through which pre-ontological chaos appears as ontic entities. In other words, the starting point is not the impossibility of the One fully actualizing itself as One, but the impossibility of Zero (Void) achieving the stability of the Void: the Void itself is irreducibly split between the pre-ontological chaos and the Void proper (what quantum physics theorizes as the difference of two vacuums), and it is this zero-level tension, the tension that splits from within the Void itself, which engenders the entire movement of the rise of One, Two, etc., i.e., the entire matrix of four versions we elaborated above: the tension between the two vacuums, the Void of the pre-ontological proto-reality and the Void proper,

---

difference prior to what it differentiates. We get over sexual difference only if we step out of sexuality as such (say, with asexual reproduction); we get over class struggle only if we enter a radically different social field.

is resolved by the rise of One (which is the pre-ontological *den* passing through the screen of the Void proper); the incompleteness of this One gives rise to its supplement, the excessive shadowy double. Out of this tension, a Two arises, another One, the translation of the shadowy double into the order of the One; however, since this duality also cannot function as a harmonious couple, the Two are always supplemented by an excessive element.

At this level, one is forced to introduce another key distinction, that between *dens*—the field of quantum waves, of pre-ontological oscillations, of "less than nothings"—and the operator of the transformation of *dens* into Ones, the "purifier" of the pre-ontological void into nothing proper. This operator is not to be identified with the *objet a*; it is rather a kind of inverted *objet a*. That is to say, the *objet a* is a virtual/spectral substance-less X that supplements actual objects, filling in the void in the heart of reality, while here we are dealing with an X that has to be added to a pre-ontological vacuum to make it the Nothing against the background of which actual objects can appear. What if this X which registers the antagonism of Nothing, its impossibility to be nothing, the counterpart of the *objet a*, is $, the (barred) subject in its proto-form, at its most basic? Do we not find a presentiment of this already in Kant where the transcendental subject, through its synthetic activity, constitutes "objective" phenomenal reality out of the confused multiplicity of sensual impressions? And is not the ontological status of this subject thoroughly ambiguous? It is not empirical, part of phenomenal reality (since it is a free subject endowed with spontaneity, while phenomenal reality is caught in causal determinism), but it is also not simply noumenal (since it appears to itself in empirical self-experience). And would it not be possible to read in the same way the most elementary coordinates of Heidegger's thought? Heidegger repeatedly insists that the ontological disclosure does not ontically cause/create entities—there is something "out there" prior to ontological disclosure, it just does not yet exist in the full ontological sense, and this X would be Heidegger's version of "less than nothing," of the pure Real. Then, in the midst of this pre-ontological Real, a *Dasein* emerges, a "being-there," the "there," the site, of the disclosure of Being. This *Dasein* (which, for well-known reasons, Heidegger refuses to call "subject") holds open the site of Nothing, of Being itself as the Void against the background of which entities appear—so, again, *Dasein* is the "operator" of the transformation of the pre-ontological Void into the Void of ontological Nothingness (Being in contrast to entities) as the background within which entities appear and disappear. In both these cases, the formal process is the same: the $, a kind of glitch in the pre-ontological field, triggers its ontological actualization, but this ontologically constituted reality is never fully actualized, it needs to be sutured by a paradoxical object, the *objet a*, which is the subject's counterpart in the world of objects, the subject's anamorphic inscription into reality.

We have thus three levels of antagonism: the Two are never two, the One is never one, the Nothing is never nothing. *Sinthome*—the signifier of the barred Other—registers the antagonism of the Two, their non-relationship. The *objet a* registers the antagonism of the One, its inability to be one. $ registers the antagonism of Nothing, its inability to be the Void at peace with itself, to annul all struggles. The position of Wisdom is that the Void brings ultimate peace, a state in which all differences are obliterated; the position of dialectical materialism is that there is no peace even in the Void.

Index

October Revolution, 23, 75, 188, 189
Offenbach, Jacques, 304–5
One Hour With You (film), 290–1
"On Language in General and Human
    Language in Particular" (Benjamin),
    239, 367
ontology, 37, 88, 91, 93, 94, 193, 329
    of Deleuze, 375, 388
    of *den*, 5, 385–6
    incompleteness thesis and, 19
    multiplicities and, 77, 265
    politics and, 26
    realist, 10, 97
"The Open Window" (Saki), 111–12
The Opposing Shore (Gracq), 155
optimism, 339
Original Sin, 119, 129, 132
Osborne, Peter, 34, 35, 343n
Other and Otherness, 14, 64, 131, 256,
    320, 328, 356
    alienation and, 140, 346–7, 396
    barred Other, 198, 401, 411, 414
    desire of, 150, 285
    knowledge of, 215–16, 221
    sacrifice and, 216–17
    subjectivity and, 12, 239, 273, 396
    See also big Other
othing, 395
Out of the Past (film), 318, 324
overdetermination, 27–8

Pacific Rim (film), 354n
Pahor, Boris, 355
Pappenheim, Bertha, 158
Pappenheim, Marie, 158, 161
Parade (film), 114
Parmenides, 385
Parrhasius, 154
Parsifal (film), 144
Parsifal (Wagner opera), 136, 140, 144,
    159
Pascal, Blaise, 51, 65
passion, 128–9, 202
    Hegel on, 238
    Kant on, 65–6

Penrose, Roger, 399, 402
performative, 59, 195, 337
Persecution and the Art of Writing
    (Strauss), 41
pessimism, 338–9
phenomenology, 77, 238–9
Phenomenology of Spirit (Hegel), 32, 56,
    141–2, 152, 232, 233, 237, 239, 333, 338
    foreword to, 28–9, 139
philosophy, 20, 88, 91
    Althusser on, 35, 87
    Descartes and, 179–81, 183
    Hegel and, 40–1, 88, 179, 181–4, 186,
        236
    Plato and, 179–80, 182
Philosophy of History (Hegel), 157, 237–8
philosophy of life *(Lebensphilosophie)*, 181
Philosophy of Religion (Hegel), 233
Philosophy of Right (Hegel), 23, 41, 368
    preface to, 40–1, 234, 243
phrenology, 242–3, 337, 339
physics, 11, 373n
    medieval, 91–2
    quantum, 221–6, 393
    theory of relativity in, 380, 402
Pippin, Robert, 17–18, 20, 27, 193, 310
    disagreement with Žižek, 19–22, 24
    on *film noir*, 317–20
Plath, Sylvia, 318–19
Plato, 9, 34, 35n, 179, 247
    anti-Platonism, 179–80
    idealism of, 182, 385
pleasure, 125, 201, 206, 219–20, 341, 342
    pain and, 233
    sexual, 198, 199, 201
pleasure principle, 122, 124, 277
Pluth, Ed, 223–5
Poe, Edgar Allan, 214–15, 249–51, 309n
poetry, 164, 232, 233
politeness, 57–8, 60–1, 62
Political Correctness, 61, 71
politics, 26, 71, 231n, 312, 369
    knowledge and, 197
    power and, 21
Ponelle, Jean-Pierre, 144